Mark Twain as Critic

*. . . he is really
a great literary critic,
so that his praise is
better worth having now
than any other man's*

(William Dean Howells to his
sister, June 25, 1906,
T-H, II 814)

Mark Twain as Critic

Sydney J. Krause

The Johns Hopkins Press, Baltimore

This book was brought to
publication with the assistance
of a grant from
Kent State University.

To Evy,

My Secret Sharer

Acknowledgments

My Cooper chapter was published as an article in the *New England Quarterly* for September, 1965, and is reprinted here, with a few minor changes, with the permission of the *Quarterly* and its editor, Herbert Brown. Harper and Row have given me permission to quote from the Zola and Cooper essays in their *Letters from the Earth* volume. The frontispiece and the dust jacket photograph of Mark Twain were taken by Albert Bigelow Paine at Dublin, New Hampshire, in 1906 and were intended to be published in Twain's autobiography. They are used here by courtesy of Mr. Paine's daughters, Louise Paine Moore and Joy Paine Cushman.

I gratefully acknowledge the financial aid I received at various important stages of my work from the American Philosophical Society, the American Council of Learned Societies, the University of Akron, and Kent State University.

I am indebted to Henry Nash Smith and Frederick Anderson, who graciously allowed me to read at will among the Mark Twain Papers, and who, on behalf of the Mark Twain Company, permit me to quote from presently unpublished material. I am also indebted to John D. Gordan, who gave me complete access to the Mark Twain manuscripts in the Henry W. and Albert A. Berg Collection of the New York Public Library. Lester B. Bridaham placed at my disposal and liberally reproduced for me many of the Mark Twain items he had collected for the Strathmont Museum in Elmira, New York. I received much appreciated library assistance from Lola Szladits, Pauline Franks, Ruth Clinefelter, and Dean Keller.

I am grateful to Walter Blair for sending me useful suggestions from time to time; to my brother, David Krause, who carefully perused an early draft of the book; to Abe Ravitz, who gave the MS a last minute reading; to William M. Gibson and Carl Bode, for some very perceptive suggestions for revision; to Howard P. Vincent, for his keen critical reading, and generally inspiring presence; to John Gallman and Jean Owen of the Johns Hopkins Press, for editorial assistance; to my typist, Louise Gardner; to Jane Nieset, for her help with proofs; and to my dear wife, Evy—for everything.

S. J. K.

Kent, Ohio
October, 1966

Contents

Abbreviations

AL *American Literature*

ANE Author's National Edition (New York, 1899). References to Twain's works are to the volumes of this edition given below:

   CY *A Connecticut Yankee at King Arthur's Court*, XVI
   FE *Following the Equator*, V, VI
   GA *The Gilded Age*, X, XI
   HF *Adventures of Huckleberry Finn*, XIII
   IA *The Innocents Abroad*, I, II
   LE *Literary Essays*, XXII
   LOM *Life on the Mississippi*, IX
   PW *Pudd'nhead Wilson*, XIV
   RI *Roughing It*, VII, VIII
   SNO *Sketches New and Old*, XIX
   TA *A Tramp Abroad*, IV, V
   TS *The Adventures of Tom Sawyer*, XII

AQ *American Quarterly*

Autob *Mark Twain's Autobiography*, ed. Albert B. Paine (New York, 1924), 2 vols.

Biog Albert B. Paine, *Mark Twain, A Biography* (New York, 1912), 3 vols.

CTG *Contributions to the Galaxy 1868–1871 by Mark Twain*, ed. Bruce R. McElderry, Jr. (Gainesville, Florida, 1961)

Letters *Mark Twain's Letters*, ed. Albert B. Paine (New York, 1917), 2 vols.

LFE *Mark Twain: Letters from the Earth*, ed. Bernard DeVoto (New York, 1962)

Love Lets *The Love Letters of Mark Twain*, ed. Dixon Wecter (New York, 1949)

MFMT Clara Clemens, *My Father, Mark Twain* (New York, 1931)

MMT William Dean Howells, *My Mark Twain* (New York, 1910)

MTAW Bernard DeVoto, *Mark Twain at Work* (Cambridge, Mass., 1942)

MTBM Samuel Charles Webster, *Mark Twain, Business Man* (Boston, 1946)

MTE *Mark Twain in Eruption*, ed. Bernard DeVoto (New York, 1940)

MTEnt *Mark Twain of the Enterprise*, ed. Henry Nash Smith (Berkeley, Calif., 1957)

MTMF *Mark Twain to Mrs. Fairbanks*, ed. Dixon Wecter (San Marino, Calif., 1949)

MTP *Mark Twain Papers*

MTTMB *Mark Twain's Travels with Mr. Brown*, ed. Franklin Walker and G. Ezra Dane (New York, 1940)

Noteb *Mark Twain's Notebook*, ed. Albert B. Paine (New York, 1935)

SFLF Franklin Walker, *San Francisco's Literary Frontier* (New York, 1939)

SOS *Sketches of the Sixties by Bret Harte and Mark Twain*, ed. John Howell (San Francisco, 1926)

Speeches *Mark Twain's Speeches*, ed. Albert B. Paine (New York, 1923)

T-H *Mark Twain-Howells Letters*, ed. Henry Nash Smith and William M. Gibson (Cambridge, Mass., 1960), 2 vols.

WG *The Washoe Giant in San Francisco*, ed. Franklin Walker (San Francisco, 1938)

WIM *What Is Man? and Other Essays* (New York, 1917)

Introduction

I

One does not ordinarily think of Mark Twain as a literary critic. I must confess, I did not think of him as much of a critic before I began this study. His most notable essay, "Fenimore Cooper's Literary Offences," may well be in a class by itself for having introduced a breath of native forthrightness into critical discourse, but it is generally felt that Twain allowed himself to be carried away by his own hyperbole, and that, in any case, the essay came rather late for the pioneer thrust it might once have given an emergent realism. Furthermore, the reader who wishes to understand Twain's "aesthetic" of literature must contend with desultory, occasionally ironic statements on artistic method —obiter dicta scattered amidst autobiographical dictations, essays, letters, marginalia, scraps of unpublished opinion, and prefatory notes. More often than not the genuinely critical remarks one does find are either cut short (if indeed they are not outright shortcuts), or seem on the verge of evaporating into a joke. Over all, the record seems embarrassingly lean, yielding not so much as a fully rounded book review.[1] For a writer of his

---

1. What passes for a review of George Washington Harris' *The Sut Lovingood Yarns* (1867) is scarcely that. Twain merely noticed the collective publication of the *Yarns* in a 134-word paragraph in the *Alta California* (July 14, 1867), only two sentences of which (33 words) attempt a judgment of the work (*MTTMB* 221). In 1870 he had done a review of Rev. George MacDonald's novel *Robert Falconer* (a book highly praised by Josiah G. Holland) which Twain left unpublished and unfinished. The novel had been recommended to him by Mrs. Fairbanks. For his private amusement Twain once did a burlesque review of a book by S. O. Stedman, *Allen Bay, A Story* (1876)—"an idiot novel" as Howells recalled (*T-H* I 209). The excerpts he selected were so self-ridiculing as to make him reject any thought of a published review. Twain's essays on Cooper and Mary Shelley were nominally begun as book reviews but turned into magazine articles. Philip S. Foner discusses Twain's unpublished review of Edwin Wildman's biography of Aguinaldo, the Philippine patriot (*Mark Twain: Social Critic* [New York, 1958], p. 289).

stature, Twain was also rather negligent in dealing with the important literary issues of his time, to say nothing of the fact that one could make a good undergraduate library of the books that repelled him. Finally, it has been variously claimed that his work might have profited from a greater exertion of self-criticism.

Still, all is not lost. Most of the negative impression has after all been just that—impression. Scholars and critics have done much to peel away Mark Twain's whimsical unconcern and expose the core of his purposive art, and they have also brought to light his theories of composition and literary art.[2] This is a book about Mark Twain's criticism of literature and his related criticism of some allied and some lesser arts, such as painting and architecture, and the theater and journalism. I wish to make known by way of reappraisal the kind, quality, and extent of his criticism, its structure, and the values he asserted or assumed.

My introduction is intended to clarify these matters in general terms, so as to dispose of some misconceptions and establish the nature of Mark Twain's role as critic.

II

Reappraisal begins with an awareness of the skill in critical argument and the criticism as such that are apparent in so much

2. Analyses of revisions (like Leon T. Dickinson's "Mark Twain's Revisions in Writing *The Innocents Abroad*," *AL*, XIX [May, 1947], 139–57) have done much to reveal Twain's art, as has Gladys C. Bellamy's *Mark Twain as a Literary Artist* (Norman, Okla., 1950). By far the most satisfying exhibition of the comic artist at work is Walter Blair's *Mark Twain & Huck Finn* (Berkeley, Calif., 1960). Explication of his theories of composition and literary art may be found in several articles: George W. Feinstein, "Mark Twain's Idea of Story Structure," *AL*, XVIII (May, 1946), 160–63; E. H. Goold, "Mark Twain on the Writing of Fiction," *AL*, XXVI (May, 1954), 141–53; and Sydney J. Krause, "Twain's Method and Theory of Composition," *Modern Philology*, LVI (February, 1959), 167–77. A recent analysis of the critical style of Twain's humor is C. Merton Babcock's, "Mark Twain, Mencken and 'The Higher Goofyism,'" *AQ*, XVI (Winter, 1964), 587–94. Even Robert Wiggins, who thought Twain a generally unsatisfactory novelist, granted that he was "an artist who discovered an artistic method uniquely his own" (*Mark Twain: Jackleg Novelist* [Seattle, Wash., 1964], p. ix).

of Twain's writing, and with the evidence that those of his contemporaries best equipped to evaluate his criticism had the highest regard for it. Though a clown and anti-intellectual, Twain was no boob. He played down, but obviously did not lack, intelligence.

That the impression of critical apathy is hardly indicative of Twain's capacity for dealing with institutions and history, with morals and ideas at large, we know not alone from his ingenuity as an ironist. There is much to be said, for example, for the way he retained an inimitable critical stance during a career that traversed brash frontier journalism, popular lecturing, humanitarian outrage, and the casuistries of a brooding determinism. Indeed, over and above a basic consistency, Twain was a masterful dialectician, even when he argued in heat from a unique and possibly dubious position. His varied harangues on Cooper, Shelley, Abelard, Gorki, Mary Baker Eddy, Colonel Vanderbilt, Theodore Roosevelt, King Leopold, General Funston, the Russian Czar, the South, the American Board of Foreign Missions, piratical publishers, political corruption, France, monarchy, Catholicism, and Christian theology all reveal a discipline over thought which not only survives but is indeed vindicated by the ardor of his convictions. Obviously, when a writer is at once a realist and a satiric humorist, he is *ipso facto* committed to judging things, and where there is judgment, there must of necessity lurk some system, some standards, a decided way of looking at the world. If Mark Twain gave the appearance that he was ignorant of abstract standards or suspicious of them, he did so because that was part both of his pose, and hence form, and of his own empirical standards, which, for the most part, were absorbed into the created experience of his books and into the created character of "Mark Twain."

As with Huck Finn, comprehension for Twain began with particular things. In his criticism he dwelt a good deal on how things were factually situated and whether they were immediately logical in their contexts. Was not the sensationalism of Adah Isaacs Menken's *Mazeppa* more a piece of unintentional comedy than of virtuosity—and comedy *because* of its strained seriousness? Should not Cooper's description of Natty Bumppo have been more faithfully borne out by Natty's "conduct and conversation?" Didn't Harte give Tennessee's Partner a dialect that was more redolent of Dickens than Pike County? Twain was meticulously observant, at times to a fault; he was what we would call a "close reader."

The attitudes of moral and social criticism that became second nature to him in the treatment of men and ideas did not suddenly vanish when he took a hard look at his profession. Twain had indeed done a considerable amount of literary criticism, far more than he has been credited with, though it has only been quite recently that this fact has been adequately recognized and anthologies have begun to offer the criticism as a representative part of his work.[3] Other reasons for the delayed recognition can be found in his use of the mask and in the fact that a portion of his criticism was done in private. But, whatever its mode or quantity, the caliber of his criticism did not go unnoticed by his peers.

Among Twain's author-friends, the two men who had substantial reputations in criticism, William Dean Howells and Brander Matthews, were both deeply impressed by his astuteness as a critic. Howells, who probably understood Twain's literary qualifications better than anyone else in his time, pronounced him a "really great literary critic"; and when he was isolating the items of major interest in Twain's collected works, he reserved a place for his "courageous forays in the region of literary criticism" (*MMT* 166). Looking back upon his total production ten years after Twain's death, Matthews, who had also correctly gauged the literary importance of Twain's work, wrote an essay on "Mark Twain and the Art of Writing."[4] In it he cited the excellence of Twain's insights and gleaned his principles of art from the Cooper essay, from a similarly acid query

3. The editors of one anthology divide their selections from Twain into three categories, one of which, "On Literature," has five pieces on literary, or aesthetic, criticism (William M. Gibson and George W. Arms [eds.], *Twelve American Writers* [New York, 1962], pp. 497–504). In another anthology one of the four groups of works by Twain is devoted to "Dramatic & Literary Criticism." It contains seven pieces, only two of which are the same as those offered in the other anthology (Perry Miller [ed.], *Major Writers of America* [New York, 1962], II, 89–111; the Twain section is edited by Henry Nash Smith).

4. *Essays on English* (New York, 1921), pp. 243–68.

about Sir Walter Scott (put to Matthews in correspondence), from the attack on Dowden's *Life of Shelley*, from the laudatory essay on Howells, from Twain's hostility to Jane Austen, and from maxims in "Pudd'nhead Wilson's Calendar." Matthews noted Twain's failure to take the historical view with styles he dismissed as too mannered or ornate; however, he thought this his only sin and concluded that if "Mark's ventures into criticism are not many, . . . they are significant, and they shed light upon his own artistic standards." Looking back from a later perspective, one would broaden Matthew's praise, for though Twain could be myopic, he made up for it by an adherence to certain criteria (directness and naturalness, for example) that would be instrumental in bringing about a major transition in American prose. Thus, while he himself had little appreciation for literary history, his critical judgment assisted in the making of it. To know Twain's criticism is to see that both historically and intrinsically it ranks rather well beside that of writers with comparable stature.

The subjects of Twain's criticism, it must be granted, were peculiar to the man. His unpredictableness is attested by the admission that he could be fascinated by "hogwash" as well as by "splendid literature" (*Autob* I 324). He reveled in Browning, whom he did not always understand (*Biog* II 847), but was not customarily attracted to the sort of writer who is engrossed by his muse. His off-center discussions of Shelley, Arnold, Whitman, and Bourget ranged over matters that had practically nothing to do with literature. Part of the fault lies with Twain's reading, which, as will be seen, might be considered somewhat shallow and dispersed for a man of letters, a role which, in the formal sense, he was not suited for and to which he did not aspire.

On the other hand, the cream of his criticism is rich in insight and sticks close to the text. There are the highly germane commentaries on Cooper, Harte, and Howells; and in addition to varied remarks on lesser lights (like Saint-Pierre and Zangwill), Twain made statements of consequence about Goldsmith, Scott, Macaulay, Zola, Edgar W. Howe, and Adolph Wilbrandt. Twain also wrote an assortment of critiques on such subjects as the popular stage and its performers, theatrical reviewers, newspaper style, oratory, architecture, art and art critics, sentimental poetry, Sunday-school tales, and school-girl composition. These critiques often bear on the quality of public taste. Some of them are burlesques of the kind he used in his own travel literature to satirize travel writers.[5] Their significance for the purposes of criticism lies in the revelation of Twain's critical discernment, his norms, and his artistry as a critic. The subjects themselves were the occasions for criticism and did not necessarily limit its scope or acumen. In fact, the distinctiveness of his critical sense injected a vitality into almost any subject he touched upon. If one had to put one's finger on the one thing that accounts for the greatness Howells spoke of, I think it would have to be Twain's *artistry*, achieved through masks, even more than his discernment.

III

Twain wrote a public and a private criticism. The public criticism was mainly mediated by masks, as was much else that he published,[6] and by their use he obtained a well-nigh perfect scheme for himself. The masks separated his personality from the issues; they anticipated the pitfalls of smugness and omniscience; they afforded him the freedom to say what had to be said; they opened the way for a bilateral technique whereby he kept up concurrent and either supporting or divergent levels of attack; and they enhanced his case by expanding the possibilities for subtlety.

There were two critical masks through which Mark Twain peered. These were the faces of the fool, or "muggins," and of the rebel, or "grumbler." The muggins dominated the earlier criticism, and the grumbler the later. These masks are roughly comparable to the classical *eiron* and *alazon* of comic tradition. In Twain's hands the one suffers from inexperience, simplicity,

5. See Franklin R. Rogers, *Mark Twain's Burlesque Patterns* (Dallas, Tex., 1960).

6. As has been pointed out by a number of critics, almost all of Mark Twain's relationships to the world of literature were in some way "masked." See especially John C. Gerber, "Mark Twain's Use of the Comic Pose," *PMLA*, LXXVII (June, 1962), 297–304; and James M. Cox, "The Muse of Samuel Clemens," *Massachusetts Review*, V (Autumn, 1963), 127–41.

and a lack of knowledge, and the other from too much experience, which leads to outrage, cynicism, and prejudice. Seemingly, the two are at opposite poles. At times, however, it is hard to tear them apart, because when the one pose was abandoned it had in large measure become absorbed by the other. Twain also mingled them. He would set up the fastidious "Gentleman" of southwestern humor as *alazon* and then make him look foolish, or he would endow his fool with a high degree of understanding. The mingling was quite common with Twain, and occurred in his fiction and in his non-literary criticism as well: for instance, when as rebel and satanic comedian he remarked that man prizes copulation above all other pleasures but excludes it from his heaven, substituting prayer (*LFE* 10), the rebel was taken over by the fool.

The first two parts of this book deal with the criticism rendered by the muggins and the grumbler, respectively. Together these masks display the art of Twain's criticism, or what may be called his "critical sensibility." The major devices of this art are ironic indirection, understatement, overstatement, oversimplification, and exaggerated naïveté, which in their effectiveness clearly transcend the ordinary processes of analysis. The third section is devoted to Twain's appreciative criticism, where his sensibility as critic is more apparent in the substance than in the form of what he says. He liked Macaulay, Howells, Howe, Zola, and Wilbrandt mainly because he found attitudes in their works that were subversive of social or artistic conventions—which were just the matters he had grumbled about. In addition, Macaulay's antithetical style seems to have been attractive to Twain because it suggested an ideal method of representing human complexities, and a manner of encompassing that which in his grumbling criticism he had merely opposed.

IV

One of the personal reasons Twain advanced for masking his true feelings also helps to explain why he preferred to keep some of his criticism private. In 1900, glancing back upon the reactions to his public character, Twain observed that fate had a way of avenging itself upon the humorist, as people mistook the mask for the man. His truths in effect became smothered under Cassandra's mantle. "I have been forced by fate," he claimed, "to adopt fiction as a medium of truth. Most liars lie for the love of the lie; I lie for the love of truth. I dissemble my true views by means of a series of apparently humorous and mendacious stories."[7] Among other things, this melancholy confession signifies the degree to which Twain could expect that when he published seriously intended comments—let alone his views on literature—they would be taken at face value. In addition to structural considerations, he thus had personal reasons for concealing criticism behind a mask. His threshold of irritability being notoriously low, invective coruscated as naturally from Twain's lips as did the breath he exhaled; however, though much of it was inspired, he just as naturally shrank from exposing his rage in print, and was at times embarrassed when something slipped out (*Letters* I 181f.).[8] He was particularly careful, for example, in so angry a piece as "To the Person Sitting in Darkness," to control his blast through understatement, logical absurdity, and anticlimax.

Twain once confided (to Matthews) that he did not think he had any right to be criticizing books, which sounded very much like an admission of incompetence, but he went on to point out that he did not do it except when he hated them, and added even more significantly: "I often want to criticize Jane Austen, but her books madden me so that I can't conceal my frenzy from the reader; and therefore I have to stop every time I begin" (*Letters* II 667). With living writers there were other predictable complications. For example, in 1899, the year after Sir Walter Besant had publicly—and unexpectedly—acclaimed *Huckleberry Finn* to be his favorite novelist's best book (for which Twain appreciatively thanked him[9]), Twain felt compelled to abandon a

7. This statement was given in an interview published in the Jacksonville, Florida, *Times Union and Citizen*, October 18, 1900. The newspaper article was sent to Twain by his press clipping bureau.

8. Criticism might bring on retaliation and public controversy. When he had ventured to assail our treatment of the Filipinos, he told Joe Twichell, "I'm not expecting anything but kicks for scoffing, and am expecting a diminution of my bread and butter by it" (*Letters* II 704f.).

9. In a four-page letter to Besant from Vienna, February 22, 1898. (The letter is in the Henry W. and Albert A. Berg Collection of the New York

review he had begun of a book by Besant (probably *The Pen and The Book*). "I hadn't the heart to go on," he said. "Besant is a friend of mine, and there was no way of doing a review that wouldn't cut into his feelings and wound his enthusiastic pride in his insane performance."[10] He could not go after a friend's book in print, and it would be unseemly to attack an enemy's, or anybody else's for that matter, to say nothing of the free publicity he would be furnishing. It was no simple matter for Mark Twain to publish his unmasked criticism. Even though he made capital of his personality, he wanted to be personally insulated, and he needed to be, for the purposes of his own work. Precisely because a relaxation of his ironic pose might alienate readers or other writers and make him look foolish before the public, Twain used his favorite correspondents as exhaust pipes through whom he could cleanse his system of spleen. Without a catharsis, he claimed that he might be deprived of creative effort for days. So, in sum, anger incited him to write literary criticism, but he had compunctions about exposing his emotions in print.

It was not merely by default that Twain averted Howells' concern that his writing too much criticism might sap him of the energies needed for creative work. Rather, Twain made much of his criticism a part of his creative work, and even in his strictly critical writing he liked to employ a creative frame. (The grumbling pose, after all, has everything to do with the acceptability of the Cooper criticism.) This was one result of his reservations. Another was that some of the criticism that got tucked away in obscure places simply remained there. Twain was

---

Public Library, hereafter referred to as *Berg*.) Twain wrote to Besant immediately after reading the article, which had appeared in a column of *Munsey's Magazine* entitled "My Favorite Novelist and His Best Book," where prominent writers mostly admired great books. Besant said his choice would be unexpected because it was a work not recognized as a masterpiece (*Munsey's*, XVIII [February, 1898], 659–64). Others who had already contributed to this column were Howells, Bourget, Harte, and A. Conan Doyle.

10. Letter to John Kendrick Bangs from Vienna, March 1, 1899, published by Francis Hyde Bangs in *John Kendrick Bangs* (New York, 1941), p. 203. Besant had in the same year (June, 1899) given Twain a very gracious introduction at a dinner tendered in Twain's honor by the Author's Club in London.

forever scribbling comments in the margins of his books as he read, or jotting down thoughts about them in his notebooks and elsewhere. A number of these notes turn up in passages deleted from the manuscripts of published books. The marginalia, plus the literary wrath siphoned into letters and personal notations, often give us Twain at his impassioned best. They indicate the perfect accommodation between the public pose and the private ire.

Twain's criticism of Harte stands somewhat apart from his other criticism. He grumbled ferociously in private and only mumbled in public about Harte—rather like the reviewers who, he said, "*talk* Alps to you, & then print potato hills" (*T-H* II 586) —but not without reason. For a while, Twain and Harte thought they had much in common and were close friends, that is, until they tried to write a play together. As Harte catapulted to national fame, Twain grew envious and began to scrutinize Harte's stories. He continued to keep tabs on what Harte was writing and then in 1879 said he had a burning desire to write an article on "Bret Harte as an Artist" (*ibid.* 262). What seemed to have foiled him was the fact that the article could only have been done caustically, and he could not find a form that would allow him to attack a former friend and rival without seeming petty. The numerous references to Harte strewn about in marginalia, letters, notes, and the eruptive part of Twain's autobiography tell us much of what he might have said, which, briefly, is that Harte was a manipulative and hence a fake realist. It was in the 1870's that Twain was most interested in Harte, the significance of that decade being that Twain had then ceased to regard himself as a journalist and, taking on the calling of author, had begun to read critically to determine what respected writers were and were not doing. Those were the formative years for American realism, and Harte's stories elicited from Twain a demand for consistency of realism that no other critic was then prepared to make.

V

The fact that Twain's work as critic has not been adequately investigated is an outgrowth of the general problem of his supposed inattention to art. One hears the contention, for instance, that Mark Twain might have written a more salty prose had he not sold out to the forces of Eastern gentility and been inhibited by his own uxoriousness;[11] and, on the other hand, one is told that he capitulated to the marketplace, giving "more conscious attention to the distribution, publication and cash value of his books than to their success as art."[12] It is true that Twain cultivated a non-literary, even an anti-literary image, but one has to be careful not to confuse the character he created for himself with its creator.

Bernard DeVoto was the most unremitting perpetuator of the non-literary image, explicitly blaming Twain's "greatest defect as an artist" on alleged lapses in criticism. According to DeVoto, not only did he exercise "little voluntary control" over his writing, but he "was unable to criticize what he had written" and his "lack of self-criticism betray[ed] him into errors of esthetics" (*MTAW* 92f.). To some extent, DeVoto is self-refuting. For when one seeks the reason for his low opinion of Twain's aesthetic sense, one finds him backtracking, unwittingly, towards the least tenable part of the argument for which he had belabored Van Wyck Brooks: to wit, DeVoto makes a dichotomy between the work of the "literary artist" and the "pleasant but trivial activity of the humorist," and he sees the latter as subverting the former, assuming that Twain could not have been what in fact he was—an artist *and* humorist (*MTAW* 56, 91, *et passim*). Actually, Brooks's thesis of an ordeal that was to

11. See, e.g., Dwight MacDonald, "Mark Twain: An Unsentimental Journey," *New Yorker*, XXXVI (April 9, 1960), 160–96 (MacDonald calls Van Wyck Brooks's *The Ordeal of Mark Twain* "still by far the best study of Mark Twain"); and Leslie Fiedler, *Love and Death in the American Novel* (Meridian ed.; New York, 1960), p. 557. As might be expected, Fiedler holds that "he lacked critical judgment completely" (p. 560).

12. Kenneth R. Andrews, *Nook Farm: Mark Twain's Hartford Circle* (Cambridge, Mass., 1950), p. 157. Somewhat more to the point, it seems to me, is Hamlin Hill's thesis that the exigencies of subscription publishing helped Twain—for better and worse—to find a way of *combining* his desire "to write enduring literature" and "to earn an impressive income" (*Mark Twain and Elisha Bliss* [Columbia, Mo., 1964], pp. 2, 67, 135–39, 159–69).

render Twain a literary eunuch goes back to H. L. Mencken's essay, "Puritanism as a Literary Force" (1917), wherein, among other charges of debilitation, Twain was thought to have denied himself the capacity for literary criticism in the measure that he fell a victim to his nationality, a sterilizing two-headed monster that spouted Puritanism and Philistinism. Engaging in the trick of overstatement, for which Twain had given him such a lively precedent, Mencken declared that American Puritanism had stripped Twain of the ability to distinguish "between the good and the bad in the work of other men of his own craft."[13]

Samples of Twain's revisions show that he modified passages too openly suggestive of sex, nudity, or irreverence; however, these changes have been a red herring to the more numerous ones he made for the purposes of style, structure, and humor. A thorough-going survey of Twain's revisions will no doubt dispel DeVoto's charge that Twain had "a massive inability to evaluate his work" (*MTAW* 51) and substantiate the impression of artistic improvement given by studies of individual works. Meanwhile, a knowledge of his criticism, particularly of his unerring detection of shoddiness and poor taste, as well as his skill in presenting his judgment, may help to explode the myth that he had no capacity for critical analysis. He was not faultless of course, but he was certainly a far better critic than he has been thought to be, and his criticism helped him artistically, just as his literary sense helped him in criticism.

Two other legitimate points that might be raised against Twain as critic have to do with his qualifications. If correctly interpreted they imply no great attenuation in the quality of his criticism, but merely explain inhibitions on its genesis and hence the reason why there was not more of it. These are the character and extent of Twain's reading, and his known detestation of critics and criticism.

The latter is easily dispensed with, because there is really not much of an apology to be made for it. On one occasion, he could say that since he had no skill in criticizing books he stayed away from it (*Letters* II 667); and on another, he could belittle criticism by declaring he believed it would require much less work

13. "Puritanism as a Literary Force," *A Book of Prefaces* (Garden City, N.Y., 1917), p. 204.

to do a book of it than a short story,[14] in which he was probably right. Some of his acknowledgments of incapacity have to be accepted as part of his pose as fool, while others arise from a specific source of resentment.[15] It is easy to magnify his hostility and see it as exceptional, whereas, in truth, many critics have been dissatisfied with the trade, and few creative writers have not cursed and scorned it. Dr. Johnson called it one of "the subordinate and instrumental arts." Irving and Longfellow thought it was mostly confined to captious men, obedience to whom would make a writer timid. Howells admitted, "I hate criticism . . . I never did a piece of it that satisfied me."[16] Twain wrote in a period, after all, that has been looked upon as the "golden age of anti-critical criticism."[17] One can make allowance for specific circumstances and still perceive little inducement for him to join the critical fraternity, and great inducement for him to stay away from it. Still, when Twain donned the masks of muggins or grumbler to engage in criticism, he was far from shirking responsibility; rather he was disinfecting the office of its invidiousness and improving its form and effectiveness.

Twain's reading suggests that he was possibly ill equipped for criticism. Some of the writers, for example, that he seems not to have interested himself in were Spenser, Marlowe, Jonson, Donne, Marvell, Dryden, Sheridan, Blake, Keats, and Coleridge —a majority, in fact, of the major poets and dramatists who had flourished before his time and to whom he would have been

14. Part of letter to unnamed correspondent, Paris, January 16, 1885, in Mark Twain Papers, hereafter referred to as *MTP*.

15. "I believe," Twain had ranted, "that the trade of critic, in literature, music, and the drama, is the most degraded of all trades, and that it has no real value—certainly no large value" (*Autob* II 69). But Twain had a specific case and a specific personality in mind when he said this. He held that the editor of the *Daily Graphic*, in addition to breaking his word not to review *The Gilded Age* until after the *Atlantic's* review should come out, had compounded the offense by spreading the rumor, as if he had it on authority, that Warner had written most of the book, and that Twain's name was being used "to float it and give it currency." For the relative accuracy of this charge see Hill's *Mark Twain and Elisha Bliss*, p. 80.

16. *Life in Letters of William Dean Howells*, ed. Mildred Howells (New York, 1928), II, 144.

17. Northrop Frye, *Anatomy of Criticism* (Princeton, 1957), p. 3.

introduced through formal schooling. Obviously, these were not
the kind of writers Twain would have written about even if he
had read them. The only piece he wrote on Shakespeare concerns
the Baconian controversy; and in his sole public eulogy of a
leading contemporary poet, Walt Whitman (requested of him
for Whitman's seventieth birthday), Twain blandly ignored the
poems—he could not have read many of them—and employed
the occasion for a panegyric on nineteenth-century progress that
was worthy of Whitman himself.[18] Though his coverage of prose
writers is respectable enough, he does not seem to have read
Melville, Crane, Butler, Gissing, Moore, Trollope, or Conrad,
and he probably read less than other writers had of Thackeray
and of Dickens (who he said paled on him[19]). Among writers of
fiction whom he abhorred, the best known are Austen, Scott,
Cooper, Poe, James, Eliot, and Meredith. He read some of the
"modern novels" that Howells praised, but what effect these may
have had is not known. He had an interesting explanation for
not delving more ambitiously into current literature: "I have
always had a fear that I should get into someone else's style if I
dabbled among the modern writers too much, and I don't want
to do that."[20] If he was enthusiastic about *The Cloister and the
Hearth, Two Years before the Mast,* and *Jude the Obscure,* he had

18. Horace L. Traubel (ed.), *Camden's Compliment to Walt Whitman, May
    31, 1889. Notes, Addresses, Letters, Telegrams* (Philadelphia, 1889), p.
    64f. Twain did read other contemporary poets than Browning. Among
    the books in his personal library, there was a volume of *Selected Poems*
    (New York, 1875), containing the poetry of Tennyson, Hood, and other
    Victorians. The book was acquired by Twain soon after its issue.
       Arthur L. Scott, who has made a thorough investigation of Twain's
    interest in poetry, points out that once he overcame an early distaste
    for it, Twain grew to have a positive relish for poetry, and ultimately
    wrote quite a bit of poetry himself (*On the Poetry of Mark Twain: With
    Selections from His Verse* [Urbana, Ill., 1966], pp. 1–39).
19. In an interview published in the Sydney (Australia) *Morning Herald,*
    September 17, 1895. He liked Lewis Carroll, he said, but no longer
    found it possible to laugh and cry with Dickens as he used to. After
    1870, only *A Tale of Two Cities* continued to appeal to him.
20. *Ibid.* This and another interview of September 17, 1895, in the Sydney
    Daily Telegraph also contain some very direct statements on his theory
    of the function of humor and on his methods of writing. In brief, he
    held that humor is very frequently alloyed with the serious and pathetic,
    half its bite coming from the combination. Writing, he said, was the
    only job he was never lazy about (though he might be lazy about
    everything else), and as a rule he did not write rapidly or trust much the
    writing that he might occasionally have done rapidly.

disproportionate praise for such writers as Edward Everett Hale, Coventry Patmore, Charlotte Teller, Elizabeth Robbins, and Elinor Glyn. The most discouraging aspect of all this is Twain's blunt statement that he detested reading novels and poetry and cared little for plays, preferring instead works of history, biography, science, and the like (*Biog* I 512). Strangely enough, he had been absorbed by Jonathan Edwards' essay on "The Freedom of Will" (*ibid.* III 1156f.). One does not soften the blow by reminding oneself that Emerson—and the New England of both Edwards and Emerson in general—did not care for novels either (Emerson also shared Twain's prejudice against Austen), or that American critics were as a rule somewhat laggard in taking an interest in the novel, having been prompted thereto only gradually in the mid 1820's, about a decade after the appearance of Scott's *Waverley*.

Howells assayed Twain's reading habits better than anyone else did. He saw that Twain was unorthodox, "unliterary," in what he read, and that he slighted the "accepted masterpieces of literature." However, he also saw that Twain was liberated from hidebound ideas and had an aptitude for lighting on the essential: "he was always reading some vital book. It might be some out-of-the-way book, but it had the root of the human matter in it: a volume of great trials; one of the supreme autobiographies; a signal passage of history, a narrative of travel, a story of captivity, which gave him life at first-hand" (*MMT* 15ff.). In this respect, Twain's reading reflects an intellectual vigor remarkably like that of the contemplative man of action, whose type Melville so aptly described in Captain "Starry" Vere.[21]

If anything, Twain's were the tastes of a man of letters in search of literary materials, and his criticism partakes of just that quality. He both read and wrote criticism primarily as a writer would. His reading may have been unsuited to the purposes of the literary critic at large, but it was exactly suited to

21. *Billy Budd, Sailor*, eds. Harrison Hayford and Merton M. Sealts, Jr. (Chicago, 1962), p. 62:

> With nothing of that literary taste which less heeds the thing conveyed than the vehicle, his bias was towards those books to which every serious mind of superior order . . . naturally inclines: books treating of actual men and events no matter of what era—history, biography, and unconventional writers like Montaigne, who, free from cant and convention, honestly and in the spirit of common sense philosophize upon realities.

his own purposes as critic, which were deeply involved with the discipline of writing. Thus, the critical element in Twain's reading is most apparent in the fact that he read mainly for *use*, and that meant he was a particularly studious reader. After making a "critical study" of Twain's reading, Harold Aspiz reported: "The books he read served him . . . as models for good writing, as touchstones for his own development, as grist for his critical mill, and as supplements to his personal observation."[22] With the mounting discovery of literary analogues and parodies in Twain's books, we are becoming aware of how well he prepared himself for his writing.[23] At the same time, this information more firmly establishes the fact that Twain was from the beginning a steady reader and that in a number of areas he was assuredly as well read as many of his Hartford peers. His better-known preferences suggest breadth enough. They ran from Suetonius, Plutarch, and Cervantes through Pepys, Macaulay, Lecky, Dumas, Carlyle, Holmes, Stevenson, Kipling, and, among his friends, Aldrich and of course Howells. He invariably read closely and critically. While reading a book on psychology, for example, he apologized for his slowness, saying, "I cannot take things in swiftly if I wish to understand them—and also make marginal notes."[24]

On this basis much of Twain's reading became inseparable from the act of criticism. His failure to put more of his reading to use in the writing of conventional essays is a circumstantial drawback to the study of his criticism, for which this book attempts to compensate; for the substance of his criticism is all there in the places that have been indicated, and needs only to be exposed. The very certainty of his grasp of literary principles explains why he did not have to write a good deal about them. This can be ascertained from a letter to Livy describing what he told a young lady authoress who had sent him a manuscript.

> . . . Literature is an *art*, not an inspiration. It is a *trade*, so to speak, and must be *learned*—one cannot "pick it up." Neither

---

22. "Mark Twain's Reading—A Critical Study" (unpublished Doctoral dissertation, University of California at Los Angeles, 1949), p. 2f.
23. See in particular Blair's *Mark Twain & Huck Finn.*
24. Laurence Clark Powell, "An Unpublished Mark Twain Letter," *AL*, XIII (January, 1942), 406. Albert B. Paine put together a set of Twain's more lively marginal notes in a chapter of his *Biography*, III, 1536–40.

can one learn it in a year, nor in five years. And its capital is *experience*—and you are too young, yet, to have much of that in your bank to draw from. When *you* shall have served on the stage a while (if you ever should), you will not send another heroine, unacquainted with the histrionic art, to ask a manager for a "star" part & *succeed* in her errand. And after you yourself shall have tried to descend a rain-water pipe, once, unencumbered, you will always know better, after that, than to let your hero descend one with a woman in his arms. Is it hypercriticism to notice these little blemishes? No—not in this case: for I wish to impress upon you this truth: that the moment you venture outside your *own* experience, you are in peril—don't ever do it. Grant that you are so young that your capital of experience is necessarily small: no matter, live within your literary means, & don't borrow. Whatever you have *lived*, you can write—& by hard work & a genuine apprenticeship, you can learn to write well; but what you have not lived you cannot write, you can only pretend to write it—you will merely issue a plausible-looking bill which will be pronounced spurious at the first counter. (*Love Lets* 228.)

It was just as typical of Twain to toss these thoughts off in a letter as it was for James, Howells, and Garland, who held similar views, to produce them in essays of formal criticism. Twain's letter catches a dual emphasis which figures prominently in all of the criticism he applied to his reading: he could tolerate no substitute for the texture of experience accurately perceived, no subjective faking where the sense of actuality is concerned; and he enjoined severe practice on those who would master the art of representing honestly what they had trained themselves to know. It is this tack that reveals the essential Twain in the richness of his informal criticism. It also illustrates that the value of Twain's criticism has its foundation in the sort of observation T. S. Eliot made about the ability of the poet to make the most useful criticism of poetry.

Finally, with respect to Twain's intentions, I do not think that he premeditatedly set up prescribed forms of criticism for himself, using the mask of the muggins for the one and the mask of the grumbler for the other. I can only say that when read in sequence the criticism does rather consistently assume these forms, and that in terms of continuity it would be quite surprising if a writer with Twain's individuality did not have certain identifiable patterns of thought.

PART I

Twain's Early Criticism: The Critic as Muggins

"But I have been playing the noble game of 'Muggins.' In that game, if you make a mistake of any kind, however trivial it may be, you are pronounced a muggins by the whole company, with great unanimity and enthusiasm. If you play the right card in the wrong place, you are a muggins; no matter how you play, in nine cases out of ten you are a muggins. They inform you of it with a shout which has no expression in it of regret."

(SOS *123*.)

1

Mark Twain and
the Critical Fool

I

If there was one thing that more than any other moved Twain to write, it was a critical reason. One would be hard pressed to find a book or sketch where he failed to indulge an animus against *some*thing. His motive, like that of all fellow satirists, implied the Juvenalian pretext, "si natura negat, facit indignatio versum." But not only did criticism inspire him and make him articulate, it also helped determine his organization, merging with art in his travesties on social and literary fads, his characterized personae, caricatures, tall tales, beast fables, and, in fact, in the whole gamut of jabs and stabs connected with ironic style.

The further one goes in noting the evidence of his critical art, the clearer the complexity of its devices becomes, both in themselves and in their interaction. The one transcendent device on which all others depend is Twain's use of varied personae. As Aristotle noted in his simple statement on point of view, in the *manner* of narration a poet "can either take another personality as Homer does, or speak in his own person, unchanged" (*Poetics* iii. 1, Butcher translation). Twain of course always took another personality, and the persona with which he accomplished not just masterful effects but feats of comic genius was the fool. All of his finest characters have something of the fool in them—Simon Wheeler, Colonel Sellers, the cub pilot, Tom Sawyer, Huck, Jim, Hank Morgan, Roxy, and the traveling "Mark Twain"—and so do some of his best pieces of criticism.

Twain's fool is an ideal mouthpiece for serious criticism because one does not expect it of him. He dramatizes the criticism and in his unawareness generates a certain amount of sympathy. At the least, he imparts some gaiety to a drab and sullen craft. The distinctive muggins complex which Twain gave his critical

21

fool was appropriated from the "good-natured self-satire" that Howells called the "prevailing mood" of his humor (*MMT* 144). It was the very quality most appreciated in Twain by Edwin P. Whipple, one of the first respectable critics to claim a place in literature for him. As Whipple pointed out—virtually giving us a picture of Mark Twain on the lecture platform—"he strikes his most effective satirical blows by an assumption of helpless innocence and bewildered forlornness of mind."[1]

Quite as important to the muggins as his foolishness are his longing for truth and his persistence in finding some part of it. He is in this respect a forerunner of the "inspired idiot" in *A Tramp Abroad*, who, though at best only a distant cousin of the traditional divine madman and wild sage, could none the less make some points worth pondering. Clearly, the otherwise unexplainable popularity of *Tramp* with Europeans was due to its having a crassly American hero whose innocence, like that of James's heroines, elicited the truth about glossed-over defects of their European-ness—their ultraseriousness implicitly alternating with his stupidity about such matters as the code of honor, institutionalism, opera, art, and historical legends.

In a sense, the muggins is a specialization of the "vernacular voice" which Henry Nash Smith has shown to have figured so significantly in Twain's development as a writer.[2] The effect Twain contemplated in using the muggins is gained by indirection and is usually in some way a formulation of anti-conventionalism. More specifically, as he conceived mugginsry in a little sketch he did for the *Californian* in 1864, it is the manner of a fool who loses just where he assumedly should win, and vice versa, for he makes others look foolish for their presumption of superiority.[3] In the one case, the fool plays the right card in the wrong place and is called a muggins "with great unanimity and enthusiasm"; and in the other, he calls a policeman a muggins for catching him in the act of climbing through the window of his

1. "American Literature," *Harper's New Monthly Magazine*, III (March, 1876), 526.
2. *Mark Twain: The Development of a Writer* (Cambridge, Mass., 1962).
3. The term muggins is most often used in games of cards, cribbage, or dominoes in which a person failing to claim a score can lose it to an adversary, who calls him a muggins for not immediately claiming it.

22

own quarters; though, having the upper hand, the policeman is, typically, unwilling to admit his mistake and drags the fool off to the station house (*SOS* 123f.).

Not all of Twain's fools are mugginses, but the one found most often in his criticism is. What makes the muggins so brilliant a projector of criticism is that, unlike the policeman, he may be the loser but, appearances aside, his wrongheadedness can almost never be quite wrong. He is completely ironic. He acts, we note, as a sort of decoy, a fellow who makes obvious *faux pas* that prompt unwary readers to pounce on him, only to have their own foolishness revealed to them. This, and occasionally much else, goes on *around* the actual subject of criticism, which has to be treated in its own right. In some of Twain's theatrical criticism, for instance, the muggins pretends to be a moralist, an ostensibly laughable pose, except that the moral *he* thinks should be laughed at—that exhibitionism drives good drama off the stage —is entirely just. So Twain has it both ways: through the fool he heaps scorn on pecksniffery and disassociates himself from it, while at the same time the fool's argument contains a legitimate criticism. The very fact of his being used as a critic makes this fool a good one, just as the very act of "Mark Twain" 's trying to be a critic makes a fool of him.

II

I have no desire in treating Twain's early criticism to make a case for the trivia of his apprenticeship. I wish merely to indicate that, as a rule, such of the early work as is redeemable owes its redemption to the subtlety of form demanded of him by criticism, and that this subtlety left its mark on his subsequent literary development. Therefore, before taking a closer look at the muggins and his criticism, we should consider for a moment the larger significance for Twain's career of his critical stance, especially as it relates to his purpose in writing, to his other early writings, and to those of other humorists who used a similar pose. These relationships have never been adequately investigated and can only be touched upon in general terms just here.

It was, after all, a level of competence in form and argument equal to that found in his use of the muggins which distinguished the other journalistic satire Twain wrote in his early period, including the material of *Innocents Abroad* and *Roughing It*.(4) And it was the critical intention in his early writing as a whole that set Twain apart from other humorists, who used the character of the fool (occasionally of the muggins too) almost exclusively for laughs.(5) As Twain himself told Archibald Henderson, "I succeeded in the long run, where Shillaber, Doesticks, and Billings failed, because they never had an ideal higher than that of merely being funny." He soon outgrew, he said, an early desire just "to make people laugh" instead of trying "to tell the truth."(6) While other humorists, and particularly the aphorists like Shillaber and Billings, did try to portray the native sense-amidst-nonsense of uneducated minds, they generally had no stomach for the unwelcome truths of a really satiric humor. The missing ingredient, in other words, was criticism, which was the prime mover and agent of such truth as appeared in Twain's early journalism, and which would ultimately involve him, as writer, in a re-evaluation of old standards and older literature, and in fact of the entire literary climate of ante bellum America.

How else did Twain rise above his literary origins and above the level of the "Down Easterners," the "Southwesterners," and the "Literary Comedians" of his own time, but by the force of his pugnacious wit and sense of outrage? Among "humorists" only Lowell in *The Biglow Papers* qualitatively rivaled him in converting humor into literary satire. Consider what the critical afflatus meant for Twain's career.

When Sam Clemens, the frustrated miner and occasional correspondent, stalked into the office of the Virginia City *Territorial Enterprise* in September, 1862, to become a regular member of

4. As might be expected, his satiric criticism turned out to be fairly complicated stuff for Twain to be using in newspapers and magazines; and he openly complained that not only Californians, but the supposedly sophisticated readers of the New York *Galaxy* were losing his point amidst the glare of his satiric fireworks ("Memoranda," June, 1870, *CTG*, 47).

5. The "Literary Comedians" always "acted a part," as Walter Blair pointed out in quoting a description of Artemus Ward (from the London *Spectator*, November 24, 1866) which had him adopting the style of the muggins (*Native American Humor* [2d ed.; San Francisco, 1960], p. 115f.).

6. *Mark Twain* (London, 1911), p. 99.

the staff, he had been taken on mainly on the strength of a number of humorous "Josh" letters that he had been contributing to the paper (without pay), one of the most impressive of which had been a criticism of rhetoric. According to Twain's story, he had burlesqued the oratory of no less a personage than the Chief Justice of the Territorial Supreme Court (*MTEnt* 390f.). As is well known, his landing a position on the *Enterprise* had rescued him from oblivion and had been a turning point in his life. From there he moved up to the post of Hawaiian correspondent of the Sacramento *Union* and used that experience to satirize the natives and their civilizers. His next major upward move was to become Holy Land correspondent for the *Alta California*, an experience he used to lampoon the Grand Tour in one of the most widely read books of its day. In time, he joined the "revolt from the village" by writing two masterpieces in that vein, *Adventures of Huckleberry Finn* and "The Man That Corrupted Hadleyburg." Twain's talent for criticism had opened some important doors and given him an opportunity for greatness.

Wherever the critical mode appeared in his early writing, one was certain to find Twain's evolving literary point of view. This was even true of his juvenilia. From the time of his adolescence in Hannibal, when as a callow printer he had written squibs sneering at the editor of a rival paper, on through an interlude as rambunctious comic writer for midwestern journals, going by such names as W. Epaminondas Adrastus Blab, Grumbler, and Thomas Jefferson Snodgrass, his mission was to depict the hollowness of social propriety, or the earthy departures from it in the life of a vernacular character. In his early style, to be sure, he was probably no better than any of a number of ephemeral humorists. The point is, however, that he understood the workings of the persona, and an initial critical intention produced embryonic variants on what were to become major satiric devices. Later on, he had ample opportunity to perfect these devices, partly because he was never just a reporter (at least not by choice) nor just a feature writer or humorist, but always tended to be a commentator, and kept looking around for something to sink his teeth into—such as cooked dividends, the fossil craze, the San Francisco police, notaries, undertakers, civic corruption, or the tormentors of the Chinaman.

In his subsequent development, Twain was assisted by literary trends; about the time when he turned professional writer popular literature was gravitating from sentiment toward humor, just as in belles-lettres the vogue of gentility and sensibility was giving way to realism and the portraiture of common life. Twain contributed much to the trend, and he also distinguished himself from it. His uniqueness stemmed from his critical sensibility, for, as it unfolded, his humor was more than an end in itself. It rendered implicit value judgments and betrayed a concern for standards. Twain looked further afield than the ordinary humorist did, venturing quite often into the areas of normative experience and hence of problems of art. Bret Harte, Charles Webb, Artemus Ward, John Phoenix, and other western writers had engaged in literary burlesque, and Twain read their work and wrote some felicitous burlesque himself.[7] However, unlike Twain's, their burlesques were not usually meant to be deliberately critical, nor did their work exhibit much craftsmanship, with the possible exception of some of Harte's *Condensed Novels*. Many such burlesques were the work of former Easterners, men who were looking back on a doctrine of culture which in the spaciousness of their new experience seemed almost effeminate. In contrast, Twain's criticism was specifically a criticism of art, and it covered a diversity of subjects. The theater, play reviewers, newspaper style, art, architecture, oratory, sentimental poetry, Sunday-school tales, and student compositions were all brought within the sphere of artistic analysis, and, what is more, Twain was mindful of their influence on public taste. In every respect he was more enterprising than other humorists had been in exploiting the potential of a persona for the purposes of tone and structure in the writing of criticism.

As commentators on Twain's relationship to the tradition of southwestern humor have pointed out, the older humorists kept the uncouth local character at arm's length from the gentlemanly narrator, who represented their own point of view, whereas Twain elevated that character to the position of narrator. He did so without divesting him of his former role as comic butt, and this decision had immense consequences for the critical fool. As a

7. See, e.g., Rogers, *Burlesque Patterns*, pp. 43–49, for the types of burlesque used in *IA*.

muggins, the fool is daft but has insight. He has an element of the mad, clairvoyant poet in him. Only a muggins would knowingly make himself an object of derision and only a poet would risk derision for the sake of truth. These conditions reveal the incipient cynic that the fool was to become with age and experience. Because of what he is, the muggins gives rise to a low order of superior laughter, "a shout which has no expression in it of regret." By this sacrificial gesture he catches the real fools—and may enlighten them. "The way of understanding," as Robert Frost once said, "is partly mirth."

Not the least remarkable aspect of the final, enlightening laugh is that it signifies a lightness of touch in Twain's early criticism that derives not so much from his humor as from the fact that foolishness with Twain is an affair of youth. In all of Twain's works the perspective of youth illuminates a slovenliness in art and in life that people customarily tolerate in silence, because it is difficult to be critical of it without seeming obvious or petty. Nowhere is Twain's skill in handling this problem more evident than it is in his theatrical criticism, to be considered in the following chapter.

2

Theatrical Criticism:
A Dude before Nudes

I

Twain's background for the criticism of plays was extensive. A lifelong theatergoer and devotee of the drama, he kept abreast of most theatrical activities. He belonged to the Players Club, founded by Edwin Booth, and was widely, in some cases personally, acquainted with the best-known actors and producers of his time. Among other things, he had worked on the dramatization of certain of his books and had criticized the dramatizations others had made of them; he had written and collaborated on the writing of plays, and was constantly coming up with ideas for the theater; he had conducted home theatricals and acted in them, with Shakespeare being one of his specialties; and he had been highly instrumental in breaking the surviving Puritan ban on the professional theater in Hartford.[1]

Twain's newspaper assignments had included a fair amount of theatrical reviewing. While he was with the San Francisco *Call*, he was responsible for writing notices of current plays, and he is thought to have done some reviewing for the San Francisco *Dramatic Chronicle*.[2] In addition, he covered the theater from time to time for the Virginia City *Territorial Enterprise*, the *Golden Era*, and the *Californian*, sending in reports that varied from brief four- or five-line calendars of theatrical events to full-fledged reviews.

1. Some of his ideas for plays, like the one about the Emperor Franz Joseph's mistress, were, fortunately, still-born (Henry W. H. Fischer, *Abroad with Mark Twain and Eugene Field* [New York, 1922], p. 57). Clara Clemens recalled parlor productions of *Hamlet*, for example, in 1881 and of *Macbeth* in 1885 (*MFMT* 88). Andrews describes Twain's influence on Hartford (*Nook Farm*, pp. 97–99).
2. *WG* 13, 89; Rogers, *Burlesque Patterns*, 21. No examples have survived of the work he may have done for the *Chronicle*.

Theatrical Criticism

Because Twain's departure from the critical amenities made good copy, Western editors delighted in reprinting his reviews, with at times a knowing wink toward the thigh-slapping crowd. Such was the case with one of a series of letters Twain had contracted to write for the *Call* from Virginia City in 1863. He contemplated the awaited opening of *East Lynne* (Clifton W. Tayleure's popular dramatization of Mrs. Henry Wood's tearful novel of 1861 about a woman who deserts her husband for another man and who, on her return, is hired as a nurse for her own children), and his squib was reprinted in the Virginia City *Evening Bulletin* with an appreciative introductory salute:

> The Great Eastern Slope theatrical critic, Mark Twain, in a letter to the San Francisco Call, makes the following "fist" at criticising the drama of "East Lynne," now being performed in the city. It is a sublime thing. Just listen to him:
> On next Tuesday evening the sickest of all sentimental dramas, "East Lynne," will be turned loose upon us at the Opera House. It used to afford me much solid comfort to see those San Franciscans whine and snuffle and slobber all over themselves at Maguire's Theatre, when the consumptive "William" was in the act of "handing in his checks," as it were, according to the regular programme of "East Lynne"—and now I am to enjoy a season of happiness again, I suppose. If the tears flow as freely here as I count upon, water privileges will be cheap in Virginia next week. However, Mrs. Julia Dean Hayne don't "take on" in the piece like Miss Sophia Edwin. Wherefore she fails to pump an audience dry like the latter.[3]

Here is the muggins in his simplest manner. The object of his criticism is not so much the emotional abandon of the play, as uppish San Franciscans, the theatergoing peerage, viewed by a lowly Virginian. Mark Twain is a backwoods clown who consents to betray his want of feeling and take his lumps on behalf of the subliterate pit. He shows, of course, that the apparently least sensitive response is the truly sensitive one.

3. Austin E. Hutcheson, "Twain Was 'News' to Other Newspapers While a Reporter on the 'Enterprise,'" *Twainian*, VII (November–December, 1948), 3. Twain's satire may to some extent be attributed to the desire for novelty. He and the other reporters tortured their souls, he said, "in the effort to find something to say about these performances which we had not said a couple of hundred times before" (*MTE* 255).

II

Twain was to produce a more complicated muggins in the person of a gentlemanly critic whom he appropriately reserved for the most famous performance he reviewed: Adah Isaacs Menken's, in Henry M. Milner's *Mazeppa* (written in 1830 and first produced in 1831), a play very broadly adapted from Byron's poem (1819).

First, a word about the play and the performer. When Twain saw *Mazeppa*, it was Menken's flamboyant style that had made the play, for by 1863 *Mazeppa* was a tired old equestrian drama. Frank Maguire had brought it to San Francisco during a meager wartime season and engaged "the finest corps dramatique," he said, in a bid to revive the spirited theater of the 1850's. It was a time when, as Constance Rourke observed, "a restless public . . . seemed to have rifled the rich offerings of a decade, and to have flung them aside."[4] So San Francisco needed something new in the early 1860's, *Mazeppa* needed a new treatment, and the play and the city apparently found one another, an event to which Twain became a discriminating witness. As he was almost alone in regarding the play as a false start, it will be helpful to understand what he was dealing with.

Standard productions of *Mazeppa* had exploited processions, combats, tableaux, and exotic costumes. As matters stood, there was little to justify another routine performance in 1863; for,

4. *Troupers of the Gold Coast: Or the Rise of Lotta Crabtree* (New York, 1928), p. 149. Lest it be assumed that the theater in post-Gold Rush San Francisco was in a frontier state, it should be pointed out that in the 1850's theatrical offerings on the Coast easily rivaled the best that was available anywhere else in the country—including New York—in richness, diversity, and professional excellence. Among the well over 1,000 theatrical pieces presented in that decade, 907 were plays (22 being Shakespeare's) and 48 were operas. Several factors were responsible for the theater's having fallen on bad times in the 1860's: an economic recession, the growing uncertainties of gold production, attended by wild speculation and followed by the war, and the discovery of silver in Nevada, which temporarily drained capital and enterprise away from San Francisco. General sources for this type of information are Joseph Gaer (ed.), *The Theatre of the Gold Rush Decade* (San Francisco, 1935); and George R. MacMinn, *The Theatre of the Golden Era in California* (Caldwell, Idaho, 1941).

nine years after it had been revived by Caroline Chapman (1851),[5] with lesser revivals along the way, it was still being trotted out as a play calculated to make a "stunning sensation," an effect which, in 1860, the reviewer in the *Golden Era* called the "chief desideratum of modern playgoers."[6] As the reviewer implied, its sensationalism could not bear much repetition. The play was ripe for burlesque—overripe, in fact—and it received the full treatment from Joe Jefferson when the famed comic actor made his first appearance in Maguire's Opera House in the summer of 1861 in *Mazeppa, or the Fiery Untamed Rocking Horse*. For Maguire to bring it back in serious form, only two years after so memorable a burlesque, meant that some new sauce had to have been added. This he found in the performance with which Miss Menken had first regaled New York in June, 1862.[7] She had taken the male lead and, although that in itself was not an unusual thing for actresses to do (especially for a virtuoso of protean comedy), here she subjected herself to being stripped on stage and then bound helplessly to the back of a horse that had to climb a narrow runway inclining well up toward the ceiling of the theater. Menken's *Mazeppa* outdid the triple bill. It combined the high and the low, romance and sensation, and in the famous equestrian scene it provided something of a circus and variety show.

Menken's semi-nudity was enough by itself to assure packed houses. The more astonishing response was that of a normally captious press, which, famished by a dearth of challenging plays,

5. When Twain learned that Miss Chapman was still doing *Mazeppa* in December, 1865 (she then being probably all of seventy-five years of age), and in the frosty Montana Territory at that, his heart went out to her:

> The idea of the jolly, motherly old lady stripping to her shirt and riding a fiery untamed Montana jackass up flights of stairs and kicking up and cavorting around the stage on him with the quicksilver frozen in the thermometers and the audience taking brandy punches out of their pockets and biting them, same as people eat peanuts in civilized lands! Why, there is no end to the old woman's energy. She'll go through with Mazeppa with flying colors even if she has to do it with icicles a yard long hanging to her jackass's tail. (*Golden Era*, January 28, 1866, *WG* 102.)

6. MacMinn, *Theatre of Golden Era*, p. 216.
7. She first did the role in Albany, New York, in April, 1861 (Allen Lesser, *Enchanting Rebel* [New York, 1947], p. 75).

tended to overpraise a histrionic exhibition. The reviewer for the *Golden Era* quoted Shakespearean lyrics in Miss Menken's honor, called her the "most magnificently developed woman in the world," and puffed about her "rare originality" and the "imperishable fame" she had achieved in "this great creation of the immortal poet."[8]

Unfortunately, the "great creation"—which Twain criticized along with the "rare originality" of the acting—was nothing like Byron's poem. In the poem (based on an episode in Voltaire's *Histoire de Charles XII*, 1731), Mazeppa was a Polish nobleman given command of the Eastern Ukraine. He had left Peter the Great to join Charles XII in 1709 at the battle of Pultowa, after which he told a tale of his youth. As a page to King Casimir V of Poland he had been apprehended in a budding affair with the wife of a court official and for punishment was bound naked to the back of a wild steed, which, having been lashed mercilessly, carried him off to the Ukraine. Once there, Mazeppa, almost dead, was taken in by peasants. Milner's plot, on the other hand, revolved around the foundling theme—Mazeppa became the lost heir to the throne of Tartary—and the heroine was the daughter of the castle warden, who had promised her in marriage to a count she did not love. Mazeppa, now known as Casimir, proved himself as a warrior and, after announcing that he was the count's rival, wounded him in a duel, whereupon he was strapped to the back of a wild steed and carried off to Tartary, arriving just in time to stop his grieving father, King Abder Khan, from appointing a chieftain to succeed him. With his newfound father, Mazeppa returned to Poland, prevented the heroine's marriage, and after defeating the Poles, married her himself.

III

Legend has it that when Adah Menken arrived in Virginia City with *Mazeppa* in February, 1864, "the boys"—Twain among them—had agreed to pan her in concert, but afterwards had decided instead to greet her with excessive praise, a trick that had the effect of taking in the rest of the cast and throwing them

8. "Dramatic and Musical—Menken in Mazeppa," *Golden Era*, XI (August 8, 1863), 5.

into jealous confusion, for many of them, like Junius Booth, were actors of long experience and privately resented being associated with a stunt show. On meeting the actress Twain was rather taken with her as a person.[9] This meeting took place about half a year after he had reviewed her performance in San Francisco.

Twain's review was the last and longest portion of a three-part letter written for the *Territorial Enterprise* for September 13, 1863, and was entitled, rather significantly, "The Menken— Written Especially for Gentlemen" (*MTEnt* 78–80). Four matters were taken up: the Menken's appearance, her gestures, her big scene, and the exaggerated plot. With each of these topics Twain raised damning questions about integrity of purpose and generally indicated that Menken was lowering public taste under the pretense of raising it.

Overshadowing everything else, however, was Twain's device of discussing the play through the (for him) unorthodox persona of a gentleman, who is at once a fool and the source of criticism. In the first paragraph the gentleman gives Menken's attire a more careful analysis than it merits, on the ironic bases that it is put forward as the main feature of the show, and that a critic who comes to see a serious play is expected to inquire into the function of all facets of its production. As the embarrassed gentleman must rule prurience off grounds and yet treat the "costume" literally, it suggests to him something garishly unlike what is intended. Meanwhile, his fussiness reveals him to be a muggins: a dude before nudity.

> They said she was dressed from head to foot in flesh-colored "tights," but I had no opera-glass, and I couldn't see it, to use the language of the inelegant rabble. She appeared to me to have but one garment on—a thin tight white linen one, of unimportant dimensions; I forget the name of the article, but it is indispensable to infants of tender age—I suppose any young mother can tell you what it is, if you have the moral courage to ask the

---

9. Rourke, *Troupers*, p. 182; Lesser, *Enchanting Rebel*, p. 125; Paine, *Biog* I 248. Possibly Twain was impressed, too, by the fact that Adah Menken's husband of the moment—her third in a string of mates— was Robert Henry Newell, the literary editor of the New York Sunday *Mercury*, whose humorous writing appeared under the name of Orpheus C. Kerr.

question. With the exception of this superfluous rag, the Menken dresses like the Greek Slave; but some of her postures are not so modest as the suggestive attitude of the latter. She is a finely formed woman down to her knees; if she could be herself that far, and Mrs. H. A. Perry the rest of the way, she would pass for an unexceptionable Venus.[10]

Our poor unsmiling dude is a little like the exasperated cup-bearer of *1601*. He has to talk about what offends him, but, unlike the reviewer of *East Lynne*, can take no secondary "comfort" in what he sees. None the less, he carries on.

The foolishness of Mark Twain's putting on airs is somewhat less important than the foolishness of the dilettante whose role he enacts in presuming to pass judgment in an area where he has no competence or where, as a gentleman, he shouldn't have any. However, one no sooner takes him for a muggins than one finds that he has spoken the simple truth. The actress, we see, comes off as anything but what she is supposed to be; she is, as the gentleman observes, a diapered half-goddess capering about in the role of romantic hero.

To bring out the full grotesquerie of the performance Twain chose his allusions with greater care than one might guess. The comparison with the Greek Slave, for instance, refers to one of the better-known poses in the "Model Artist" shows, which featured so-called live statuary, and Twain's implication is that it is not the costume alone—at times it resembles the drapery of a statue—but Miss Menken's immodest "postures" in it that are out of keeping with the aesthetically statuesque impression given by the clothing.[11]

10. "The Greek Slave" was widely hailed as perhaps the greatest piece of sculpture of its time. It had been created by the American sculptor Hiram Powers, who had worked for Dorfeuille in his Wax Museum in Cincinnati, and had there met Frances Trollope. In 1851, Dr. Collyer, a famous model-artist entrepreneur, had his wife appear as "The Greek Slave," a pose in which she won notoriety. Mrs. Perry, née Marion Agnes Land Rookes, an actress of Australian birth, made her San Francisco debut as a dancer in 1858. During the 1860's she acted regularly at Maguire's Opera House, where she was no doubt seen by Twain. She married J. B. (June) Booth, Jr.

11. What Twain said about her figure, by the way, was based on precise observation. Photographs of her as *Mazeppa* confirm the impression of a body that down to the knees presented an aspect of sylph-like femininity, but, as she discarded the tights in her San Francisco appearance

For his next point, Twain moves on from the farcical costume to Menken's frenetic stage movements. The dude assumes that because her gesticulations stand out from their dramatic context, they cannot be demonstrations of virtuosity in acting, but are to be appreciated in and for themselves; and so that is the way he studies them, trying to keep his balance amidst the flurry of motion. The trick of playing the muggins also takes on another dimension, for in writing back to Virginia City from San Francisco, Twain naturally touches on rivalries and local pride. In any event, not wishing to press the fact that he is swimming against the current of critical applause (everybody else may be "right"), Twain has the dude brace himself and tell what he sees, no matter how ridiculous.

> Here every tongue sings the praises of her matchless grace, her supple gestures, her charming attitudes. Well, possibly, these tongues are right. In the first act, she rushes on the stage, and goes cavorting around after "Olinska" [Mazeppa's love]; she bends herself back like a bow; she pitches headforemost at the atmosphere like a battering-ram; she works her arms, and her legs, and her whole body like a dancing-jack; her every movement is as quick as thought; in a word, without any apparent reason for it, she carries on like a lunatic from the beginning of the act to the end of it. At other times she "whallops" herself down on the stage, and rolls over as does the sportive pack-mule after his burden is removed. If this be grace then the Menken is eminently graceful.

The most ungraceful part of the play is what everyone has come to see, the unmanageable ride on the fiery Tartarean steed. In describing it, the dude again tries to report the observed facts and keep his composure, but it is taxing for him and his disgust begins to show through. He takes the play too seriously, so that at one stroke he continues his humorous commentary on the play, while at the same time becoming the object of it himself.

> After a while they proceed to strip her, and the high chief Pole calls for the "fiery untamed steed"; a subordinate Pole brings in the fierce brute, stirring him up occasionally to make him

---

and wore a white blouse that left her shoulders bare and a pair of shorts that reached mid-thigh, far too great an emphasis fell upon a pair of bulbous knees, bulging, masculine calves, and the thick ankles of a dancer. Thus Twain pointed out an important flaw in the sex appeal which her costuming was to have brought out.

35

run away, and then hanging to him like death to keep him from doing it; the monster looks round pensively upon the brilliant audience in the theatre, and seems very willing to stand still —but a lot of those Poles grab him and hold on to him, so as to be prepared for him in case he changes his mind. They are posted as to his fiery untamed nature, you know, and they give him no chance to get loose and eat up the orchestra. They strap Mazeppa on his back, fore and aft, and face uppermost, and the horse goes cantering up-stairs over the painted mountains, through tinted clouds of theatrical mist, in a brisk exciting way, with the wretched victim he bears unconsciously digging her heels into his hams, in the agony of her sufferings, to make him go faster. Then a tempest of applause bursts forth, and the curtain falls. The fierce old circus horse carries his prisoner around through the back part of the theatre, behind the scenery, and although assailed at every step by the savage wolves of the desert, he makes his way at last to his dear old home in Tartary down by the footlights, and beholds once more, O, gods! the familiar faces of the fiddlers in the orchestra. The noble old steed is happy, then, but poor Mazeppa is insensible—"ginned out" by his trip, as it were.

After this, the review is brought around to the humorous improbability of its romantic plot, and then, following further allusions to the willingly duped audiences and local pride ("crowded houses went crazy over it every night"—impatient "Virginians" will soon have a chance to do the same), Twain ends as he had begun, on the Menken, praising her work in another play, *The French Spy*, for her silence and restraint of movement, qualities that would appeal to a gentleman, but that would be anathema to the vivacious actress. Twain wants to bring people to their artistic senses, and the dude helps him by trying to be kind to a lady and find something—anything—to praise her for, because he wishes to be fair. Mentioning her role in *The French Spy* as that of a "frisky Frenchman," who is as "dumb as an oyster," he believes her "extravagant gesticulations" were less "overdone" there than they were in *Mazeppa*. Since she does not deliver a line very well anyway and depends on her "shape and acting" (i.e., movements), "the character of a fidgety 'dummy' is peculiarly suited to her line of business. She plays the Spy, without words, with more feeling than she does Mazeppa with them." She is at her best when she does not try so much to *act*. The gentleman would have praised her with as good a will as not, and indeed he tried his best to do so.

For Twain to have accurately characterized Miss Menken's performance while pretending to be an innocent gentleman required no mean skill. To do this when she was the toast of the West and was blotting out every other theatrical interest suggests a rather high order of discrimination.[12] During the play's two-month run, more than half the people in San Francisco, over thirty thousand of them, had come to see Menken in *Mazeppa*. Among them was Charles Warren Stoddard, who later recalled his reaction in "gentlemanly" terms that were somewhat at variance with Twain's:

> Garments seemed almost to profane her, as they do a statue. . . . The moment she entered upon the scene she inspired it with a poetic atmosphere that appealed to one's love of beauty, and satisfied it. . . . She was a vision of celestial harmony made manifest in the flesh—a living and breathing poem that set the heart to music and throbbed rhythmically to a passion that was as splendid as it was pure.[13]

Similar, if quieter, sentiments filled the reviews not only in San Francisco but also in New York and points in between, and even in London and Paris. Outright deflation of the sort Twain wrote was practically non-existent. *Punch* and a few other British journals might frown on the vulgarity of Miss Menken's costume, the New York *Herald* might regard her as an allurement for "juveniles and lovers of the marvelous," and *The New York Times* might not deign to review her.[14] However, no one had got at the heart of the matter as Twain had. The typical review more closely resembled the blurb in the New York *Illustrated News*, in which Miss Menken was pictured as a crowning sensation, even for the New Bowery patrons, who steadily demanded, and got, almost nothing but sensationalism. The quality of her

12. Objections were few and far between. Several months after Twain's review, the critic for the Sacramento *Bulletin* had objected to being given a peep show (Lesser, *Enchanting Rebel*, p. 113), but there was nothing approaching Twain's probing analysis.
13. "La Belle Menken," *National Magazine*, XXI (February, 1905), 479.
14. "Theatrical and Musical," *Herald*, June 16, 1862, 5. The *Times* would notice her presence by no more than a perfunctory statement or vague allusion ("Amusements," *Times*, June 17, 1862, 2; "Amusements," *Times*, September 20, 1862, 2).

acting, the *News'* critic pointed out, was well spoken of by the best of critics; and he himself found her Mazeppa a "quiet and ladylike" piece of acting.[15]

IV

Twain's critique of Adah Menken's *Mazeppa* was not the only occasion on which he tried, by means of the moralistic fool, to set forth the relationship between stage morals and integrity of form. He did so again several years later in a report from New York on the famous *Black Crook*. This spectacular extravaganza and first large-scale "girlie show," with its chorus in showy tights, appeared within a few months after Menken had brought *Mazeppa* back to New York in 1866. With the praise of several European capitals behind her, and being dinned into the public ear, Menken gave prestigious reinforcement to the new vogue of the "nude drama."

After seeing *The Black Crook*, Twain was more seriously disturbed than he had been in 1863 about the possible effect of nudity on the legitimate stage. George Odell, who called the season of 1866–67 "A Season of Sensations," noted that *The Black Crook* was "the first attempt to put on the stage the wild delirious joy of a sensualist's fancy."[16] With other more notorious forms of corruption running rampant in the country after the war, the theater could hardly have escaped the general contamination. This did not go unnoticed. Whereas previously in San Francisco Twain had stood alone in censuring counterfeit drama, in New York there had been a good deal of shrill moralistic objection to it. Recognizing the usual inverse effects of moralism, Twain had to proceed subtly if he was to take an essentially moral line himself.[17] It is therefore interesting to see how he conquered the problem of tone by means of the muggins.

When he came east in January, 1867, on what was to have been the first leg of a journey around the world, with a commission to write letters for the *Alta California*, Twain had been away from

15. "New Bowery Theatre," *Illustrated News*, July 5, 1862, 130.
16. *Annals of the New York Stage* (New York, 1931), VIII, 152.
17. He had observed that the newspaper critics had to take some of the blame for the success of *The Black Crook* (*Speeches* 48).

New York for some fourteen years and was naturally interested in changes. More than anything else, he was struck by the way "model artists" in one guise or another (some dressed as fairies!) were crowding out everything else, in much the same way that Menken had. In his first letter back to the *Alta* on February 2, Twain devoted a considerable amount of space to this matter. The second and third parts of his five-part letter surveying changes in city life were entitled "The Model Artists" and "All Dramadom Affected" (*MTTMB* 84–87):

> When I was here in '53, a model artist show had an ephemeral existence in Chatham street, and then everybody growled about it, and the police broke it up; at the same period "Uncle Tom's Cabin" was in full blast in the same street, and had already run one hundred and fifty nights. Everybody went there in elegant toilettes and cried over Tom's griefs. But now, things are changed. The model artists play nightly to admiring multitudes at famous Niblo's Garden, in great Broadway [in *The Black Crook*]—have played one hundred and fifty nights and will play one hundred and fifty nights more, no doubt—and Uncle Tom draws critical, self-possessed groups of negroes and children at Barnum's Museum.

Although a naïve melodrama like George L. Aiken's dramatization of *Uncle Tom* may not seem to afford a happy contrast (in 1852 the conservative press had considered it a crude caricature), the very simplicity of the play indicates that the transformation in theatrical affairs was drastic. As matters stood, poor "Tom," though offered by Barnum, was being seen by a relatively highbrow audience, while everyone else was stampeding to watch a dramatic void.[18] So far did Twain go with the fact of change. To enter on a more roundly denunciatory note, he had to anticipate and exploit it himself, and so at the end of the paragraph, while the reader looks for him to make a more explicit

18. It was the reviewer for the New York *Herald* (September 3, 1862) who had considered "Tom" a caricature. Garrison's *Liberator* (September 9, 1853) was predictably enthusiastic in playing up its salubrious effect on the audience: they left the theater "as gravely and seriously as people retire from a religious meeting." For a summary of the critical response to *Uncle Tom*, see Barnard Hewitt, *Theatre U.S.A., 1668 to 1957* (New York, 1959), pp. 171–79. *The Black Crook* grossed $1,100,000, playing 475 performances in sixteen months. A performance lasted about six and a half hours.

criticism, Twain turns to humor and unexpectedly aims it at his persona, thus playing the old game of muggins: "I fear me I shall have to start a moral missionary society here. Don't you suppose those friends of mine in San Francisco were jesting, when they warned me to be very choice in my language, if I ever lectured here, lest I might offend?"

In this aside to his Western reader, Twain's mention of his lectures brings one back to the mask of the uncouth clown, innocently preoccupied with discovering the way of the world. Having himself been advised to mend his ways, he is not unflatteringly surprised that the East should prove to be less the seat of culture than of brazen immorality, over which he, of all persons, must shake his head. It would not have been lost on those San Franciscans who followed Twain's journalism that there was an obverse parallel between the need of missionary work in New York and his recent reflections upon missionary encroachments in the Sandwich Islands.

Twain had only to bring up the issue of public morality to put a quietus on moral enthusiasm. In this passage and in later parts of his letter, he mocks excessive proprieties by an excessive nicety in his devotion to them, and therein lies the second stage of his criticism as muggins. The same San Franciscans he had just regaled by taunting New Yorkers are now ensnared by the backlash of his joke on moralism, inasmuch as they themselves had banished model artists for immorality, and not out of a desire to protect the theater.

In the midst of the criticism that follows the introduction of the muggins, Twain points out how not to criticize *The Black Crook*, by noting that when a newspaper and a parson "pitched into" it, they automatically gave the show national publicity and put money into its owner's pocket. What makes it possible for him to render a moral critique is that, having fended off hyperthyroid moralists and shameless immoralists, he attempts to portray the feelings of a man of ordinary decency appalled by unrestraint and an impossible agglomeration of gaudiness. Speaking as he does, this dude should not be watching *The Black Crook*; he is therefore a muggins. He is thrust into emotional turmoil as he tries to withstand the sensory assault of naked beauties, and so he complains puritanically:

> . . . it is about as spectacular as anything I ever saw without
> sinking right into the earth with outraged modesty. It is the
> wickedest show you can think of. You see there is small harm
> in exhibiting a pack of painted old harlots, swathed in gauze,
> like the original model artistes, for no man careth a cent for
> them but to laugh and jeer at them. Nakedness itself, in such
> a case, would be nothing worse than disgusting. But I warn you
> that when they put beautiful clipper-built girls on the stage in
> this new fashion, with only just barely clothes enough on to be
> tantalizing, it is a shrewd invention of the devil. It lays a
> heavier siege to public morals than all the legitimate model
> artist shows you can bring into action.

His reasoning being just sane enough to put one off one's
guard, Twain then springs his joke. For this muggins has been
working himself up to a reiteration of his indignation: "This
exhibition . . . touches my missionary sensibilities." To be fully
appreciated, the duality of Twain's criticism here should be
seen as a continuation of what he had been doing to establish
the gentlemanly pretensions of his persona in the *Alta* letters
that lead up to this one. During the voyage to New York, Mark
Twain, the correspondent, had been tormented by the vulgarity
of Mr. Brown, a Caliban who "always unearths the disagreeable
features of everything that comes under his notice." It is significant that the provocation for this complaint had been that
Brown had caught the dude in the act of admiring two native
damsels with "voluptuous forms, and . . . precious little drapery"
and had warned him that one would not want to "prospect one
of them heifers with a fine-tooth [comb]" (*MTTMB* 41). Despite
a similar hypocrisy, the muggins of the *Black Crook* letter con-
demns the show for all of the right reasons. He notices that the
producers have gone out of their way to prolong spectacular
diversion and to find ingenious excuses for nudity, only to compound the purposelessness of the whole. Toward the end of his
critique the dude becomes increasingly bewildered:

> The scenery and the legs are everything; the actors who do
> the talking are the wretchedest sticks on the boards. But the
> fairy scenes—they fascinate the boys! Beautiful bare-legged
> girls hanging in flower baskets; others stretched in groups on
> great sea shells; others clustered around fluted columns; others
> in all possible attitudes; girls—nothing but a wilderness of
> girls—stacked up, pile on pile, away aloft to the dome of the

theatre, diminishing in size and clothing, till the last row, mere children, dangle high up from invisible ropes, arrayed only in a camisa. The whole tableau resplendent with columns, scrolls, and a vast ornamental work, wrought in gold, silver and brilliant colors—all lit up with gorgeous theatrical fires, and witnessed through a great gauzy curtain that counterfeits a soft silver mist! It is the wonders of the Arabian Nights realized.

Those girls dance in ballet, dressed with a meagreness that would make a parasol blush. And they prance around and expose themselves in a way that is scandalous to me. Moreover, they come trooping on the stage in platoons and battalions, in most princely attire I grant you, but always with more tights in view than anything else. They change their clothes every fifteen minutes for four hours, and their dresses become more beautiful and more rascally all the time.

Having examined the effect of *The Black Crook* on art and morals, Twain exposes its effect on the theater. He is distressed at the plight of the girls, who have become commercial pawns. But the besetting difficulty remains one of aesthetic discord, and this becomes well-nigh intolerable in the lesser shows where the stage action varies from the ludicrous to the pathetic. Twain works his way into his critique from the posture of a "blushing" muggins, noting that the Worrell Sisters "cannot hope to achieve supreme success" because "they do not take off enough." Sallie Hinckley, "playing a nude fairy piece . . . makes a lovely statue of herself . . . [being] dressed about like the Menken." Her chorus is so repulsive, though, that our dude is for the first time moved to a desire for violence.

She has got about thirty padded, painted, slab-sided, lantern-jawed old hags with her who are so mortal homely that nothing tastes good to them. And to see those lank, blear-eyed leathery old scalliwags come out and hop around in melancholy dance, with their cheap, ragged, nine-inch dress-tails flapping in the air—Oh, it is worth going miles to see! And when one of them finishes her poor little shindig and makes her wind up stamp in the orthodox way, sticking out a slipper like a horse trough, with a criminal attempt at grace, I want to snatch a double-barrelled shot-gun and go after the whole tribe.

Bad as this was, Twain held that the worst effect of nudity was its threat to legitimate theater. Although Edwin Booth and the legitimate theater were doing well enough, Twain was convinced that their prosperity would be short-lived unless they broke down and began to "peel some women." Wherever he looked during this tour of the New York theater, Twain saw signs of a degeneration in taste. If it wasn't nudity itself, it was something akin to it that thrived in the same atmosphere, like sadist sensation. The latter he complained of in connection with *The Christian Martyr*, then on the boards at Barnum's Museum, cheek by jowl with freak shows, peanut stands, a statue of Venus, and a waxworks that featured a model of Queen Victoria (*MTTMB* 116–18).

The whole tendency of postwar theatrical productions was bad. Those people associated with the theater who wanted the situation brought under control invoked the principle Twain had cited, that the incursion of nudity bred confusion and undermined dramatic standards. Of course, drama critics have always made a professional obligation of bemoaning the state of the theater. A lament such as Whitman's, for example, in the Brooklyn *Eagle* in 1847 that "of all 'low' places where vulgarity . . . is in the ascendent, and bad-taste carries the day . . . , the New York theatres . . . may be put down . . . at the top of the heap!"[19]—such a lament was scarcely novel and could likely have been made in almost any season. But the case against nudity was something that had to be pleaded over and above the one usually raised against vulgarity, for it struck at the autonomy of the theater. Twain's criticisms of *Mazeppa* and *The Black Crook* were capital blows struck on behalf of the good cause. He buttressed them later with other attacks, in which, while defending a popular medium, he was anti-popular enough to insist on a high level of art in it. This can be seen in the next phase of his attack on nudity.

19. Montrose J. Moses and John Mason Brown (eds.), *The American Theatre as Seen by Its Critics 1752–1934* (New York, 1934), p. 70f. For another, more mixed comment by Whitman on the subject of model artists, written in New Orleans in March, 1848, see Emory Holloway (ed.), *The Uncollected Poetry and Prose of Walt Whitman* (Garden City, N.Y., 1921), I, 191.

V

Following *The Black Crook*, nudity aggrandized its position in the theater, despite periodic harangues from dramatic and moralistic quarters. The season of 1869–70, for example, was another sensational one, almost on a par with that of 1866–67. The major attraction was Lydia Thompson and her British Blondes,[20] who were attacked in the New York press and by Twain in the Buffalo *Express*. Reviewers of the Blondes objected, in the way that Twain had earlier with *The Black Crook*, to the incongruous hodgepodge of cheap effects.[21] After having disparaged their performance, Twain received word that they felt themselves to have been unjustly insulted. He therefore fired back editorially in the *Express*, with exaggerated gentlemanly outrage, "Seriously, would not you suppose that if you would do what Miss Lydia Thompson and Miss Pauline Markham do every day, that you could bear a good deal in the way of criticism? Do you know what it is they do? They come on stage naked, to all intents and purposes, padded; powdered; oiled; enameled; and glorified with false hair. They are coarsely, vulgarly, voluptuous." He disliked their "dismal dances," and also their "doleful procession of tasteless jokes made toothsome with obscenity" because it is hard to hear "vulgarity, slang and obscenity, issue from female lips."[22] The newly married editor (husband of an angel before whom "evil deeds stand abashed,— then surrender"[23]) is of course personally piqued at the Blondes. But his criticism is more heavy-handed than it needs to be, and it is just humorless enough to become funny in itself—a probably unintended piece of mugginsry.

20. This troupe had a repertoire of burlesque on popular classics, such as *Sinbad and the Forty Thieves*. One of its typical featured performances was entitled *Ixion Ex-King of Thessaly, or the Man at the Wheel*.

21. "It is impossible to give an idea of this sustained burlesque. It resembles an Irish stew as one minute they are dancing a cancan and the next singing a psalm tune. It is a bewilderment of limbs, belladonna and grease" (Bernard Sobel, *A Pictorial History of Burlesque* [New York, 1956], p. 19f.).

22. "The Blondes," Buffalo *Express*, February 27, 1870, Documents File, *MTP*.

23. Theodore Hornberger (ed.), *Mark Twain's Letters to Will Bowen* (Austin, Tex., 1941), p. 20.

Outweighing the business of nudity was the consistency of Twain's concern with functionalism and the intrinsic propriety of a performance, but the extrinsic issue was not unimportant. Indeed, Twain's interested moralism ran exactly counter to the evangelical moralism represented by an organization like the YMCA of his day and the type of person it recruited. Backed by business men, the "Y" put out a pamphlet in 1866 declaring that a great field for moral reform existed among young clerks and apprentices of the city, who, as they no longer boarded with their employers, were wasting their spare time on such diversions as drink and the theater. In that year, which had witnessed the return of Menken in *Mazeppa*, an obscure shipping clerk and dry goods salesman named Anthony Comstock wrote the "Y," his future employer in the reform movement, to express his agreement with their views. He dramatized the typical situations of bored young men giving themselves over to billiards, drink, cards, and attendance at the opera and the theater. At first, Comstock was too busy with books, magazines, art, and contraception to make war on the theater, as he did later. Bawdy theatricals did much to arouse him, though, and in 1873 he was grumbling in his diary, "Why is it that every public play must have a naked woman?"[24] By its effect on reformers like Comstock, the vogue established by Menken's *Mazeppa*, *The Black Crook*, and Lydia Thompson's "Blondes" was eventually to place not just the drama but all of the arts in jeopardy.

Twain's criticism had urged that as a defense against Comstockery and as a virtue in its own right, the theater should purge itself of dramatic impurities and thereby of the charge that it was a purveyor of salacity. This clearing of the moral air in popular literature was something that was constantly in need of being done. With his mock-modest dude, Twain had demonstrated one of the best ways of doing it.

24. Heywood Broun and Margaret Leech, *Anthony Comstock, Roundsman of the Lord* (New York, 1927), pp. 28, 76, 77.

3

Extravagant Romanticism: Playing Dumb

I

The gentleman was one kind of fool—an unusual "high" type. Twain had other lower types, who, like the gentleman, were characteristically green, credulous, and humorless, though outwardly not as perceptive as he was. Whereas, for example, the gentleman might feel uneasy about using "the language of the inelegant rabble" when he said, "I couldn't see it," there is manifestly a good deal that the "low" fools—who use the phrase unapologetically—can't see. The common lot of these fools is the undeviatingly simple life. They are natural mugginses. The representative figure among them is a model dullard; that which is too stupid for criticism he attacks, generally on grounds that it is incomprehensible. His most formidable criticism is to simplify the powerful overflow of absurd feelings. He is death on triteness. Twain brings this fool to life with complete effortlessness, merely by playing dumb.

We have noticed how the high-level fool operates as critic. Now let us see how the normal one, an ordinary dunce, performs. Three prime examples are provided by Twain's review of the play *Ingomar, The Barbarian*, his review of the opera *The Crown Diamonds*, and his report of a speech by a Nevada politician, L. O. Sterns. In all three there is a striving for loftiness which Twain as fool pretends is beyond his depth. What he specifically satirizes is an embarrassingly extravagant romantic style, one that seems to combine the qualities of *The Black Crook*, Menken, and the Blondes: the straining for novelty, the attempt to gain an effect for its own sake, and the effort to produce a fantastic display of superficial emotions. As far as the opera and the speech were concerned, the situation was tailor-made for the use

46

of the muggins. Mark Twain was challenged to cover the opera, and he had to cover the speech on his reporter's beat and didn't want to.

Friedrich Hahn's *Ingomar, The Barbarian* (1843)[1] was a heroic romance based on the gallantry of a wild oriental chieftain. Being even more blatantly oriental than *Mazeppa*, it was acted in the most extravagantly romantic stage tradition. Its performance was all the more difficult for Twain to stomach because by the middle of the nineteenth century the oriental romance had become something of an anachronism. The vogue of orientalism which had been stimulated by Marlowe's *Tamburlaine* and had flourished in the heroic drama of the Restoration had already seen better days when it was adopted by the Romantic poets. Thereafter, it reappeared only in isolated cases and in modified form, as in a novel like Charles Kingsley's *Hypatia* (1853), or as a popular curiosity in the historical and biblical romance exemplified by novels like Lew Wallace's *Ben Hur* (1880) and Henryk Sienkiewicz's *Quo Vadis* (translated in 1896). *Ingomar* hovered on the fringes of this latter movement and was its beneficiary, drawing well in numerous revivals right up to the end of the century.

When Twain saw *Ingomar* at Maguire's new opera house in Virginia City in November, 1863 (several months after he had seen *Mazeppa*), he wrote a burlesque, entitled " 'Ingomar' over the Mountains," which was published in the *Territorial Enterprise* and in the *Golden Era*, and was reprinted in New York's *Yankee Notions* five months later. The burlesque was characterized as one of a "succession of humorous, pungent and peculiar critiques" written for the *Enterprise* during Maguire's fall season.[2] Twain was therefore presented as indulging in a favorite

---

1. Originally *Der Sohn Der Wildness*, this five-act play was first done in English around 1850, after it had been translated (into verse) by William H. Charlton (Ina Ten Eyck Firkins [comp.], *Index to Plays, 1800–1926* [New York, 1927], p. 133). Friedrich Hahn was the pseudonym of the Austrian dramatist Baron Eligius Franz Joseph von Münch-Bellinghausen (1806–71).

2. The piece was reprinted both by Ivan Benson, *Mark Twain's Western Years* (Stanford, Calif., 1938), pp. 181–83, and by Franklin Walker,

topical exercise. In keeping with this background, he chose a form which in itself implied that the extravagance of the play was badly dated: he had a homespun Westerner reduce the play to a spare, realistic scenario and *localize* it, the result being an ironic extension of Hahn's treatment of the tired old theme of the noble savage.[3]

Ingomar is about a barbarian (Alemanni) chief who falls in love with a Greek girl, Parthenia (her name signifying her virginity), who was being held hostage by the tribe in order that her kidnapped father, Myron, might try to raise the money for his ransom. Ingomar's love inspires him to kill a tribesman intent on carrying her off and to attempt to purchase her freedom. In the big scene of the play, his love becomes so fierce that Parthenia threatens to commit suicide at his approach. Ingomar prefers to give up his position as chief rather than part with her, and he goes to work as an armorer for her father, until Polydor, Myron's creditor and the girl's rejected suitor, threatens to enslave his debtor's wife and daughter, whereupon Ingomar takes their place. The Greeks offer the barbarian his freedom if he will fight the Alemanni, who are readying an attack. He refuses to dishonor himself, but, as he is about to be exiled, the Timarch of the decadent Greeks steps in to free Ingomar, to marry him to Parthenia, and to work out a settlement with the barbarians, who under their new king and queen are to build a neighboring city-state.

Judged by the standards of his mock review of gladiatorial combat in *Innocents* (I 357–60), or even by those of his review of *The Crown Diamonds*, Twain's burlesque of *Ingomar* is not uniformly adept. He at first stresses the surface incongruities of one

---

The Washoe Giant in San Francisco (San Francisco, 1938), pp. 59–60. (I cite Walker's text.) The editor of *Yankee Notions* wrote, "We miss a figure if anything more thoroughly droll has been perpetrated in many a long year" (XIII [April, 1864], 125).

3. In terms of topicality, localization also gave Twain an opportunity to make the most of such analogues as those between the scenario and the plot of the dime novel, and between the Comanches and the anything but heroic Indians of Virginia City, the Pi Ute's mentioned at the end of the burlesque, who lived in brush huts at the geographic and social bottom of the hill, below the red light district and the Chinese settlement.

actress's looking like "a healthy Greek matron (from Limerick)"
and another's seeming a truly "accomplished Greek maiden"
because "she speaks English without any perceptible foreign
accent."[4] To dismiss the burlesque as too heavy-handed is, however, to overlook the deflational effect of Twain's exposing the
falsely high (glorious orientalism) by means of the genuinely
low (the drab American West). Once he gets under way, the
persona scores most of his hits by exposing *himself* as a thick-
witted yokel who has trouble bringing the action down to his own
level. In the following sequence, simplification has enabled him
at last not just to understand the plot, but to learn what is
really going on.

> Scene 4. Dusty times in the Myron family. Their house is
> mortgaged—they are without dividends—they cannot "stand
> the raise."
> Parthenia, in this extremity, applies to Polydor. He sneer-
> ingly advises her to shove out after her exiled parent herself.
> She shoves!

> Act II. Camp of the Comanches. In the foreground, several of
> the tribe throwing dice for tickets in Wright's Gift Entertain-
> ment. In the background, old Myron packing faggots on a jack.
> The weary slave weeps—he sighs—he slobbers. Grief lays her
> heavy hand upon him.
> Scene 2. Comanches on the war-path, headed by the chief,
> Ingomar. Parthenia arrives and offers to remain as a hostage
> while old Myron returns home and borrows thirty dollars to
> pay his ransom with. It was pleasant to note the varieties of
> dress displayed in the costumes of Ingomar and his comrades.
> It was also pleasant to observe that in those ancient times the
> better class of citizens were able to dress in ornamental carriage
> robes, and even the rank and file indulged in Benkert boots,
> albeit some of the latter appeared not to have been blacked for
> several days.

In addition to his interest in the robes and boots, no small part
of Twain's playing dumb is his wavering between a normal
Western idiom and the style of the play, which, being innocently
susceptible to its influence, he occasionally apes.

4. There is also an uncomfortable break in point of view when Twain
remarks, in the midst of playing dumb, that one scene is "too noble
to be trifled with in burlesque."

The muggins's dull mind is put to excellent use in reducing the famous love scene to its essentials. The barbarian is being taught what love is. He is supposed to stride about with the tempestuousness of a beast, while the maiden tries to cool his relentless passion by exerting her feminine charms upon it:

> Scene 3. Parthenia and Ingomar alone in the woods. "Two souls with but a single thought, etc." She tells him that is love. He "can't see it."
> Scene 4. The thing works around about as we expected it would in the first place. Ingomar gets stuck after Parthenia.
> Scene 5. Ingomar declares his love—he attempts to embrace her—she waves him off, gently, but firmly—she remarks, "Not too brash, Ing., not too brash, now!" Ingomar subsides. They finally flee away, and hie them to Parthenia's home.

By the time he reaches the last part of the play, Twain has the muggins naïvely succumb to the pseudo-intensity of the action, though it also begins to seem a bit too much for him:

> Scene 6. The Comanches again, with Thorne at their head! He asks who enslaved the chief? Ingomar points to Polydor. Lo! Thorne seizes the trembling broker, and snatches him bald-headed!
> Scene 7. Enter the Chief of Police again. He makes a treaty with the Comanches. He gives them a ranch apiece. He decrees that they shall build a town on the American Flat, and appoints great Ingomar to be its Mayor! [Applause by the supes.[5]]
> Scene 8. Grand Tableau—Comanches, police, Pi-Utes, and citizens generally—Ingomar and Parthenia hanging together in the centre. The old thing—The old poetical quotation, we mean. —They double on it—Ingomar observing "Two souls with but a single Thought," and she slinging in the other line, "Two Hearts that Beat as one." Thus united at last in a fond embrace, they sweetly smiled upon the orchestra and the curtain fell.

Before Twain burlesqued *Ingomar*, humorists had for some time been using the play as a standard whipping boy. It had been mentioned in a familiarly satiric way by John Phoenix, in a mock review called "Musical Review Extraordinary" (1854), and by Bret Harte in "A Night at Wingdam" (1861). Phoenix's piece,[6]

---

5. The "supes" are the supernumerary or walk-on actors.
6. *Phoenixiana, or Sketches & Burlesques, by John Phoenix*, ed. Francis P. Farquhar (San Francisco, 1927), pp. 117–19.

which took reviewers to task for their tiresome enthusiasms, provided a model for another type of criticism Twain liked to engage in, a criticism of dramatic criticism itself. (A good example of this type of criticism appears in his review of *The Crown Diamonds*.) However, while the kind of burlesque review Phoenix wrote was generally more consistent in tone and smoother than the one Twain did on *Ingomar*, Phoenix could not bring himself to pose as an outright dullard, and so fell short of the ironies Twain achieved with his muggins.

II

Twain found that San Francisco drama and opera critics tended to fall into two categories. They were either too mincing or too enthusiastic.[7] The enthusiasts were less accessible to criticism than the mincers because they so completely revealed what they were. One could hardly make them look any worse. In order to attack them without seeming to do so, Twain was almost forced to play dumb.

The dramatic criticism of Frank Soulé typifies what Twain had to contend with in trying to subvert the enthusiastic style. Soulé was such an incurable enthusiast that he wrote effusively even when mincing. Describing the Shakespearean actress Matilda Heron, Soulé wrote: "It may require five acts to get accustomed to her voice, and then it will grow like music, and mingle with her exquisite elocution like the soft notes of the nightingale with the liquid fall and cadence of a brook.[8] Twain knew and admired Soulé when he worked with him on the San Francisco *Morning Call*, and even sought his praise in 1863 (*Biog* I 259); yet within a year he was burlesquing the Soulé type of review in what would be his roundest criticism of Western reviewers.

7. Among other things, he remarked that California critics "always go into ecstatsies [sic] with an actor the first night he plays, and they call him the most gifted in America the next morning. Then they think they have not acted with metropolitan coolness and self possession, and they slew around on the other tack and abuse him like a pickpocket to get even" ("On California Critics," *Golden Era*, February 25, 1866, *WG*, 102).

8. MacMinn, *Theater of Golden Era*, p. 99.

The piece in question was published in the *Californian* for October 15, 1864, under the unpromising title, "Still Further Concerning That Conundrum" (*SOS* 131–35). The conundrum is peremptorily displaced by a burlesque review showing what an enthusiastic critic might have done with *The Crown Diamonds*, a comic opera by the French composer Daniel F. E. Auber. Compounding the usual extravagance of operatic stage movements, Auber concocted an elaborate plot for the solution of a commonplace problem. Catarina, Queen of Portugal, is in financial difficulty. In order to make her throne financially secure, she plans to substitute false gems for the crown jewels. She joins a group of counterfeiters and becomes their leader. Don Henrique, nephew of the Minister of Police, is captured by the counterfeiters and saved from death by the disguised Queen. She later seeks refuge in Don Henrique's house and finds romance. Don Henrique breaks his engagement to the girl to whom he has been pledged, and in the final scene, after the confusion of identities and the mystery of the jewels have been cleared up, he is chosen to marry the Queen.

Twain, who was of course no lover of opera to begin with,[9] had a lark with *The Crown Diamonds* and turned out a rather complex piece of criticism. Its success stems from his posing as a muggins who stupidly imitates the bloated style of the effusive critic. His imitation contained a wide-ranging criticism, which embraced not only the predictable epiphanies of the enthusiast, but also uncritical audiences, singers who can't act, and writers of uncomical romantic comedy. Since the prose of opera reviewers tended to echo the unvarying solemnity of the art form, comedy notwithstanding, Twain's need to find something novel to say was as great as the need to deflate pomposity. His search for novelty finally led him to discuss a performer who had never gotten his due, a "supe" who doubled as court attendant and furniture shifter.

In his opening paragraph, the muggins tries to establish contact with two levels of readers. By direct address and a tortuously formal style he appeals for the attention of the *cognoscenti*, and especially of one person among them—his editor, it would seem

9. See *Biog* II 625, *TA* I 78, and "At the Shrine of St. Wagner," *WIM* 209–27.

—who had urged him to go to the Academy of Music and "prepare" himself "to write a careful critique" of *The Crown Diamonds*. (In due time he will disclose that he is really addressing an even more interested party than his editor.) Meanwhile, by his ostentation, Mark Twain also puts on a show for the groundlings who want one of their own to give them the truth about operatic appreciation. He is directly responding to these challenges from above and below to improve on the professional review when he breaks forth with this throat-clearing bombast:

> That you considered me able to acquit myself creditably in this exalted sphere of literary labor, was gratifying to me, and I should even have felt flattered by it had I not known that I was so competent to perform the task well, that to set it for me could not be regarded as a flattering concession, but, on the contrary, only a just and deserved recognition of merit.

Having strained himself to the limit, the muggins then pretends to "throw disguise aside and speak openly," but instead continues his parody of the ornate diction of the reviewer and his pretense of upholding cultural standards, which he makes seem easy of attainment by suggesting that it can be done by formal language and the expression of fine feelings. The opera reviewer therefore stands accused of tending to "vitiate" (in the narrator's word) the very tastes he is striving to sustain:

> Now, to throw disguise aside and speak openly, I have long yearned for an opportunity to write an operatic diagnostical and analytical dissertation for you. I feel the importance of carefully-digested newspaper criticism in matters of this kind —for I am aware that by it the dramatic and musical tastes of a community are moulded, cultivated and irrevocably fixed— that by it these tastes are vitiated and debased, or elevated and ennobled, according to the refinement or vulgarity, and the competency or incompetency of the writers to whom this department of the public training is entrusted. If you would see around you a people who are filled with the keenest appreciation of perfection in musical execution and dramatic delineation, and painfully sensitive to the slightest departures from the true standard of art in these things, you must employ upon your newspapers critics capable of discriminating between merit and demerit, and alike fearless in praising the one and condemning the other.

With his satiric apparatus running in high gear, Twain's clichés almost drown out their own redundancy, while ironic ambiguities are muffled by lofty talk about "departures" from art and the like. In the phrase "painful sensitivity," for example, the emphasis falls on the seemingly inexact, yet literally quite exact, idea of painfulness. Despite its obviousness, there is some amazingly skillful criticism at work in this sketch.

Twain's next step is to further ensnare the sentimentalists by *really* speaking more squarely to the point, his effect being doubled by the fact that a previous promise of straight talk had been studiously evaded. Just before making that shift, he carries the pose of sophomorism to its extreme in order to bolster the contrary expectation ("such a person [i.e., so cultivated a critic] —although it may be in some degree immodest in me to say so— I claim to be"); and he follows through with an unexpected thumper in which he identifies his challenger: "You will not be surprised, then, to know that I read your boshy criticisms on the opera with the most exquisite anguish—and not only yours, but those which I find in every paper in San Francisco." The heretofore ambiguous "you" of the person initially addressed is thus seen to be not Twain's editor, but none other than the opera critic of his own journal, the *Californian*. Twain has written his review not just for the benefit of all the opera critics in San Francisco, but primarily for the critic who works in the most fastidiously aesthetic department of the most fastidiously aesthetic journal on the West Coast.

Having uncovered his antagonist, Twain momentarily comes out into the open himself. He does so to say what is explicitly wrong with opera reviews and to drive home the point of his mugginsry, which is to set the reviewers an example of the foolish mind thinking clearly:

> You can do nothing but sing one everlasting song of praise; when an artist, by diligence and talent, makes an effort of transcendent excellence, behold, instead of receiving marked and cordial attention, both artist and effort sink from sight, and are lost in the general slough of slimy praise in which it is your pleasure to cause the whole company, good, bad and indifferent, to wallow once a week. With this brief but very liberal and hearty expression of sentiment, I will drop the subject and leave you alone for the present, for it behooves me now to set you a model in criticism.

The novelty of Twain's model review is his concentration on one "Signor Bellindo Alphonso Cellini, the accomplished basso-relievo furniture-scout and sofa-shifter." He has seen "with what studied care a venomous and profligate press have suppressed his name and suffered his sublimest efforts to pass unnoticed and unglorified." To redeem Alphonso, Twain describes some of his great scenes, and re-assumes the enthusiastic mood:

> . . . in the scene where the Prime Minister's nephew [Don Henrique] is imploring the female bandit [the Queen in disguise] to fly to the carriage and escape impending wrath, and when dismay and confusion ruled the hour, how quiet, how unmoved, how grandly indifferent was Bellindo in the midst of it all!— what solidity of expression lay upon his countenance! While all save himself were unnerved by despair, he serenely put forth his finger and mashed to a shapeless pulp a mosquito that loitered upon the wall, yet betrayed no sign of agitation the while. Was there nothing in this lofty contempt for the dangers which surrounded him that marked the actor destined hereafter to imperishable renown?

The "crowning glory" of Alphonso's performance comes after a tense scene in which he provides a chair for the Queen and apparently has been directed to look on in a way that will convey an approving response to her words, which are lost in song. Twain's rendition of this scene, the last of four he describes, is the satiric apex of his review, as he balances the rhapsodics and analytic delicatesse of the reviewers against the pedestrian interests of his muggins:

> But the crowning glory of Cellini's performance that evening was the placing of a chair for the Queen of Portugal to sit down in after she had become fatigued by earnestly and elaborately abusing the Prime Minister for losing the Crown Diamonds. He did not grab the chair by the hind leg and shove it awkwardly at her Majesty; he did not seize it by the seat and thrust it ungracefully toward her; he did not handle it as though he was undecided about the strict line of his duty or ignorant of the proper manner of performing it. He did none of these things. With a coolness and confidence that evinced the most perfect conception and the most consummate knowledge of his part, he came gently forward and laid hold of that chair from behind, set it in its proper place with a movement replete with grace, and then leaned upon the back of it, resting his chin upon his hand, and in this position smiled a smile of transfigured sweetness upon

the audience over the Queen of Portugal's head. There shone the inspired actor! and the people saw and acknowledged him; they waited respectfully for Miss Richings to finish her song, and then with one impulse they poured forth upon him a sweeping tempest of applause.

At the end of the piece the idolized furniture-scout and sofa-skirmisher was called before the curtain by an enthusiastic shouting and clapping of hands, but he was thrust aside, as usual, and the other artists, (who chose to consider the compliment as intended for themselves), swept bowing and smirking along the footlights and received it. I swelled with indignation, but summoned my fortitude and resisted the pressure successfully. I am still intact.

By the time he comes to the end of his review, the enthusiastic muggins is so pleased with himself that he begins to carry on like a mincer. He says that the principals in the cast—all established singers—"deserve a passing notice": "With study, perseverance and attention, I have no doubt these vocalists will in time achieve a gratifying success in their profession." Feeling that he has covered just about everything (as indeed he has), the muggins commends his review to the opera critic of the *Californian*, trusting he will thereafter surely want to "hire out" his assignments to "Mark Twain."

III

The naïveté and dim-wittedness Twain exploited in his criticism of extravagant romanticism indicate the relationship between the critical muggins and his highest achievements in humor, especially as they became fixed in the pose contrived for his lecture appearances. This relationship is apparent in most of Twain's early criticism. One of the most apt instances of his playing dumb, in the manner of his humor, is contained in a critique of oratory.

In his essay on "How To Tell a Story" Twain gave a classical explanation of the method employed by an artist of oral humor. The gist of it is that the storyteller shall preserve an expression of gravity and decorum that makes him impregnable to humor. Above all else, he is oblivious to the humor of his rambling manner, for the difficulty of keeping things straight is something of a trial to him and he is not doing very well. He wanders around, forgets, backtracks, digresses, and takes any lead that promises to keep him moving, however unimportant it may be. Since it is manner over matter, the humorous tale has no formal ending. The ending lies in the manner itself, though the listener may not immediately realize that it does. One is also accustomed to an emphatic treatment of the "nub" of a story, whereas the humorist will underplay and even pretend not to see the "nub." "Simplicity and innocence and sincerity and unconsciousness" are the key attitudes of the storyteller (*LE* 7–15).

For Twain to impose the techniques of humor on a "story" was one thing. Their imposition on a real-life situation presented itself to him as a method of condemning one of the most abuse-ridden of the social arts, that of political oratory. He needed to make only one major variation in method: since the politician normally does have an end in mind when he speaks, if not much else, the humor of his manner arises from the efforts he makes to develop his thesis which break down into redundancy. In oratory, Twain once again had a topic that so patently cried out for criticism that a critic might well despair of finding the means to attack it. The method he selected was to make a muggins of both the object of his satire and the narrator of it, the former being a politician who thinks himself wronged and anything but a muggins in trying to right the wrong. The difference between the two is that the politician is a muggins without recourse, while the reporter permits himself to become one by concession and has his recourse in the exposure of folly. The one *plays* the part and the other does not.

While covering the Nevada Territory's Constitutional Convention, Twain and the other reporters routinely condensed the speeches. When one member, by the name of L. O. Sterns, objected to this practice, Twain agreed that the condensation probably did not do him justice, and he tried to make amends by giving a more faithful report. The speech is the third part of a three-part dispatch from Carson City of December 5, 1863 (*MTEnt* 92–95). In Part One, Twain's tone is by turns moralistic and joshing. In the second, he prepares us for the speech and moves from a factual tone to that of the muggins. Although his device is somewhat thinner than elsewhere, he poses as the complaisant reporter trying his best to satisfy a man who is not easily pleased and who probably will not be in this instance, even though the reporter has tried to restore Sterns's own style for him:

> Now, in condensing the following speech, the other day, we were necessarily obliged to leave out some of its most salient points, and I acknowledge that my friend Sterns had ample cause for being annoyed at its mutilation. I hope he will find the present report all right, though. . . . I have got his style verbatim, whether I have the substance or not.

Twain then offers the speech: "Mr. Sterns said,"

> Mr. President, I am opposed, I am hostile, I am uncompromisingly against this proposition to tax the mines. I will go further, sir. I will openly assert, sir, that I am not in favor of this proposition. It is wrong—entirely wrong, sir (as the gentleman from Washoe has already said); I fully agree (with the gentleman who has just taken his seat) that it is unjust and unrighteous. I do think, Mr. President, that (as has been suggested by the gentleman from Ormsby) we owe it to our constituents to defeat this pernicious measure. Incorporate it into your Constitution, sir, and (as was eloquently and beautifully set forth in the speech of the gentleman from Storey) the gaunt forms of want, and poverty, and starvation, and despair will shortly walk in high places of this once happy and beautiful land. Add it to your fundamental law, sir, and (as was stated yesterday by the gentleman from Lander) God will cease to smile upon your labors. In the language (of my colleague), I entreat you, sir, and gentlemen, inflict not this mighty iniquity upon generations yet unborn! Heed the prayers of the people and be merciful! Ah, sir, the quality of mercy is not strained, so to speak (as has been aptly suggested heretofore), but droppeth like the gentle dew from Heaven, as it were. The gentleman from Douglas has said this law would be unconstitutional, and I cordially agree with him. Therefore, let its corse to the ramparts be hurried— let the flames that shook the battle's wreck, shine round it o'er the dead—let it go hence to that undiscovered country from whose bourne no traveler returns (as hath been remarked by the gentleman from Washoe, Mr. Shamp), and in thus guarding and protecting the poor miner, let us endeavor to do unto others as we would that others should do unto us (as was very justly and properly observed by Jesus Christ upon a former occasion).

Twain capped off his parody with three brief paragraphs that quietly reinforce its purpose. The first contains an anticlimax.

For all its evident style, Sterns's eloquence went for nought, as the "Convention not knowing of any good reason why they should not tax the miners, . . . went to work and taxed them." Adding to the anticlimax is the fact that there seems to have been a good case against taxation, since it tended to drive out the small miner and discourage investment in mining companies.

Twain next attended to the allusions. He checked to make certain they were correct, he said, and now, thanks to him, they were among the few accurate matters in the speech: "I guarded against inaccuracy by consulting the several authorities quoted in the speech, and from them I have the assurance that my report of Mr. Sterns' comprehensive declamation is eminently correct." However, research can not be entrusted to a muggins. The "Golden Rule" is misworded on the face of it, and while the quality of mercy may not be "strain'd," it does not drop like "the gentle dew from Heaven" but as Portia rather said like the "rain from heaven" (*Merchant of Venice*, Act IV, scene 2, lines 184–86). In trying to recast the popular version of the phrase in the Sermon on the Mount into the King James idiom (Matt. 7:12), Twain gives the semblance of fidelity without its substance, which is in keeping with the central problem in Sterns's insubstantial speech. The fool has a marvelous gift for impropriety. He intermixes Hamlet's skepticism about the immortality of the soul with the reference to Christ, and inadvertently links Christ with the distinguished members of Nevada's Constitutional Convention.

In short, the business of hanging the most substantial allusions onto a speech feeble in substance had appealed to Twain as a means of stimulating the mind of the fool, of delivering the whole of him to the reader. The allusions were nothing, yet everything. Since Twain had to go somewhat out of his way to jam in the phrase "let its corse to the ramparts be hurried," and since the phrase comes from the second line of Charles Wolfe's once-popular "The Burial of Sir John Moore at Corunna" (1817), a poem Twain had parodied in his youth and had returned to from time to time,[10] one has the suspicion that most and possibly all

10. Minnie M. Brashear, *Mark Twain, Son of Missouri* (Chapel Hill, N.C., 1934), p. 138; Cyril Clemens, *Young Sam Clemens* (Portland, Me., 1942), p. 62f.

of the allusions were Twain's invention and merely resembled their vainglorious counterparts in the original.

In his last paragraph the fool indicates that he has learned his lesson; the more he studies the situation, the more assured he is of the wisdom of reporting speeches verbatim. Besides, it might keep the peace:

> I think I have hit upon the right plan, now. It is better to report a member *verbatim*, occasionally, and keep him pacified, than have him rising to these uncomfortable questions of privilege every now and then. I hope to be able to report Bill Stewart *verbatim* in the course of a day or two, if he will hold on a spell.

The conditions under which Twain played the fool here were not the most favorable ones. The Constitutional Convention had so many overtones of comic opera that not even a fool could be so obtuse as to be wholly oblivious to them. The transparency of his *playing* the fool is therefore veiled by his doing it at the tacit invitation of a member of the Convention and by his falling in with the politician's antic mood, which warrants satiric latitude. Furthermore, the foolish reporter does more than imitate Sterns's style; he attempts to enter the speaker's character. Recalling his *Enterprise* parody on Chief Justice Turner's speech, many years after the event, Twain said he needed little more than the Judge's subject in order to re-create his patter and his method of organizing the speech (at which, incidentally, he had not himself been present), for he knew all of Turner's "pet quotations" (*MTE* 390f.). His affinity for entering the consciousness of the fool had given Twain the humorous rationale of his burlesque oratory; and it enhanced the role of characterization in his little drama of playing the muggins.

It would not be claiming too much to observe, on the basis of the types of criticism examined thus far, that with his use of the muggins Mark Twain had given a wholly new—and as yet completely unrecognized—dimension to satiric criticism in American journalism. Indeed, his critical form seemed to indicate that he was cut out for better things, which he would demonstrate by allowing his muggins to go to work on journalism itself.

4

Of Journalism and Art:
A Mad and a Frustrated Fool

I

Much of Twain's early criticism (including most of the pieces so far considered) grew out of a habit he had of burlesquing various kinds of newspaper articles. He was criticizing his trade in the act of pursuing it. His approach varied from that of a low-keyed spoof to an at times high-keyed use of the fool in his extreme condition, that of sheer idiocy. The object of this criticism was belittlement. Not only had familiarity bred contempt, but Twain was embarrassed by journalism and craved a wider horizon and a more prestigious field in which to exercise his talents. On the other hand, when he tried to write about a subject requiring cultivated sensitivity—like art, for example— Twain found himself beyond his depth. He therefore took refuge in the pose of a frustrated fool (which in a way he felt he was), and from that point of view defined a valid area of criticism.

In this chapter, I treat the contrast between Twain's criticism of a subject he thought was culturally below him and one he thought was culturally above him. Since some attention has been given to his criticism of journalism, less will be done with it than with his criticism of art. First, let us look at some variations in basic technique. These will indicate Twain's purpose in afflicting the muggins with outright madness.

In 1863, once Twain had begun to publish with some frequency in *The Golden Era*, California's first, and at the time foremost, literary journal, he also began to look down on mere newspaper work, though he still continued to write for the press. In the next year when he moved up to the *Californian*, which surpassed the *Era* in literary distinction, he became even more contemptuous of journalism, in much the same way that, while writing *Innocents Abroad* and *Roughing It*, he would become scornful of "magazining." Until he could at last consider himself a full-fledged author, Twain alternated between newspaper and magazine writing, and sharpened his criticism of the former. From 1863 to 1871 many of his magazine sketches were burlesques of contemporary types of journalism, some being reprints of items first published in newspapers. News, he lampooned in "The Killing of Julius Caesar, Localized" (1865); sensation, in the famous "Petrified Man" hoax (1862); the medical adviser's column, in "Curing a Cold" (1863); the fashion column, in "The Lick House Ball" (1863); the exposé, in "The Facts in the Case of the Great Beef Contract" (1870); the interview, in "The First Interview with Artemus Ward" (1870); the agricultural column, in "How I Edited an Agricultural Paper Once" (1870); and the book review, in "A Book Review" (1871). Before he was finished, Twain had parodied journalism in the hinterlands and almost every stripe of journalist in sight, including the reporter, the agricultural expert, the reviewer, the feature writer, the political analyst, the editorial writer, and the muckraker. Many of the satires he reprinted in *Sketches New and Old* (1873) were of this sort, and publishing them in book form was his way of recognizing the merit of this branch of his early critical writing.

To be sure, he was far from being alone in writing such travesties. They were the stock in trade of feuding reporters and had long been a staple of Western journalism by the time Twain arrived on the scene. The fact that he did not always make the happiest choice of critical techniques was a result of his following the course of other reporters, whose invective was usually direct and obvious. What at first seemed to be the most promising method of criticism for Twain—simple irony—proved to be the least effective, and what seemed to be the least effective—foolishness—eventually proved to be the most promising method. In either case, Twain's criticism of journalism was weakest when he was visibly angry without at the same time pretending to be somewhat mad.

Take, for example, his disgust with the carping theater critics. As word got around that arrangements were being made to bring Edwin Forrest out to the Coast, Twain was outraged at the thought of his probable reception. Lashing out at the critics, he tried to sting them with their own type of invective.

> In God's name let him stay where he is. . . . I have looked upon
> him as the bulwark which enables us to defy the waves of
> European criticism . . . and now, after all this, they would bring
> the illustrious tragedian out here and turn the inspired critics
> of the San Francisco press loose upon him. This will never do.
> These mosquitoes will swarm around him and bleed dramatic
> imperfections from him by the column. . . . Their grand final
> shot is always in the same elegant phraseology: they would
> pronounce Mr. Forrest a "bilk"! You cannot tell me anything
> about these ignorant asses who do what is called "criticism"
> hereabouts—I know them "by the back." But I do hope they
> will never get a chance to expose to the world what a poor,
> shabby, stuck-up impostor Mr. Forrest is.[1]

In February, 1866, on learning that the great Forrest, acknowledged titan of the tragic stage and a man of exceeding vanity,
was indeed coming to San Francisco in *Othello*, Twain, who had
seen him in the role eight years earlier in Washington,[2] hung out
a warning for him. In form, his open letter was a grade or two
above the previous missive, improving in subtlety as it moved
from ironic assertion to parody.

> [The California critics] will soon let you know that your great
> reputation cannot protect you on this coast. You have passed
> muster in New York, but they will show you up here. They will
> make it very warm for you. They will make you understand that
> a man who has served a lifetime as dramatic critic on a New
> York paper may still be incompetent, but that a California
> critic knows it all. . . .
>   How would you feel if they told you your playing might
> answer in places of small consequence but wouldn't do in San
> Francisco? They will tell you that, as sure as you live. And then
> say, in the most crushing way:
>   "Mr. Forrest has evidently mistaken the character of this
> people. We will charitably suppose that this is the case, at any
> rate. We make no inquiry as to what kind of people he has been
> in the habit of playing before, but we simply inform him that
> he is now in the midst of a refined and cultivated community,
> and one which will not tolerate such indelicate allusions as were

---

1. Cited by Pat Ryan, Jr., "Mark Twain: Frontier Critic," *Arizona
   Quarterly*, XVI (Autumn, 1960), 201.
2. *Mark Twain's Letters to the Muscatine Journal*, ed. Edgar M. Branch
   (Chicago, 1942), p. 22.

made use of in the play of 'Othello' last night. If he would not play to empty benches, this must not be repeated." (*WG* 101f.[3])

In order to take the curse off a criticism of criticism, Twain introduced an element of foolishness into it. There was abundant foolishness in his wilder parodies, like those on the fashion column, where he caught the spirit of the type in the very process of exaggerating its style.[4] However, as we have seen, the biggest stride Twain would take toward perfecting his satiric criticism came with his converting mockery into self-mockery, and letting the reader see not how much, but how little he seemed to know. Since it was pride that had to be chastened in critics, Twain dramatized that fact when he stirred up the muggins and set him to crowing. Thus, to his burlesque of the imagined gladiatorial review illustrating that time had not altered the "general style and phraseology of dramatic criticism," he appended a reminder that neither had it altered the smugness of reviewers: "I have been a dramatic critic myself, in my time, and I was often surprised to notice how much more I knew about Hamlet than Forrest did; and it gratifies me to observe, now, how much better my brethren of ancient times knew how a broadsword battle ought to be fought than the gladiators" (*IA* I 360).

II

The most complicated role Twain would assign the muggins in his criticism of journalism was to turn him into a virtual idiot. The occasion was a feud the *Californian* had gotten itself into by pointing out the typical vices of prominent newspapers in the area. When the papers bristled back, Twain tried to vindicate

3. These comments appeared in his article "On California Critics," in the *Golden Era*, February 25, 1866. As Ryan points out, Twain's prediction came true, for Forrest, past his prime, was not favorably received by the San Francisco reviewers ("Frontier Critic," p. 203).

4. Consider the following:

> Mrs. F. F. L. wore a superb toilette habillée of Chambry gauze; over this a charming Figaro jacket, made of mohair, or horse-hair, . . . over this again, a Raphael blouse of cheveux de la reine, trimmed round the bottom with lozenges formed of insertions, and around the top with bronchial troches. . . . On the roof of her bonnet was a menagerie of rare and beautiful bugs and reptiles, and under the eaves thereof a counterfeit of the "early bird." . . . (*WG* 35.)

the *Californian*. He created an idiotic muggins who unintentionally parodied the styles deplored by the *Californian* and then
perversely sided with those who defended themselves from its
criticism. The principle behind the idiocy was quite simple: the
more asinine the pride of the journalists, the greater the need of
asininity in their critic. Twain's persona was not only an idiot,
but a comical phoenix who, in the course of the sketch, rose
several times from the position of willing butt to mock those to
whose mockery he had exposed himself.

The full title of Twain's sketch was "The Facts Concerning the
Recent Trouble between Mr. Mark Twain and Mr. John
William Skae of Virginia City—Wherein It Is Attempted To Be
Proved That the Former Was Not To Blame in the Matter"—
which, as usual, was a blind, in this case for a chaotic lampoon
of a Western news story.[5] Purportedly, Mark Twain, the innocent correspondent, was given a story about a "Distressing
Accident" by his friend Skae, who walked into the office late one
night "with an expression of profound and heartfelt suffering
upon his countenance." Without troubling to read the dispatch, the sympathetic fool stopped the press and inserted
it into the "first edition" of that issue of the *Californian*.

He had been hoaxed. The writer of the dispatch had made an
imbecile attempt to crowd all of his facts into his opening sentence (all 231 words of it). He buried the news—in fact never got
to it—confused past and present, forgot what he had started out
to write, and in desperation ended with a moral on the evils of
drink.

> Last evening about 6 o'clock, as Mr. William Schuyler, an old
> and respectable citizen of South Park, was leaving his residence
> to go down town, as has been his usual custom for many years,
> with the exception only of a short interval in the Spring of 1850
> during which he was confined to his bed by injuries received in
> attempting to stop a runaway horse by thoughtlessly placing
> himself directly in its wake and throwing up his hands and

---

5. "The Facts" was printed in the *Californian*, August 26, 1865, *SOS*,
   180–87. Twain republished the "Distressing Accident" from it in the
   Galaxy in October, 1870, in response to a clipping sent him by a reader
   who had found almost as garbled a piece of writing as Twain's parody
   (*CTG* 85f.). He printed the entire piece again, but in a greatly revised
   form, as "Mr. Bloke's Item" in *SNO* 216–20.

shouting, which, if he had done so even a single moment sooner must inevitably have frightened the animal still more instead of checking its speed, although disastrous enough to himself, as it was and rendered more melancholy and distressing by reason of the presence of his wife's mother, who was there and saw the sad occurrence, notwithstanding it is at least likely, though not necessarily so, that she should be reconnoitering in another direction when incidents occur, not being vivacious and on the lookout, as a general thing, but even the reverse, as her own mother is said to have stated, who is no more, but died in the full hope of a glorious resurrection, upwards of three years ago, aged 86, being a Christian woman and without guile, as it were, or property, in consequence of the fire of 1849, which destroyed every blasted thing she had in the world. But such is life. Let us all take warning by this solemn occurrence, and let us endeavor so to conduct ourselves that when we come to die we can do it. Let us place our hands upon our hearts and say with earnestness and sincerity that from this day forth we will beware of the intoxicating bowl.

There is a pause, and then in the second edition of the journal Twain reports his editor's reaction:

The boss editor has been in here raising the very mischief and tearing his hair and kicking the furniture about, and abusing me like a pick-pocket. He says that every time he leaves me in charge of the paper for half an hour I get imposed upon by the first infant or the first idiot that comes along. And he says that distressing item of Johnny Skae's is nothing but a lot of distressing bosh, and has got no point to it. . . . He says every man he meets has insinuated that somebody about *The Californian* office has gone crazy.

The fool is taken aback. This is what he gets for trying to do someone a kindness. He determines to read the dispatch. He is puzzled and reads it six more times without being able to "get the meaning of it." Though "driven to the verge of lunacy," he amiably hopes his friend will annotate the next such story he brings in. At length the muggins sees the light, but the wrong one. He must confess that on reflection "after all this fuss that has been made by the chief cook about this item, I do not see that it is any more obscure than the general run of local items in the daily papers after all."

The benign idiot has twice thrust his head forward to have it bashed, and he will do it again. He thinks the newspapers under attack by the *Californian* are liable to the same charge his editor had brought against Skae—which makes him take their part against the *Californian*! "You don't usually find out much by reading local items, and you don't in the case of Johnny Skae's item. But it is just *The Californian's* style to be so disgustingly particular and so distressingly hypercritical." This gets him launched. He proceeds to show how the *Californian* has unjustly berated the papers for the very thing each prides itself on. Its accusations are that the *Alta*'s humorist, Stiggers, writes jokes that are devoid of meaning and humor; the *Flag*'s poets write poetry that has neither meaning nor meter; the *Call*'s grammar is made up of ungrammatical combinations never seen in the language before; and the *Bulletin*'s country correspondent sends in letters that are rambling, precious, and cluttered with meaningless details.

Though obvious enough, Twain's irony would lose half its effectiveness were it not for his so completely entering the character of the idiot, which enables him both to question the *Californian*'s hypercriticism and to sanction its justness. Hard as it is for the editor to put up with the idiot, it is even harder to endure his being one's advocate. Contradiction cannot overpower him; it is rather a device to overpower the reader and prevent him from reaching too soon for the tenor of the irony. The fool's abandonment of sense and his general disorganization become a paradigm of the mentality of the newspaper writers. What better man to defend them than a journalist who is of one mind with them?

If the idiot is disorganized, Twain's sketch is not. After the idiot's defense of the newspapers, he brings the reader back to something he may have overlooked in the all but forgotten dispatch by Johnny Skae. Continuing to damn what he praises, the idiot reveals that the dispatch was actually a compendium of the several vices the newspapers were accused of! Presumably, the San Francisco reader might have perceived this had he taken the pains to read it as carefully as an idiot had.

Now who but *The Californian* would ever have found fault with Johnny Skae's item. No daily paper in town would, anyhow. It is after the same style, and is just as good, and as interesting and as luminous as the articles published every day in the city papers. It has got all the virtues that distinguish those articles and render them so acceptable to the public. It is not obtrusively pointed, and in this it resembles the jokes of Stiggers; it warbles smoothly and easily along, without rhyme or rhythm or reason, like the *Flag*'s poetry; the eccentricity of its construction is appalling to the grammatical student, and in this it rivals the happiest achievements of the *Call*; it furnishes the most laborious and elaborate details to the eye without transmitting any information whatever to the understanding, and in this respect it will bear comparison with the most notable specimens of the *Bulletin*'s country correspondence; and finally, the mysterious obscurity that curtains its general intent and meaning could not be surpassed by all the newspapers in town put together.

As Twain once remarked in a notebook, "It takes a heap of sense to write good nonsense."[6]

III

If there was one place where the fool would have to be ruled *persona non grata*, it would be in the realm of art, over which to play the fool was to *be* the fool. Deepening the enigma of art criticism for Twain was the fact that he privately had no confidence in his taste, suspecting that if he liked a painting there was bound to be something wrong with it, and vice versa (see, e.g., *IA* I 306f.). Nevertheless, regardless of whether the fool's mask was adopted in earnest or sport, it remained, with certain modifications, just about the only device through which Twain expressed a number of legitimate objections on matters of art, art appreciation, and art reviewing. For one thing, his muggins in art criticism was a fairly levelheaded chap; in direct contrast to the correspondent for the *Californian*, he was the sanest of Twain's critical fools. He looked hard for the values he was supposed to find in paintings and was frustrated that they should escape him. Almost no one seemed to be so wholly at sea about art as the muggins was, and yet he uncovered a number of real problems.

Since the best and most notorious examples of these early comments on art appeared in *Innocents Abroad*, it should be noted that they came at a time when Twain was using foolishness

6. Unpublished Notebook No. 14 (February–September, 1879), 11, *MTP* (Copyright © 1967, Mark Twain Company).

of character for purposes beyond those of criticism, and at a time, too, when he was beginning to merge the special abilities of the muggins to draw fire from above and below with the composite traits of a somewhat different Mark Twain from the one he had been out West. Though he might be a fool, the Eastern Mark Twain had compunctions about being an idiot. The sanity of the muggins consequently owed something to Twain's awareness that in addressing a wider audience than that of San Francisco he had first to tone down the Western wildness that had forced him to part company with the earthy Mr. Brown. He might curse the old masters as much as he pleased in private, and later on, in *A Tramp Abroad*, he might say some idiotic things about them in print (II 243–53) and throw in some nonsense about Turner for good measure (I 243f.). He could even return to the pose of the dunce as late as 1903, in a little sketch called "Instructions in Art" and make himself out a madcap painter with an uncanny ability to penetrate the obscurities of his own unobscure paintings and dress them up in jargon.[7] But in 1869, a transitional year for Twain, it was not prudent for him to publish his complaints against European art—however just they might be—unless he could at the same time certify that he was no Philistine. This he did with complete ease, for once he put his mind to it, Twain could be an exceedingly impressionable—indeed enthusiastic—appreciator of fine art.

Before the Cathedral of Milan, whose architecture and sculpture were in good condition (unlike some of the old paintings), the innocent traveler was captivated. Having looked at it for half a night and all of a day, he exclaimed,

> What a wonder it is! So grand, so solemn, so vast! And yet so delicate, so airy, so graceful! A very world of solid weight, and yet it seems in the soft moonlight only a fairy delusion of frostwork that might vanish with a breath! How sharply its pinnacled angles and its wilderness of spires were cut against the sky, and how richly their shadows fell upon its snowy roof! It was a vision!—a miracle!— an anthem sung in stone, a poem wrought in marble! (*IA* I 226.)

---

7. Originally published in *Metropolitan*; reprinted by Paine in *Europe and Elsewhere* (New York, 1923), pp. 315–26.

As for the ornamental bas reliefs, a person might study one of them for "a week without exhausting its interest." *Each* of the Cathedral's beauties seemed inexhaustible. In the statuary "every face," Twain noted, "is eloquent with expression, and every attitude is full of grace" (I 227).[8]

If Twain was capable of such abandon in his appreciation of art, one is entitled to wonder why he should have allowed himself to look like a backwoods scourge in heaping derision on the old masters. One explanation is that, in keeping with the total purpose of his book, he was more distressed by the tourist's unexamined reverence for the paintings of the masters (largely inspired by guides and guidebooks) than he was by the art itself. As Twain said in his Preface, he wanted "to suggest to the reader how *he* would be likely to see Europe and the East if he looked at them with his own eyes" (I xxxvii). With respect to paintings, in particular, he protested, "It is impossible to travel through Italy without speaking of pictures, and can I see them through others' eyes?" (I 307). Twain knew that the admiring tourist was too intimidated to report what his senses told him. For a person of ordinary honesty this was disgraceful, and somewhat frustrating. In order to get through to the tourist Twain had to speak of the paintings with a frankness shocking enough to penetrate his dishonesty. In objecting to the non-realistic

8. On studying the Palace of Versailles, the ravished republican went into even greater raptures:

> Versailles! It is wonderfully beautiful! You gaze, and stare, and try to understand that it is real, that it is on the earth, that it is not the Garden of Eden—but your brain grows giddy, stupefied by the world of beauty around you, and you half believe you are the dupe of an exquisite dream. The scene thrills one like military music! A noble palace, stretching its ornamented front block upon block away, till it seemed that it would never end; a grand promenade before it, whereon the armies of an empire might parade; all about it rainbows of flowers, and colossal statues that were almost numberless, and yet seemed only scattered over the ample space; broad flights of stone steps leading down from the promenade to the lower grounds of the park—stairways that whole regiments might stand to arms upon and have room to spare; vast fountains whose great bronze effigies discharged rivers of sparkling water into the air and mingled a hundred curving jets together in forms of matchless beauty. . . . (I 204.)

Twain's transport continued for more than a page, in the course of which he forgave Louis XIV for the "two hundred millions of dollars" he had spent on "this marvelous park" when bread was scarce.

compositional conventions of the religious paintings (a piece of unconscious Pre-Raphaelitism on Twain's part), he tried to put into words what the tourist was probably thinking. Twain's strategy was to make himself the butt of the tourist's laughter in order to disabuse him of his folly.

In imitation of the tourist, Twain strained to see qualities no longer visible in "The Last Supper." Rather than fake admiration for it, he admitted his frustration by taking the supposedly laughable view that to his "untrained eye" the copies seemed "superior . . . to the original." Relying on his humble vision, he felt compelled to articulate what sensible people would shrink from saying after having seen what he had seen:

> "The Last Supper" is painted on the dilapidated wall of what was a little chapel attached to the main church in ancient times, I suppose. It is battered and scarred in every direction, and stained and discolored by time, and Napoleon's horses kicked the legs off most the disciples when they (the horses, not the disciples) were stabled there more than half a century ago. (I 247.)

To drive home his point Twain gave a dispassionately realistic description of what was left of the picture, and then brought on the tourists:

> The colors are dimmed with age; the countenances are scaled and marred, and nearly all expression is gone from them; the hair is a dead blur upon the wall, and there is no life in the eyes. Only the attitudes are certain.
> People come here from all parts of the world, and glorify this masterpiece. They stand entranced before it with bated breath and parted lips, and when they speak, it is only in the catchy ejaculations of rapture:
> "Oh, wonderful!"
> "Such expression!"
> "Such grace of attitude!"
> "Such dignity!"
> "Such faultless drawing!"
> "Such matchless coloring!"
> "Such feeling!"
> "What delicacy of touch!"
> "What sublimity of conception!"
> "A vision! a vision!" (I 248.)

As far as his actual criticism of the painting is concerned, the persistent reasonableness and resultant frustration of the muggins combine to make something of a purist of him:

> I am willing to believe that the eye of the practiced artist can rest upon the Last Supper and renew a lustre where only a hint of it is left, supply a tint that has faded away, restore an expression that is gone; patch, and color, and add to the dull canvas until at last its figures shall stand before him aglow with the life, the feeling, the freshness, yea, with all the noble beauty that was theirs when first they came from the hand of the master. But *I* cannot work this miracle. Can those other uninspired visitors do it, or do they only happily imagine they do? (I 249f.)

It is indicative of the sort of attitude Twain thought his persona should take in criticizing art that these remarks were not present in his original *Alta* letter on Leonardo, from which, incidentally, he also deleted Brown's expression of gratitude on learning that Leonardo had been dead for three hundred years, as well as such sentiments as, "We don't know any more about pictures than a kangaroo does about metaphysics."[9]

Of still greater interest is the fact that Twain made a virtue of necessity in taking the stance of a sensible fool who is frustrated at finding so little truth in discussions of the old masters. While revising the *Alta* letters for the book, he had fumed at the thought of his *having* to discuss the old masters when one could scarcely utter a word about them that was not platitudinous. To Emeline Beach, his young friend and shipmate, whom he asked to tell him all she could about the Murillos she liked, he had let off some steam: "Hang the whole gang of Old Masters, I say! The idea that I have to go to driveling about those dilapidated antediluvian humbugs at this late day, is exasperating." These feelings notwithstanding, he conceded that if jokes about the painters had been passable in newspaper letters, they would have to come out of the book. "I cannot afford to expose my want of cultivation too much," he said.[10] Since he could neither

9. Daniel M. McKeithan, *Traveling with the Innocents Abroad: Mark Twain's Original Reports from Europe and the Holy Land* (Norman, Okla., 1958), p. 57f.
10. Bradford A. Booth, "Mark Twain's Friendship with Emeline Beach," *AL* XIX (November, 1947), 228, 224.

lie nor rage, Twain invented a suitable middle course, and thereby satisfied his conflicting desires to be frank and not to seem
crude. But the operative principle, as he told Emeline, was to
"invent." In conceiving his prize invention—his persona—
Twain dispensed with fact in order to obtain a critical effect.
Thus, instead of railing at the old masters, he characterized himself as a dullard, not quite able to discover the admitted beauty
in the old paintings. He made a correction of just this kind in an
allusion to Emeline, excising "people abuse me because I am
so bitterly prejudiced against the old masters that I cannot see
any beauty in their productions. It makes me perfectly savage
to look at one of those pictures," and substituting "my friends
abuse me because I am a little prejudiced against the old
masters—because I fail sometimes to see the beauty that is in
their productions."[11] For his purposes as critic, there was in the
long run much to be gained by Twain's saying that in deference
to his good friends on board ship it gave him "real pain to speak
in [an] *almost* unappreciative way of the old masters" (I 306; my
italics).

What then were Twain's major complaints against the old
masters—apart from his complaint against the tourist's adulation
of them? In essence, he raised four questions, of varying degrees
of relevance. Each concerns a neglected problem faced by the
layman, and each is broached by a layman who wants to make
a creditable attempt to like their work and is thwarted by the
very sincerity of his demands.

First, he saw too many of the old masters crowded together
in the Louvre and in the Roman palaces he visited. One painting
detracted from another, so that the well-intentioned observer
could not do justice to any of them. Baffled and abused, the fool
capitulates, claiming foul play, and asks our indulgence:

> If, up to this time, I had seen only one "old master" in each
> palace, instead of acres and acres of walls and ceilings fairly
> papered with them, might I not have a more civilized opinion of
> the old masters than I do now? I think so. . . . It begins to dawn
> upon me, now, that possibly, what I have been taking for

---

11. McKeithan, *Traveling with the Innocents*, p. 70; *IA* I 331.

uniform ugliness in the galleries may be uniform beauty after all. I honestly hope it is, to others, but certainly it is not to me. Perhaps the reason I used to enjoy going to the Academy of Fine Arts in New York was because there were but a few hundred paintings in it, and it did not surfeit me to go through the list. I suppose the Academy was bacon and beans in the Forty-Mile Desert, and a European gallery is a state dinner of thirteen courses. One leaves no sign after him of the one dish, but the thirteen frighten away his appetite and give him no satisfaction. (II 15.)

Second, adding to the oppression of numbers was the preposterous sameness of subject, which the inquisitive Mark Twain tried to bear as well as he could. The positions and expressions given saints and martyrs were indistinguishable from one picture to the next. "We have seen pictures of martyrs enough, and saints enough," he sighed, "to regenerate the world." Versailles and the Cathedral of Milan were unique; these paintings were not. Once again, it took a muggins to point out what everyone observed, but no one had the nerve to mention—that the monotony of subject matter precluded anything resembling an aesthetic experience. With remarkable restraint, the apologetic muggins uncompromisingly states his case. Ostensibly, he doesn't know any better than to say what is on his mind:

I may . . . as well acknowledge with such apologies as may be due, that to me it seemed that when I had seen one of these martyrs I had seen them all. They all have a marked family resemblance to each other, they dress alike, in coarse monkish robes and sandals, they are all bald-headed, they all stand in about the same attitude, and without exception they are gazing heavenward with countenances which the Ainsworths, the Mortons, and the Williamses, *et fils* [the supposed connoisseurs] inform me are full of "expression." (I 304.)

A corollary of this view, and the third of Twain's points, was that in their obsession with otherworldliness the masters had mainly ignored the rich life going on around them in the Renaissance world (II 16). (Breughel and Hogarth would have been more to his liking.) "To me," the muggins pleaded, "there is nothing tangible about [their] imaginary portraits, nothing that I can grasp and take a living interest in" (I 304). When the thankful muggins did discover some "Venetian historical pictures" that gripped his imagination, he noticed that the painters could not resist patching on the "formal introduction of defunct Doges to the Virgin Mary in regions beyond the clouds," which, he would humbly submit, "clashed rather harshly with the proprieties" (I 305).

Twain's other point, which has to do with the morals of the masters, is not important. However, as part of the general indictment, and particularly as part of the muggins' growing suspicion that he is being humbugged (the reward of his good will), it shows that even a fool can take only so much. Mark Twain lustily despised the masters for glorifying the "damned Medicis." The thought that Raphael should have "pictured such infernal villains as Catherine and Marie de Medici seated in heaven and conversing familiarly with the Virgin Mary and the angels" was enough, by itself, he felt, to prejudice any honorable man (he hoped his female companions, who had chided him about this prejudice, would take note) against the old masters. He insisted that he simply had to "keep on protesting against the groveling spirit that could persuade those masters to prostitute their noble talents to the adulation of such monsters as the French, Venetian, and Florentine princes of two and three hundred years ago . . ." (II 331).

IV

At bottom, except for the matter of repetitiveness, it cannot be said that Twain had much of a case against the paintings as such. His own feelings of inferiority when confronted with the old masters greatly narrowed the possibility of his making a valid aesthetic judgment of their work. It was a different story with American paintings, for he felt himself to be completely competent to deal with them, and he said as much in contrasting the Italian galleries with the Academy of Fine Arts in New York. In America, it was not necessary for him to feign personal frustration so much as to point up the comic frustrations inherent in his judging home-grown art. That was what Twain did when he had a brush with art criticism in New York, just prior to his boarding the *Quaker City* on June 7, 1867.

On May 28, he took in the annual show of the National Academy of Design, and five days later attended a showing of Albert Bierstadt's gigantic painting, "The Domes of the Yosemite," the latest of Bierstadt's versions of his almost exclusive subject. Both reviews went back to the *Alta* in San Francisco (appearing on July 28 and August 4, 1867, respectively) as installments on the correspondence he was to send back from his trip to the Holy Land (*MTTMB* 238–42, 249–51). In the first review he coyly made the most of his stated ignorance about art; in the second he by and large played it straight, presenting himself as a down-to-earth Westerner whose familiarity with the setting of Bierstadt's painting gave him a clearer perspective than that of the immigrant painter. In addition to discussing the paintings, Twain's object in both reviews was to show up the critics, as he claimed that their abuse had kept him away from the exhibits. He actually came to the same disapproving conclusion that the critics had, but, being averse to their cocksureness, pretended in his first review to be ill at ease in an art gallery, somewhat like the proverbial whore in church.[12]

The mode of apprehension in each experience—that is, the way that Twain lets us know what he knows—is based upon a certain sense of frustration, emanating in the one instance from his foolishness and in the other from his irony. His foolish attitude toward the Academy's show he would hide from New Yorkers and confide to his folksy Western readers. He is the bumpkin in the big city:

> There were two pictures that suited me, but they were so small and so modest that I was ashamed to let the other visitors see me looking at them so much, so I gazed at them sidewise, and "let on" to be worshipping the "old master" rascalities. I had no catalogue, and did not want any—because, if a picture cannot tell its own story to us uncultivated vagrants, we scorn to read it out of a book. (*MTTMB* 239f.)

In the case of the Bierstadt, it was upsetting that the painting should look so much "more beautiful than the original" scene.

---

12. He had earlier (1865) been "ordered" to do "an elaborate criticism" of the exhibit at the California Art Union, but apparently felt himself to be so completely out of his element that he funked it ("An Unbiased Criticism," *Californian*, March 18, 1865; *SOS* 158–65).

"Some of Mr. Bierstadt's mountains swim in a lustrous, pearly mist, which is so enchantingly beautiful that I am sorry the Creator hadn't made it instead of him, so that it would always remain there" (*ibid.*, 249, 250).

The letter on the Academy show is a review by evasion. If the reader wants to find out how good the paintings are, he may well be frustrated himself, unless he catches the meaning of Twain's presumed frustration, in which case he will have gotten a sound review—a feat Twain did not quite have the self-assurance to attempt with the old masters. The key to his form is a satire on critics, established in his first paragraph, in which the muggins renounces all desire to rid himself of his born ignorance and acquire the knowledge that critics have. Using a metaphor which exactly prefigures his dramatic speculation in *Life on the Mississippi* on whether he had gained or lost more in coming to know the river (83–85), Twain asserts the virtues of an uninformed appreciation of art:

> I am thankful that the good God creates us all ignorant. I am glad that when we change His plans in this regard, we have to do it at our own risk. It is a gratification to me to know that I am ignorant of art, and ignorant also of surgery. Because people who understand art find nothing in pictures but blemishes and surgeons and anatomists see no beautiful women in all their lives, but only a ghastly stack of bones with Latin names to them, and a network of nerves and muscles and tissues inflamed by disease. The very point in a picture that fascinates me with its beauty, is to the cultured artist a monstrous crime against the laws of coloring; and the very flush that charms me in a lovely face, is, to the critical surgeon, nothing but a sign hung out to advertise a decaying lung. Accursed be all such knowledge. I want none of it. (*MTTMB* 238.)

The art critics had been "so diligently abusing everything in and about the Academy of Design" that the muggins had "expected that a visit there would produce nothing but unhappiness." He hoped that his ignorance would protect him from misery, and at the outset it did, as he freely admired "all the sea views, and the mountain views, and the quiet woodland scenes, with shadow-tinted lakes in the foreground, and . . . just revelled in the storms." His joy is shortlived, however. After he takes in a "dreamy tropical scene" that he is not sure he ought to like, the principle of frustration becomes more pronounced, and delivers his review for him. He tries to reinforce his pleasure in simple representational beauties, but soon tires of them when he sees that they are overwhelmed by triteness and sentiment. This reversal begins with his scowling at an imitation "old master" and ends with his denouncing the hideous Moorish architecture of the Academy.[13] It was particularly frustrating to find out what he had taken pains to keep himself in the dark about: that the critics were right in condemning the exhibit.

The first stage of his disillusionment is a fine example of the technique of the muggins—a speaking falsely as to particulars, but truly as to fundamentals: "And I know I ought to have admired that picture, by one of the old masters, where six bearded faces without any bodies to them were glaring out of Egyptian darkness and glowering upon a naked infant that was not built like any infant that ever I saw, nor colored like it, either. I am glad the old masters are all dead, and I only wish they had died sooner" (239).

He obviously should *not* have admired this painting, which was out of place in a gallery of contemporary American art. In all probability this "old master" was Edwin White's "St. Stephen's Vision," which aped the beatific subject and pious style of Italian Renaissance paintings. As the reviewer for *The New York Times* put it, White would have been better off painting what he had really seen instead of roaming back two thousand years to paint what he had imagined.[14]

Twain said that out of three hundred paintings he had found thirty or forty that were beautiful. Since there were actually some six hundred paintings, he had arbitrarily doubled the

13. The museum, he wrote, "is barred, and cross-barred, and streaked, and striped, and spotted, and speckled, and gilded, and defiled from top to bottom, with infamous flummery and filagreed [sic] gingerbread, to that degree that the first glance a stranger casts upon it unsettles his mind for a week." The stranger, Twain thought, would first think it was a church, but one that no God-fearing Christian would worship in. He would also dismiss the possibility that it might be a hotel, a mansion, or a lunatic asylum planned by the inmates, and conclude that it was a pretentious stable built by a parvenu sportsman (*MTTMB* 241f.).

14. *Times,* May 23, 1867, 5.

proportion of good ones, but to his shame had to admit that he had "gone and done the very same thing the art critics do—left unmentioned the works I liked, and mentioned only those I did not like" (241). He did single out for praise one of the few paintings that showed genuine talent and was to be commended by the critics, "The Hunter's Flask" by William Holbrook Beard, uncle of Daniel Carter Beard, who later illustrated *A Connecticut Yankee* and became a good friend of Twain's.[15]

The climactic admission—in which we observe how the muggins' trusting innocence was destroyed by sentimentality—came with his noting that "half the paintings in the Academy are devoted to the usual harmless subjects, of course."

> You find the same old pile of cats asleep in the corner; and the same old party of kittens skylarking with a cotton ball; and the same old excited puppy looking out of a window; and the same old detachment of cows wading across a branch at sunset; and the same old naked libels marked "Eve"; and the same old stupid looking wenches marked "Autumn," and "Summer," etc., loafing around in the woods, or toting flowers, and all of them out of shirts, in the same old way; and there were the everlasting farmers, gathering their eternal squashes; and a "Girl Swinging on a Gate"; and a "Girl Reading"; and girls performing all sorts of similar prodigies; and most numerous and most worn-out of all, there was the usual endless array of vases and dishes full of grapes and peaches and slices of watermelon, and such stuff; and the same tiresome old tom-cat "laying" for a gold-fish. (240f.)

---

15. "The Hunter's Flask," the *Times* critic noted, "is worthy of high praise, taking it for just what it is. The squirrels are admirably individualized. Nothing could be more drunken than the expression of the poor fellow who has sunk back in the grass . . ." (*ibid.*).
   Twain gave this description of the picture:
   > [It] was racy. In a little nook in a forest, a splendid gray squirrel, brimful of frisky action, had found a basket-covered brandy flask upset, and was sipping the spilled liquor from the ground. His face told that he was delighted. Close by, a corpulent old fox-squirrel was stretched prone upon his back, and the jolly grin on his two front teeth, and the drunken leer of his half-closed eye told that he was happy, and that the anxious solicitude in the face of the black squirrel that was bending over him and feeling his pulse was all uncalled for by the circumstances of the case. (*MTTMB* 240.)

V

Since the muggins subsumed reasoning, when Twain loosened his ties with him he augmented the overtly analytic side of his criticism. On viewing Bierstadt's "Domes" he found himself in the position of dealing with a picture painted by an outsider and purporting to represent a Western scene well known to himself and his readers. At the Academy of Design show Twain had been the outsider, for which he had compensated by acting the fool. With Bierstadt, while the fool was not totally banished, the comparative base he operated on was converted into a framework for analysis. That base was explicitly one of realism: what the Westerner had seen as opposed to what Bierstadt wanted people to see.

"The Domes of the Yosemite" was the best of about a hundred enormous canvases Bierstadt painted of that general scene. This one measured almost ten by fifteen feet and was seen to best advantage from the balcony of a theater. It was shown at the Studio Building in New York in May, 1867, for the benefit of the "Ladies Southern Relief Association." Formerly, Twain had criticized from behind the mask of unknowing; on regarding Bierstadt's painting, he could not raise the issue that needed to be raised without seeming to be an expert. He therefore retained the aura of dullness associated with the muggins by giving some of his most incisive criticisms in statements of ironic frustration. It was to avoid going over to the side of the critics that he made his first ironic allusion to Bierstadt's having made the scene look "considerably more beautiful than the original."

Twain felt that, instead of magnifying an already magnificent effect of spatial grandeur (a technique for which Bierstadt was accused of "theatricalism"[16]), the painter should have contented

16. Oliver W. Larkin, *Art and Life in America* (New York, 1959), p. 209. One reviewer had objected that Bierstadt's perspective was faulty and that "The Domes" lacked real grandeur (Clarence Cook, "Mr. Bierstadt's 'Domes of the Yosemite,' " New York *Daily Tribune*, May 11, 1867, 4). That, at any rate, Bierstadt had created considerable confusion by mixing moods can be seen in a recent commentary which has it that "his Wagnerian interpretations often captured the grandeur, if not the light and air, of the real thing" (Alexander Eliot, *Three Hundred Years of American Painting* [New York, 1957], p. 95).

himself with trying to capture no more than the real grandeur of the twin mountain peaks. Moving from the general prospect, with the two peaks in each of the upper corners of the picture, to such particulars as the valley, the bluff, the trees, and the boulders, Twain found that everything was "correct and natural," but that this accuracy was precisely the reason why Bierstadt erred in manufacturing unnatural "atmospheric effects." He will admit that he has been smitten by those effects, for they are "startling"; the difficulty is that the frustrated observer will find nothing like them in Yosemite. Though he "may be mistaken," it does seem to be "more the atmosphere of Kingdom-Come than of California." One gets "dreamy lights and shadows" playing around the precipices "instead of the bald, glaring expanse of rocks and earth splotched with cloud-shadows like unpoetical ink-spots which one ought to see in a California mountain picture when correctly painted." Bierstadt's "soft and rounded and velvety" mountains are so "great an improvement on nature" that one laments being deprived of the pleasure of seeing them *in* nature.

To justify the realistic basis of his criticism, Twain made a distinction between a "picture," in which liberties taken for the sake of artistic form are permissible, and a "portrait," in which the painter leads us to believe that he is doing something from life that is impressive in and of itself. His argument was for the dominance of subject and for the functionalism of its separate effects, criteria which, when rigorously applied, exactly validate his frustration. "As a picture, this work must please, but as a portrait I do not think it will answer. Portraits should be accurate. We do not want feeling and intelligence smuggled into the pictured face of an idiot, and we do not want this glorified atmosphere smuggled into a portrait of the Yosemite, where it surely does not belong. I may be wrong, but still I believe that this atmosphere of Mr. Bierstadt's is altogether too gorgeous" (251).

5

Of Poetry and Sunday-School Tales: Anger and the Fool

I

As I have indicated, the grace of Twain's early criticism is that, enraged as he might be personally, he generally kept his foolish persona in a state of benign ignorance. There were, however, some kinds of outrage that not even a fool could tolerate without seeming wholly bloodless. These involved subjects which—like the old masters—were completely intolerable to Twain himself: the pretentiousness of popular poetry and the simple-mindedness of Sunday-school tales. Twain permitted his fool to get properly angry at a poet who tried to fool him, and the anger inspired a retaliatory parody. The Sunday-school tale was something else again. The discomposure it excited in Twain went beyond anything a fool could handle.

Though not as severe a condition perhaps as idiocy, anger in the fool was practically his undoing as fool. Twain could not have him *very* angry without relieving him of his dullness. In any case, since the Sunday-school tale of his day—the equivalent of a Horatio Alger story—was for Twain an incomparably tedious piece of foolishness, a fool's anger could not begin to touch it. The need was for demolition, and Twain's satire was sufficiently destructive in the two concerted parodies he wrote on Sunday-school tales, "The Story of a Bad Little Boy That Bore a Charmed Life" and "The Story of the Good Little Boy Who Did Not Prosper."[1] However, in accenting the pathetic foolishness of

---

1. The "Bad Boy" story first appeared in the *Californian*, December 23, 1865 (*SOS* 202–05), which is the text I cite below. He later referred to it as "The Bad Little Boy who Did not Come to Grief" (*CTG* 44), and merely as "Story of the Bad Little Boy" on reprinting it in *SNO* 54–59.

   The "Good Boy" story appeared in the Buffalo *Express*, April 23, 1870, and in the *Galaxy*, May, 1870, and was reprinted in *SNO* as "The Story of the Good Little Boy" (60–67). Twain dated its composition from "about 1865." In quotations I use the *SNO* text.

the tales themselves, Twain improvidently deprived himself of a viably foolish position from which he might get the better of them. In the second parody he conferred the defensive mask of the fool upon the object of his criticism, the good boy; and when the muggins was given over to the opposition, that was the end of him as a critic.

This desertion was to be more than compensated by Twain's doing critical justice to the sentimental Sunday-school tale in *Tom Sawyer*. Since he so pointedly satirized the good and bad boy stories in *Tom Sawyer*, Twain's comment in a letter of 1876 gives us an inkling of the private rage that had likely been muted in order that his book might arouse a proper distaste for sentimentality in his readers. "There is one thing which I can't stand," Twain wrote,

> and *won't* stand from many people. That is sham sentimentality —the kind a school-girl puts into her graduating composition; the sort that makes up the Original Poetry column of a country newspaper; the rot that deals in "the happy days of yore," "the sweet yet melancholic past," with its "blighted hopes" and its "vanished dreams"—and all that sort of drivel. Will's [Will Bowen's letters] were *always* of this stamp. I stood it years. When I get a letter like that from a grown man and he a widower with a family, it gives me the bowel complaint.[2]

A major question, then, in Twain's early parodies of popular poetry and Sunday-school tales is one of how much his personal anger might be allowed to show—particularly in proximity to the character of the fool—and still be effective as criticism. Both the poetry and tales presented him with the kind of situation for which he would develop the dominant persona of his later criticism, the grumbler; but Twain had not yet worked out a critical role for the grumbler comparable to that of the fool. In dealing with the poetry, he took the angry fool about as far as he could go in criticism.

II

Twain was a first-class parodist of various poetic styles. In the course of his parodies, most of them written before 1870, he went

2. *The Portable Mark Twain*, ed. Bernard DeVoto (New York, 1946), p. 750f.

up and down the literary scale, taking in such figures as Shakespeare, Swift, Gray, Byron, Poe, Longfellow, Campbell, Aldrich, Thomas Moore, Charles Wolfe, folk ballads, and religious hymns; and he often dipped down into the world of obituary and moralistic newspaper verse as well.[3] En route he performed all the variations, burdening serious verse with trivial subjects and doggerel with philosophy. By and large, the parodies were exercises in wit, and had no deeper critical motive than the ordinary *jeu d'esprit*.

There were, however, several occasions on which Twain's lightness of tone did become imbued with criticism. On one such occasion he stumbled upon a piece of clever newspaper poetry and, playing the muggins, became "irritated" because the poet had "fooled" him. It must be remembered that much of the native "poetry" Twain had seen in books and newspapers out west was imitative of romantic poets, specifically of Wordsworth, Shelley, Byron, Poe, Hood, and Moore. The poet Twain criticized, Paul Duoir, not only imitated romantic affectations (he referred to pleasures undefiled by the world, to the rare feelings and timeless value of constant love, and the like), but he also tried to outdo the romantics in ingenuity. He organized his poem around an extended metaphor and turned it into a riddle to be climactically unraveled in the last line. The poem, "My Kingdom," was published in 1865 in the San Francisco *Evening Bulletin*,[4] a paper Twain had accused of having a special weakness

3. In the third chapter of his dissertation on "Mark Twain's Reading" Aspiz brought together many of these parodies (pp. 113–70). Most of them have also recently been discussed and published by Arthur L. Scott (*On the Poetry of Mark Twain*).

4. Twain entitled his sketch containing the parody, "Real Estate versus Imaginary Possessions, Poetically Considered." He published it in the *Californian*, October 28, 1865; *SOS* 188–90. Another interesting parody appeared in a piece he did for the *Galaxy*, entitled "A Memory" (August, 1870; *CTG* 66–67). In it he purportedly recalled a boyhood experience and posed as the idiotic son of an austere judge, who was not particularly fond of poetry, though the boy thought he liked Longfellow well enough. The boy composed a poem on the inspiration of a Warranty Deed given his half-brother by a Texas lady and gentleman whose lives he had saved "by an act of brilliant heroism." After running through eleven stanzas of "This Indenture, made the tenth/Day of November, in the year/Of our Lord one thousand eight/Hundred

for sentimentality. The poem—vaguely reminiscent of Edward Dyer's "My Mind to Me a Kingdom Is"—began:

> I have a kingdom of unknown extent,
>   Treasures great, its wealth without compare;
> And all the pleasures men in pride invent
>   Are not like mine, so free from pain and care.
>
> 'Tis all my own: no hostile power may rise
>   To force me outward from its rich domain;
> It hath a strength that time itself defies,
>   And all invaders must assail in vain.
>
> 'Tis true sometimes its sky is overcast,
>   And troublous clouds obscure the peaceful light;
> Yet these are transient and so quickly past
>   Its radiance seems to glow more clear and bright.
>
> It hath a queen—my queen—whose loving reign
>   No daring subject ever may dispute;
> Her will is mine, and all my toil her gain,
>   And when she speaks my heart with love is mute.

The "kingdom," as one soon guesses, is "One True Woman's Heart." This the muggins does not guess. Having been strung along, expecting "real estate," he is incensed at being tricked at the end. The very cleverness upon which the poet prided himself becomes the provocation for criticism by a reader not clairvoyant enough to see through the device, though, supposedly, he should for that reason be an ideal reader of the poem. Twain could not have more cleverly exposed the absurdity of its form. Another advantage of his using the muggins here is that over so hopelessly trivial an item no person of ordinary sense could waste his time. The muggins' discovery of the cheapnesss of the trick leads him to think better of himself than he should. As his anger mounts, he begins to think he can write as good a poem as Duoir's, which gives Twain the opportunity for a corrective parody.

---

six-and-fifty," the boy breaks off midway through the twelfth, remarking: "I kind of dodged, and the boot-jack broke the looking-glass. I could have waited to see what became of the other missiles if I had wanted to, but I took no interest in such things" (67).

His little sketch is by no means a high grade of satire, but in terms of critical method it adds up to a small triumph. For example, the innocence of the muggins is in inverse proportion to the presumptuousness of the poet; and this contrast is unfolded dramatically through the revelation of character. "Oh, stuff!" the muggins begins after quoting the poem, "Is that all?"

> I like your poetry, Mr. D., but I don't "admire" to see a man raise such a thundering smoke on such a very small capital of fire. I may be a little irritated, because you fooled me, D., you fooled me badly. I read your ramifications—I choose the word, D., simply because it has five syllables, and I desire to flatter you up a little before I abuse you; I don't know the meaning of it myself—I noticed your grandiloquent heading, "My Kingdom," and it woke me up; so I commenced reading your Ramifications with avidity, and I said to myself, with my usual vulgarity, "Now here's a man that's got a good thing." I read along, and read along, thinking sure you were going to turn out to be King of New Jersey, or King of the Sandwich Islands, or the lucky monarch of a still more important kingdom, maybe —but how my spirits fell when I came to your cheap climax! And so your wonderful kingdom is—"A True Woman's Heart!" —with capital letters to it! Oh, my! Now what do you want to go and make all that row about such a thing as that for, and fool people?

The fool finally works himself into such a rage that he turns the tables on Duoir (whom he calls "my innocent royal friend" and advises to be "more practical"), and offers him a poem of his own that extolls a piece of real property. He rattles off four stanzas before giving up.

> You can keep your boasted "kingdom," since it appears to be such a comfort to you; don't come around trying to trade with me—I am very well content with

MY RANCH

> I have a ranch of quite unknown extent,
>   Its turnips great, its oats without compare;
> And all the ranches other men may rent
>   Are not like mine—so not a dern I care.
>
> 'Tis all my own—no turnstile power may rise
>   To keep me outward from its rich domain;
> It hath a fence that time itself defies,
>   And all invaders must climb out again.

'Tis true sometimes with stones 'tis overcast
  And troublous clods offend the sens'tive sight;
Yet from the furrows I these so quickly blast,
  Their radiant seams do show more clear and bright.

It hath a sow—*my* sow—whose love for grain
  No swearing subject will dispute;
Her swill is mine, and all my slops her gain,
  And when she squeaks my heart with love is mute.

(SOS 189–90.)

For the criticism of popular poetry the muggins was without peer. The invention Twain showed in this criticism—as in the other areas of his early criticism—suggests that he may indeed have lost at least as much as he gained in putting the fool behind him. On the other hand, if he was to have any doubts about having an angry muggins criticize serious poetry, these would likely have been erased by the Whittier birthday speech fiasco. While few people seem to have fully appreciated how much the point of the speech rested on an absurdity (*MTMF* 217), which emanated in the first place from the outraged innocence of the miner (who is a muggins), the gaucherie of the situation was accentuated by the miner's becoming angry with the deadbeats who gave a burlesque application to the verses of Emerson, Longfellow, and Holmes.

There were two later, exceptional—and, in relation to the Sunday-school tales, highly instructive—criticisms of popular poetry wherein Twain employed a useful alternative to rage. The poets concerned were Julia A. Moore, the Sweet Singer of Michigan and author of *The Sentimental Song Book*, which Twain quoted in *Following the Equator* (I 340f.), and her fictive pen sister Emmeline Grangerford, whose "Ode to Stephen Dowling Bots, Dec'd" was modeled on Mrs. Moore's style. Mrs. Moore had "the same subtle touch," Twain noted, that he found in *The Vicar of Wakefield,* "the touch that makes an intentionally humorous episode pathetic and an intentionally pathetic one funny" (*FE* I 339f.). She and Emmeline were so charmingly oblivious to this "touch" that Twain could neither be angry at them nor play the fool at their expense. The lady poets were very nearly mugginses, and the closer one came to being a muggins, the less susceptible one was to criticism from that quarter. With Mrs. Moore and Emmeline, Twain wisely chose the path of comic sympathy, presenting the pricelessly pathetic character of the one from Huck Finn's all-accepting point of view and the valiant naïveté of the other from the point of view of a world-weary pessimist who finds relief in her "William Upson," an elegy on a lad killed in the Civil War, one stanza of which went:

> Now, William Upson was his name—
> If it's not that, it's all the same—
> He did enlist in a cruel strife,
> And it caused him to lose his life.

No amount of criticism could tell us more about the true heart of a popular poetess.

III

During the writing of *A Tramp Abroad*, Twain declared that "a man can't write successful satire except he be in a calm judicial good-humor." He wasn't getting anywhere with his work because, he said, "I don't ever seem to be in a good enough humor with ANYthing to satirize it; so I want to stand up before it & curse it, & foam at the mouth, or take a club & pound it to rags & pulp" (*T-H* I 248f.). It would have been superfluous for Twain to explain how he felt while writing his parodies of Sunday-school literature.

His parodies did not lack wit so much as they lacked a workable persona. In its simplest terms, Twain's problem was that he could not permit the apparently foolish narrator to be quite as angered as he was in the "Bad Boy" story without stripping him of his foolishness and thereby making him too obvious—and intelligent—an agent of criticism; nor could he get the reader properly angry at a muggins like the one who was the object of criticism in the "Good Boy" story. In these combinations, anger and the fool were incompatible with effective criticism. The parodies of Sunday-school tales therefore provide us with interesting transitional material which falls just between two major strands of Twain's criticism. If one may judge by subsequent results, it would seem that the mistakes he made in them helped to clear the way for his more successful treatment of sentimental moralizing in his fiction and in his pose as grumbler.

In his first parody, the one on the "Bad Little Boy," Twain lamely undertook the pose of an old fool. The story was written as a lesson "For Good Little Girls and Boys" from "The Christmas Fireside" of "Grandfather Twain." Where one expects the addleheaded style of a well-meaning old codger, one instead runs into a headstrong narrator who knows all too clearly what he is about. In his invidious asides he establishes his personality as that of a nay-sayer. He does so immediately in his opening sentence: "Once there was a bad little boy, whose name was Jim —though, if you will notice, you will find that bad little boys are nearly always called James in your Sunday-school books" (*SOS* 202). Replacing preachment with complaint, Twain systematically underscores the grumbling tone in successive paragraphs, each of which begins with the negation of Sunday-school stereotypes and builds to an anti-typical retort introduced by an intensifying "No," or "Oh, no," and with sinful Jim himself coming out as a kind of sneering grumbler:

> Once, this little bad boy stole the key of the pantry and slipped in there and helped himself to some jam, and filled up the vessel with tar, so that his mother would never know the difference; but all at once a terrible feeling didn't come over him, and something didn't seem to whisper to him, "Is it right to disobey my mother? Isn't it sinful to do this? Where do bad little boys go who gobble up their good kind mother's jam?" and then he didn't kneel down all alone and promise never to be wicked any more. . . . No; that is the way with all other bad boys in the books, but it happened otherwise with this Jim, strangely enough. He ate that jam, and said it was bully, in his sinful, vulgar way; and he put in the tar, and said that was bully also, and laughed, and observed that "the old woman would get up and snort" when she found it out; and when she did find it out he denied knowing anything about it, and she whipped him severely, and he did the crying himself. Everything about this boy was curious—everything turned out differently with him from the way it does to the bad Jameses in the books. (*SOS* 203.)

By the time Twain reaches the end of the tale the persona turns from argument to counter-preachment. "And he grew up, and married, and raised a large family, and brained them all with an axe one night, and got wealthy by all manner of cheating and rascality, and now he is the infernalist wickedest scoundrel in his native village, and is universally respected, and belongs to the Legislature."[5] The best that can be said for this blunt statement is that intention and tone are at one in it. But at this level one might conceivably prefer Twain's sarcasms on the championship of Sunday school by John B. Wanamaker and John D. Rockefeller.[6] In his legal battle with Wanamaker over his sale of Grant's *Memoirs*, Twain jubilantly admonished him for "picking Mrs. Grant's pocket in the intervals of keeping Sunday School," and called him "that unco-pious butter-mouthed Sunday school-slobbering sneak-thief . . . now of Philadelphia, presently of hell" (*T-H* II 573, 572).

Slender as it may seem as a subject for criticism, the parody of Sunday-school literature was of maximal—in fact, seminal—importance for Twain's fiction. It was part of the critical impetus that launched him on his first significant novels, *Tom Sawyer* and *Huckleberry Finn*. It also figured in some of his most trenchant reminiscences of boyhood, as in the Hannibal chapters of *Life on the Mississippi* (liii–lvi), where young Sam Clemens was given many of the traits of the "bad boy," and "Dutchy" those of his "good boy";[7] and there are notable overtones of the good boy-

5. Twain apparently sensed that he deprived the tale of subtlety in ending it as he did. In "Backlog Studies," where Charles Dudley Warner set forth some of the conversations of his Nook Farm neighbors, he recalled that Twain, his "Next Door Neighbor," had observed: "I tried a Sunday-school book once; but I made the good boy end in the poorhouse, and the bad boy go to Congress; and the publisher said it wouldn't do, the public wouldn't stand that sort of thing. Nobody but the good go to Congress" (*Complete Writings of Charles Dudley Warner*, ed. Thomas R. Lounsbury [Backlog Ed.; Hartford, 1904], I, 249f.).

6. Twain commented upon Rockefeller's performance as "Admiral of a Sunday-school in Cleveland, Ohio" (*MTE* 83f.), and upon his contributions to the American Board of Foreign Missions—which, according to Twain, were given right along with those of Satan ("A Humane Word From Satan," *The $30,000 Bequest and Other Stories*, ANE, XXIV, 237–38).

7. This is not the place to consider all of the ramifications of the good boy and bad boy syndromes as they occur in parodies, in fiction, and in autobiographical reminiscences. Worth noting, however, are a few of

bad boy relationship, especially of the reversal of their fortunes (as experience burlesques morality), in such other works as *The Prince and The Pauper, Pudd'nhead Wilson,* and *The Mysterious Stranger.* Indeed, Twain was enchanted by situations that confuted the morality of Sunday-school tales, and he relentlessly played up the ironic distribution of rewards and punishments meted out by life.[8] Some of his variations on Sunday-school piety may be found in sketches like "The Late Benjamin Franklin" (1870), "About Magnanimous Episode Literature" (1878), and "Edward Mills and George Benton: A Tale" (1880); and every now and then he threw a sketch of this kind into a travel book (e.g., "The Legend of the Seven Sleepers" [*IA* II 162–68] and the tales of how Cecil Rhodes made his fortune and how "Ed Jackson" made his [*FE* I 139–48, 227–37]).

It is not difficult to unearth the probable causes of Twain's obsession. In addition to his having attended the "Old Ship of Zion" Methodist Sunday school and the Presbyterian Sunday school in Hannibal, where he was once a Cadet of Temperance, young Sam Clemens had been exposed to *Peter Parley's Magazine* —his father was a subscriber—in which Samuel G. Goodrich endeavored to "spiritualize" the minds of children; and *Youth's Companion,* a magazine specializing in sentimental stories about good boys and girls, was as accessible in the Hannibal of Twain's youth as it was to his daughters in the Hartford of their youth.

the ironic differences between Twain's own experiences, on which he drew for his portraits of the good and bad boys, and the form they took in his parodies. In the case of Dutchy's drowning we are sympathetic toward the good boy, as the guilt-stricken Mark Twain is, on recalling that he had participated in the treachery of the bad boys. The chapter on the drowning opens with the thunderstorm that followed the drowning of Lem Hackett, the worst of the bad boys, and with young Sam's resolve to reform: "I would be punctual at church and Sunday-school; visit the sick; carry baskets of victuals to the poor," etc. (*LOM* 401). Needless to say, his resolve vanishes with daylight.

8. It was not uncommon to find him scratching down in his notebooks instances of good persons who came to grief and of bad ones who prospered, a case in point being a note on a good girl who was "poor & honest & pious" and had a "hard wretched time," and a bad girl who "lives in style in the county jail" (Unpublished Notebook No. 17 [May, 1883–August, 1884], 34 [Copyright © 1967, Mark Twain Company]).

Moreover, part of Sam's early aversion to school is attributable to the daily regimen of prayers, readings in the Bible, and in William Holmes McGuffey's *Eclectic Readers* and Noah Webster's *Spelling Book*, both of which contained moral tales with just the kind of incidents he was to parody.[9] One well-known work that epitomized the tradition of burlesqueable didacticism was Timothy Titcomb's *Letters to Young People* (1858), by Josiah G. Holland, whom Twain later assailed for denouncing humorous lecturers.[10] While Twain was not necessarily burlesquing Holland in his Sunday-school parodies, Holland, a staunch opponent of vernacular humor, produced exactly the sort of

9. "Fable I" in the Spelling Book was "Of the Boy That Stole Apples," an event treated in Twain's "Bad Boy" story (*SOS* 203), and one he recalled from his boyhood. (He told Will Bowen in 1870, "we have forgotten all the sorrows and privations of that cannonized epoch [their youth] and remember only its orchard robberies, its wooden sword pageants, and its fishing holidays" [*Letters To Will Bowen*, p. 18]).

 McGuffey generally chose stories that provided moral edification for the young, taking his selections from an assortment of sources—the Bible, Bacon, Addison, Johnson, Schiller, Jefferson, Irving, Channing, *et al.* He sought out stories in which goodness triumphed over calamity, perseverance resulted in the achievement of one's aims, and, in general, those in which faith, hope, or charity won the day. A typical story dealt with a poor widow with five "tattered" children between whom and starvation one cold Saturday night there lay nothing but a herring (her last, smoking on the coals), but this she would willingly share with a stranger who came to the door, in hopes that someone might do the same for the long-lost son she believed to be wandering somewhere around the world—whereupon the stranger revealed himself to be her son (*The Eclectic Fourth Reader: Containing Elegant Extracts in Prose and Poetry, From the Best American and English Writers* [6th ed.; Cincinnati, 1838], pp. 141–43).

10. Henry Nash Smith describes an unpublished harangue that Twain wrote on Holland, when he sensed that he was one of the humorous lecturers Holland had decried in an editorial in *Scribner's Monthly Magazine* for February, 1872 (*Mark Twain: The Development of a Writer*, p. 191). Holland hoped that the "drollerists" and "literary buffoons" (he mentioned Artemus Ward and his imitators) would retire from the literary platform, which they defamed. Twain wrote a nineteen-page diatribe in response, noting that his breed of lecturers drew bigger houses than Holland's pious and instructional crew did, and that the people wanted no "further stuffing from a blessed old perambulating sack of chloroform." He entitled this piece "An Appeal From One That Is Persecuted," and gave it the subtitle "A Soft Answer Turneth Away Wrath" (*Berg* [Copyright © 1967, Mark Twain Company]).

ponderous moralizing that fueled the perennial satires on "goody-goody" literature written by humorists like Benjamin P. Shillaber. Twain, who admired Shillaber's Mrs. Partington, was well versed both in the "goody-goody" tradition and in the satires on it. The immediate suggestion for his writing a "Bad Boy" story may well have come from Charles H. Webb, publisher and editor of the *Californian*, and from Bret Harte, a leading contributor and part-time editor of the journal, both of whom had used its columns to poke fun at tales of moral instruction (*SFLF* 182).

Twain had imitated Webb and Harte on other occasions, and it may be that in his "Bad Boy" story he was not sufficiently independent of his models. In any case, his "Story of the Good Little Boy Who Did Not Prosper" seems to have been an attempt of sorts to cast the satire in a mold that came more naturally to him during his apprentice years than out-and-out grumbling did. Jacob Blivens, the good boy, is an innocent fool. Also improved is the role of the narrator, who has no argumentative presence in the tale. We are only casually aware of him, as when he is puzzled by Jacob's fanatical goodness, or when he matter-of-factly ends the story, being obliged to come forward because the good boy has been blown up.

> You never saw a boy scattered so. . . . Thus perished the good little boy who did the best he could, but didn't come out according to the books. Every boy who ever did as he did prospered except him. His case is truly remarkable. It will probably never be accounted for. (*SNO* 66f.)

The apparent absence of critical thunder in this piece does not mean that it was not as critical as the other. Its tenor was a grumbling hostility to moralism on the grounds that it was not moral, that the Sunday-school tale was specifically immoral in unfitting boys for the rigors of life by making fools of them, and that success was not reserved for the prigs and weaklings of the world, who became little gentlemen before they had been boys. By withering the hope that the meek shall inherit the earth, Twain made a far more devastating attack on the way of the world than ever the children's tracts did.

However, in spite of its improved structure, Twain's "Story of the Good Little Boy" has a major flaw in it. Since the total simpleton tends to become an object of concern, one's attitude toward him is much like that of the narrator and of the other boys, who saw him as "afflicted" and tried to keep him out of harm's way. His disappointment, for example, that the good boy in "Sunday-school books" "always died in the last chapter, . . . with all his relations and the Sunday-school children standing around the grave in pantaloons that were too short, and bonnets that were too large, and everybody crying" (61) is acutely pathetic. The "moral" of the story requires that Jacob Blivens be not only killed but blown to smithereens while trying to do good: having sat down on an empty nitroglycerin can after lecturing boys not to tie the cans to dogs' tails, he is whacked by an Alderman. But one resists a moral that requires the unmerited death of this harmless boy-Emmeline Grangerford. The inherent appeal of his character as muggins cripples the effort to project a criticism that is supposed to work against, instead of merely through, him.

A better working relationship between the intention of grumbling and the pose of foolishness by which it is dissembled apparently required something more, in Twain's hands, than just a fictive persona. The ideal relationship awaited his transformation of the parody of Sunday-school literature into the condition of fiction itself, where it became dramatized in the quests for worldly knowledge by such figures as the tenderfooted Mark Twain of *Roughing It* and *Life on the Mississippi*, Huck Finn, and Theodor Fischer. It might have made some difference if there had been a truly good-hearted muggins like Huck around to feel personally reproached by Jacob Blivens' goodness. Or, to look at the matter from the point of view of the character to be satirized, one finds an excellently foolish expositor of self-criticism in a rogue like Senator Dilworthy of *The Gilded Age*, who told the Sunday-school children back in Cattleville how the bad little boy wound up a drunkard, while the good boy was elected to Congress and, in fact, stood before them at that moment, a monument of virtue and success (II 237–40). An even more adroit formulation of the character and actions appropriate for a satire on the stories of good boys appears in a scenario about the mad solicitousness of a Jacob Blivens, whose story Twain set down in his notebook preceding an extended notation on the Hannibal version of *The Mysterious Stranger.* "Write Xmas story," it began,

> Title, The Good Little Boy who went to Hell. Treats the little devils to fans & ice cream. Gives papa-Satan an asbestos prayer-book, partly converts him, & secures certain ameliorations, palliations, privileges & advantages for Christian babies, St. Bartholomew Catholics who got snatched out of life without the saving last sacraments, &c. . . . . Goes to heaven & gets privileges there for good little children—they are allowed to spend their Sundays in hell.[11]

IV

A concluding thought on Twain's early criticism. In retrospect, it is impressive that his use of the muggins should have enabled him to write so much really telling criticism without for a moment exposing his own ego. That protection was quite important to him in the period when he was a relative nonentity. Equally important was his technical coup in pushing such a lamb as the ego-less muggins into the ego-harrowing arena of criticism, where he could not begin to challenge anyone until the crucial moment for one's challenging *him* had passed and been superseded by one's awareness of what Twain was up to. Clearly, in no other critical connection did Twain more fruitfully employ the fool, except in the more devious critical course he followed in his fiction. The fool's mask slid into his fiction as into its natural element, where the art of the criticism completely assimilated the criticism itself, and gave it a life of its own.

As far as the subjects of Twain's criticism go, it is quite evident that he was for the most part concerned with the public arts,

11. Unpublished Notebook No. 32 II (August, 1898–July, 1899), 49f. (Copyright © 1967, Mark Twain Company).

It is interesting that, in the year following the serialization of *Ragged Dick*, Twain put down in his notebook the outline for a mock Alger story about a girl who tried literally to live the life of the typical heroine of Sunday-school literature. For example, she counsels the paper boy that when he delivers a paper he should accompany it with a sermon on the perils of the unregenerate, and she packs him off with a tract depicting the agonies of the damned. Eventually she turns away a man who has come to pay her aunt a thousand-dollar debt, which results in her aunt's ruination (Unpublished Notebook No. 10 [1868], 1–8).

popular forms, and popular audiences. He hoped for an improvement in public taste, a subject to which he later addressed himself at some length in a letter to Andrew Lang, defending *A Connecticut Yankee* from charges that it was a coarse travesty. He distinguished two types of books, those written for the "Head" and those written for the "Belly and Members," and argued that no critic had as yet troubled himself to set up, much less to investigate, standards pertinent to the latter. "If a critic should start a religion," he said, "it would not have any object but to convert angels: and they wouldn't need it." He had never had "any ambition" himself to "cultivate the cultivated classes," but had "always hunted bigger game—the masses." He asked that "critics adopt a rule recognizing the Belly and the Members, and formulate a standard whereby work done for them shall be judged" (*Letters* II 527ff.). While he could attempt nothing as ambitious as that in his early criticism, and while he was to lament that his subtlety had often been lost on the ordinary reader, Twain none the less did try to provide some critical norms that might get through to the Belly and Members; and in those critical sketches where his muggins drew a laugh that came from the region of the belly, it cannot be doubted that he hit his mark.

PART II

Twain's Later Criticism:
The Critic as Grumbler

*Sometimes my feelings are so hot that I have to take the pen
and put them out on paper to keep them from setting me afire
inside; then all that ink and labor are wasted because I can't print
the result.*

(Biog *II 724.*)

*"It's a melancholy thought to me that we can no longer express
ourselves with the bass-drum; there used to be the whole of the
Fourth of July in its patriotic throbs."*
("*Our Next Door Neighbor*" [*Clemens*],
Complete Writings of Charles Dudley Warner, *I, 279.*)

6

The Grumbling Mark Twain

While gathering materials for *A Tramp Abroad*, Twain conceived a character who might have helped him to sublimate the
disabling rage that he said prevented him from writing satis-
factory satire. He put into this character's mouth the spontaneous scoffing that Europe excited in the American (the kind
he had previously given to Brown and Blucher and occasionally
to Mark Twain) and assigned him the name of "grumbler."
When he spoke of getting drunk, he wrote "grumbler" in the
margin of his notebook; when he started grappling with the
German language, he had the grumbler curse it, or get a steve-
dore to teach him how to curse *in* it; and when he wanted to complain about the food or a church (the interior of the Church of
St. Nicholas looked like an "ugly barn") he again called upon the
grumbler.[1] In short, when the indignant Mark Twain wanted to
draw blood, the grumbler was his man. Once he perceived that
he could not inject both a clownish persona and a grumbler into
his book, and that he had quite enough to keep things moving
with just the interplay between his clown and Europe and between him and his straight man, "Harris," Twain apparently
jettisoned the grumbler. But not entirely, and certainly not for
good. The more vehement of the grievances directed against the
German language, Wagnerian opera, the Rhine legends, St.
Mark's Cathedral, and Italian paintings were clearly the work
of a whimsical grumbler. The world traveler in *Following the
Equator* was a complete grumbler in fact if not in name; and the
legalistic critic who prepared briefs against Dowden and Shelley

1. Unpublished Notebook No. 12 (1877–78), 10, 15, 19, 33, 34, 35. Twain
had briefly used the nom de plume "grumbler" at an early age, having
signed both a letter "To Rambler" (Hannibal *Journal*, May 10,
1853) and a letter to "Mr. Editor" (Hannibal *Journal*, May 7, 1853)
"Grumbler" (Edgar M. Branch, "A Chronological Listing of the Writings of Samuel Clemens to June 8, 1867," *AL*, XVIII [May, 1946],
115f.).

in his "Defence of Harriet Shelley" and against Goldsmith, Cooper, and Scott on other occasions was precisely the same grumbler capitalizing on the same critical pose. This was the pose in which Mark Twain would come to be known as the aggressive, eruptive forerunner of the "tooth-and-claw" tradition in American criticism—the critic, in other words, who paved the way for H. L. Mencken.

Before considering this criticism in any detail, I should like to say some things about the form and effect of Twain's grumbling, its purpose, and its prototypical expression in the mind of a fractious child.

The history of Twain's grumbling criticism is a record of feelings that were too hot not to be written down. He went far afield, of course, from the province of writing and declared himself on countless social issues, but the types of fakery he attacked in life and letters were basically the same, and so was the manner of his grumbling, which invariably won him converts to the cause of righteous wrath. When, around the turn of the century, for example, he began increasingly to appear in print as a foe of imperialists and missionaries (who provoked the most popularly distributed of his unpopular views), Moberly Bell, editor of the London *Times*, recalled Twain's having admitted that he "qualified as the first yellow journalist"; yet Bell believed he had caught on so well with the British because he seemed "a fearless upholder of all that is clean, honest, noble and straight-forward in letters as well as in life."[2] He grumbled because he saw problems that cried out for a kind of criticism they were not getting. That was what got the reader on his side. It was also what justified him in regarding dissent as a sort of constitutional need of the "race," and its frequently unexercised right. "The symbol of the race," he once remarked, "ought to be a human being carrying an ax, for every human being has one concealed about him somewhere, and is always seeking the opportunity to grind it" (*Biog* II 564). In time Twain filled the outlines of his own symbol. Reporters who watched him hack away at imperialism and the missionary movement thought they were

2. Fischer, *Abroad with Mark Twain*, p. 194f.

discovering him in a new role ("the genial humorist of the earlier day" had become "a sort of knight errant who does not hesitate to break a lance with either church or state"[3]), whereas all he had done was to make conspicuous a type of criticism he had been practicing all along.

One might say that habitual grumbling made Mark Twain a sort of intellectual melancholiac, in the old, Renaissance sense of the term. By nature he felt himself to be of Satan's party, a partiality he thought was "ancestral"—"in the blood, for I could not have originated it" (*Autob* I 83).[4] At any rate, few matters were more despicable to his Satanism than a tepid non-partisanship. In his days as a hectoring frontier reporter, it was typical of him to blast the Carson City *Independent* for taking exception to his criticism of undertakers, calling it a "harmless, non-committal sheet" and noting that "even the religious papers bearing [its name] give a decided, whole-souled support to neither the Almighty nor the Devil" (*MTEnt* 161). Naturally, he took to ax-grinding writers like Cervantes, Carlyle, Macaulay, Dana, Ingersoll, and Lecky more readily than to others, and in reading them he underscored such passages as: "No characters were more highly appreciated in antiquity than those of men who, through a sense of duty, opposed the strong current of popular favour. . . ."[5] He also relished forthrightly "profane" characters like Fielding's Squire Western,[6] and, needless to say, he put the best moral light on his own non-adjusted characters, particularly if, like Huck or Pudd'nhead, they opposed the strong current of popular favor.

But the most significant upshot of Twain's malcontent was a partisanship that became the vital center and genius of his

3. Louisville *Courier Journal*, April 1, 1901.
4. Twain had been duly impressed by Milton's Satan. While on the river he had written his brother: "What is the grandest thing in 'Paradise Lost'—the Arch-Fiend's terrible energy!" (*Biog* I 146).
5. William Edward Hartpole Lecky, *History of European Morals from Augustus to Charlemagne* (New York, 1869), I, 195. For Twain's marginal notes on Lecky's *History*, see Chester L. Davis, "Mark Twain's Religious Beliefs as Indicated by Notations in His Books," *Twainian*, XIV (May–June), 1–4; (July–August), 1–4; (September–October), 1–4; (November–December, 1955), 3–4.
6. Unpublished Notebook No. 14 (February–September, 1879), 4.

humor. Not only would he admit to being a "Professional Moralist," and a "revolutionist by birth, reading, and principle";[7] he claimed to be a humorist who "preached." "Humor must not professedly teach, and it must not professedly preach, but it must do both if it would live forever" (*MTE* 202). He had always preached, and he believed that that was why, in contrast to such "mere" humorists as Ward, Billings, and Nasby (whom he named), he had by 1906 lasted "thirty years"—or from about the time that he took on the calling of fictionist. What is more, the preaching was primary; it was his end in writing: "If the humor came of its own accord and uninvited, I have allowed it a place in my sermon, but I was not writing the sermon for the sake of the humor. I should have written the sermon just the same, whether any humor applied for admission or not" (*ibid.*, 202f.).[8] Had his humor lacked moral energy, we would indeed have thought less of it than we do. The same can be said of his grumbling criticism, and of the persona through whom it was morally informed.

Twain's grumbling persona was the auto-inspirational medium of his non-adjustability, the power of his negative thinking. This may be detected in a "scheme" he had of pretending that he addressed his dark thoughts to the one person most likely to be appalled by them:

> When you are on fire with theology you'll not write it to [Henry H.] Rogers, who wouldn't be an inspiration; you'll write it to Twichell, because it will make him writhe and squirm & break the furniture. When you are on fire with a good thing that's indecent you won't waste it on Twichell; you'll save it for Howells, who will love it. As he will never see it you can make it really indecenter than he could stand; & so no harm is done, yet a vast advantage is gained. (*Biog* III 1489.)

---

7. Louis J. Budd, *Mark Twain, Social Philosopher* (Bloomington, Ind., 1962), pp. 199, 186.
8. Twain had marked the following while reading Thackeray's essay on Swift (in *English Humorists*, 1868): the humorous writer "comments on all the ordinary actions and passions of life almost. He takes upon himself to be the weekday preacher, so to speak" (Coley B. Taylor, *Mark Twain's Margins on Thackeray's "Swift"* [New York, 1935], p. 31).

The Grumbling Twain

It is not without significance that Twain should have needed this little fiction to prime himself for criticism. One notices that as ideal sounding boards Twichell and Howells are the imagined counterparts of Twain's two dominant critical personae, the grumbler and the fool. They inspired him by releasing his other self as a separate being empowered to act a part in accordance with his character and become the anti-conventional hero in the agon of grumbling. Thus, the very destructive intent of Twain's grumbling criticism gave rise to the persona who would deliver it. Since the condition of that grumbling persona's existence lay in a reaction to unmerited respectability, Mark Twain as grumbler usually took cover (no less than he did as muggins) in the point of view of a low character, or at least one who ranked lower than the object of his criticism. As Twain tellingly observed, "When I take up one of Jane Austen's books, such as *Pride and Prejudice*, I feel like a barkeeper entering the kingdom of heaven. I know what his sensation would be and his private comments. He would not find the place to his taste, and he would probably say so" (*Biog* III 1500).

For all of the seriousness of Twain's grumbling, its form and effect took their shape mainly from the comedy of his maintaining the bartender-in-heaven pose. The comedy was in fact proportional to his seriousness; and Twain was fully as serious as his criticism was over-stated. Consequently, as a secondary effect, his comedy partook of a parody of the critic's posture itself, concerning which he had grumbled, "The critic's symbol should be the tumble-bug; he deposits his egg in somebody else's dung, otherwise he could not hatch it" (*Noteb* 392).

Only superficially did Twain come close to being a tumble-bug himself. His surliness was funny. It had a resolute innocence about it; and the profusion of metaphor and invective issuing from that façade was a piece of comic extravaganza. One enjoyed Twain's enjoying himself, his expressing himself with the bass drum, as it were; for if he took great pleasure in the performance of a fool, he did not derive half the pleasure from actually playing the fool that he derived from playing the grumbler. These and other aspects of Twain's inspired melancholia—his mingling of logic and absurdity, his argumentative gusto, his moral energy, and his commonsensical indictment of critics and critical prose

—are best viewed in the vividness of their native state, as in the following passages from "In Defence of Harriet Shelley":

> I have committed sins, of course; but I have not committed enough of them to entitle me to the punishment of reduction to the bread and water of ordinary literature during six years when I might have been living on the fat diet spread for the righteous in Professor Dowden's *Life of Shelley*, if I had been justly dealt with.
>
> . . . .
>
> This Shelley biography is a literary cake-walk. The ordinary forms of speech are absent from it. All the pages, all the paragraphs, walk by sedately, elegantly, not to say mincingly, in their Sunday-best, shiny and sleek, perfumed, and with *boutonnieres* in their button-holes; it is rare to find even a chance sentence that has forgotten to dress. If the book wishes to tell us that Mary Godwin, child of sixteen, had known afflictions, the fact saunters forth in this nobby outfit: "Mary was herself not unlearned in the lore of pain"—meaning by that that she had not always traveled on asphalt; or, as some authorities would frame it, that she had "been there herself," a form which, while preferable to the book's form, is still not to be recommended. If the book wishes to tell us that Harriet Shelley hired a wet-nurse, that commonplace fact gets turned into a dancing-master, who does his professional bow before us in pumps and knee-breeches, with his fiddle under one arm and his crush-hat under the other, thus: "The beauty of Harriet's motherly relation to her babe was marred in Shelley's eyes by the introduction into his house of a hireling nurse to whom was delegated the mother's tenderest office."
>
> This is perhaps the strangest book that has seen the light since Frankenstein. Indeed, it is a Frankenstein itself; a Frankenstein with the original infirmity supplemented by a new one; a Frankenstein with the reasoning faculty wanting. Yet it believes it can reason, and is always trying. It is not content to leave a mountain of fact standing in the clear sunshine, where the simplest reader can perceive its form, its details, and its relation to the rest of the landscape, but thinks it must help him examine it and understand it; so its drifting mind settles upon it with that intent, but always with one and the same result: there is a change of temperature and the mountain is hid in a fog. Every time it sets up a premise and starts to reason from it, there is a surprise in store for the reader. It is strangely near-sighted, cross-eyed, and purblind. Sometimes when a mastodon walks across the field of its vision it takes it for a rat; at other times it does not see it at all.

104

· · · · · · · · · · ·

There is an insistent atmosphere of candor and fairness about this book which is engaging at first, then a little burdensome, then a trifle fatiguing, then progressively suspicious, annoying, irritating, and oppressive. It takes one some little time to find out that phrases which seem intended to guide the reader aright are there to mislead him; that phrases which seem intended to throw light are there to throw darkness; that phrases which seem intended to interpret a fact are there to misinterpret it; that phrases which seem intended to forestall prejudice are there to create it; that phrases which seem antidotes are poisons in disguise. The naked facts arrayed in the book establish Shelley's guilt in that one episode [his infidelity] which disfigures his otherwise superlatively lofty and beautiful life; but the historian's careful and methodical misinterpretation of them transfers the responsibility to the wife's shoulders—as he persuades himself. The few meagre facts of Harriet Shelley's life, as furnished by the book, acquit her of offense; but by calling in the forbidden helps of rumor, gossip, conjecture, insinuation, and innuendo he destroys her character and rehabilitates Shelley's—as he believes. And in truth his unheroic work has not been barren of the results he aimed at; as witness the assertion made to me that girls in the colleges of America are taught that Harriet Shelley put a stain upon her husband's honor, and that that was what stung him into repurifying himself by deserting her and his child and entering into scandalous relations with a school-girl acquaintance of his. (*LE* 16, 18f., 21f.)

In a sense, the grumbler took over where the muggins left off. He articulated the unarticulated rage that had been left hanging in midair between the fool and the target of his criticism. Similarly, the grumbler can be seen as an extension of the fool; he could get incontinently and foolishly angry. Among the various traits shared by the muggins and grumbler, the one touchstone of both was a radical affinity with the intelligence of the child—that open intelligence, blissfully unaware of itself and uninstructed in cant and sophistry. Usually, it was the generic boy, as Twain represented him, who had the disposition to be a grumbler. He had the singlemindedness and independence not to be cowed by authority. Better still, if a bad boy, he was a born scoffer of the type we glimpse in the group of sixth-century British boys who flung clods at the mailed and mounted Connecticut Yankee and sassed him. They expressed the epitome of boy-ness: "In my experience," the Yankee reported, "boys are the same in all ages. They don't respect anything, they don't care for anything or anybody.... they sass me in the holy gloom of the Middle Ages; and I have seen them act the same way in Buchanan's administration; I remember, because I was there and helped" (*CY* 91). In contrast, girls do not complain. Usually they are compliant. They wish to stand in the good graces of their elders—that is, except when they are themselves, when they are frankly and fractiously children, as boys are.

Perhaps the most ingeniously exceptional of the boyish girls Twain "adored" was Marjorie Fleming, the Wonder Child, to whom he dedicated a little sketch toward the end of his life. Marjorie was a girl Tom Sawyer, touched by Mrs. Moore;[9] more than that, "she was the human race in little." To be sure, she could not rid herself of girlishness, but she was not conscious of having been imposed upon. "She was made out of thunder-storms and sunshine, and not even her little perfunctory pieties and shop-made holiness could squelch her spirits or put out her fires for long." Marjorie was a first-class grumbler. That was what made her great. In describing her "faculty," Twain gave her the unmistakable *élan* of a budding artist:

> she doesn't have to study, and puzzle, and search her head for something to say; no, she had only to connect the pen with the paper and turn on the current; the words spring forth at once, and go chasing after each other like leaves dancing down a stream. For she has a faculty, has Marjorie! Indeed yes; when she sits down on her bottom [her phrase] to do a letter, there isn't going to be any lack of materials, nor of fluency, and neither is her letter going to be wanting in pepper, or vinegar, or vitriol,

---

9. Here is Marjorie the elegist:

> Three Turkeys fair their last have breathed,
> And now this world forever leaved;
> Their father, and their mother too,
> They sighed and weep as well as you;
> Indeed, the rats their bones have cranched.
> Into eternity theire [sic] launched.
> A direful death indeed they had,
> As wad put any parent mad;
> But she was more than usual calm,
> She did not give a single dam.

"Marjorie Fleming, The Wonder Child," *The Complete Essays of Mark Twain*, ed. Charles Neider (New York, 1963), p. 464. Marjorie was, as Twain indicated, an actual person.

or any of the other condiments employed by genius to save a literary work of art from flatness and vapidity. And as for judgments and opinions, they are as commodiously in her line as they are in the Lord Chief Justice's.[10]

Twain was so thoroughly smitten by Marjorie because she "frankly and freely" criticized all that she read, "sometimes with vitriol," but her style was the expression of a person, not of a persona. Twain, on the other hand, exchanged the child's freedom for subtlety—which gained him a larger freedom—and his criticism was the richer for his decision to grumble *in character*, rather than in his own person. Fully as important as the persona for his criticism was the thematic tension between seeming goodness and seeming badness—a replaying of the conflict in his "Good Boy" and "Bad Boy" parodies. This conflict went rather deep. From the good boy-bad boy relationship that existed in Twain's home between Henry and himself ("the unbroken monotony of [Henry's] goodness and truthfulness and obedience would have been a burden to [Mother] but for the relief and variety which I furnished in the other direction" [*Autob* II 92]),[11] one can follow an interesting line of development running through such parallel situations as those of the boys in Twain's Sunday-school parodies, Tom and Sid in *Tom Sawyer*, Tom and Huck in *Huckleberry Finn*, and Theodor and Satan in *The Mysterious Stranger*, in which the bad boys represent a point of view that is Twain's grumbling criticism enacted in life. On the basis of this line of development and of the shortcomings in Twain's use of the fool in his criticism of Sunday-school literature, a logical beginning may be made in the exposition of his grumbling criticism by examining his comments on the writings of boys and girls.

10. *Ibid.*, p. 457.

11. This was Orion Clemens' comment on his two younger brothers:

> If a cat was to be drowned or shot Sam (though unwilling yet firm) was selected for the work. If a stray kitten was to be fed and taken care of Henry was expected to attend to it, and he would faithfully do so. So they grew up, and many was the grave lecture commenced by ma [sic], to the effect that Sam was misleading and spoiling Henry. But the lectures were never concluded, for Sam would reply with a witticism, or dry, unexpected humor, that would drive the lecture clean out of my mother's mind, and change it to a laugh. . . . But the boys grew up—Sam a rugged, brave, quick-tempered, generous-hearted fellow, Henry quiet, observing, thoughtful, leaning on Sam for protection. . . . (*Biog* III 1591f.)

7

Boys, Girls, and Goldsmith: Sense vs. Sensibility

I

In addition to his discovery of Marjorie Fleming, Twain had on three widely separated occasions lingered over some specimens of school-boy composition in which he detected an intriguing discord between thought and style. On the first of these, he visited a private school in Carson City, Nevada, and wrote a dispatch about it to the *Territorial Enterprise* (1864); on the second, he picked up a book of howlers which inspired his essay, "English as She Is Taught," first published in the *Century Magazine* (1887); and on the third, in 1896, he read a similar book of howlers taken from the pathetic English of school children in India, around which he had written a chapter for *Following the Equator* (II xxv). The American compositions engaged Twain both nostalgically and critically. At the most suggestive level, it was as if they gave him a glimmer of pure self. At a more mundane level, Twain shared the child's conspiracy against unintelligible rules that got in the way of truth. The child, and particularly the boy, wrote as he thought, in defiance of rhetoric and form. His knowledge of his own perceptions was at odds with the style that would have pleased the schoolmarm—she who was generally a proponent of sensibility and could inflict it on girls. The schoolboy might have written more correctly, but in doing so he would have lost the point of his opposition, and he would not have written as truly.

In other words, typical school-boy compositions evinced for Twain the beginnings of a rebellion against the conquest of sense by sensibility. The mischief had originated with the instruction the boy received, and, not being wise enough to know he was right in resisting it, he had at once the innocence and gumption to be the sort of critic often favored by Twain. But the schoolboy had a unique advantage; being by nature both a grumbler and a fool, he was indeed the one character whom Twain could neither be himself nor consistently represent one of his personae as. There is some measure of poetic justice, therefore, in the fact that in one of Twain's most blatant pieces of grumbling—that directed against Goldsmith's *Vicar of Wakefield*—he would grumble in such a way as to voice the inner thoughts of a repressed boy shedding received ideas about literature.

On his visit to Miss Hannah K. Clapp's private school for boys and girls in Carson City, Twain relived his own school days: "The exercises [that] afternoon were of a character not likely to be unfamiliar to the free American citizen who has a fair recollection of how he used to pass his Friday afternoons in the days of his youth." After mentioning the performance of "your rightly constructed schoolboy" in spelling and recitation, Twain turned to the compositions. Such was the "unusually vivid impression" that a boy's "literary effort" had left with him that he wrote a typical composition in its afterglow:

> "I like horses. Where we lived before we came here, we used to have a cutter and horses. We used to ride in it. I like winter. I like snow. I used to have a pony all to myself, where I used to live before I came here. Once it drifted a good deal—very deep —and when it stopped I went out and got in it."
> That was all. There was no climax to it, except the spasmodic bow which the tautological little student jerked at the school as he closed his labors. (*MTEnt* 137.)

Taken by itself, the sample composition seems hardly worth the effort of reconstruction. However, in the critical analysis with which Twain prepares us for it, we see that he conceived of the boy's composition as a silent protest against the pretense of sensibility exemplified by school-girl compositions—particularly the kind he would later cite in *Tom Sawyer*. Chief among the virtues of school-boy writing, we learn, were:

> the cutting to the bone of the subject with the very first gash, without any preliminary foolishness in the way of a gorgeous introductory; . . . the brief, monosyllabic sentences . . . ; the penchant for presenting rigid, uncompromising facts for the consideration of the hearer, rather than ornamental fancies;

[and] the depending for the success of the composition upon its general merits, without tacking artificial aids to the end of it, in the shape of deductions or conclusions, or clap-trap climaxes. . . . " (*Ibid.*, 136.)

Interestingly, in the piece Twain pronounced the "best" composition, a girl had atypically taken up the boy's role of hurling clods at authority. It seems that the "Hon. Wm. H. Gillespie, member of the House Committee on Colleges and Common Schools" had been "assuming imposing attitudes, and beaming upon the pupils with an expression of benignant imbecility which was calculated to inspire them with the conviction that there was only one guest of any consequence in the house." The girl ended her composition on "holidays" with the "proviso" that her Christmas "was dreary, monotonous and insipid to the last degree. Mr. Gillespie called early, and remained the greater part of the day!" "The charm of the thing," Twain observed, "lay in the fact that the last naive sentence was the only suggestion offered in the way of accounting for the dismal character of the occasion" (*ibid.*, 137f.).[1]

This girl was exceptional. She too, like Helen Keller, to whom Twain alluded in the composition chapter in *Following the Equator*, knew not "merely *things*" but the "*meanings* of them" (II 303). The schoolgirls that Twain remembered, or invented, usually wrote compositions that were the quintessence of literary flummery. In "English as She Is Taught," Twain quoted a schoolboy's composition "On Girls," in which the boy definitively stated their natural failings in the ineffable manner of the generic boy. Twain had been questioning whether children were not being pushed beyond their depth in school in being asked to learn useless and impenetrable facts, with "instruction" consisting of "obscure and wordy 'rules' " being stuffed into vacant heads. The composition illustrated what native understanding could do unaided, when a boy's mind had not been enervated by instruction. Twain noted, "It is full of naivete, brutal truth, and unembarrassed directness":

---

1. Twain cherished a similarly charming letter written by his thirteen-year-old niece, Annie Moffett, in 1865 (*Mark Twain and the Art of Writing*, ed. M. B. Fried [Buffalo, N.Y., 1961], pp. 26–28).

Girls are very stuck up and dignefied in their maner and be
have your. They think more of dress than anything and like to
play with dowls and rags. They cry if they see a cow in a far
distance and are afraid of guns. They stay at home all the time
and go to church on Sunday. They are al-ways sick. They are
al-ways funy and making fun of boy's hands and they say how
dirty. They cant play marbels. I pity them poor things. They
make fun of boys and then turn round and love them. I don't
beleave they ever kiled a cat or anything. They look out every
nite and say oh ant the moon lovely. Thir is one thing I have
not told and that is they al-ways now their lessens bettern boys.
(*WIM* 254f.)

Just to say that girls "stay home all the time and go to church
on Sunday," are "al-ways sick," "cant play marbels," and "now
their lessens bettern boys" is to say everything about them. The
boy is a perfect example of an innocent grumbler. What girls
mean to him is a compact metaphor of the quality that brought
out the grumbler in Twain.

II

In the spring of 1870, Twain, then editor of the Buffalo *Express*, and his friend David Gray, editor of the rival Buffalo
Courier, were asked to pick the prize compositions in the annual
contest of the Buffalo Female Academy. Because he and Gray
had gone about their work with "pitiless honesty," having indeed, "judged these compositions by the strict rules of literary
criticism," Twain thought that their choices would not have been
those either of the Academy or of the general public.[2] He consequently felt obliged to speak "in vindication" of the "verdict"
he and Gray had reached and said in effect they had declared
themselves for the party of sense and against the pretenders to
sensibility. In addition to being the "least ambitious," the prize
essays were the "least showy" and "the least artificial, the least
labored, the clearest and shapeliest, and the best carried out";
they did not sermonize but told "a very simple little incident, in

2. The several quotations I make are from Fried's reprint of Twain's
"Report to the Buffalo Female Academy," which had appeared in the
Express, June 18, 1870 (*ibid.*, pp. 1-24).

unpretentious language"; and they were concise, apt and accurate in diction, modest and fresh in subject, and "instinct with naturalness." Twain improved the occasion by singling out the villainy of "the old sapless composition model" and suggesting its cultural identity and perpetuation through schools, schoolmarms, and schoolgirls sodden with sensibility. Using such terms as "daring" and "plain duty" to preface his severest criticism, Twain complained that "the dead weight of custom and tradition have clogged method and discipline," compelling students to write compositions "constructed upon one and the same old heartrending plan." He steadily circled back to this central point, grumbling with cumulative effect toward the end that "considering the 'Standard School Readers' [McGuffey's, no doubt] and other popular and unspeakably execrable models which young people are defrauded into accepting as fine literary composition, the real wonder is, not that pupils attempt subjects which they would be afraid of at forty, and then write floridly instead of simply, and start without premises and wind up without tangible result, but that they write at all without bringing upon themselves suspicions of imbecility."

To Twain the blighted style of school-girl compositions seemed pervasive. He considered it the curse of much Victorian and pseudo-Victorian prose, and his repugnance doubled and trebled with each new discovery of it outside the schoolroom in the writing of journalists and popular novelists. His grumbling took several forms, but the consistent tests he used for the school-girl fallacy were the proportion of moral sentiment to theme, style to meaning, and sensibility to sense. The earliest of his overt, unposed grumbling statements about the verbosity of journalists and popular novelists set the tone for much that was to follow (its form was a distinct harbinger of the Cooper criticism), and it came at about the time when Twain was publishing a major piece of covert grumbling over school-girl compositions in chap. xxi of *Tom Sawyer*, where the "pretended" compositions (actually taken from a book by a sentimental lady) symbolized a good deal of what had made bad boys of Tom and his gang.

The overt grumbling arose in the course of his perusing Henry
H. Breen's *Modern English Literature: Its Blemishes and Defects*
(1857), which he called "one of the most useful books," and which
prompted him to write some "Comments on English Diction."[3]
Breen, a regular tumble-bug, had rifled the best authors to collect
faux pas for the instruction of the novice. The pretext for Twain's
criticism of the redundant and ostentatious prose which he said
one might find in Scott, Dickens, and almost any "sermon,
lecture, book or newspaper" was apparently a section in Breen
on "Errors in Composition" devoted to such matters as "Syn-
onymous and Redundant Terms," the blunders coming mainly
from writers who flourished between the times of Smollett and
Wordsworth. With a glance in the direction of the schoolboys,
Twain suggested that "ungrammatical simplicity" was "more
endurable" than wordiness; and for a diction with true forceful-
ness he instanced that of the Bible, Shakespeare, and Lincoln.
While he was entertained by Breen's subversiveness, Twain had
his own oppositional stance. He started out, in questioning the
validity of Scott's prose, as a sort of unregenerate schoolboy
made confident and articulate. So plainly sensible are Twain's
criteria that one must remind oneself that in his time and his
context (that of the criticism of Victorian prose), they were not
self-evident.

> I open Sir Walter Scott's *Guy Mannering* at a venture, and
> find this sentence: "This proposal seemed to dispose most of
> the assembly instantly to evacuate the premises." Why not have
> said, "These words moved most of the company to go at once"?
> No highflown language, no triple syllables are required in such a

---

3. These "Comments" were privately printed by Twain's nephew Jervis
Langdon in a pamphlet he entitled *Samuel Langhorne Clemens: Some
Reminiscences and Some Excerpts from Letters and Unpublished Manuscripts* (Elmira, N.Y., 1938), pp. 20–22. Twain had inscribed his copy
of Breen "Hartford, 1876" (*MTP*).
   Twain made a number of statements on the values of precision and
compression. In one of them, remarking on the comment Emeline
Beach's teacher had made on her compositions, Twain had written:
"To get the right word in the right place is a rare achievement. To
condense the diffused light of a page of thought into the luminous flash
of a single sentence is worthy to rank as a prize composition just by
itself" (Booth, "Mark Twain's Friendship with Emeline Beach,"
p. 226).

case. Cases will come when such are required: then, if you have been dealing in them all along, they come without force and fall dead upon the ear. There is majesty, there is sublimity, in thunder. That is because God thunders at intervals only. Sir Walter Scott and Mr. Dickens were distressingly given to using too many words. You will find the same fault in nearly any sermon, lecture, book or newspaper. If you wish to see how forcible short words and an unostentatious diction are, glance into the Scriptures. There you find such expressions as "Like the shadow of a great rock in a weary land"; "Deep calleth unto deep"; "Come unto me, all ye that labor and are heavy laden, and I will give you rest"; "Entreat me not to leave thee, or to return from following after thee: for whither thou goest I will go and where thou lodgest I will lodge; thy people shall be my people and thy God my God; where thou diest will I die, and there will I be buried; the Lord do so to me, and more also, if ought but death part thee and me."

Sir Walter could not have said these things in anything short of four chapters.

One should suit his language to his theme; and not be always riding the high horse like Sir Walter. One should mount the high horse at the proper time and only then. Then he will be fresh, not jaded. One should discourse gently of violets and zephyrs, and save his long syllables and sounding phrases for battle hymns, the destruction of cities, the fall of empires.

The richest instance of Twain's indirect grumbling over school-girl sensibility occurs in chap. xxi, the "'Examination' day" chapter of *Tom Sawyer*. There Twain crystallized in action the socioliterary implications of the conflict between boys and girls, and sense and sensibility, which had begun with his parodies on Sunday-school literature. He actively assisted the conspiratorial intention of his boys (between whom and Mr. Dobbins there was continuous warfare, with the boys "badly worsted" and thirsting for revenge) by presenting two essays and a poem as the work of Tom's female classmates, only to acknowledge in a note at the chapter's end that the ingenious gaudery was no mere invention of his but that, being the published writing of a paragon of school-girl education, it went beyond anything one could merely imagine.[4] The compositions

4. In an end note to the chapter, Twain wrote: "The pretended 'compositions' quoted in this chapter are taken without alteration from a volume entitled 'Prose and Poetry, by a Western Lady'—but they are

are symbols. They help document Twain's case against good girls and portend their fate, and they function in his general burlesque of juvenile literature and in his theme of appearance versus reality.

The boys resent being made puppets on parade for the benefit of the schoolmaster, "throned in his great chair" before parents and dignitaries. Twain has them rebel at the high point of the school year (climax of so many painful Friday afternoons) and in its final moment steal the master's thunder and snatch victory from defeat. It is a smashing triumph. When the master begins to bungle his map drawing, a cat is lowered from the garret scuttle and whisks off his whig, exposing a bald pate previously gilded by the sign painter's boy. At that point Dobbins loses more than his dignity. For all practical purposes he is disrobed, defrocked, and unmanned, and appropriately so, for he has been less than manly in upholding school-girl compositions. After the orgies (first those of the girls and then those of the boys) and the breaking of taboo, school is out, and there is vacation, when as events will have it, the boys literally begin to run the lives of the adults. Chap. xxi is thus a pivotal point in the novel. It culminates one phase and marks the rise of another. The reverse culmination devised by the boys is itself, however, the culminating event in a series of rebellious triumphs over the ideal of goodness so perfectly summed up in the school-girl compositions. Tom, who, according to his aunt, was "full of the Old Scratch," had, in the beginning of the book, beaten the well-dressed new boy; and from then on he went from one triumph to another, each capping its predecessor. His conning the boys into painting the fence is topped by his capturing the Bible prize, which gives way to his breaking up the sermon when the dog sits on his cinch bug (thereafter "even the gravest sentiments were constantly being received with a smothered burst of unholy mirth"), and a crescendo is reached when the parents are brought to their knees on the boys' return from Jackson's Island to attend their own

---

exactly and precisely after the school-girl pattern, and hence are much happier than any mere imitations could be" (*TS* 210). The book in question was *Prose and Poetry. By a Georgia Lady* [Mary Ann Harris Gay] (Nashville, Tenn., 1858). The book was privately printed and dedicated "To the Ladies of Georgia . . . by a Native Georgian."

funeral. "As the 'sold' congregation trooped out [of the church] they said they would almost be willing to be made ridiculous again to hear Old Hundred sung like that once more" (177).

Although it does not seem possible at the time, the parents *are* made more ridiculous, on Examination day, with the humiliation of their collective surrogate and the exposure of absurd piety and grandiloquence. The compositions suggest more than words without reference; the prose is a synoptic metaphor of the shadowy unreality into which the child is willy-nilly plunged and from which the wayward boys are determined to break out. The titles of the girls' essays alone—"Memories of Other Days," "Religion in History," "Dream Land," "Melancholy," "Filial Love," "Heart Longings"—are enough to terrorize a boy, but the boys had been intimidated by the atmosphere even before the compositions were given. The first boy to recite is "cruelly scared." He is "a very little boy" who speaks "with the painfully exact and spasmodic gestures which a machine might have used." Stage fright makes Tom break down in the middle of "Give me liberty or give me death," a subject with exaggerated relevance to the boys' situation. Thus the boys' conduct is by contrast a condition of Twain's satire, and—in keeping with the climactic structure of the chapter—one of four media for his criticism of sensibility, the others being the adulation of the grown-ups (the mayor makes a speech himself praising the eloquence of the girls, and each recitation is greeted with a "buzz of gratification"), the orgiastic "compositions" themselves, and Twain's own analytic comment on them as narrator.

The extracts Twain offers as "compositions" were craftily selected. The first, taken from the pious lady's essay, "Is This Then Life," epitomizes the precious prose and garishly plaintive moralism of its type. In its complete form the essay had also been given to discursiveness, melodrama, poeticism, and other quirks of sensibility. The passage Twain quoted aptly fit his fictional and critical themes, for the authoress dwells upon her heroine's recognition of the difference between appearance and reality—and that is what the rebellion of Tom and the other boys is all about.[5] The second extracted "composition," "A

5. The first paragraph went as follows:

   In the common walks of life, with what delightful emotions does the youthful mind look forward to some anticipated scene of festivity!

Vision," is more literary. It is the self-parodying soul of girl-ness. The writer evolves an extended conceit wherein the person having the vision finds herself in a dark and stormy night. Apparently, this experience stands for the life of a sensitive soul caught up in the materialistic world. Hungering for spiritual respite, the visionary gets it from a comforter who "moved like one of those bright beings pictured in the sunny walks of fancy's Eden by the romantic and young." She is sad, this comforting spirit, and, pointing to the storm, bids the heroine "contemplate the two beings presented," which we infer are the storm and the sad calmness of the spirit. Twain spares us the rest, remarking that the "nightmare" ended "with a sermon so destructive of all hope to non-Presbyterians that it took the first prize." It matters little that the actual essay had no such conclusion, or that the two spirits were subsequently identified as "War" and "Peace" and the comforter as "Meditation."[6] It sufficed that he could show the villagers' mindless infatuation with Miltonic ornamentation in a country version of the prose of sensibility.

In Twain's intervening analysis, he speaks as a man of sense who has had his own sensibilities wounded by the deathless iteration of these compositions from generation to generation of girls, embracing "doubtless all their ancestors in the female line clear back to the Crusades." The helpless narrator can point to the inevitable "nursed and petted melancholy," the "wasteful and opulent gush of 'fine language,'" the "tendency to lug in by the ears particularly prized words and phrases," and the "inveterate and intolerable sermon that wagged its crippled tail at the end," and yet have to admit that "the glaring insincerity of these sermons was not sufficient to compass the banishment of the fashion from the schools, and it is not sufficient to-day." Though troubled at heart, he can only shrug his shoulders and move on: "Homely truth is unpalatable" (*TS* 205f.).

Imagination is busy sketching rose-tinted pictures of joy. In fancy, the voluptuous votary of fashion sees herself amid the festive throng, 'the observed of all observers.' Her graceful form, arrayed in snowy robes, is whirling through the mazes of the joyous dance; her eye is brightest, her step is lightest in the gay assembly. (*TS* 206.)

6. *Prose and Poetry*, p. 192.

Some twenty years later, when he saw school-girl sensibility—or, more accurately, one of its sources—in an adult classic, *The Vicar of Wakefield*, Twain raged and stormed and foamed at the mouth. Unlike the girls, Goldsmith did not have the excuse of innocence. What was worse, he preyed upon innocence in *The Vicar* and muddled its virtues by making them a gauge of adult sensibility and righteousness. For Twain, *The Vicar* was clearly a Sunday-school tale writ large. Hence in grumbling that the book was "one long waste-pipe discharge of goody-goody puerilities and dreary moralities," he appropriately sounded very much like a ruthlessly sensible boy, a sinful Jim.

III

But Twain had not always scoffed at Goldsmith. So enamored was he with "The Citizen of the World" (1760, 1762) at the age of twenty-five that he ranked it with *Don Quixote*. A status-conscious steamboat pilot, he let it be known that these two works were his "*beau ideals* of fine writing," and that he liked them for their "quiet style" (*Letters* I 45).[7] He had, by then, already heard Goldsmith appreciatively paired with Shakespeare; as, two years earlier, George Ealer, a seasoned pilot, had given him "readings" from them, his "two Bibles," in the intervals while their boat lay at landings (*LOM* 169). Twain's affection for "The Citizen" lasted more than a decade, for in the *Galaxy* "Memoranda" his only eventful social criticism dealt with the persecution of the Chinese, and the best of it was a series of seven "Letters" called "Goldsmith's Friend Abroad Again."[8]

7. Twain may have read his father's copy of *Don Quixote* as a boy. As the two most frequently reprinted translations up to the middle of the nineteenth century were those by Charles Jarvis (1742) and Tobias Smollett (1755), the chances are that Twain read one of them, which might explain his linking of Goldsmith's style with what he supposed to be that of Cervantes.

8. These are considerably better than two earlier articles, wherein Twain had editorialized upon the stoning of the Chinese ("Disgraceful Persecution of a Boy," May, 1870, *CTG* 42–44) and upon the degrading jobs given them ("John Chinaman in New York," September, 1870, *CTG* 70), and wherein he had gone over much the same set of offenses as those reported in the "Letters." Nor was his eulogy on the industry and

118

With all due allowance for differences of time and purpose (Twain's concern was injustice, Goldsmith's social foibles), one notices a divergence in critical method between the two sets of letters that suggests the basis for Twain's attack on the moral shallowness of *The Vicar*. While Goldsmith's Lien Chi Altangi may be incapable of being ruffled, he is so continuously critical a person that his criticism has an inversely quiescent and molli-fying effect. The reader sleeps well after reading him. In con-trast, Twain's Ah Song Hi is so quiet (he breathes not a whisper of criticism, even though he is clubbed, kicked, set upon by a dog, and imprisoned for disturbing the peace) that the unspoken criticism obtained through him rises to a considerable clamor. To be sure, Goldsmith's mannered rhetoric and balanced periods perfectly mirror his over-all form,[9] but this does not alter the fact that his criticism is loud in manner and quiet in matter. By contrast, Twain's criticism specifically departs from that of his model in being quiet in manner and loud in matter. When— without detracting from the suppleness of Goldsmith's style— one places a representative instance of muted criticism in "The Citizen" next to one in "Goldsmith's Friend," the former seems decorous and captious, while the latter seems restrained and provocative:

---

self-reliance of the abused Chinese in *Roughing It* (II, chap. xiii) as effective as the "Letters," the first four of which appeared in October, 1870, the fifth and sixth in November, 1870, and the seventh in January, 1871.

Another instance of Goldsmith's influence on Twain may be found in the similarities between Beau Tibbs and Colonel Sellers; see Edward H. Weatherly, "Beau Tibbs and Colonel Sellers," *Modern Language Notes*, LIX (May, 1944), 310–13.

9. For Goldsmith to treat British pride, for example, was to specify such vices as a high susceptibility to flattery and a deathly fear of contempt and to balance them with such virtues as personal independence and a devotion to the cause of liberty ("Letter" iv). Lien was engaged in "a kind of experimental inquiry" ("Letter" xxx), as was Goldsmith, in crossing the universal type of *l'homme sensible* with a Mr. Spectator type of English gentleman ("The Citizen of the World; or, Letters from a Chinese Philosopher Residing in London to His Friends in the East," *The Works of Oliver Goldsmith*, ed. Peter Cunningham [New York, 1900], III, 103, 192; subsequent references to "The Citizen" and *The Vicar* are to this edition).

I find no pleasure . . . in taxing the English with departing from nature in their external appearance, which is all I yet know of their character; it is possible they only endeavor to improve her simple plan, since every extravagance in dress proceeds from a desire of becoming more beautiful than nature made us; and this is so harmless a vanity, that I not only pardon but approve it. A desire to be more excellent than others is what actually makes us so, and as thousands find a livelihood in society by such appetites, none but the ignorant inveigh against them. ("Letter" iii; *Works* III 100.)

I have been here about a month now, and am learning a little of the language every day. My employer was disappointed in the matter of hiring us out to service on the plantations in the far eastern portion of this continent. His enterprise was a failure, and so he set us all free, merely taking measures to secure to himself the repayment of the passage money which he paid for us. We are to make this good to him out of the first moneys we earn here. He says it is sixty dollars apiece. ("Letter" iv; *CTG* 80.)

Twain wrote "Goldsmith's Friend" to combat prejudice and not to attack Goldsmith. But, inferior as his "Letters" might be in other respects, Twain's prose appears to have had more, in reality, of a functionally quiet style than the prose he once admired for that quality. Having deviated from Goldsmith in that respect, Twain may have become disenchanted with his style in the process of borrowing his form (just as he developed a dislike for Harte's style when he tried to imitate it). Regardless of whether or not he became disenchanted, Twain did deviate from the style of "The Citizen of the World" on the same basis on which he later criticized *The Vicar of Wakefield*, his objection being that the moral understanding Goldsmith wished to generate was actually dissipated—and indeed made repulsive—by his working too strenuously for it.

IV

In one of the aphorisms from Pudd'nhead Wilson's Calendar used as chapter epigraphs in *Following the Equator*, Twain defined a classic as "a book which people praise and don't read" (I 245). *The Vicar of Wakefield* was a classic he had not only reread several times, but one on which he twice passed judgment in

Following the Equator. On the first occasion—not long after the appearance of the epigraph on the classic—he associated *The Vicar* with Julia Moore.

The reluctant voyager had had a chance to relax in a deck chair and be warmed by the sun ("three days of paradise"), and he was charitably disposed. Feeling very much like the citizen of the world that he was, he could afford to smile upon innocent error; and so he placidly assigned *The Vicar* a place in that sappy-serious realm of Sunday-school and school-girl literature which only a cad, or a bad boy, would directly criticize:

> I have been reading the poems of Mrs. Julia A. Moore, again, and I find in them the same grace and melody that attracted me when they were first published, twenty years ago, and have held me in happy bonds ever since. "The Sentimental Song Book" has long been out of print, and has been forgotten by the world in general, but not by me. I carry it with me always—it and Goldsmith's deathless story. . . . [sic] Indeed, it has the same deep charm for me that the Vicar of Wakefield has, and I find in it the same subtle touch—the touch that makes an intentionally humorous episode pathetic and an intentionally pathetic one funny. (*FE* I 339f.)

As Goldsmith is surely not to be classed with Mrs. Moore, Twain's levity is comparable in tone to an oriental smile, the sort in which one reads apparent sweetness as the measure of implicit disgust.

If one restricts the comparison with Mrs. Moore to *The Vicar* alone, Twain's condescension is not wholly unjust, as may be seen from a glance at the history of the novel's reception.[10] First of all, some of Twain's thoughts coincide with those of Austin Dobson, who in his biography had pointed out the obvious inconsistencies in the plot of *The Vicar* and had called it a literary

---

10. The comparison is in fact quite relevant, apart from the history of the novel's reception. James Hart has pointed out that while "Sterne was the high priest of sensibility" in America, "Goldsmith stood close to him in the hierarchy," and that in conjunction with Gray and the graveyard poets they bodily transplanted the cult of sensibility to this country. They had for their audience young ladies who would particularly relish the elegiacs of Mrs. Moore, having a penchant, as did Emmeline Grangerford, for drawing "nothing so much as a weeping willow trailing boughs over an obelisk or an urn" (*The Popular Book: A History of America's Literary Taste* [New York, 1950], p. 61f.).

curiosity more talked about than read.[11] At the beginning of its history, after Samuel Johnson had snatched the manuscript from Goldsmith's quivering hand, corked the wine bottle, and obtained sixty pounds from John Newbery with which Goldsmith could save himself from debtor's prison, *The Vicar* was not greatly esteemed as a work of art. (Newbery held it for more than four years before publishing it.) Johnson pronounced it to be "very faulty"; it had "nothing of real life in it and very little nature," being a "mere fanciful performance."[12] Contemporary reviewers mainly agreed with him. To one of them *The Vicar* was a wild romance containing some unspecified beauties, but "defects enough to put the reader out of all patience with the author."[13] The book enjoyed some degree of popular success, but it took the nineteenth-century romantic critics to discover its poignancy and make a popular classic out of it. Scott set the pattern. Discounting improbabilities, he held that "the admirable ease and grace of the narrative, as well as the pleasing truth with which the principal characters are designed, make *The Vicar of Wakefield* one of the most delicious morsels of fictitious composition on which the human mind was ever employed." He was most moved by such matters as the "fireside picture" of the Vicar and his family and the goodness and truth of Goldsmith's "sentiments."[14] This general image of the book persisted throughout the century, even among its less enthusiastic readers. Taine, for example, whose *History of English Literature* Twain had read, called *The Vicar* a "prose Idyl" and lauded Goldsmith for creating in it "an admiration and love for pious and orderly, domestic and disciplined, laborious and rural life."[15]

11. *Life of Oliver Goldsmith* (1st ed., 1888; London, 1898), p. 117f.
12. *Diary and Letters of Madame D'Arblay*, ed. Austin Dobson (London, 1904–5), I, 77.
13. The reviewer for the *Monthly Review*; cited by Ralph M. Wardle, *Oliver Goldsmith* (Lawrence, Kan., 1957), p. 169.
14. "Oliver Goldsmith," *The Lives of the Novelists* (New York, 1872), pp. 231–34. (Scott's *Lives* were originally prefixed to Ballantyne's *Novelists' Library*, 1821–24.)
15. *History of English Literature*, trans. H. Van Laun (New York, 1879), II, 183, 185. Twain incidentally, called Taine "The Father of English Literature because he made so many people read serious books which without his advice and encouragement they would never have tackled" (Fischer, *Abroad with Mark Twain*, p. 138).

However well Twain may have known the bias of the romantic critics, he was convinced that the prevalent view of *The Vicar* bore little relationship to its worth. At about the time that he was preparing to ambush Cooper, he began to think of doing "a really honest review of the Vicar of Wakefield." He noted that since "our second-hand opinions, inherited from our fathers, are fading," he would in doing the review "try to find out what our fathers found to admire and what not to scoff at" (*Noteb* 240). Other books that he thought needed to be honestly reviewed were *Roderick Random, Joseph Andrews, Pamela,* and "Miss Burney's books." Meanwhile, on rereading *The Vicar* (in 1895), he declared it, along with "some of Jane Austin [sic]," "thoroughly artificial," and shortly thereafter he was nudging himself to read "that devilish Vicar of Wakefield again."[16] These notes were made while he was working on *Following the Equator*; hence it would seem that he reread *The Vicar* at least twice, to make sure of himself, before publishing his criticism. If the second rereading preceded the second comment on *The Vicar*, then one may suppose that he was not only sure of himself but somewhat less than cheered by what he had had to endure in order to confirm his opinion.

A rather significant omen of the character he would assume in condemning *The Vicar* comes from Twain's note that it was high time readers were done with the opinions of their "fathers" and tried to find out whether there was anything "not to scoff at" in the book. In his second attack on *The Vicar*, Twain broke all of the tacit injunctions of his "fathers." Concluding, in substance, that Goldsmith had written a prolonged Sunday-school tale, he released a magnificent burst of comic grumbling (transcribed directly from his notebook) that immediately placed him before the reader as the model bad boy of American criticism.

16. Unpublished Notebook No. 27 (March, 1893–July, 1894), 61; Unpublished Notebook No. 28 B (December, 1895–March, 1896), 3; Unpublished Notebook No. 29 I (January, 1896–April, 1897), 3 (Copyright © 1967, Mark Twain Company).

Also, to be fair, there is another word of praise due to this ship's library: it contains no copy of the Vicar of Wakefield, that strange menagerie of complacent hypocrites and idiots, of theatrical cheap-john heroes and heroines, who are always showing off, of bad people who are not interesting, and good people who are fatiguing. A singular book. Not a sincere line in it, and not a character that invites respect; a book which is one long waste-pipe discharge of goody-goody puerilities and dreary moralities; a book which is full of pathos which revolts, and humor which grieves the heart. There are few things in literature that are more piteous, more pathetic, than the celebrated "humorous" incident of Moses and the spectacles. (*FE* II 312.)

V

Not the least fantastic aspect of Twain's performance is that its brilliance of style acts both as a defense against instant dismissal and as a goad to send one back to the text—which fully substantiates the truth of each seemingly bombastic phrase.

In analytic terms, Twain's critique covers elements of characterization, tone, theme, and plot. Goldsmith's plotting is unadulterated melodrama: he gives us a sterling hero in the hour of his felicity and then with the aid of a villain gradually deprives him of it over the middle span of the action, only to reverse his fortune when it seems beyond salvaging. One is asked to believe that the Reverend Charles Primrose's persistence in rectitude was sufficient to overcome his adversities, so that character and tone are made the means for a conquest of physical hazards created by plot. Wanting to find a woman who will love him for his person rather than his money, Sir William Thornhill, the Vicar's manorial lord and a man of sensibility, assumes the disguise of a virtuous but impoverished gentleman. In his absence, the Squire, his nephew, is left in charge of the estate, and being a wastrel, depraved by power, he harasses one of the Vicar's daughters, Olivia, and subsequently the Vicar himself. In the downward plunge, the Vicar loses the fortune of ten thousand pounds he had inherited from his brother when the agent in charge of it absconds to avoid bankruptcy. Olivia is seduced and deserted by the Squire, and the Vicar, after a long journey to recover his shamed child, arrives just in time to see his house burn down. The Squire thereupon puts him in prison for his debts and in recrimination for the minister's accusations. He is joined there by his son George (whom the Squire imprisoned for his audacity in challenging him to a duel), and shortly he hears a false report of Olivia's death. The Vicar is reviled in his attempts to give the prisoners Christian instruction but persists and finally softens them, at which point Goldsmith begins to turn the tide. The agent is captured, much of the inheritance is recovered, the two daughters are married, and the villain asks forgiveness and is denied it.

One cannot quarrel with Goldsmith's effort to do for the middle-class family what he would do for the peasantry of "Sweet Auburn." But one is within one's rights in objecting, as Twain did, to the "showing off" of the Vicar and Sir William, for whose endless preachments the plot seems to have been contrived. Sir William is not above intoning a Shaftesburian memorial to his own youth: a lover of "all mankind," "the slightest distress, whether real or fictitious, touched him to the quick, and his soul laboured under a sickly sensibility of the miseries of others" (*Works* II 112). Scarcely anyone speaks without sermonizing, and all of the sermons do sound "theatrically" alike —that is, like the Vicar's.

In the original version of his second comment on the book Twain had said it "makes virtue nauseous."[17] No one had a greater knack for doing that than the Reverend Charles Primrose. To Twain he must have seemed to have walked right out of a Sunday-school tract. Because of his private income, he makes over his living of thirty-five pounds a year to the orphans and widows of deceased clergymen. He is rather easily carried away with self-satisfaction, especially when he warms to his argument that widowers should not remarry. Indeed, as far as his own wife is concerned, he has already written an epitaph for her, extolling her "prudence, economy, and obedience, till death," and he likes it so much that he has it framed and hung over the chimneypiece, where it will serve the double purpose of admonishing his wife of her duty to him and of his fidelity to her. He hopes to inspire her with a "passion for fame and constantly [to] put her in mind of her end" (105).

17. MS of *More Tramps Abroad* (the title of the British edition of *FE*), 1549, *Berg* (Copyright © 1967, Mark Twain Company).

The Vicar is pompous, pedantic, fatuous, and, in a word, Twain's complete fool. He is proud of deriving moral lessons from misfortune, as from the loss of their home or the fall of his daughter, in whose presence he reminds his wife that heaven is "much more pleased to view a repentant sinner than ninety-nine persons who have supported a course of undeviating rectitude" (211). There are countless situations like these in which the pathos, as Twain pointed out, is truly humorous, and the humor pathetic. A confidence man relieves Moses, the Vicar's son, of the money he received from the sale of a horse, giving him in exchange a gross of worthless green spectacles. One hesitates to laugh at the "blockhead," as his mother calls him, for the family has suffered too grievous a loss. The embarrassment of the humor is scarcely mitigated when the same man makes a fool of the Vicar himself by taking a second horse from him with an invalid note.

The Vicar's crowningly foolish acts occur during his pathetic imprisonment. He wants to reform the ruffian prisoners, and though his initial sermon is met with mockery, he vows to repeat it. Goldsmith devotes an entire chapter to the climactic sermon, in which the Vicar tries to prepare his son and himself "for eternity" and, not wanting to be "niggardly," requests that his fellow prisoners be permitted to stand where they may hear the sermon too (241). The Vicar at this point resembles a type of character that had greatly fascinated Twain and about whom he had written his parody on the Sunday-school tale, as well as such unpublished sketches as the "Autobiography of a Damned Fool," in which the fool tried to reclaim his irate and irreligious boss by reading him a tract entitled "The Pit Yawns for You," the "Albert Story," in which a virtuoso tried to civilize a colony of monkeys, and "The Story of Mamie Grant, the Child-Missionary," in which the pious Mamie tells her aunt at breakfast that it is impossible for her to eat batter cakes while her aunt's soul is in peril.[18] The major difference between the Vicar

18. The "Autobiography of a Damned Fool" and the "Albert Story" both date from the late 1870's and were connected with Twain's interest in the life of his brother, Orion (MSS DV 310, DV 310A, *MTP*). The "Mamie Grant" story appeared in Twain's Unpublished Notebook No. 10 (1868), 1-9. Professional reformers were anathema to Twain.

and Twain's sermonizers is that their efforts realistically end in disaster, whereas Primrose thrives (he reforms the prisoners in a week), as do the good boys in Sunday-school stories.

It is helpful to remind oneself of the matters Twain grumbled about, for critics in our day still minimize the sentimentality and improbable plotting in *The Vicar* and extoll Goldsmith's moving portrait of the virtues of rural life and the wisdom, fortitude, and humanity of the Vicar. There would appear to be at least some reactive value in looking at the book from Twain's point of view when a recent biographer of Goldsmith can advise that "anyone who would truly appreciate it should not try to criticize or analyze it, but should read and enjoy it as people have been doing ever since it was published."[19]

In his criticism of Goldsmith, Twain grumbled in the manner of his schoolboy, economically "cutting to the bone with the very first gash." In his criticisms of Cooper and Scott, as we shall see in the next two chapters, he wrote more expansively and with greater variation in his gashing tactics.

Charles Dudley Warner had him responding to them with a thought reminiscent of the anarchistic ideal of Rabelais' Abbey of Thélème: "I'm sick of every sort of reform. I should like to retrograde awhile. Let a dyspeptic ascertain that he can eat porridge three times a day and live, and straightway he insists that everybody ought to eat porridge and nothing else. I mean to get up a society every member of which shall be pledged to do just as he pleases" ("Backlog Studies," *Complete Writings*, I, 191).

19. Wardle, *Oliver Goldsmith*, p. 171.

8

Cooper's Literary Offenses: Mark Twain in Wonderland

I

The author of "Fenimore Cooper's Literary Offences" is the cantankerous Mark Twain of critical legend, the curmudgeon whom we know so well, or at least think we do. Since the Cooper he describes is somewhat more and somewhat less than the novelist we know *him* to be, Twain's Cooper seems equally legendary. We have read about Cooper's incredible defiance of the "eternal laws of Nature," only to rub our eyes at the boners we missed, and at the incredible oddity of Twain's belaboring them. But first impressions of either man can be deceptive. The sulphurous grumbling over Cooper is hardly the work of a judicious person, of a responsible citizen like Samuel Clemens, who, after the debacle of 1892, had made it a point of honor to pay his creditors one hundred cents on the dollar; rather, it belongs to a hoodwinking persona who puts up a good front but is not always entitled to the horror he exhibits and is not the unsuspecting reader he pretends to be. Actually, he is an unabashable hack and in his bacchanal of sophistry latches on to just enough fact to silence doubt. Thus, what this creature has gotten away with on the basis of gall alone is literary mayhem, pure and simple. How he does it is a luminous example of Twain's fascination as critic. For between the result obtained and the barely recognizable subject of Twain's grumbling lies the genius of a critical method that is quite as skillful as it is devastating, and, externally, quite as puzzling too.

Of course, the use of the persona will not absolve Twain of all his sins. It cannot be denied that, strictly in terms of values, whereas his condemnation of *The Vicar* is fully germane, both in principle and detail, his condemnation of the Leatherstocking Tales is of mixed validity. He places *The Deerslayer* in the "domain of romantic fiction" and yet has no comprehension of the romantic imagination. By magnifying faults in style, invention, and realism, he surely mistakes the part for the whole, ignoring symbolic—to say nothing of mythic—implications that transcend eccentricities of technique. From one situation to the next the theme reverberates that Natty's is the celebrated idyl of the new Adam, redeemed by Christian sensibility and restored to Eden. To these reverberations Twain is deaf. Nor is he aware of the ritual of initiation through which Natty passes. How perceptively imperceptive of him to put down as an absurdity the scene he calls Deerslayer's "half-hour with his first corpse." There would seem to be little point, therefore, in one's seriously trying to confront Twain with the text—and perhaps that is why it has not been done. Instead, one tends to accept his confrontation of it and to acknowledge that he is right about Cooper's having violated his "rules governing literary art," and just as callously wrong about the totality of Cooper's effect.

On the other hand, the very idea of rightness amid wrongness, of logic in the treatment of particulars and illogic in the treatment of the whole, of fullness amid emptiness of analysis, of fact amid fancy, sense amid nonsense—all of this, if we do not too easily shy at apparent contradiction, brings us to the paradoxical heart of Twain's unexplicated critical method. For if, under his scrutiny, Cooper's forest episodes take place in a wonderland of snapping twigs and lost moccasin tracks (a wonderland quite like Alice's, by the way, in that "so many out-of-the-way things . . . happened" that one might think "very few things indeed were really impossible"[1]), then Twain's ambiance is assuredly the wonderland of common-sense criticism. If Natty is a romantic version of Alice, Twain comes off as a realistic version of the Mad Hatter. He is aghast at Cooper's "marvelous creatures" and his "miracles"; yet he convinces the reader that that is what they are because he has first convinced himself that "nothing is impossible to a Cooper person" (*LE* 90). The world he has made of Cooper's frontier becomes the world of his own habitation as critic: it is his fantasy, nor is he out of it. The realm of the free

---

1. *The Annotated Alice: Alice's Adventures in Wonderland & Through the Looking Glass*, ed. Martin Gardner (New York, 1960), p. 30.

and easy, it is also the universal meeting ground of fools and grumblers, of children and adults, and its form and setting are those of the tall tale.

Think for a moment of the infamous ambush of the ark in "the *Deerslayer* tale" (as Twain puckishly insists on calling it), the first red-white encounter and first major incident in the book. Everyone has chuckled over Twain's critical redaction of the scene, but, so far as I know, no one seems to have overly exerted himself in checking Twain's account against Cooper's. It was all very well for Twain to say that Cooper "saw nearly all things through a glass eye, darkly"; yet when it came to distortion, he easily "laid over" anything Cooper had done. His account of the ambush is almost a complete canard, brilliantly carried off by his high-handed confidence in admonishing readers for their failure to question Cooper's reliability—a bluff which seems to have inhibited them from inquiring into his own. The fact is, however, that, vague or imprecise as his physical relationships may get, Cooper did not arbitrarily tamper with the width of the Susquehanna at the outlet where it issued from Glimmerglass.[2] He did not, as charged, shrink it from fifty to twenty feet (as readily, say, as Alice changed size), but merely gave its actual width as fifty feet and then noted that the shores were so thickly lined with bushes growing out over the stream, and with trees arching over it from the steep banks that the space between would only "admit the passage of anything that did not exceed twenty feet in width" (49). Nor can one find the contradiction Twain implies there is in Cooper's denoting this "the narrowest part of the stream," which geologically it should be. The narrowness that Twain attributed to narrative convenience Cooper had gone to some length to explain, pointing out why and how the trees were arched over the outlet almost obscuring it from sight (in the dense forest at the lake's edge the trees everywhere grew naturally toward the light, some "in nearly horizontal lines, for thirty or forty feet" [53]); and he carefully set up the arch as "a nat'ral and-bush" (in Hurry-Harry's phrase)

2. For Twain's account of the episode, see *LE* 85–88. For the relevant passages from Cooper's account, with which Twain's is to be compared, see *Writings of J. Fenimore Cooper* (Iroquois ed.; New York, n.d.), I, Chapters 3 and 4, particularly 49–51, 52–54, 66–69.

by indicating how the sapling from which the Indians were to jump came to overhang the water "in nearly half a circle" (it had "first grown toward the light; and then been pressed down into this form by the weight of the snow; a circumstance of common occurrence in the American woods" [67]). The only real improbability of the episode was the method Hutter devised for getting the ark back upstream through the outlet and into the lake again. (Having set the anchor in the lake, he pulled on the anchor line to retrace his course.) With this Twain was not half so concerned as he was with the dimensions of the scow, which he, and not Cooper, made an ungainly hundred and forty feet long and sixteen feet wide. For Cooper's purposes the ark had only to be big enough to accommodate a cabin housing Tom Hutter and his daughters and light enough to be pulled upstream by rope, being flat-bottomed and drawing no more than two or three inches of water (354). Moreover, since the sapling presumably grew from the shore and not from the outer (river) edge of the vegetation, the Indians could not, as Twain would have it, have simply stepped aboard the ark instead of descending from a tree. But the most fanciful distortion is Twain's description of the Indians' seemingly preposterous miscalculation in missing the ark. By the time he reaches that point, his momentum—like that of the Indians—is such that he is quite at the mercy of his own rage. The Indians' plan, as he points out, is "to drop softly and secretly from the arched sapling to the dwelling as the ark creeps along under it at the rate of a mile an hour, and butcher the family." So far so good, but as he proceeds, Twain, despite his mock restraint, rewrites Cooper's shoddy invention and insidiously improves it:

> It will take the ark a minute and a half to pass under. It will take the ninety foot dwelling a minute to pass under. Now, then, what did the six Indians do? It would take you thirty years to guess, and even then you would have to give it up, I believe. Therefore, I will tell you what the Indians did. Their chief, a person of quite extraordinary intellect for a Cooper Indian, warily watched the canal-boat as it squeezed along under him, and when he had got his calculations fined down to exactly the right shade, as he judged, he let go and dropped. And *missed the house*! That is actually what he did. He missed the house, and landed in the stern of the scow. It was not much

of a fall, yet it knocked him silly. He lay there unconscious. If the house had been ninety-seven feet long he would have made the trip. The fault was Cooper's, not his. The error lay in the construction of the house. Cooper was no architect.

There still remained in the roost five Indians. The boat has passed under and is now out of their reach. Let me explain what the five did—you would not be able to reason it out for yourself. No. 1 jumped for the boat, but fell in the water astern of it. Then No. 2 jumped for the boat, but fell in the water still farther astern of it. Then No. 3 jumped for the boat, and fell a good way astern of it. Then No. 4 jumped for the boat, and fell in the water *away* astern. Then even No. 5 made a jump for the boat—for he was a Cooper Indian. In the matter of intellect, the difference between a Cooper Indian and the Indian that stands in front of the cigar-shop is not spacious. (87f.)

Twain tells this so well, one could almost wish it were true. Unfortunately, he was—again, like the Indians—a little wide of the mark. It seems that the ark had gone about half the way under the sapling when Deerslayer, peering from a cabin window amidships, spied the parcel of Indians. They were not yet *in* the tree waiting, but were on the shore, just climbing it. Thus at that moment they had possibly some twenty or more feet of sapling to traverse before they could get over the scow and into position for a jump: "When Deerslayer first saw this party, it was just unmasking itself, by ascending the part of the tree nearest to the earth, or that which was much the most difficult to overcome . . . " (68). Upon hearing his call, Harry and Hutter "applied all their force to the line," and the scow, having "redoubled its motion," could no longer have been going at the pokey "mile an hour" pace Twain gave it. In fact, it "seemed to glide from under the tree," according to Cooper, at exactly the moment that the Indians, "perceiving that they were discovered," all ran "forward on the tree," and in rapid succession "leaped desperately toward their fancied prize" (*ibid.*). Everything happened so quickly, with the simultaneous effort of the two men on the ark and the confused rush of the Indians—who are to be seen as unable to stop themselves at the last moment—that, while it taxes one's imagination a bit, the scene is nowhere so bad as Twain makes it out to be by slowing down its pace and imputing deliberation to the frantically leaping savages.

To the question of what Twain has gained, one's answer must be, on viewing these disparities, that his blowing up the improbabilities of Cooper's invention heightens the madly wondrous element in his romanticism as nothing else can. As Twain observed, Cooper "is more interesting when he is not noticing what he is about than when he is" (92).

A comparable job of distortion elicits the incipient fantasy of Hawkeye's attempt to locate Fort William Henry in a fog by sighting on the direction of a furrow cut by a cannonball shot from the fort (Chapter 14 of *The Last of the Mohicans*).[3] As Twain represents the scene, the lost party hears "a cannon-blast, and a cannon-ball presently comes rolling into the wood and stops at their feet"; whereupon Twain, pointing to "the admirable Bumppo," declares, "I wish I may never know peace again if he doesn't strike out promptly and *follow the track* of that cannonball across the plain through the dense fog and find the fort." In the book, it wasn't exactly that way. In truth, the furrow seemed momentarily to have misled them. Hawkeye, in desperation, with the enemy pressing in around him, merely proposed that as a last resort they might look for the furrow: "This shot that you see ... has ploughed the 'arth in its road from the fort, and we shall hunt for the furrow it has made, when all other signs may fail." Before finding it they again lose their direction, until Uncas finds the furrow "where it had cut the ground, in three adjacent anthills." Shortly after trying to guide themselves by it (Hawkeye ridiculously calls, "Give me the range"!), they see a strong glare of light, which is followed by the report of several cannon, telling them that they have been going toward the woods rather than the fort. They then reverse their steps and make their way to safety.

Twain shrewdly interlarded the true with the false, both within and among the "situations" he cited as examples of miraculous invention. (In case one is curious, Twain's summary of the longest of them, the "passage at arms" in marksmanship in *The Pathfinder*, Chapter 11, between David Muir, Jasper Eau-douce,

3. For Twain's account see *LE* 83. For Cooper's, see *Writings* II 167–70.

and Natty, is completely on the level.[4]) In the end, though, one doesn't know which is more hilarious, Twain's description of an offense or its deviation from Cooper's text. For better or worse, the weight of his grumbling persuasion has spread confusion in the ranks and carried the day. The spectacle of Mark Twain in Wonderland has apparently been irresistible.

His trick, in sum, was to catch Cooper walking on thin ice and to break it up under his feet. He would make a somewhat ridiculous situation absolutely and irreclaimably ridiculous; and judging by the number of readers who still take Twain's word over Cooper's text, his hectoring has done its shameless work better than he had any right to expect.

If we ask *why* he did this to Cooper, we may possibly reconcile ourselves to *how* he did it, since his means should properly be judged by his ends. Twain's pointing with alarm to Cooper's literary offenses was more than a caveat against the pitfalls of romantic fiction; it was a plea for readers to accept the verdict of history that old-style romanticism—at best an exotic movement with a code of feeling engendered by the cult of sensibility, to which America opposed the cult of experience—that this brand of die-hard romanticism was a literary dead letter in post-Civil War America. Cooper was the realists' whipping boy, the visible symbol of defunct romanticism, and insofar as he falsified the life they would represent truly, he was its most vulnerable and appropriate symbol. Twain could surreptitiously caricature Cooper's invention because the vested interests of realism seemed at stake, particularly since the revival of the historical novel in the 1890's buttressed the reputations of Cooper and Scott, fanned their always latent popular appeal, and threatened the achievement of the realists by a seductive romanticization of the province of fact. In short, this was war, and Twain gave no quarter. He offered proof of the other side's most threatening move by indicating in the epigraphs to his Cooper essay that the opinions of professional scholars (*vide* T. R. Lounsbury), critics (*vide* Brander Matthews), and novelists (*vide* Wilkie Collins) were paving the way for the establishment of Cooper as a classic

4. For Twain's account see *LE* 88–92. For Cooper's, see *Writings* III 164–70.

American writer. Twain seemed to feel, and with some justification, that at so late a juncture in the course of American literature, the apotheosis of Cooper could do incalculable harm, and perhaps cancel out many of the successful battles that he and other realists had fought. It had not helped the realists' cause that for the better part of the century Cooper (our Scott) had somehow been kept in the forefront of American authors, both at home and abroad, and that he had been widely translated and had given great popular currency to certain idealized conceptions of the American experience. This was one of the main reasons for Twain's having gone after Cooper as though—to use one of his own expressions—he had had no more conscience than a cat.

An even more important reason was that Twain's intent was an expression of artistic conscience. How long, he was asking, would readers allow themselves to be deceived about their own traditions and about a native approach to literature? His critical method adroitly educed these historical and aesthetic demands. It consisted of a fusion of the factual with the fantastic and a juxtaposition of overstatement with understatement. There was a sort of wonderland dialectic about it which did much to make the Cooper essay, for all its shortcomings, the outstanding piece of satanic criticism known to the literary trade and the foremost instance of the art of Mark Twain's grumbling criticism.

After what we have seen Twain make of the ark episode, these redeeming qualities will bear more looking into. But first, we should bear in mind that from the beginning of his identification with the cause of realism, Twain had sensed that Cooper stood in his sun. Much of his later argument and method (even the glories of grumbling) had indeed developed from his earliest defined antagonism towards that hybridization of Shaftesbury, Rousseau, and Gray which had given Cooper, along with Freneau, Bryant, and Longfellow, the myth of the Noble Red Man. After observing the regal son of the forest at first hand on the frontier, Twain had had his doubts about him. He expressed them on three notable occasions within a span of three years, most successfully on the first, in a sketch entitled "The Noble Red Man" (September, 1870, *Galaxy*), and awkwardly (by having a fool attempt to do a grumbler's job) on both the second, in an essay entitled "A Visit to Niagara" (1871, *SNO*), and the third, which was part of a chapter in *Roughing It* (I xix, 1872).[5]

II

We have in "The Noble Red Man" the earliest formally complete specimen of Twain's speaking through his fire-eating persona for the purposes of literary criticism. The essay constitutes the effort of the realist in Twain to disjoin the past from the present.[6] Specifically, his two-pronged attack deals one blow at the romanticization of the Indian and a second at the goody-goody folk who lament the ravages of the whites upon the "poor abused Indian" and ignore the atrocities he perpetrates upon the whites. Twain's organization is that of a straight, unconditional contrast: antithesis rammed hard against thesis. His first five paragraphs are a matter-of-fact summary of the Indian's physical and moral person as it is set down by the romantic writers; his next nine paragraphs systematically negate their portrait, item by item, fact for fiction. Since there is no secret about the facts, much depends on how they are put to readers who have been beguiled by the literary Indian. Thus Twain industriously packed the first five paragraphs with all of the data given in the books. When spread over any one book or narrative poem, the absurdity of these data is diluted; when they are collected and

5. The criticism in the Niagara sketch fails because, after starting out with the discerningly unfoolable fool, Twain retreats to the point of view of the less knowing dandy, and then to that of the absolute simpleton, who, like the good boy, has his solicitousness repaid with disaster. Unlike the situation in "The Noble Red Man," in this sketch the narrator is the fool blundering into criticism, rather than being the fool as critic, or even the critic as fool. Then, too, Twain has other fish to fry, such as tourism, commercialism, and the Irish. The fool in the *Roughing It* passage who tells us he is "a disciple of Cooper and a worshiper of the Red Man—even of the scholarly savages in the 'Last of the Mohicans,'" is by that very statement as incredible as the Indians are. He professes to be an innocent disciple of Cooper's, and yet by his analysis of the terrors of Cooper's dialogue he shows himself to be so fully aware of Cooper's faults as to be disillusioned in him.

6. This function of Twain's realism is lucidly defined by Roger B. Salomon, "Realism as Disinheritance: Twain, Howells and James," *AQ*, XVI (Winter, 1964), 531–44.

jammed together, one soon sees it in full measure. Oversimplification of this kind is one of Twain's critical techniques. In addition, he artfully intersperses with the reportage a considerable amount of damning exaggeration which takes on the appearance of truth from its surroundings. An example occurs toward the end of the second paragraph. After giving the details of the Red Man's colorful appearance in literature (with his "sheaf of brilliant feathers," his belt and moccasins "wonderfully flowered with colored beads," and he himself "rainbowed with his war-paint"), Twain completes the portrait of this "being" we want to "fall down and worship" by sketching in his famed "eagle eye gazing at specks against the far horizon which even the pale-face's field-glass could scarcely reach" (*CTG* 71). Twain slips so smoothly into his overstatement that once it is recognized the preceding "facts" become an understated criticism. It is a painless step from there for him to begin to suggest by how much the "facts" as given are an exaggeration in themselves: "In some publications [the Red Man] seldom says anything but 'Waugh!' and this, with a page of explanation by the author, reveals a whole world of thought and wisdom that before lay concealed in that one little word" (*ibid.*).

At the beginning of the essay, despite tongue-in-cheek exaggerations, Twain's criticism is for the most part played down. It is put into a new register when he considers the Red Man not as he is "in print" but out on the plains, where, since he is not "on dress parade," he is his "natural self." The exaggerated derogation of the grumbler takes over, but Twain's criticism retains its balance and liveliness because the recitation of vices has an aura of fact that seems to circumscribe the overstatements and provides the counter-implication of restraint. This impression is abetted by Twain's refusal to give certain disgusting features of the Indian too close an inspection. The complexity of his satire helps to offset an overt attempt to mow down the romantic opposition by sheer weight of details:

> He is little, and scrawny, and black, and dirty; and, judged by even the most charitable of our canons of human excellence, is thoroughly pitiful and contemptible. There is nothing in his eye or his nose that is attractive, and if there is anything in his hair that—however, that is a feature which will not bear too

close examination. . . . He wears no bracelets on his arms or
ankles; his hunting suit is gallantly fringed, but not intentionally; when he does not wear his disgusting rabbit-skin robe, his
hunting suit consists wholly of the half of a horse blanket brought
over in the Pinta or the Mayflower, and frayed out and fringed
by inveterate use. He is not rich enough to possess a belt; he
never owned a moccasin or wore a shoe in his life; and truly he
is nothing but a poor, filthy, naked scurvy vagabond, whom to
exterminate were a charity to the Creator's worthier insects
and reptiles which he oppresses. Still, when contact with the
white man has given to the Noble Son of the Forest certain
cloudy impressions of civilization, and aspirations after a nobler
life, he presently appears in public with one boot on and one shoe
—shirtless, and wearing ripped and patched and buttonless pants
which he holds up with his left hand—his execrable rabbit-skin
robe flowing from his shoulders—an old hoop-skirt on, outside of
it—a necklace of battered sardine-boxes and oyster-cans re-
posing on his bare breast—a venerable flint-lock musket in his
right hand—a weather-beaten stove-pipe hat on, canted
"gallusly" to starboard, and the lid off and hanging by a thread
or two; and when he thus appears, and waits patiently around a
saloon till he gets a chance to strike a "swell" attitude before a
looking-glass, he is a good, fair, desirable subject for extermination if ever there was one. (*CTG* 71.)[7]

The thought of extermination comes as a seemingly gratuitous
extremity. In terms of method, it is an ingenious piece of
hyperbole. The argument does not rest with the effort to expunge
the fantasy of savage nobility; from the grumbler's detestation
of the real Indian, there grows the idea that his extermination
would not be an undesirable alternative to the problem he
creates. By the time that the moral justification for ridding the
world of Indians is repeated at the end of the critique, the idea
has picked up a kind of mad plausibility. Extermination is
logically humane and merciful, a blessing for all. It is a proposal
to relieve humanity of the loathsome example of the Indian at
the same time that he himself is relieved of a loathsome existence
which could not be further degraded by death. In the madness
of this reasoning and in the self-accelerating wrath that drives
Twain to ask for the obliteration first of an idea and then of the

7. To stave off the skeptics, Twain added a verifying footnote: "This is not
a fancy picture; I have seen it many a time in Nevada, just as it is here
limned" (*ibid.*).

savages whose being mocks the idea, he demonstrates the blind-ing agility that makes his grumbler so good at bringing out the fantastic in what *is*—a talent that is largely responsible for the art of this otherwise unsavory suggestion of a Final Solution to the Indian Problem.

The phases of his argument are well meshed. The persona is not merely riding the crest of cathartic rage when he enters the second phase of his reasoning, for that phase is a coherent part of his antidote to the fallacy he would destroy in the first phase of it, the worship of the non-existent noble savage. Independently, extermination is intended as a foil to the equivalent hyperbole of the humanitarians and romantics. Twain's proposal, it need hardly be said, is no more to be taken seriously than is Swift's "Modest Proposal." The irony of his making it in a form that understates his overstated meaning is but further evidence of the Swiftian complexity of his exaggeration.

The variations in Twain's technique are for the most part made viable by the tonic wildness of the grumbler. To get an idea of their richness, one might consider the following types:

1. The inverse restatement of a previous exaggeration: "He is ignoble—base and treacherous, and hateful in every way. Not even imminent death can startle him into a spasm of virtue" (71).

2. An exaggerated hypothesis further exaggerated both in its particularity and revolting pathos: "to give him a dinner when he is starving, is to precipitate the whole hungry tribe upon your hospitality, for he will go straight and fetch them, men, women, children, and dogs, and these they will huddle patiently around your door, or flatten their noses against your window, day after day, gazing beseechingly upon every mouthful you take, and unconsciously swallowing when you swallow!" (72).

3. The realistic impossibility: "he trades a crippled horse, or a damaged musket, or a dog, a gallon of grasshoppers, and an inefficient old mother for [a bride] . . . and all the 'blushing' she does can be removed with soap and a towel, provided it is only four or five weeks old and not caked" (72).

4. The crushing citation of a factual account that makes his exaggerations seem pale: "the Indians *massacred nearly 200 white*

persons and ravished over forty women captured in peaceful outlying settlements along the border. . . . Children were burned alive in the presence of their parents. Wives were ravished before their husbands' eyes. Husbands were mutilated, tortured, and scalped, and their wives compelled to look on" (72).

III

What Twain had at first done with a rude hand, he later did more subtly, with a gloved fist. The greater smoothness of the "Offences" essay is due largely to his doing a tighter job of undercutting his exaggeration, in addition to varying it. The point is that all criticism worthy of the name usually has a self-corrective tendency, something that brings it back on course after its overreaction to the alleged ineptitude of a preceding generation of writers. As R. P. Blackmur once noted, "Like walking, criticism is a pretty nearly universal art; both require a constant intricate shifting and catching of balance."[8] With Twain, the grumbler was at once a reactive and a self-corrective agent. The self-corrective element inheres in Mark Twain's seeming to be not so much a critic as a caricature of one. From him distortion can be no crime. Apparently Twain gave some thought to the matter of point of view, for he fortunately discarded a pose in which he would doubtless have made a buffoon of himself and thereby have taken the vinegar out of his reaction: he originally wanted to present himself as "Mark Twain, M.A., Professor of Belles Lettres in the Veterinary College of Arizona," publishing his lectures, "Studies in Literary Criticism."[9]

8. "A Critic's Job of Work," *Form and Value in Modern Poetry* (Doubleday Anchor ed.; New York, 1957), p. 346.
9. Twain had prepared two essays on Cooper's literary offenses, but published only the most complete one. Bernard DeVoto published the other under the title, "Fenimore Cooper's Further Literary Offenses," *New England Quarterly*, XIX (September, 1946), 291–301. The essay is reprinted in *Letters from the Earth* under the title, "Cooper's Prose Style" (pp. 137–45). DeVoto discusses the relationship of the two essays in a note (*LFE* 290). The essays must have been written earlier than August, 1894, when Twain wrote Livy from New York about cutting down "those old Cooper articles" to a single article of five magazine pages (*MTP*).

Instead of giving himself professorial airs, Twain acted like a wholesome plebeian, and wasting no time on preliminaries, came out swinging at the professional students of literature. Lounsbury had called *The Pathfinder* and *The Deerslayer* "pure works of art," Matthews had mentioned "an extraordinary fulness of invention," and Collins saw Cooper as "the greatest artist in the domain of romantic fiction yet produced by America." Twain began his essay by representing himself in a state of petrified reaction. But his thought seemed to be going one way and his expression the other. The form of his stated skepticism was one of immovable simplicity. Could it be that two professors and a popular novelist would praise Cooper without reading him? "It seems to me that it was far from right." "It would have been much more decorous to keep silent and let persons talk who have read Cooper." As for what was wrong, "Cooper's art," he succintly noted, "has some defects," temporarily echoing Lounsbury's "the defects . . . are comparatively slight," and then went on: "In one place in *Deerslayer*, and in the restricted space of two-thirds of a page, Cooper has scored 114 offences against literary art out of a possible 115. It breaks the record. There are nineteen rules governing literary art in the domain of romantic fiction—some say twenty-two. In *Deerslayer* Cooper violated eighteen of them" (*LE* 78f.). Why eighteen out of nineteen or twenty-two—no more and no less? It may be that he doesn't fool anybody with his irony, but then who is going to take Mark Twain's opinion over those of three *real* critics?

Twain does marvels with the understatement of his overstatements.[10] He deals out a chorus of them—in fact, the entire diapason—but they are never wholly the same in kind or degree from one point to the next. His pervasive technique, moreover,

10. Even in its simplest form—that is, a series of direct charges followed by a catalogue of "circumstantial evidence"—Twain's mingling of over- and understatements is impressive.

> Cooper's word-sense was singularly dull. When a person has a poor ear for music he will flat and sharp right along without knowing it. He keeps near the tune, but it is *not* the tune. When a person has a poor ear for words, the result is a literary flatting and sharping; you perceive what he is intending to say, but you also perceive that he doesn't *say* it. This is Cooper. He was not a word-musician. His ear was satisfied with the *approximate* word. I will furnish some circumstantial evidence in support of this charge. My instances are gathered from half a dozen pages of the

is recapitulated in the general structure of the essay, as he leaves the reader with the implication that he can scarcely plumb the depths of Cooper's badness or present more than a few illustrations without being tedious, and all the while he is piling it on for all he is worth, in deceptively simple sentences. Aside from the persona, what one has to do with here is the inobtrusiveness of the obtrusive, the long-standing rhetorical principle that, as Longinus observed, "when two things are brought together, the more powerful always attracts to itself the virtue of the weaker (*On the Sublime*, trans. W. Rhys Roberts, sec. xv).

It is significant of the quality of Twain's understatement that it is more often assumed than stated, and for the reader more often felt than conceived. The most forceful understatements are guilefully placed in the opening and concluding paragraphs, where, by virtue of structural emphasis, they soften the stridency of what goes on in between and appear to be more representative of Twain's tone than they actually are. At the end, they are a gesture of grace in parting, as Twain seems to replace the grumbler's visage with one of relative sweetness and light. His conclusion is beautifully orchestrated. Each damning thrust is begun with a protestation of humility ("Now I feel sure, deep down in my heart"; "I may be mistaken, but it does seem to me") followed by a bare reductive summary ("Cooper wrote about the poorest English that exists"; "*Deerslayer* is just simply a literary *delirium tremens*"), until he gets himself wound up again, only to slacken off in the spare two-sentence finale, where, out of steam at last, he wearily drops his closing thought. It is a deadly concession, though, silently but magniloquently overstating his case in exact proportion to his condensed understatement of it:

> A work of art? It has no invention; it has no order, system, sequence, or result; it has no lifelikeness, no thrill, no stir, no

---

tale called *Deerslayer*. He uses "verbal," for "oral"; "precision," for "facility"; "phenomena," for "marvels"; "necessary," for "predetermined." . . . (94f.)

The list goes on for a full thirty-one instances, seemingly culled at random and without effort. From just a look at the physical appearance of that list of errors blocked out on the page, one is ready to concede the point, without checking, that what is true of six pages may well be true of many others—in fact, of the entire book.

seeming of reality; its characters are confusedly drawn, and by their acts and words they prove that they are not the sort of people the author claims that they are; its humor is pathetic, its pathos is funny; its conversations are—oh! indescribable; its love-scenes odious; its English a crime against the language.

Counting these out, what is left is Art. I think we must all admit that. (96.)

IV

Despite the undercurrent of understatement, a virtual cataract of abuse rushes through the interior of this tempestuous essay. Twain's exaggeration was, among other things, his way of meeting the excessive deference paid to Cooper. It was born, as well, of a natural response to the uncriticized badness of Cooper's style, and became fitting commentary on a baroque prose which Twain charged—without exaggeration—was distinguished by its unvarying extravagance.[11] Somewhat less obvious is the nature of the exaggeration produced by the interaction of Twain's persona with his subject. A griper by nature, he would not be worth listening to if his dissatisfaction were not somehow revelatory and presented with some wit and charm. Actually, the revelation is itself the charm of the persona's style; his instructive irony is doubled by the fact that this grumbler has not lost the capacity for wonder. He has, indeed, come away from the Leatherstocking Tales flushed with discovery, having followed his own precept that one might "find it profitable to study [Cooper] in detail—word by word, sentence by sentence" (*LFE* 137). His findings

---

11. As he put the matter:

> The style of some authors has variety in it, but Cooper's style is remarkable for the absence of this feature. Cooper's style is always grand and stately and noble. Style may be likened to an army, the author to its general, the book to the campaign. Some authors proportion an attacking force to the strength or weakness, the importance or unimportance, of the object to be attacked; but Cooper doesn't. It doesn't make any difference to Cooper whether the object of attack is a hundred thousand men or a cow; he hurls his entire force against it. He comes thundering down with all his battalions at his back, cavalry in the van, artillery on the flanks, infantry massed in the middle, forty bands braying, a thousand banners streaming in the wind. . . . Cooper's style is grand, awful, beautiful; but it is sacred to Cooper, it is his very own, and no student of the Veterinary College of Arizona will be allowed to filch it from him. (*LFE* 139.)

are as much a matter to be wondered at as appalled by. Unlike the critics and other devotees of Cooper who have unwittingly joined him in wonderland, the persona knows he has been there. For example, as Twain explores the "little box of stage properties" in which Cooper "kept his six or eight cunning devices, tricks, artifices for his savages and woodsmen to deceive and circumvent each other with," he has the acute impression that Cooper rather innocently counted on a certain bizarre innocence in his readers: "he was never so happy as when he was working these innocent things and seeing them go" (*LE* 81f.). As Twain sees them worked, they entail a farcical oblivion to reality. To believe in their unreality, one would have to either be a victim of wonderland or quite immune to the wonderful, perhaps both. (Cooper's having taken many of his pastoral epigraphs from the topsy-turvy world of Shakespearean comedy— he quoted *A Midsummer Night's Dream* quite frequently in *The Last of the Mohicans*—was apparently not lost on Twain.)

In instance after instance, the persona shakes his head in amazement. How can anybody have been taken in by the saga of broken twigs?

> He prized his broken twig above all the rest of his effects, and worked it the hardest. It is a restful chapter in any book of his when somebody doesn't step on a dry twig and alarm all the reds and whites for two hundred yards around. Every time a Cooper person is in peril, and absolute silence is worth four dollars a minute, he is sure to step on a dry twig. There may be a hundred handier things to step on, but that wouldn't satisfy Cooper. Cooper requires him to turn out and find a dry twig; and if he can't do it, go and borrow one. (82.)

Twain is baffled by the "sailorcraft" by which "a vessel, driving towards a lee shore in a gale, is steered for a particular spot by her skipper because he knows of an *undertow* there which will hold her back against the gale and save her" (*ibid.*). The attempt to find Fort William Henry by means of the cannon ball furrow disturbs him to such a degree that he must embellish it. Chingachgook's finding buried tracks in the stream bed while Cooper holds natural law in abeyance simply fells him. "Bless your heart," he cries, "Cooper hadn't any more invention than a horse" (84). In his bewildered state the grumbler might be forgiven for sympathetically adding his own inventions to Cooper's. When Cooper cuts his ties completely with earthly probabilities, as in the marksmanship contest, Twain must step aside and tip his hat to the master: "There, you see, is a man who could hunt flies with a rifle, and command a ducal salary in a Wild West show to-day if we had him back with us" (89). He is flabbergasted to read that Natty was able, at a distance of one hundred yards, to see David Muir's bullet enter the very hole made by Jasper's bullet. His wide-eyed "wasn't it remarkable" seems scarcely adequate.

It was perhaps inevitable that if Twain read enough of Cooper's wondrous madness, he would eventually capitulate. And he did, coming back at him in the debris of broken rules like a logic-chopping Mad Hatter. Adding yet another string to his bow, in what might be called the method of preponderance, Twain talks about the rules in such a way that he gives more of negation than he merely *seems* to be giving in any one case, and yet still far less than he *might* give. Rule 2 will illustrate:

> 2. They [the rules] require [1] that the episodes of a tale shall be necessary parts of the tale, and [2] shall help to develop it. But [3] as the *Deerslayer* is not a tale and [4] accomplishes nothing, and [5a] arrives nowhere, [5b] the episodes have no rightful place in the work, since there was nothing for them to develop. (79.)

This is typical. A rule is not just broken, it is compoundly fractured, often in at least three or more ways. Rule 2 happens to be broken in five ways, as indicated. In Rule 5 Twain multiplies the basic offense nine times, and caps it off by saying that all nine forms may be found in conjunction anywhere in the novel. It is now our turn to experience wonderment.

> 5. They require that when the personages of a tale deal in conversation, [1] the talk shall sound like human talk, [2] and be talk such as human beings would be likely to talk in the given circumstances, [3] and have a discoverable meaning, [4] also a discoverable purpose, [5] and show of relevancy, [6] and remain in the neighborhood of the subject in hand, [7] and be interesting to the reader, [8] and help out the tale, [9] and stop when the people cannot think of anything more to say. But this requirement has been ignored from the beginning of the *Deerslayer* tale to the end of it. (79f.)

By this kind of progression, one idea suggests its corollary, fault feeds on fault, criticism on criticism, until one comes up with a total count of not eighteen, but thirty-eight violations; and Twain intimates that he could—like Colonel Sellers' clock—keep striking indefinitely, as he obligingly breaks off, "but choose for yourself; you can't go amiss." Nor is this his sole method of intensification. Here and there a rule is not just violated, it is profoundly, flagrantly, disgustingly and barbarously flaunted: it is "flung down and danced upon." For that sort of thing, Twain really lets himself out in the compounding of a single offense. In Rule 7, where he does so, there is but one offense predicated, but it sounds like an army of them.

> 7. They require that when a personage talks like an illustrated, gilt-edged, tree-calf, hand-tooled, seven-dollar Friendship's Offering in the beginning of a paragraph, he shall not talk like a negro minstrel in the end of it. But this rule is flung down and danced upon in the *Deerslayer* tale. (80.)

Once the eighteen broken rules have been set forth, the last seven rattled off in briefest order, one has only finished the *proem*. The pattern established with the rules reasserts itself in each of the successively illustrated faults (poor invention, erroneous knowledge, absurd situations, non-observation, unnatural dialogue, inconsistent characterization, and stilted diction). There is the naming of the fault and the multiplication of examples, but with variations in tone and in the length of treatment of each fault and example, the leaving off before satiety has been reached, and the giving of the impression that only the surface has been scratched. Twain marches from one fatal negation to the next and winds up with a drumbeat rhythm: Cooper cannot write English, the English of *The Deerslayer* is the poorest he ever wrote, *The Deerslayer* is not a work of art, it lacks invention, order, system, sequence, etc., etc., etc. The final wonder is that so much of this is admitted to be true by Cooper scholars[12] and that so much of it *is* preponderantly and basically, if not always specifically, true.

12. For example, James Grossman agreed with what Twain had said about Cooper's breaking Rule 7 (*James Fenimore Cooper* [New York, 1949], p. 150). William Charvat, in his introduction to *The Last of the Mohicans*, observed that "the slovenly imprecision of [Cooper's] diction,

---

which Mark Twain so mercilessly exposed, cannot be justified, only explained" ([Riverside ed.; Boston, 1958], p. xvi). Stanley T. Williams accepted the validity of Twain's charges of "literary offences" and in discussing *The Last of the Mohicans* concurred: "Who does not, like Mark Twain, discern extravagances in the plot?" ("James Fenimore Cooper," in Robert E. Spiller *et al.* [eds.], *Literary History of the United States* [rev. ed.; New York, 1953], pp. 255, 263).

9

"The Sir Walter Disease":
A Sick South and Sickened
Mark Twain

I

Twain harbored a long-smoldering grudge against Sir Walter Scott and "the chivalry business." Questions as to why he abominated Scott and how he criticized him lead us to a central strain in his anti-romanticism and provide a good test of virulence as critical method. The hatred and the method go together, since it was always an inspiring moment for Twain when he had the urge to let fly at somebody. On reading Scott, as he did during the boredom of an illness, he became positively exultant: "the days have lost their dullness since I broke into Sir Walter and lost my temper" (*Letters* II 738). How far back his antipathy reached cannot be known for certain; however, an early exposure to Scott would seem to have been likely. In 1854, he had a roommate in St. Louis who had a special liking for Scott, and in the 1890's, making notes on the Hannibal years, he recalled that Scott had been among the town's favorite authors.[1]

As Twain's literary tastes developed, Scott's novels became a distillation of all that he thought had gone wrong with the romantic mind. The kind of influence those novels exerted struck him as having all the earmarks of a "disease" (*LOM* 347). It seemed a crazed and crazing hothouse atmosphere that the vast reading public breathed (particularly down South) on letting itself loose in Scott's medieval world—or, what was worse, in his medievalized modern world. Scott crazed Twain too. His criticism was to reach its irrational apex in the charge that Scott had

---

1. Brashear, *Mark Twain, Son of Missouri*, p. 170; "The Hannibal of his boyhood . . . was abominably fond of Sir Walter Scott" (*MTAW* 91); "Villagers of 1840–3" (DV 47, *MTP* 10).

helped cause the Civil War. He might as well have pinned the war on his Hartford neighbor, Mrs. Stowe.[2] But apparently Twain wasn't joking. He was, on the contrary, a little heartsick at what he thought Scott had done to his native South.

By his grumbling form, Twain not only managed to establish what truth there was to his criticism, but he gave us insights into Scott's influence that no amount of devotion to facts alone could have produced. Twain, after all, put great stock in the efforts of romantic historians (like Carlyle) to realize the otherwise dead past. He vouched for the importance of critical realization by weaving his opinion of historical romancers into the anti-romantic backdrop of certain episodes of *Huckleberry Finn*. He did this in the *Walter Scott* episode, for example, merely by having Huck want to emulate Tom Sawyer's attempt to actualize the world of Scott's novels and others like them.[3] However, the matter of Twain's having had a positive, creative outlet for his negative criticism is a subject unto itself; and my concern just here is primarily with the no less intriguing idea of the merit of what he said about Scott in relation to how he said it.

Apart from the sporadic sniping at Scott in notebooks and letters (one of which contained a burlesque synopsis of *Ivanhoe*[4]), Twain's major criticism of him is located in the second part of *Life on the Mississippi* and in two letters to Brander Matthews written in May, 1903. The letters are best dealt with first because through them the criticism of Scott is hinged to the previous criticisms of Goldsmith and Cooper, and also because the example of a fictive persona grumbling in a non-fictional context helps to account for Twain's ability to extract a maximal effect from an, at times, limited investment of truth.

In the first letter, Twain fell back on one of the didos of his Cooper criticism by legalistically preparing a bill of specifications composed of qualities that he felt were lacking in Scott and were

2. Pursuing Lincoln's joke to its logical conclusion, Jay Hubbell facetiously suggested that, if Sir Walter ultimately caused the war, "that malign influence could have come only through *Uncle Tom's Cabin*. Before she wrote that novel, Mrs. Stowe had read *Ivanhoe* no less than nine times" (*Southern Life in Fiction* [Athens, Ga., 1959], p. 13).

3. See my article, "Twain and Scott: Experience versus Adventures," *Modern Philology*, LXII (February, 1965), 227–36.

4. *Ibid.*, p. 229, n. 12.

demanded by literary norms. He listed twelve overlapping questions, which, taken with other statements in the letter, are reducible to six desiderata that resemble the more significant of the rules with which he had browbeaten Cooper. The desiderata are: a concise prose that is accurate in diction and capable of true passion; human and admirable protagonists, instead of "cads and cadesses"; characters who behave like real people and are not "bloodless shams"; a narrative pace that "will chain the reader's interest" and exclude the author's sentiments, which are usually insincere; adroitness in the invention of plot situations and an adequate but subtle preparation for them; and humor that is humorous. Just as Twain had previously questioned Matthews' opinion of Cooper, so was he now challenging his opinion of Scott. What is more, he was directly challenging Matthews to disprove his rebuttal. The legalistic hocus-pocus was meant to stir him up a bit, and with it went a tacit allegation of guilt for deep and devious wrongs. Think of how everyone has been deceived!

For the most part Twain rested his case solely upon judgments: one had only to read Scott afresh (as he had) to see what was wrong. Unfortunately, his judgments, when independently examined, are less than self-evidently reliable. For one thing, they are not completely applicable to the novels reviewed, since Twain indiscriminately ranked *Guy Mannering* with the manifestly inferior *Rob Roy*. His views are partial (in both senses), and by his own admission, for the twelve questions were based, he said, on incomplete readings of just those two books, the first of which he finished only after some delay and a struggle, and the second of which he could not finish at all. Moreover, by the time of his second letter he related that he had meanwhile read *Quentin Durward*, and liked it immensely (after the other two books, "it was like leaving the dead to mingle with the living"), although he was not thereby induced to revise anything he had said in the previous letter.

Possibly one should take Twain's comments from the sickbed in the same offhand spirit in which they seem to have been tendered; and one would be willing to do so, were there not an ingenuity of dramatic form about his letters that transforms what might have been a banal squib into a critique of some complexity. To appreciate that complexity one should observe the persona's contribution to drama, the statements by Matthews that occasioned it, and the new light in which certain qualities of the novels are placed by Twain's criticism.

One is not long in doubt about Twain's interposing a persona between himself and Matthews. This is perceived at once in his departure from the expository style of normal criticism, even in a familiar letter. After posing his questions, he breaks forth with the mock-Shelleyan agony: "Brander, I lie here dying, slowly dying, under the blight of Sir Walter." With the iterated pretense of acute pain, his form becomes that of a plaintive cry uttered by a sick man who had all innocently sought relief from pain in reading Scott's immortal novels. A man in that state is entitled to grumble, especially to a friend who had helped to inflame the public adulation for Scott's unhealthy romanticism. The point is that Twain *knows* he is sick. He cannot say the same for those who have fallen prey to the Sir Walter disease. Thus he is not immediately bellicose. He has first to show cause, and that he hopes to do pragmatically by getting Matthews to reread Scott with certain fatal questions in hand. Should Matthews find the answers he might then be in a position to instruct and console a sick friend, and maybe even make him feel better: "it occurs to me to ask you to sit down, some time or other when you have 8 or 9 months to spare, and jot me down a certain few literary particulars for my help and elevation." The thought of Matthews' needing that much time, of his being able to find the non-existent particulars, and of his helping Twain, who, with Scott, is beyond help, sets up the larger ironies in the string of loaded questions.

The questions themselves are justification for the climactic second part of the letter, in which Twain bares his exaggerated anguish. He phrases them with specious simplicity to show—as in the following—how little a man in his condition asks:

> 1. Are there in Sir Walter's novels passages done in good English —English which is neither slovenly or involved?
>
> . . . .
>
> 3. Are there passages which burn with real fire—not punk, fox-fire, make-believe?

. . . .

5. Has he personages whose acts and talk correspond with their characters as described by him?
6. Has he heroes and heroines whom the reader admires, admires, and knows *why*?

. . . .

9. Are there pages where he ceases from posing, ceases from admiring the placid flood and flow of his own dilutions, ceases from being artificial, and is for a time, long or short, recognizably sincere and in earnest?
10. Did he know how to write English, and didn't do it because he didn't want to?
11. Did he use the right word only when he couldn't think of another one, or did he run so much to wrong because he didn't know the right one when he saw it? (*Letters* II 737f.)

The last question, No. 12, is different from the others. By the time he comes to the end of the list, his own questions have summoned forth the disgust he had barely repressed in forming them:

> 12. Can you read him? and keep your respect for him? Of course a person could in *his* day—an era of sentimentality and sloppy romantics—but land! can a body do it today? (*Ibid.*, 738.)

His transition being thus effected, Twain releases a full broadside against Scott, reciting the trauma of a sick man's encounter with his novels. Now the grumbling persona takes over, and the ground has been so well laid for him that no extravagance seems uncalled for.

> Brander, I lie here dying, slowly dying, under the blight of Sir Walter. I have read the first volume of Rob Roy, and as far as chapter XIX of Guy Mannering, and I can no longer hold my head up nor take any nourishment. Lord, it's all so juvenile! so artificial, so shoddy; and such wax figures and skeletons and spectres. Interest? Why, it is impossible to feel an interest in these bloodless shams, these milk-and-water humbugs. And oh, the poverty of the invention! Not poverty in inventing situations, but poverty in furnishing reasons for them. Sir Walter usually gives himself away when he arranges for a situation—elaborates, and elaborates, and elaborates, till if you live to get to it you don't believe in it when it happens.
> I can't find the rest of Rob Roy, I can't stand any more Mannering—I do not know just what to do, but I will reflect,

and not quit this great study rashly. He *was* great, in his day, and to his proper audience; and so was God in Jewish times, for that matter, but why should either of them rank high now? And *do* they?—honest, now, *do* they? Dam'd if I believe it. (*Ibid.*)

Four days later he was still in bed, his head still smoking; he had finished *Guy Mannering* and thought it "a book crazily put together out of the very refuse of the romance-artist's stage properties." Though he may have begun his study rashly, he was true to his word in not quitting it rashly, for he had taken up *Quentin Durward,* and to indicate the qualitative difference between it and *Guy Mannering* had said, "it was like withdrawing from the infant class in the College of Journalism to sit under the lectures in English literature in Columbia University." His misgivings are not so much over how Scott can be considered a good novelist, as over how he could have written a good book, like *Quentin Durward* (*ibid.,* 739).

II

Twain's motive for re-examining Scott's novels was outwardly much the same as what it had been with *The Vicar*; he wanted to know whether such popular and critical favorites might withstand the test of a rigorously honest criticism. As Paine put it, he "determined . . . to try to understand this author's popularity and his standing among critics" (*Biog* III 1196). But why, one wonders, should he have specifically reproached Matthews, and why on the subject of Scott, at so late a date as 1903? The answer would seem to lie in Matthews' publication of a group of essays in a book entitled *The Historical Novel and Other Essays* in 1901, which he dedicated to Twain, "in testimony," he said, "of my regard for the man and of my respect for the literary artist." In the middle of this book one finds an essay, "New Trials for Old Favorites," dated 1898, that turns out to be a response to Twain's then recent criticisms of Cooper and Goldsmith, a response directly invited, of course, by Twain's having chided Matthews for his praise of Cooper. Matthews, interestingly, took his topic from the same aphorism of Pudd'nhead's that Twain had used in setting up his criticism of *The Vicar* in *Following the Equator*: the classics of literature are admired but not read. Although Matthews agreed ("much of our veneration for the classics is a sham") he none the less held, after quoting Twain on *The Vicar*, that he had "overstated his case against Goldsmith as he once overstated his case against Cooper." Because he had, out of professional self-interest, to defend the critical amenities, Matthews could not reconcile himself to Twain's defiance of them. But since he had also to acknowledge Twain's discernment and originality, he boxed himself into something of a dilemma. Striving for balance, he had to do a good deal of backing and filling, a common practice among "reasonable" critics, and one which Twain's slashing style tended to expose. For example, no sooner had Matthews noticed the remarkable similarity between Twain's opinion of *The Vicar* and Austin Dobson's than he subjoined his dissent from the thesis that there was not a sincere line in the book, and, indeed, maintained that it was *all* sincerity. To compound his inconsistency, he was shortly afterwards approving the same exaggerated manner of criticism that had caused him to take issue with Twain on Goldsmith's sincerity: "To arouse us from our laziness and our lethargy there is nothing like a vehement assault on the inherited opinion—even if the charge is too sweeping, like Mark Twain's annihilation of Goldsmith's little masterpiece."[5]

It cannot be that Matthews mistook the vehicle for the intent of Twain's criticism, for he conceded his annihilation of a masterpiece, and on another occasion, when he was giving his "Memories of Mark Twain" (1919), he understood that Twain "could be a good hater, superbly exaggerating the exuberance of his ill-will."[6] What probably did alarm Matthews was the note of a new, and to him, threatening voice in Twain, "the tocsin of revolt," as he called it, which did not bode well for the old certainties of literature. By placing a prima-facie value on "severe restraint" in criticism and by disvaluing unrestraint in proportionally absolute terms, Matthews was brought into conflict with his own acceptance of Twain's highly unrestrained condemnation of Scott's medieval novels, particularly *Ivanhoe*. Reiterating a point made at some length in his title essay, "The

5. *The Historical Novel and Other Essays* (New York, 1901), pp. 57, 50, 60.
6. *The Tocsin of Revolt and Other Essays* (New York, 1922), p. 259.

Historical Novel" (1897), he declared that no critic in his day would praise Scott for his "tournaments or his pinchbeck chivalry" or for any other of his "romantic gauds."[7]

What Matthews did hold out for was Scott's "vigorous and veracious portrayal of human character" in his Scottish novels,[8] and it was mainly on the issue of the quality of those novels that Twain proceeded to assail his judgment. In his letters, he picked up each of the features of such native and modern works as *The Antiquary, The Heart of Midlothian,* and *The Bride of Lammermoor* that Matthews had instanced as praiseworthy in his essay on the historical novel; all that Twain added were questions about the heaviness of Scott's style. For Matthews' claim that Scott was a realist in those works and had a gift for storytelling, Twain had questions about plot invention and narrative pace; for his claim that Scott drew "memorable characters," especially "types of the Scottish character, with its mingled humor and pathos," and that he was adept at revealing "the subtleties of human nature," Twain had questions about his creating real human beings and sympathetic protagonists; and for Matthews' claim that Scott was a humorist, Twain had questions as to whether his humor was funny.[9] If the vehement tone of Twain's letters was somewhat influenced by Matthews' conservatism, Twain's selection of novels was no doubt also based on Matthews' idea of the superiority of those treating Scott's native land in modern times to those treating the medieval world. What Twain was saying, by way of contradiction, was that he found two modern novels to be bad and one medieval novel to be good.

When viewed as an outgrowth of these differences, Twain's evaluation of the novels he mentioned to Matthews puts them in a new light. One might go so far as to say that he makes a contribution to Scott criticism. Even his misjudgment of *Guy Mannering* contains an element of truth if it is read in conjunction with *Rob Roy,* for while it is a much better work, *Guy Mannering* has some of the disturbing mannerisms of style which

7. *Historical Novel,* pp. 50, 64f.
8. *Ibid.,* p. 65.
9. *Ibid.,* pp. 9–11.

in *Rob Roy* are accentuated by a boring plot and insipid characters. On the other hand, when one compares those modern
novels with *Quentin Durward*, both of them pale considerably.
It is a sign of significant objectivity that Twain's seemingly
unshakable hatred of Scott's medievalism would give way before
a genuinely well-written book. It also signifies an impressive
adherence to quality.

However, the justness of Twain's evaluations of the novels is
not confined to inferences, for his peremptory treatment of them
carries with it the directive that they be reread in the light of
his criticism.

Each of the counts he brought against *Rob Roy* is amply
corroborated by a second reading. With regard to pace, one finds
the first part of the book demonstrably dull and slow-moving.
The hero and heroine, Francis Osbaldistone and Diana Vernon,
are a stiff and unnatural pair, a perfect "cad" and "cadess," who
assume an air of excruciating formality with one another. Of
Diana, the favorably inclined reviewer in the *Edinburgh Review*
reported, in sentiments approximating Twain's, that "a girl of
eighteen . . . with more wit and learning than any man of forty
. . . —and with perfect frankness and elegance of manners,
though bred among boors and bigots—is rather a . . . violent
fiction. . . ."[10] One readily guesses from the undue attention
given to an obscure traveler named Campbell that he will turn
out to be the Robin Hood-like brigand, Rob Roy; and the
scenes leading up to his identification abundantly illustrate
Twain's charge about Scott's elaborate obviousness in preparing
situations. An analogous flaw is Scott's bunching up of the un-
raveling of complications at the end of the story, so that the
entire book seems a preparation for the denouement. Also, Scott's
style is singularly stuffy. The hero begins the narration of his
story with a type of fustian that is unwaveringly maintained for
the greater part of the book: "The recollection of those adventures, as you are pleased to term them, has indeed left upon my
mind a chequered and varied feeling of pleasure and of pain,
mingled, I trust, with no slight gratitude and veneration to the
Disposer of human events who guided my early course through
much risk and labour, that the ease with which He has blessed

10. *Edinburgh Review*, XXIX (February, 1818), 410.

my prolonged life, might seem softer from remembrance and contrast."[11]

The "big bow-wow" style of which Scott freely admitted he was guilty, and which made Twain long to do a burlesque "wherein the pantaletted children talked the stilted big-word hifalutin of Walter Scott's heroes,"[12] was somewhat less noticeable in *Guy Mannering* than in many of Scott's other novels. Some of his preparations for situations are also better hidden in *Guy Mannering*, perhaps because the major plot situation is not so much an invention as the working out of what is early made known. (The frame for the plot is the fulfillment of Guy Mannering's astrological analysis of the dark future awaiting the son of Godfrey Bertram, who was to be punished for unreasonably turning against the gay gypsies living on his estate.) Faults of pace, plot, style, and character there assuredly are in *Guy Mannering*, and they can be readily found if one is inclined to follow Twain's directions in looking for them. Scott is often slower and more leisurely than he needs to be with the development of his narrative. He labors overmuch in unfolding action and indulges in overdrawn descriptions and analyses of his characters' backgrounds and behavior, particularly with the so-called local types, such as Meg Merrilies, the famous old gypsy woman. Other character traits that one surmises may have bothered Twain are apparent in Godfrey Bertram (a kindly and inefficient young laird who has some of the bungling unworldliness of Mr. Burchell and the Reverend Primrose of *The Vicar*) and in Dominie Sampson (a cleric too shy and inept to be a preacher, who, as the butt of his schoolfellows' jokes, is a variant on the pathetically humorous type that Twain could not abide in Moses, the Vicar's son). By his admiration for Dandie Dinmont (the stout yeoman of blunt honesty who aids the missing heir, Harry Bertram) Twain indicates a preference for the un-self-conscious and objective style of characterization that one does not find often enough in Scott's modern novels, since he too obviously treasured many of the local Scottish types—the types that Matthews and most other critics enjoyed.

11. *Rob Roy* (Riverside ed.; Boston, 1923), p. 1.
12. Unpublished Notebook No. 21 (February, 1886–May, 1887), 10 (Copyright © 1967, Mark Twain Company).

The instinctive rightness of Twain's tastes is most completely confirmed, however, by the swift and unbounded approval he gave *Quentin Durward*, after plodding through the other two books. The characters in *Quentin Durward* are developed in some depth, and they are more complex and dramatically alive than those in *Rob Roy* or *Guy Mannering*. Nor is the action of *Quentin Durward* weighed down, to the extent that it is in those two, by glosses on the ideality of the past and Scott's love of Scotland. Its mood was bound to be pleasing to Twain, in that Scott had the Macaulayan purpose of reaching beyond academic history and attempting to evoke the living past.[13] He tried to recreate the *drama* of history, played not so much by historical personages as by believable human beings.

Quentin Durward had another attribute which explains why Twain very particularly wanted to bring it to Matthews' attention. It was the very antithesis of *Ivanhoe*; it was, in fact, a strongly—and consciously—anti-romantic romance (Introduction, p. xiv); so that for Twain Scott was being most unlike himself. Gone were the zeal for chivalry, the worshipful attitude toward knighthood, and the idealization of medieval society as naturally ethical. However much Scott might have wanted to defend the feudal code and to berate a monarch who weakened it by Machiavellian politics, that notion gets fairly well pushed aside once his narrative begins to move, and the motif taking its place is that the abuses of the monarchial system seem to be its regular practices. For instance, all of the rascality with which Twain decked out "priestcraft and kingcraft" was almost luridly displayed in *Quentin Durward*. Scott had unquestionably been more realistic there than Twain would be in a *A Connecticut Yankee*.

This purposeful realism of Scott's has been sufficiently applauded in the Scottish novels, and we are reminded of its sources by the desire he asserted, in the opening chapter of *Waverley*, to undermine the cheap gothicism then in vogue (an aim reiterated in the "Dedicatory Epistle" to *Ivanhoe* and elsewhere). But from the time of its initial sale on the Continent, when *Quentin Durward* took the French by storm, its special realism

13. Introduction, *Quentin Durward* (Riverside ed.; Boston, 1923), p. xx.

(which debunked the nostalgia so often associated with Scott) had been generally ignored. On that circumstance alone depends both the efficacy of Twain's asking Matthews, "I wonder who wrote Quentin Durward?" and his refusal to water down his charges against the other novels, which were typical of Scott, as *Quentin Durward* was not. Twain would have Matthews read it, in other words, as a standing criticism of Scott's romantic novels.[14]

The authority of Scott's realism in *Quentin Durward* is impressive. The story mainly concerns the remarkable career of the profligate but alert and politically shrewd Louis XI in contest with his rivals, chiefly with the valorous and imprudent Charles the Bold of Burgundy, who, though personally and militarily stronger than Louis, was the King's nominal vassal. As a king, Louis neutralizes the varied mischiefs of the time in much the way that one poison (to use Scott's metaphor) counteracts another. The grossness and hypocrisy of persons in high places, including a Cardinal, are so freely exposed that in some parts of the book the governing tone is one of sheer cynicism. Almost all of the warriors have a jaundiced attitude toward combat and women; and genteel flummery is almost completely dispensed with (except in the romance of Durward and the Princess Isabelle de Croye, a minor affair). Louis' is a many-sided and a charming villainy. Though he is vain, base, cruel, vindictive, and unscrupulous, Scott gives him a very human weakness for superstition and a fondness for "low life." Above all, he is made appealing, in the manner that many Renaissance villains are, by virtue of his uninhibitedness. Scott even manages to shift our sympathies toward Louis when we see him as the underdog in the grasp of Charles the Bold, the French Hotspur, and then watch him extricate himself by his wits. Adding to the sort of material that gave Twain a good deal of private delectation was Scott's continuously going out of his way to demonstrate the

14. To this day a good deal of Scott criticism remains shackled to the proposition that, as it is stated by Ian Jack, the novels dealing with "Scotland in the eighteenth century or at the end of the seventeenth" give us "Scott's true area of inspiration," and that, concomitantly, when in "most of the later romances he turned to other settings, he ceased to be a major writer" (*Sir Walter Scott* [London, 1958], p. 16).

prevailing ignorance and cruelty of the period. Twain was thus not only finding his social prejudices substantiated, he was finding them substantiated by Scott, and by Scott's artistry!

Although *Quentin Durward* tended to deflate the idealization of knighthood which had been popularized by *Ivanhoe*, practically speaking, it could no more moderate the public's love of *Ivanhoe* than it could compensate for the weaknesses of *Rob Roy*. It is therefore idle to speculate on whether there might have been less gnashing of teeth over what Scott supposedly did to the South had Twain read *Quentin Durward* before writing *Life on the Mississippi*. In *Life on the Mississippi* Twain attacked the influence of Scott's infatuation with an unrealistic style of life. In our Southern states, this influence had grown to epidemic proportions. It had unsettled the collective mind of the South and made it sick and a sickening sight for Mark Twain to behold.

III

Twain had such difficulty completing Part Two of *Life on the Mississippi* (he was plagued by illness and lassitude) that he grew to hate the "wretched God-damned book" (*MTBM* 207), aware no doubt that much of it seemed cold porridge alongside "Old Times on the Mississippi." Exceptions to this want of spirit were passages of criticism, where his usual zest came back to him. Nowhere was his writing zestier than when he was lighting into Sir Walter Scott. While it was no novelty at the time to berate the postwar South for remaining under the sway of neo-feudalism,[15] Twain's protest was unique, as is partly attested by its being the one most consistently cited, and what is more important, by its inflammatory and visionary character.

In 1883, it behooved Twain, a returning Southerner, to describe the malaise he experienced when faced by the image of a

15. Louis J. Budd, "The Southward Currents under Huck Finn's Raft," *Mississippi Valley Historical Review*, XLVI (September, 1959), 236, n. 39. C. Vann Woodward made note of the regularity with which reporters, travelers, and commercial agents in the late 1870's criticized the South for its resistance to industrialization, which in the next decade began to invade the South on a large scale, producing the mixed culture Twain alluded to (*Origins of the New South* [Baton Rouge, La., 1951], pp. 107f., 115).

South bent on retaining an umbilical link with its chivalric past. He felt pressed to apologize for his homeland, explain its lot, and goad it—he hoped—into changing its ways. Out of this background of conflicting emotions came the criticism of Scott and the extremity of its grumbling form. Half-way measures would not do; moreover, grumbling liberated him. Under its afflatus he had the prerogative of speaking the unspeakable, of venturing the half-mad intuition that lights up the dark side of truth.

For most readers Mark Twain must have seemed to be going off half-cocked again. He was saying that "Sir Walter had so large a hand in making Southern character, as it existed before the war, that he is in great measure responsible for the war" (348). He was saying, too, that even in the postwar era the "debilitating influence" of Scott's "mediaeval romances" continued to "run the people mad" in the South, in consequence of which (1) they falsified culture by erecting "imitation castles" for their public buildings and "Female Institutes" and by issuing empty boasts from the latter that "the Southern" was "the highest type of civilization this continent has seen" (310); (2) their journalists paid chivalric tribute to the ladies by writing about them in a swollen and precious prose (340–43); (3) the region was restrained from fully participating in the North's advance toward industrialization and progress (346f.); and (4) too many Southern writers failed to realize themselves because they clung to the "old inflated style" inspired by Scott (348f.).[16] One swallows hard to down Twain's notion of causality; and yet as the insights of a son of the South sickened by its prolonged postwar convalescence, his impression can be somewhat wide of the facts—which it may not be—and still be no less meaningful a fact in itself.

One of the major points to be made about the Scott criticism in *Life on the Mississippi* is that form validates meaning. The

16. With the narrowness of the confines to which Twain restricts Scott's appeal I cannot here concern myself. A recent article that summarizes the varied and complex bases of Scott's appeal (the evocation of Scotland's past, the glitter of his Toryism, and his representation of a continuity between past and present, as well as the inevitability of progress—Twain notwithstanding) is John Henry Raleigh's "What Scott Meant to the Victorians" (*Victorian Studies*, VII [September, 1963], 7–34).

key to this form is Twain's stated purpose of dealing interpretively with history. The certitude with which he developed his case against Scott, its nagging recurrence, and its ingrained bias all suggest the way he worked when he had a source at hand, and it is quite possible that he was getting drunk on Lecky (*Biog* II 743); however, for the specific hazard at interpretive history Twain seemed to have generated his own steam. The "long foreground" that must have been present somewhere for him to make so confident an attack on Scott is properly to be sought in the opening chapters of *Life on the Mississippi*, written with a fresh will and lively theme, and in the same vein as the Scott criticism.

Although Twain assumed a number of guises in *Life on the Mississippi* (a bungling fool, a veteran of the pilot house saddened by changes in the river and the profession, a nostalgic visitor to scenes of his youth, and a seemingly innocent tourist), the expository manner of his opening chapters runs rather close to that of the foreign tourist-historians, whose books he praised as "usually calm, truthful, reasonable, [and] kind," though they seemed "just the reverse to our tender-footed progenitors" (213). Twain tried to treat the facts as a historian would, dispassionately and with a disposition to be fair. However, as one might suspect, the pose of historian was cat's-paw for his satire, his comic equivalents of the tourists' manner being the poker-faced presentation of absurdity, the juxtaposition of simple and condemnatory facts seemingly selected at random, and a detached and cynical calm. The result was an exposure of matters that never seem to get recorded in "history" as facts, such as that the great explorers were not merely in "intimate communication" with the Indians, but that "in the South the Spaniards were robbing, slaughtering, enslaving, and converting them; [while] higher up the English were trading beads and blankets to them for a consideration [i.e., their lands], and throwing in civilization and whisky, 'for lagniappe'" (21). Another such illustrative fact Twain provides is that La Salle greeted the Indians with "a flourish of arms," followed by the pipe of peace and the expropriation of "the whole country for the king . . . while the priest piously consecrated the robbery with a hymn" and explained how the savages were to be compensated "with possible possessions in heaven for the certain ones on earth which they had just been robbed of" (27). Here, then, was the factual upshot of the solemnities mouthed by Saint-Lusson and the Jesuits in Parkman's *La Salle.*[17] This going curtly to the truth of the matter was one of the means Twain would employ to rewrite history in his grumbling about Scott.

Even more relevant for the criticism of Scott is the over-all point of view on history with which Twain set out to write a travel book around "Old Times on the Mississippi." He reasoned that if men wanted to force history to tell the truth for a change they would have to treat it interpretively: to state a fact "without interpreting it" is much like describing a sunset by astronomical measurements and the scientific values of its colors (18). As he put facts together they became as much a satire on themselves and on the honorific associations of history as they were upon human kind. What better way to place the Mississippi in time morally than by reciting the contemporaneous enormities of the feudal-aristocratic order. These showed, as plain history could not, how thoroughly effaced the society revered by Scott and the South had been by the time that the first white man saw the Mississippi River.

Consider the illuminative criticism Twain creates by listing some of the great personages who were rising, falling, passing, or yet to be at about the time that Europe fell upon the virginal world of the Mississippi Valley. Sticking at first to such facts as lend interpretive "color" to the past, he gradually turns other like facts into a villification of the best of the past—the unexcelled civilization of the Renaissance, which in his condensed history appears to have been so brilliantly decadent in its prime:

> The date 1542, standing by itself, means little or nothing to us; but when one groups a few neighboring historical dates and facts around it, he adds perspective and color, and then realizes that this is one of the American dates which is quite respectable for age.

---

17. Twain got a good deal of material for the opening chapters from *La Salle* and from a "Cyclopedia" (Unpublished Notebook No. 16 [January–September, 1882], 25). For Twain's handling of the material in Parkman, see Chapter 4 ("France Takes Possession of the West") in William R. Taylor (ed.), *The Discovery of the Great West: La Salle* (Rinehart ed.; New York, 1956), pp. 33–39.

For instance, when the Mississippi was first seen by a white man, less than a quarter of a century had elapsed since Francis I.'s defeat at Pavia; the death of Raphael; the death of Bayard, *sans peur et sans reproche*; the driving out of the Knights-Hospitallers from Rhodes by the Turks; and the placarding of the Ninety-five Propositions—the act which began the Reformation. When De Soto took his glimpse of the river, Ignatius Loyola was an obscure name; the order of the Jesuits was not yet a year old; Michael Angelo's paint was not yet dry on the "Last Judgment" in the Sistine Chapel; Mary Queen of Scots was not yet born, but would be before the year closed. Catherine de Medici was a child; Elizabeth of England was not yet in her teens; Calvin, Benvenuto Cellini, and the Emperor Charles V. were at the top of their fame, and each was manufacturing history after his own peculiar fashion; Margaret of Navarre was writing the "Heptameron" and some religious books—the first survives, the others are forgotten, wit and indelicacy being sometimes better literature-preservers than holiness; lax court morals and the absurd chivalry business were in full feather, and the joust and the tournament were the frequent pastime of titled fine gentlemen who could fight better than they could spell, while religion was the passion of their ladies, and the classifying their offspring into children of full rank and children by brevet their pastime. In fact, all around, religion was in a peculiarly blooming condition: the Council of Trent was being called; the Spanish Inquisition was roasting, and racking, and burning, with a free hand; elsewhere on the Continent the nations were being persuaded to holy living by the sword and fire; in England, Henry VIII. had suppressed the monasteries, burned Fisher and another bishop or two, and was getting his English Reformation and his harem effectively started. When De Soto stood on the banks of the Mississippi, it was still two years before Luther's death; eleven years before the burning of Servetus; thirty years before the St. Bartholomew slaughter; Rabelais had not yet published; "Don Quixote" was not yet written; Shakespeare was not yet born; a hundred long years must still elapse before Englishmen would hear the name of Oliver Cromwell. (18–20.)

The interpretation packed into this passage clearly anticipates the obsession of Twain's Scott criticism. All told, the generally known facts associated with these memorable names add up to an indictment of the past that Scott had tried to make his readers enamored of. The great Bayard, *le Chevalier sans peur et sans reproche* who had fought with exceptional valor under three French kings (Charles VII, Louis XII, and Francis I) before being killed in 1524, was reputedly the last knight to have embodied the selfless ideals of chivalry. Francis I, who fancied himself a worthy knight, was known for his quite unknightly licentiousness (he kept numerous mistresses, the most important of whom he was dominated by and gave titles to, and he appeared in two of the stories of "gallantry" told by his sister Marguerite in the *Heptameron*, xxv and xlii); while in his defeat at Pavia, which ended in his imprisonment and the loss of Burgundy to Spain, Francis made a virtual travesty of knighthood by sending back the legendary message that all was lost save honor. Along with Francis, the several other monarchs mentioned by Twain— Charles V, Henry VIII, and Elizabeth—were of course noted for being singular and often tyrannous autocrats, far more gifted in the art of Renaissance politics and the repression of religious and political dissidents than in nurturing the chivalric claim to dominion through fealty. Charles V specifically backed the rape of the New World by Cortes and Pizzaro. As for the other members of royalty Twain alludes to, Catherine de Medici, frustrated in her plot to assassinate Coligny, took part in planning the St. Bartholomew's Day Massacre, whereas Mary Queen of Scots, eventually executed for treason, was to become associated with the type of lost cause that Scott liked to espouse and indeed did, in *The Abbott*, which is concerned with young Roland Graeme's chivalric devotion to the imprisoned Mary. Among the writers Twain mentioned, Margaret of Navarre, Cellini, Rabelais, and Cervantes in various ways exposed the turpitude and hypocrisy of the heirs of chivalry and medieval Catholicism. The Papacy was for the most part rather unworthy of the art lavished upon it by Michaelangelo and Raphael, whose subjects suggested an ideality somewhat at variance with the Church of their day. In addition to citing "the sword and fire" as the prevailingly Christian means used by Catholics and Protestants alike to fortify the faith and extirpate heresy, Twain had first let fall a subtler factual reference to the union of chivalry and Catholicism (the Church Militant) in the activities of the Knights Hospitalers, whose two-century tenure on Rhodes had been a period of moral decline in which the crusading spirit had given way to political and commercial endeavors. In sum, a few well-placed facts tell us all we need know about the glorious heritage of the age of chivalry. If Twain could have been assured that history was history, that the past could be as peaceably put to rest as De Soto was, there would have been no attack on Scott. Since an outworn "reverence for rank and caste" had not died, he had to find a reason for its revival, and not only a reason but a symbol too.

In the opening chapters of his book Twain thus laid the basis for deploring the re-importation of a moribund ideal that would be ruinous to Southern character. No doubt there is the tart flavor of a backwoods cynic, like Josh Billings, in Twain's interpretive history, but, as is equally apparent, it was not unlike the cynicism by which Diogenes allowed no human act to escape the astringent of moral analysis.

IV

To proceed now with the question of validity in relation to form, we should note that one of the applications of the earlier material to the critique of Scott and the South has to do with theme and another with point of view. Theme is the lesser matter. Twain's book was to be a selective chronicle of the major life on and along the Mississippi. This meant it would be a record of the life of the river in history from the time when Europeans first saw it in the sixteenth century, and of the life along its banks since, including the war, which was the most significant event to touch them. As a metaphor of time itself, the river was an appropriate medium by which the seeds of the feudal-aristocratic tradition might be carried into a region that would be fertile ground for their growth and would be receptive to their second flowering in Scott's historical romances.

Twain was intimately concerned with the question of point of view on his return to the river. Given "the materials furnished by history," he wondered for example, whether anyone—even an outsider—could "reproduce for himself the life of that time in Vicksburg" when it was under siege; and he concluded that the non-participant would probably have an advantage over the participant, since often-repeated experience results in insensitivity. Then, with exceeding pertinence to his own situation, he drew the following parallel: "When one makes his first voyage in a ship, it is an experience which multitudinously bristles with striking novelties; novelties which are in such sharp contrast with all this person's former experiences that they take a seemingly deathless grip upon his imagination and memory. By tongue or pen he can make a landsman live that strange and stirring voyage over with him; make him see it all and feel it all" (279). On his return to the river Twain could claim all of the advantages of both the insider and the outsider. He found it instructive to be an outsider to all that had taken place since his days as an insider there.

It was from both perspectives simultaneously that he would criticize Scott's influence on the South. He was an insider in his unequivocal identification with the South as the place of his birth, his speech, his upbringing, an outsider in his role of grumbling analyst of culture and history on the model of "Dame" Trollope, whose *Domestic Manners of the Americans* he carried with him on the trip and read approvingly in search of ideas. The insider in him made him look outside for a cause of the South's backwardness and find it in the narcotic effect of Scott's modern chivalry.

The extent to which as insider he felt the South to be intrinsically good, despite his discontent with it, has everything to do not only with the cause of his attack on Scott but also with its meaning. For it is directly following a chapter in which he had been showing that with "manufactures" there inevitably come "miscreants" (chap. xxxix)— a sign of his increasing recognition of the ravages of commercialism—and in conjunction with his heart-warming arrival in the Eden-like "absolute South," of which he speaks so lovingly, that he looks aghast at the restored Capitol building in Baton Rouge and makes his first attack on Scott. Rising above the "dense rich foliage and huge snow-ball blossoms" of the magnolias (whose scent is so sweet it "might suffocate one in his sleep"), the pseudo-gothic "castle" of a Capitol more than merely offends the eye, it obtrudes an alien "Culture" into the Garden and epitomizes the cause of the South's alienation from its appropriate culture.

"Sir Walter Scott," Twain surmised,

> is probably responsible for the Capitol building; for it is not conceivable that this little sham castle would ever have been

built if he had not run the people mad, a couple of generations ago, with his mediaeval romances. The South has not yet recovered from the debilitating influence of his books. Admiration of his fantastic heroes and their grotesque "chivalry" doings and romantic juvenilities still survives here, in an atmosphere in which is already perceptible the wholesome and practical nineteenth-century smell of cotton factories and locomotives; and traces of its inflated language and other windy humbuggeries survive along with it. It is pathetic enough that a whitewashed castle, with turrets and things,—materials all ungenuine within and without, pretending to be what they are not,—should ever have been built in this otherwise honorable place; but it is much more pathetic to see this architectural falsehood undergoing restoration and perpetuation in our day, when it would have been so easy to let dynamite finish what a charitable fire began, and then devote this restoration-money to the building of something genuine. (308f.)

Now it turns out that, as far as can be determined, the influence of Scott had nothing to do with the architecture of the Capitol. The original building, put up in 1847–50, was designed by James H. Dakin, who excelled in Gothic Revival structures (he did the Washington Square Dutch Reformed Church in New York and St. Patrick's Cathedral in New Orleans, modeling the latter after the York Cathedral in England, which Twain himself had admired); and Dakin had said he chose the Tudor Gothic style for the Baton Rouge Capitol because "no other style . . . could give suitable character to a building with so little cost" and because he did not want it to be a "mere copy" of the trite Greek and Roman Revival structures "already erected and often repeated in every city and town of our country."[18] After it was gutted by fire during the war, it was simply more economical to restore the original building (resting impressively on a terraced bluff overlooking the river), regardless of its four battlemented towers, cast-iron turrets, and foliated traceries, than to build a new one.

But despite Dakin's motive, Twain could not have been more right about the *effect* of the structure, to which the architect seemed to have been absurdly oblivious. That—considering effect rather than motive—Twain could still use the Capitol as a

18. "James Harrison Dakin," *Dictionary of American Biography* (New York, 1944), XXI, 219f.

reminder of Scott's "debilitating influence" on Southern culture is attributable to his dual points of view. For an outsider, what the architect wanted to do was of no consequence in relation to what he did do. As a knowing insider concerned about his native South, he tried to show precisely how the region had been wronged in the construction of a capitol whose architecture could not be other than a monument to the age popularized by Scott and mocked by the South's growing commitment to the nineteenth century and industrialization. This capitol perpetuated the South's split personality. It therefore was "pathetic," Twain pointed out, that castles "pretending to be what they are not" should have been built in the "otherwise honorable" South, and "much more pathetic" that they should have been restored, instead of giving way to something "genuine."[19]

V

The inside-outside accommodation carries over into the succeeding criticisms of Scott, but the overriding concern from this point on is that the South is sick and is not likely to get well unless it can somehow be brought to see itself as others see it. Twain had his doubts. He wondered in particular how the narcissistic South was going to stop trying to relive a trumped-up romantic past when it persisted in admiring the Walter Scott reflections of its self-idealization. Having seen about as much of the Sir Walter disease as he could stand, Twain began to meet shock with shock, and to illustrate the sickness by offering some sickening evidence of it.

The inspiration for this procedure may well have come from what he had written about the Capitol; for immediately afterwards, to show that "Baton Rouge has no patent on imitation castles," he inserted, in consecutive manuscript revisions, first the puffing of two castled "Female Colleges" about their upholding the romantic charm and noble sentiments of Southern

19. As for Twain's use of the dubious norm of nineteenth-century progress, he had earlier indicated that he valued "changes . . . in the direction of increased population and wealth" in the river towns because there is an "intellectual advancement and liberalization of opinion which go naturally with these" (284).

"civilization," and then a lengthy footnote, containing "illustrations of [the civilization] thoughtlessly omitted by the advertiser,"[20] these being press dispatches describing certain barbarous, and supposedly typical, unprosecuted homicides. While the grotesquerie of the contrast, put just that way, was Twain's doing, there could really be no gainsaying the grotesque coincidence in fact of high-sounding talk from a Kentucky "Female College" about "the highest type of civilization this continent has seen" with the report of a Tennessee "Female College" professor's self-defense shotgun killing of his brother-in-law, who "had already killed one man and driven his knife into another"—surrounding which report Twain had given those of a feud between a "General" and a "Major" which took three lives one afternoon, a fight between two gallant rivals in love that ended in the ax murder of one, and a duel between two "highly connected" young Virginians in which one had been stabbed in the stomach with a butcher knife, and "every effort was made [thereafter] to hush the matter up" (note to 310–12).

The dichotomy between lofty ideals (training "young ladies . . . according to the Southern ideas of delicacy, refinement, womanhood, religion, and propriety") and sordid acts (each homicide had a relationship to the code of honor, which Twain equated with the South's medievalism) showed how little the South knew itself. The implied ailment was, as Twain had already hinted, what we would call a form of schizophrenia. That was the diagnosis metaphorically indicated by Twain's shrewd observation that while the "imitation castle is doubtless harmless" in itself, "as a symbol and breeder and sustainer of maudlin Middle-Age romanticism" in the nineteenth century, "it is necessarily a hurtful thing and a mistake" (309).

20. The manuscript of *Life on the Mississippi* is in the John Pierpont Morgan Library in New York, Twain having given it to Morgan in 1909. It runs to over thirteen hundred pages and does not of course include the chapters that had appeared in the *Atlantic Monthly* from January to July, 1875, as "Old Times on the Mississippi." The two excerpts from the "Female College" advertisements were added on manuscript pages 694–96 (ANE IX 309f.). The lengthy footnote was not in the manuscript and so was doubtless added later to further strengthen Twain's case against the hypocrisy purportedly resulting from Scott's influence.

The business of "keeping school in a castle" was bound to have its influence on impressionable young ladies, some of whom were destined to influence taste and culture and to help set the tone of Southern life.[21] Behind the ladies lay the elongated shadow of Sir Walter (who else had bedazzled the South with the love of castles?). Before them lay the vision of a self-perpetuating aristocratic tradition that widened the gap between the Old and the New South, between romantic myth and historical reality. In Twain's view, all the surviving shibboleths of the Old South pointed to but one tangible source. However, even though Scott could not possibly have been the entire cause of the "trouble," and even though the ideals of the Old South long antedated *Ivanhoe*, a strong bond of moral reinforcement and, above all, of identification remained. This bond helped Twain to identify a pervasive and otherwise not easily identifiable illness.

Hence, when he started whacking away at Scott again (in chap. xlv, "Southern Sports," after a four-chapter interval) on reading the elegant prose of a society page reporter, Twain was put on his guard by the hackneyed, and seemingly innocuous, observation that the grandstand at a mule race was "well filled

21. Take, for example, the career of a girl educated in one of the "Castles" Twain mentioned. Virginia Maury Otey, the eldest daughter of Reverend James Hervey Otey, founder and head of the Columbia, Tennessee, Female Institute, married Benjamin Blake Minor in 1842. Minor was editor and proprietor of the *Southern Literary Messenger* from 1843 to 1847. She regularly helped him with editorial chores and had charge of the editorial office during her husband's absence in the winter of 1845–46. A lover of what Byron had called "The Poetry of Heaven," she had been a contributor to the Columbia Institute's monthly magazine, *The Guardian*, one such contribution being a poetic address to the star Aldebaran, of which she had made a "pet." Under the pen name of La Visionaire she wrote a story for the *Messenger* in 1844 entitled "Stephano Colonna, or Love and Lore: A Tale of the 15th Century," for which she was awarded a twenty-five-dollar prize. When Minor retired from his editorship, he became principal of the Virginia Female Institute in Staunton, Virginia (Benjamin Blake Minor, *The Southern Literary Messenger* [New York, 1905], pp. 126–28).

Twain's famous description of "The House Beautiful" in *LOM* (chap. xxxviii) evinces a certain influence from "Women and Scott," with its volume of "Tupper, much penciled; . . . maybe 'Ivanhoe'; also 'Album,' full of original 'poetry' of the Thou-hast-wounded-the-spirit-that-loved-thee breed; two or three goody-goody works—'Shepherd of Salisbury Plain,' etc. . . ." (295).

with the beauty and the chivalry of New Orleans." His gorge rose, and his being able instantly to cite that giveaway phrase as a symptom of the disease he traced to Scott facilitated his defining what was wrong both in the reporter's style and in social attitudes at large. What he found was "confirmation of the theory . . . that the trouble with the Southern reporter is Women: Women, supplemented by Walter Scott and his knights and beauty and chivalry, and so on" (342). The reporter could not help himself, Twain perceived, for he is "obliged" to use that reference to "chivalry" "a million times a day, if he have occasion to speak of respectable men and women that often" (340). Twain knew the Southerner, and at least one "soft, sappy, melancholy" Missouri village, from inside. He knew that among his native villagers, whom he insistently considered Southerners (*LOM* 412), "Byron, Scott, Cooper, Marryatt, Boz [and] Pirates and Knights [were] preferred to other society."[22] In a flash, therefore, the reporter's talk of chivalry conjured up for him the restless ghost of Sir Walter Scott marching in lockstep with Southern Womanhood and trailing the exaggerated deference, grandiloquent journalism, verbosity, softheadedness, sentimentality, and general sickness of mind that were the combined result of that unholy alliance. The reporter was its special victim. Normally sensible, "he goes all to pieces; his mind totters, becomes flowery and idiotic" before the lethal combination of Scott and women. He will use twenty-two words to express a ten-word thought; and he "never tires" of referring to "the beauty and chivalry" because it "has a fine sound to him." Indeed, "there is a kind of swell, mediaeval bulliness and tinsel about it that pleases his gaudy, barbaric soul."

In proof of his "theory" about the effect of Scott and women upon Southern journalism, Twain quotes a passage from the reporter's account of the mule race, in which he would appear to imagine that he is Sir Walter describing the assemblage of ladies at Ashby-de-la-Zouche; so that we have, as Twain remarks, "this frantic result":

> It will be probably a long time before the ladies' stand presents such a sea of foam-like loveliness as it did yesterday. The New

---

22. "Villagers of 1840–3," 10 (Copyright © 1967, Mark Twain Company).

Orleans women are always charming, but never so much so as at this time of the year, when in their dainty spring costumes they bring with them a breath of balmy freshness and an odor of sanctity unspeakable. The stand was so crowded with them that, walking at their feet and seeing no possibility of approach, many a man appreciated as he never did before the Peri's feeling at the Gates of Paradise, and wondered what was the priceless boon that would admit him to their sacred presence. Sparkling on their white-robed breasts or shoulders were the colors of their favorite knights, and were it not for the fact that the doughty heroes appeared on unromantic mules, it would have been easy to imagine one of King Arthur's gala-days. (342f.)

A sign of the reporter's usual sanity is his consciousness of the incongruity of using the genuine heroic reference with the ludicrously unromantic mule race. For all that, he still remained quite unable to help himself. One reason Twain had previously suggested for his helplessness before the aroma of chivalry was that reporters had been continuously drugged by it for "two generations." Thus, the damage was done in the time of those who fought the war and of those who grew up after it—which brings us to the most grievous crime that Twain laid at Scott's doorstep.

VI

Although Twain in later years would change his tune about the South and its "consecrated" Cause,[23] in *Life on the Mississippi* the South was to all intents and purposes the Sick Man of America. It had never been more sick than when it went to war to preserve the glories of knighthood and chivalry. (One could

23. The apotheosis of the South in Twain's memory seems to have set in around the turn of the century. Almost in direct ratio to the growing bitterness of his social criticism, his recollections were crowded with the sunlit days of his boyhood out there in that "great and beautiful country," which, as he then saw it, had blissfully escaped "modern civilization." "In that old time it was a paradise for simplicity—it was a simple, simple life, cheap but comfortable, and full of sweetness, and there was nothing of this rage of modern civilization there at all. It was a delectable land" (November 28, 1902, *Speeches* 249).

The year before, in his speech on Lincoln's birthday, he had made a full-hearted identification with the Confederacy and in terms that had earlier revolted him (*Speeches* 230). In the area of economic progress, in which he had thought the South so backward in *LOM*, he had

say the South was more sick in that respect, for example, than it was morally remiss in its practical motives for opposing abolitionism.) What stands out about Twain's final, grumbling attack on Scott for being "in great measure responsible for the War" is that, when taken in perspective and in terms of point of view and purpose, it is surely one of the most carefully prepared pieces of free-wheeling criticism that he ever wrote, about Scott or anybody else.

With respect to point of view, the appropriate sympathies had been welling up in Twain before he got to the chapter on the war, and even before he had conceived it, so that when he did he was primed for it, and his remarks became the natural outgrowth of those sympathies. He not only reminded the reader of his Southernness, he portrayed himself as in the act of re-experiencing it. Just prior to exposing the madness of the society reporter, he was commenting on how deeply he was affected by the sound of the Southerner's tongue: "I found the *half-forgotten* Southern intonations and elisions as pleasing to my ear as they had formerly been. A Southerner talks music. At least it is music to me, *but then I was born in the South*" (my italics). As an index of purpose, it might be noted that the last of these statements was introduced in a manuscript revision (*MS* 828; *LOM* 332). Soon afterwards (in the journalism chapter itself), Twain continued to keep his Southern sympathies before the reader by

---

done a complete aboutface by 1894, declaring that the South was well off in having had few opportunities for "the rush for sudden wealth," a phenomenon that is "almost unknown" there "and had been, from the beginning" ("What Paul Bourget Thinks of Us," *LE* 157). He also changed his ideas about the Southerner's affection for "rank and caste." Northerners, he held, who poke fun at the Southerner's fondness for titles, forget that "whatever a Southerner likes the rest of the human race likes, and that there is no law of predilection lodged in one people that is absent from another people" ("Does the Race of Man Love a Lord?" *North American Review*, CLXXIV [April, 1902], 442). Along with the honeyed afterglow that accompanied his memory of the prewar South there came a concomitant disillusionment with progress. He told Joseph Twichell in 1905 that the nineteenth century had made progress "only in materialities, but not in righteousness" (*Letters* II 769). He laid much of the evil to the blighting influence of Robber Barons like Jay Gould, and to rampant cupidity (*MTE* 77, 81; Foner, *Mark Twain: Social Critic*, pp. 161, 162).

giving an appreciative explanation of why Southerners date from the war,[24] which was reminiscent of his compassion for the people of Vicksburg who had often been shut up in caves during the siege, most of them haunted by starvation and sickness (chap. xxxv).

The extent of Twain's control over the point of view from which he spoke may also be gleaned from revisions which reveal some of the personal feelings he suppressed in the interest of preserving his Southern identity. Privately he was far more severe with the South than he dared be publicly. In his notebook, for example, he was categorically damning the style of Southern speech (the sound of which, he was saying in print, had only charmed him): "South still in the sophomoric period—all speech there is flowery & gushy—pulpit, law, literature, it is all so."[25] In revising, on the other hand, he excised a passage containing unwelcome reflections on the duel and on the intermittent revival of the tournament, a "two-cent, tin-imitation of Ashby-de-la-Zouche." In another more explosive and insulting excision, he had belabored the South for enslaving itself by voting solidly for one party ("a 'solid' country . . . is a community of savages"), and he had tied this in with the charge that Southern juries often failed to convict murderers.[26] To further offset his dissatisfaction with Southern prose, he also added a statement to his journalism critique in praise of the ordinary Southern editor for having "a strong, compact, direct, unflowery style" (*MS* 859; *LOM* 341).

24. "It shows how intimately every individual was visited, in his own person, by that tremendous episode. It gives the inexperienced stranger a better idea of what a vast and comprehensive calamity invasion is" (337).

25. Unpublished Notebook No. 21, 38 (Copyright © 1967, Mark Twain Company). See also "A Cure for the Blues," in *The American Claimant and Other Stories and Sketches*, ANE XXI 389f.

26. These and other major excisions have been published as an appendix to the Limited Editions Club edition of *LOM* (New York, 1944), pp. 411f., with an accompanying comment by Willis Wager, who did a dissertation on the Morgan manuscript ("A Critical Edition of the Morgan Manuscript of Mark Twain's *Life on the Mississippi*" [New York University, 1942]). Wager felt that Twain cut the passages that might give offense to the South because he was afraid of their adverse effect on sales. I believe that considerations of taste and theme may have been quite as important to Twain, even though some of the cuts were suggested to him by James R. Osgood, his publisher.

The burden of his criticism thereby falls on an aberration, induced by Scott, which obscured the practice of sound writing in the South.

It is in chap. xlvi, meaningfully entitled "Enchantments and Enchanters," that Twain releases his all-encompassing criticism of Scott's influence on the South. The last chapter on Scott, it is climactic in every sense. In the first place, it was begun and ended, and had been conceived and intended, as an analysis of the relative dormancy of Southern letters, and not principally as a means of pinning the war on Scott. Twain was indeed also interested in connecting Scott with the war, but as a summation of all he had previously said about his influence and as an indication of how the "character of the Southerner" made inevitable the saddest of all conflicts, in which the North played nemesis to a flaw aggravated by Scott. In addition, he wanted to place the South's immoderate affection for Scott in its historical setting: Scott's "enchantments" restored an admiration for *l'ancien régime* and hereditary class which had been respectively expunged from Western history by the French Revolution and Napoleon. Finally, he attempted in some measure to redo Cervantes' job of applying the correctives of reason and history to the stultifying atmosphere of a romanticized medievalism; and, while he was at it, he took another swipe at the cult of Southern Womanhood, attributing to it "girly-girly romance" and the "inflated speech" of sham knightliness. From these several major directions and several lesser ones he proposed to mount an all-out drive on the Sir Walter disease.

Again, Twain's manuscript supplies us with an index of purpose. Originally, he had had just the first paragraph of chap. xlvi, the one on the Mardi Gras, ending with the observation that "gentlemen of position and consequence" disguised themselves "merely for the sake of romance," and he had gone on from there with what is now chap. xlvii, recounting his rendezvous with Joel Chandler Harris and George Washington Cable, writers whose vital regionalism forecast the rebirth of a bona-fide Southern literature. It was following this that Twain had originally had his defamatory chapter on the "solid South." But whether or not he added the rest of chap. xlvi in substitution for the excised chapter, he needed only to have contemplated what he already had—the Scott-infected Mardi Gras (now consumed with his "mediaeval business") placed hard by the realism of the local colorists—to have realized that their relationship was one of toxin to antibody, and on that basis to have improvised the intervening criticism of Scott (*MS* 875–90; *LOM* 345–49). And Twain may indeed have gotten at Scott in just that way. For a man who complained, as Twain had while working on *Life on the Mississippi*, that to buoy up his writing during periods of flagging health he had to "religiously save up *every* wayward & vagrant suggestion of intellectual activity & hurry to apply it to *work* before it weakened & died,"[27] Scott must have come to him as a godsend. None the less, whatever the conditions of composition, chap. xlvi, as constituted, splendidly fuses the earlier sporadic outbursts against Scott into one last, spiraling, climactic blast.

Thrust between two insulating passages of literary-historical analysis, the blast as such divides into two three-paragraph sections. The first is the cadenza in which responsibility for historical and cultural regression is heaped on Scott, and the second is a piece of literary history, spelling out the damage he did to Southern letters. It would be well to note, before becoming further involved with structure, that the meaning upon which structure depends has one major shortcoming and that, despite this shortcoming, Twain scores a direct hit on Scott's reactionism. Twain's argument runs as follows: the modern world is indebted to the French Revolution for breaking "the chains of the ancient regime and of the Church," so that "a nation of abject slaves [could become] a nation of freemen," and to Napoleon for the "setting of merit above birth" and stripping "the divinity from royalty," so that kings "can never be gods again, but only figure-heads, and answerable for their acts like common clay." After these principles had been purchased at so dear a cost in human blood, along comes Sir Walter Scott and tries to turn back time, and, like a modern Merlin, casts an "enchantment" over whole generations of readers and makes them yearn for a restoration of the despotic past. The difficulty here (overlooking the supposedly "permanent services" done by the Revolution and Napoleon on behalf of "liberty, humanity and

27. Letter to Joseph Twichell from Elmira, N.Y., September 19, 1882, *MTP* (Copyright © 1967, Mark Twain Company).

progress") is that obviously Scott alone cannot bear half the onus Twain would foist upon him. At the very least, one would have to begin with the Congress of Vienna, in 1815, attended by representatives from every significant royal house in Europe, a time roughly corresponding with Scott's early successes— *Waverley* (1814), *Guy Mannering* (1815), *Ivanhoe* (1818)—as well as with the reign of Metternich, in order to chart some effects of the real counter-revolutionary forces.

On the other hand, one besetting irony for Twain was that whereas in history what is past is truly past and times irrevocably change, restoration or no, literary history is by its very character a record of the attempt to uphold and memorialize past values by showing their relevance to the present and their immunity to historical change. Out of this irony comes his valid protest that only in literature can one really turn back the clock of history and, if a writer is so disposed (as Scott was), exert a really reactionary influence on manners and mores. Since his novels were being read with such avidity in the South, Scott did, in this respect, do "measureless harm" to Southern society, where, as Twain contends, "these harms . . . flourish pretty forcefully still" though "most of the world has outlived [a] good part of [them]." The visible result is that the South is left with a split personality of devastating proportions. The region is divided against itself, as

> the genuine and wholesome civilization of the nineteenth century is curiously confused and commingled with the Walter Scott Middle-Age sham civilization, and so you have practical common-sense, progressive ideas, and progressive works, mixed up with the duel, the inflated speech, and the jejune romanticism of an absurd past that is dead, and out of charity ought to be buried. But for the Sir Walter disease, the character of the Southerner—or Southron, according to Sir Walter's starchier way of phrasing it—would be wholly modern, in place of modern and mediaeval mixed, and the South would be fully a generation further advanced that it is. (347.)

The structural triumph of Twain's grumbling is that its form so appropriately captures the impossibility of getting at an influence that is too flimsy to be blown away by reason, and that is made maddeningly substantial by its own insubstantiality— a something one can feel but not touch, experience but not explain, and dislike but not quite rationally criticize. Since it was so deepseated and yet so amorphous, there was no telling *what all* such an influence might be accountable for. Its mode of operation, like its effect, was just the kind of fluid, quixotic fancy with which the comic grumbler was so thoroughly at home. It was a madness that made him exuberant and gave wings to his capacity for magnification.

Faced with the dilemma of Scott's impregnability, the grumbler must finally, in the best tradition of southwestern humor, simply rear back and "cuss." Twain retained this pose until it revealed a way out of the dilemma along the same path that had led him into it, for he viewed the tradition of the vernacular character drawn by Harris and Cable as the new hope for Southern literature and the remedy for Scott's influence.

The first sentence of Twain's most abusive paragraph exemplifies the grumbling pose in its most illustrious form, as abuse is heaped on abuse and is crowned by a swelling parallelism that fairly throbs with each iterative compound:

> Then comes Sir Walter Scott with his enchantments, and by his single might checks this wave of progress [ushered in by the Revolution and Napoleon], and even turns it back; sets the world in love with dreams and phantoms; with decayed and swinish forms of religion; with decayed and degraded systems of government; with the sillinesses and emptinesses, sham grandeurs, sham gauds, and sham chivalries of a brainless and worthless long-vanished society. (347.)

In the next paragraph, spurred on by his frustration over an influence spread by the processes of literary history, Twain tries to extrapolate the malefic side effect producible by the interference of that influence with the processes of ordinary history. Having seen proof of a lasting dislocation in Southern life during the postwar era and having seen Scott's influence at work in it, he arrives at the theory that the same influence, working even more strongly on the prewar South, may well have created the illusory sense of honor that inevitably leads to conflict. This much sense is there in Twain's remark that "Sir Walter had so large a hand in making Southern character, as it existed before the war, that he is in great measure responsible for the war." Apparently Twain did not want to be taken too seriously, though, for as he developed this hypothesis, he leavened it with the attitude of the comic grumbler (in such nonsense phrases as "it seems a little harsh toward a dead man" and "the former resembles the latter as an Englishman resembles a Frenchman"), and in going back over the passage he had the presence of mind to add such hedging terms (italicized below) as "plausible," "perhaps," "wild," and "rather" to those he had already used to underscore the hypothetical nature of his proposition (as "in great measure"). The upshot of it all is that by trifling with history, as Scott had, he damns Scott with impunity; and that is his private revenge on literary history.

> Sir Walter had so large a hand in making Southern character, as it existed before the war, that he is in great measure responsible for the war. It seems a little harsh toward a dead man to say that we never should have had any war but for Sir Walter; and yet something of a *plausible* argument might, *perhaps*, be made in support of that *wild* proposition. The Southerner of the American Revolution owned slaves; so did the Southerner of the Civil War; but the former resembles the latter as an Englishman resembles a Frenchman. The change of character can be traced *rather* more easily to Sir Walter's influence than to that of any other thing or person. (348.)

In the last section of his chapter, Twain saw that, while certain laws of literary history ran counter to progress, there was consolation in another law quite familiar to himself, which was that romantic nostalgia was highly vulnerable to satire. "A curious exemplification of the power of a single book for good or harm is shown in the effects wrought by 'Don Quixote' and those wrought by 'Ivanhoe.' The first swept the world's admiration for the mediaeval chivalry-silliness out of existence; and the other restored it" (348). He held that the South had particularly suffered from the fact that "Scott's pernicious work undermined" the work of Cervantes. Although in the 1830's and 40's the literary periodicals of North and South alike had been "filled with wordy, windy, flowery 'eloquence,' romanticism, sentimentality—all imitated from Sir Walter," the South, unlike the North, had failed to outgrow that style. This was true, he argued, because even in the 1880's one could see that its authors preferred to "write for the past, not the present; [and to] use obsolete forms and a dead language" (348f.).

Twain may or may not have thought himself a modern Cervantes prior to *A Connecticut Yankee*. However, his criticism of Scott's influence on the South came full cycle when he spoke not just with a Southern identity but as an advocate of the cause of Southern realism, which ultimately was his own cause. He pointed out that, as things stood, the South had everything to gain from the reputations made by Harris and Cable, "two of the very few Southern authors who do not write in the Southern style." Moreover, he felt that, by rights, "instead of three or four widely-known literary names, the South ought to have a dozen or two—and will have them when Sir Walter's time is out" (349). Twain in this way held out the prospect of a literary cure for a literary wrong—for true literary glory in exchange for the will-o'-the-wisp glory of Scott's romanticism.

VII

Although much of the Scott criticism does not quite come within the realm of the provable, and therefore need not stand or fall with the proof that Scott's influence was all that Twain said it was, I still feel obliged to indicate here what can reliably be ascribed to it, lest I seem to have wholly skirted the issue. It will bear looking into also because no other segment of Twain's total criticism has created so much controversy. Interestingly, while literary historians have almost unanimously doubted the kind of pervasive influence Twain attributed to Scott, most historians have found ample testimony, for their purposes, of the fact that Scott had not just an influence, but a potent influence, on Southern life and literature, even though the relative purity and degree of influence cannot in the nature of things be known absolutely.[28]

28. Jay Hubbell, for example, grants that Scott was "the South's favorite author" and that his historical romances were "more widely read in the South than the poems of Byron and Moore or the novels of Bulwer-Lytton or G. P. R. James," and that Scott had a significant influence on such Southern writers as Tucker, Caruthers, Kennedy, and Simms; but he finds little sanction for Twain's charge that Scott's romances had so profound an effect on Southern life as to make him in any way responsible for the war; or for the idea that Scott "created rank and caste down there, and . . . pride and pleasure in them" (*The South in*

The evidence of Scott's influence is varied but considerable. Once called "the fiction god of ante-bellum Alabama," Scott was the single most popular writer in the South during the nineteenth

---

American Literature [Durham, N.C., 1954], pp. 188–93). Hubbell conveniently lists most of the historians of note with whom Twain's analysis has by and large found some degree of favor: William E. Dodd, *The Cotton Kingdom* (New Haven, Conn., 1919), p. 62f.; H. J. Eckenrode, *Jefferson Davis* (New York, 1923), p. 11, and "Sir Walter Scott and the South," *North American Review*, CCVI (October, 1917), 595–603; Clement Eaton, *Freedom of Thought in the Old South* (Durham, N.C., 1940), pp. 48, 317; James Truslow Adams, *America's Tragedy* (New York, 1934), pp. 95f., 119f.; W. B. Hesseltine, *A History of the South* (New York, 1936), p. 344f.; Francis B. Simkins, *The South Old and New* (New York, 1947), p. 55; Wilbur J. Cash, *The Mind of the South* (New York, 1941), p. 65; Hodding Carter, *Southern Legacy* (Baton Rouge, La., 1950), p. 67f.; and Rollin G. Osterweis, *Romanticism and Nationalism in the Old South* (New Haven, Conn., 1949), pp. 51–57 *et passim*. Eckenrode probably goes further than anyone else in accepting Twain's charges, even seeing Scott's influence in the discrepancies between the Northern and Southern civilizations which supposedly brought on the war ("Sir Walter Scott," p. 603).

In addition to Hubbell, the scholars who have most seriously questioned Twain's charges are Grace Warren Landrum ("Sir Walter Scott and His Literary Rivals in the Old South," *AL*, II [November, 1930], 256–76) and G. Harrison Orians ("Walter Scott, Mark Twain and the Civil War," *South Atlantic Quarterly*, XL [October, 1941], 342–59). Their arguments are, however, weakened by the concessions of fact they are compelled to make. Far from disproving "conclusively" the sort of influence stipulated by Twain, Miss Landrum brings forward some rather substantial proof of the pre-eminent favoritism accorded Scott in the South, such as the fact that Scott's novels and poems were easily available in cheap editions, widely read, frequently reprinted, and favorably reviewed in the ante bellum South, that numerous important figures were enamored of Scott (J. P. Kennedy, Henry Clay, John James Audubon, Commodore Maury, Jefferson Davis, L. Raphael Semmes, and Robert E. Lee), and that the Southern tournament gathered some part of its following from readers of *Ivanhoe*. On reasoning that is somewhat flimsier than that which she attributes to Twain, she would enthrone Byron in Scott's place as the writer chiefly responsible for "fashioning the ante-bellum concept of woman" because he was widely read and "undoubtedly captured readers of amorous yearnings" (p. 270). Then too, she has to admit that she can not claim "unfailing thoroughness" in the sampling of evidence (p. 276).

Orians also conceded that Scott was exceedingly popular in the South, that he "undoubtedly contributed to the decorative phases of Southern life," and that his works induced Southern aristocrats "to desire a more chivalric order" (pp. 348–50). He tried to dispose of any idea that Scott might have given the South its interest in tournaments, but

century. About this there has been little dispute.[29] Scott's popularity in the South also traversed a longer span of years than that of any other writer; it held up for some sixty years, between 1810 and 1870, and was keenest in the crucial 1830's and 40's, as Twain pointed out. It may be only a legend, of course, that Scott's novels were shipped below the Potomac by the trainload, but booksellers did rather steadily list his works in Southern newspapers at prices that made him accessible to every class of reader.[30] Hence it seems probable that, as Frank Luther Mott has remarked, "Southern readers loved Scott more devotedly than the people of any other region outside of Scotland itself."[31]

Scott's appeal to the pillars of Southern society—to the few nobly descended planters, the many newly-made aristocrats (the "Cotton Snobs"), and professional men alike—coincided with and helped to inflate the already billowing myth of a Cavalier tradition, which, though begun in Virginia, was at length to be taken over by all of the Southern states.[32] "Chivalry" became an emotive watchword of the myth. Unknown in earlier periods when the aristocracy was more truly composed of aristocrats, this term came into regular use in the South during the 1830's, largely through the example of novelists who imitated Scott,[33] so that its far-reaching connotations are thought to be one of Scott's major contributions to the Cavalier tradition.

---

found that "an embarrassing amount of evidence might be advanced to prove Scott's responsibility for the pageantry of the tournament . . . [and for] the names of the knights [and] address to the winners of Tournaments" (p. 344f.). While he held that Scott was also popular in the North and West, he admitted that his popularity in the South persisted far longer than it did elsewhere.

29. Even Miss Landrum, who minimized his influence, affirmed, "It has long been conceded that the South devoured Scott voraciously" ("Notes on the Reading of the Old South," *AL*, III [March, 1931], 60).

30. John Hay, "Sir Walter Scott," *Addresses of John Hay* (New York, 1906), p. 54f.; Frank Luther Mott, *Golden Multitudes* (New York, 1947), pp. 68–70; Hart, *The Popular Book*, p. 76; Landrum, "Notes on Reading," p. 61.

31. *Golden Multitudes*, p. 68.

32. Dodd, *Cotton Kingdom*, p. 62f; Cash, *Mind of the South* (Anchor ed.; Garden City, N.Y., 1954), pp. 74–81.

33. Jay Hubbell, "Cavalier and Indentured Servant in Virginia Fiction," *South Atlantic Quarterly*, XXVI (January, 1927), 25.

In addition to having been widely read, Scott was widely imitated in the South. The magnetic influence of his novels was especially pronounced in its potentially most effectual prewar stage, when a significant group of writers availed themselves of his subject matter and tone. Some of the better-known Southern novelists manifestly influenced by Scott were George Tucker (1775–1861), Virginia economist and historian, in his first novel, *The Valley of the Shenandoah* (1824), which his enthusiasm for the Waverley novels had prompted him to write; John Pendleton Kennedy (1795–1870), Baltimore lawyer and Whig Congressman-turned-novelist, in *Horseshoe Robinson, A Tale of the Tory Ascendency* (1835), a historical romance completely and consciously imitative of Scott; Judge [Nathaniel] Beverley Tucker (1784–1851, distant relative of George Tucker), a fiery secessionist and frequent contributor to the *Southern Literary Messenger*, in *George Balcombe* (1836), a novel of mystery and intrigue ranging over the Virginia and Missouri frontier country; Dr. William Alexander Caruthers (1802–46), liberal Virginia physician, who came to be called the "Chronicler of the Cavaliers," in *The Cavaliers of Virginia* (1835) and *The Knights of the Horseshoe* (1845), both of which reflect his reading of the Waverley novels and his effort to adapt their materials to the South; and William Gilmore Simms (1806–70), critic, novelist, admirer of Scott, and generally one of the most respected literary figures of the Old South, in his "Revolutionary Romances" (particularly in *The Partisan*, 1835), dealing with activities on the Carolina frontier during the Revolution, which he treated in the manner of the "Modern Romance" as laid down by Scott and Cooper. Historians like Charles E. A. Gayarré and poets like Philip Pendleton Cooke were likewise influenced by Scott; and the *Southern Literary Messenger* not only published the works of many of Scott's devoted followers in the South but on one occasion took exception to the views of a critic who in praising Dickens had disparaged Scott.[34]

Clearly, the character and amount of literary derivation from Scott constituted far more than an approval of the historical romance. Of paramount importance to the South were his social

34. XXII (April, 1856), 291.

values. Echoing a general contention that "others read the Waverley novels with enthusiasm, but the South sought to live them," Rollin Osterweis justly discerned a supporting influence in the codes of the gentleman and duello, tournaments, military action, the hunt, the horse race, manners, attitudes towards women, concern with lineage, and lavish hospitality.[35] With respect to tournaments, for example, though the Southern version of them did not need to depend upon Scott's passage at arms at Ashby for a model, those reported in the press more often than not followed the formalities, titles, and costuming given by Scott.[36] Nor was it unusual for Scott's novels to be regarded as a repository of the distinctively Southern norm of gentility. "Johnson, Burke, and Sir Walter Scott," read an article in *De Bow's Review* of New Orleans, "should have statues in every Southern capitol. Thus would our youth learn what are the sentiments and opinions that become gentlemen and cavaliers."[37]

The Cavalier tradition and Sir Walter Scott were practically inseparable in the minds of many Southerners, and this was nowhere more evident than in the war, with respect to which we have seen Twain implicating Scott in the formation of Southern character. On the one hand, Southern war poetry made abundant reference to the "Cavalier" and to "knightly" conduct, and, on the other, wide currency was given to tales like the one about G. Raphael Semmes, who was induced to resign from the U.S. Navy and follow the Confederacy in 1860 because he thought of the lines from "The Lay of the Last Minstrel" beginning "Breathes there a man, with soul so dead." As for the war itself,

---

35. *Romanticism and Nationalism in the Old South*, pp. 251, 96. Osterweis made a comprehensive, and at times fully persuasive, study of the influence of Scott's romanticism upon the South. His *terminus a quo* is that the civilization of the Old South rested on a "tripod" with cotton and the plantation system forming one leg, slavery another, and the "chivalric cult" a third. His book focuses upon the last of these, being concerned with "the origin, nature, and significance" of the chivalric cult. For a measured evaluation of Osterweis' argument one should take into account the weaknesses pointed out by Hubbell in his review of Osterweis' book (*South Atlantic Quarterly*, XLVIII (July, 1949), 472–75).

36. *Romanticism and Nationalism in the Old South*, pp. 3–5, 45. Osterweis cites tournaments in Virginia, Maryland, and Louisiana.

37. Cited by Hubbell, *The South in American Literature*, p. 189.

the career of General J. E. B. ("Jeb") Stuart was a living em-
bodiment of the Cavalier tradition, and it gave him a lasting
reputation as "the flower of chivalry" and the "last knight" of
his kind.[38] Southerners commonly assumed that Scott's chivalry
had been the pattern for their officers' concepts of honor and
valor. At one point in the war, concern was expressed in an
editorial in the Richmond *Examiner* that the Southern forces
were being hamstrung by the "polite notions of war" which they
had "borrowed from the Waverley Novels."[39] These notions
have been traced to the chivalric code imbibed by men who went
to schools like Virginia Military Institute, but they were prevalent enough to have provided a butt for Twain's caricature of the
typical young officer ("a fair sample of the kind of stuff we were
made of") who, as he indicated in "The Private History of a
Campaign That Failed," was "full of romance, and given to
reading chivalric novels and singing forlorn love-ditties," and
who had "some pathetic little nickel-plated aristocratic instincts."[40]

Strong as the ideals of knighthood were during the war, their
appeal became even stronger in the nostalgic postwar era and
brought into greater prominence the delusions with which the
South had gone into the war. It has been shown, for example,
that while the Cavalier ideal was neither generally understood
nor embraced, even among planters, its importance in shaping
thought, politics, and society, both before and after the war, was
fully as great as if it had been.[41] Since the Cavalier tradition,
which had at first been abetted by Scott's novels, reached a

38. D. W. Brogan, "A Fresh Appraisal of the Civil War," *Harper's Magazine*, CCXX (April, 1960), 136. The Southern press and periodicals did
 their share to advance the widely accepted corollary of the Cavalier
 tradition, whereby the Southern cause was identified with the preservation of "chivalry, honor, nobility," and the like, and the Northerners
 were declared a race of commoners, oblivious to the noble graces and
 motivated solely by selfish gain. This was the theme of an essay entitled
 "The Difference between the Northern People and the Southern
 People," *Southern Literary Messenger*, XXX (June, 1860), 401–9.
39. *Examiner*, May 12, 1863; cited by Osterweis, *Romanticism and Nationalism in the Old South*, p. 91.
40. "Private History," in *American Claimant*, p. 237.
41. See Cash, *Mind of the South*, p. 72f.; William R. Taylor, *Cavalier and
 Yankee* (New York, 1961), p. 340.

fever pitch in the postwar era, one even finds a literary historian occasionally restating Twain's thesis that the backward-looking "social system" of the South seemed to have been "buttressed by [Scott's] pictures of mediaeval society."[42] C. Vann Woodward, one of the most authoritative historians of the "New South," actually went further than Mark Twain had gone in positing widespread ramifications of the romantic revival. Interestingly, Woodward did so while citing the same architectural evidence Twain had used—the Female Institute of Columbia, Tennessee:

> The romanticism and sentimentality of that generation of Southerners [of the 1880's and 90's] . . . was too copious to spend itself upon the Lost Cause. Genealogy became the avocation of thousands. Its more esoteric branches yielded their treasures to seekers after the heritage of grandeur. The fabled Southern aristocracy, long on its last legs, was refurbished, its fancied virtues and vices, airs and attitudes exhumed and admired. Homage even from the plain man, who for ages had been unimpressed by doings of the upper crust, was added in this period. Drippings from the plantation legend overflowed upon race and labor relations, public charities, and even the organization of factory villages. The Natchez Cotton Mills were adorned with "three spires or turrets of mansard style to give them grace and beauty," and the Female Institute of Columbia, Tennessee, boasted in an advertisement of "its resemblance to the old castles of song and story, with its towers, turreted walls, and ivy-mantled porches."[43]

Typical of the homage paid to the Lost Cause by members of the "upper crust" was the tenacity with which Sidney Lanier clung to the hope for a resurgent chivalric ideal. He flatly asserted that "the days of chivalry are not gone, they are only spiritualized. . . . In these times, the knight of the 19th century fights, not with trenchant sword, but with trenchant soul." Using almost the same antithesis Twain had used in his references to the nineteenth century and medievalism, but with a wholly opposite proposal in mind, Lanier felt that since commercialism had overthrown chivalry "it is now [1874] the gentleman must arise & overthrow Trade."[44]

42. Hart, *The Popular Book*, p. 76.
43. *Origins of the New South*, p. 157.
44. *The Centennial Edition of the Works of Sidney Lanier*, ed. Charles R. Anderson (Baltimore, 1945), I, xiii; *Letters 1874–1877*, ed. Charles R. Anderson and Aubrey H. Starke (Baltimore, 1945), IX, 122.

Like Lanier, Twain also had the South's best interests at heart. His annoyance with the state of Southern letters was, in a sense, his way of repaying a debt to the South. After all, those regionalists who, like Cable, Harris, and himself, placed craft above sentiment had either moved out of the South or published a good deal in Northern journals. And, besides diminishing their potential influence on other Southern writers, this withdrawal practically gave the field to the historical romancers, whose popularity was assured by the rebirth of the Cavalier tradition. As Harris had once explained, an inveterate fondness for romance proved to be one of the biggest obstacles that Southern writers had to surmount.[45] Altogether too many preferred not to surmount it, for postwar fiction was largely given over to the Old Plantation romance written by such writers as John Esteen Cooke, George Cary Eggleston, Mary Johnston, and Thomas Nelson Page.[46] Looking back upon the Old Plantation days, Page traced their philosophic tone to Greece, their dominant spirit to Rome, and their guardfulness of individual rights to England; "and over all," he continued, "brooded a softness and beauty, the joint product of Chivalry and Christianity."[47] When one considers that the Cavalier tradition was destined to attract a significant following in the North, and that the historical romance was coming to the fore again in England,[48] the terms Twain used to attack one of the ultimate sources of both seem none too strong.

45. Hubbell, *The South In American Literature*, p. 791.
46. The sort of favor that Scott enjoyed among writers of the "plantation novel," and among southwestern humorists as well, has been ably summarized by Kenneth S. Lynn, *Mark Twain and Southwestern Humor* (Boston, 1960), p. 54. In brief, the novelists used Scott to bolster their claims about the beneficence of a feudal economy and slavery; and the humorists learned from Scott a way of fostering a love for the Southern past (as a means of asserting sectional identity), and a way, too of using low characters in heroic roles.
47. Thomas Nelson Page, *The Old South: Essays Social and Political* (New York, 1892), p. 5. Although Page thought it had been unwise for Kennedy, Caruthers, and Tucker to have imitated Scott so closely (p. 85), he approved of Scott's influence on society (p. 161).
48. For the popularity of the Cavalier tradition in the North see Taylor, *Cavalier and Yankee*, p. 146. For a comment on the revival of the historical romance see G. R. Carpenter, "The Neo-Romantic Novel," *Forum*, XXV (March, 1898), 120–28.

Strong charges were a strength in Twain's criticism of Scott's romanticism. Cooper and Whitman had raised similar caveats against Scott,[49] but one probably has a better recollection of Twain's remarks because the spontaneity of his grumbling inspired a hypothesis that in its very wildness has the unmistakable tang of a felt truth. In linking Scott to the regional malady, Twain had to be more than merely wild, of course, His inside point of view made all the difference between the criticism he wrote in *Life on the Mississippi* and the frivolous rantings he had indulged in when, speaking as a renegade, in his Buffalo *Express* editorials (1869) he had disparaged education in Tennessee ("Will it outlast the velocipede?"), blamed lynchings on chivalric pretenses, and scorned the tournaments of mock knights as "absurdity gone crazy."[50]

It is not strictly true that in *Life on the Mississippi* Twain did not face up to a "dilemma" assumedly created, as one critic has held, by his being "torn between lamenting and praising and preaching the future."[51] Rather, the Mark Twain who looks back longingly upon the prewar river is a different Mark Twain from the one who castigates the South for living in Sir Walter Scott's past and welcomes the new era. The mobility of point of view permitted Twain to record his mixed feelings, as well as differences in time and within himself. By the time he became the man of the world he had as a youth wanted landlubbers to think he was, Twain had seen enough of the world, and of time and change, to form opinions somewhat more reliably than Southerners who had not been "outside." He even felt free to make judgments upon history, and emerged as one of his own favorite types of historian, a Suetonious, Carlyle, Macaulay or Lecky—above all as a "poetic" historian who did not allow the demands of petty accuracy to stop him from reaching out for larger truths about the character of a nation, a segment of time, or the influence of Sir Walter Scott upon the South.

49. *England with Sketches of Society in the Metropolis* (London, 1837), II, 15f.; "Poetry To-day in America" [1881], *The Complete Poetry and Prose of Walt Whitman*, ed. Malcolm Cowley (New York, 1948), II, 296f.
50. Summarized by Budd, *Mark Twain: Social Philosopher*, p. 87.
51. Marian Montgomery, "The New Romantic vs. the Old: Mark's Dilemma in 'Life on the Mississippi,'" *Mississippi Quarterly*, XI (Spring, 1958), 79.

10

Bret Harte: The Grumbling
Realist's Friend and Foe

I

The one insistent criterion of the grumbling so far examined
has been that of a simple, unvarnished realism; and its source
an equally uncomplicated hostility to old-school, sentimental
romanticism. Twain differed, though, from the rest of the early
realists in the important, but as yet unnoticed, respect that his
criticism of the onflowing stream of popular romanticism did not
stop at the water's edge. He, far better than anyone before Irving
Babbitt, was able to see that an important phase of the new
realism was not the independent stream it seemed to be, but
rather an elusive tributary of the old romantic parent stream.
It was while rafting the familiar headwaters of Western realism
—for some, indeed, its main current—the fiction of Bret Harte,
that Twain discovered that, like Huck, he'd been there before.

The discovery did not come all at once. In fact, it did not come
until some six years after Twain had met and become fast
friends with Harte. The friendship had very likely blinded him
to the true character of what Harte was writing. But it was easy
to be blinded. By word and deed Harte had given Twain every
reason to believe that, like himself, he was a staunchly anti-
romantic realist. Had not the recrudescence of sensibility in the
works of Scott, Cooper, Bulwer-Lytton, and Disraeli given both
of them plenty to grumble about? In his greater—and earlier—
concern with the shortcomings of romantic fiction, Harte would
seem to have been considerably ahead of Twain. To suggest, for
instance, as he had in 1870, that Disraeli's *Lothair* represented
"the slowly decaying romance of the past, that dealt with conditions and accessories of men and women rather than with the
men and women themselves"[1] was not just to downgrade the

1. Review of *Lothair*, 1870, in *Bret Harte: Representative Selections*, ed.
Joseph B. Harrison (New York, 1941), p. 29.

"romance," but to rule, out of hand, that its techniques presumably made the difference between what was and what was not creditable literature. One may imagine Harte's astonishment had he known that in the same year Twain would, on reading *The Luck of Roaring Camp and Other Sketches*, find parts of it—*mirabile dictu*—to be romantically rotten at the core. It took a good deal more raw discernment for Twain to make that judgment of stories generally assumed to be the finest fruit of Western realism than it had for Harte to criticize the romanticism of *Lothair*. It took an even greater amount of forbearance for a man of Twain's volatility to hold his peace and grumble in private about his findings, particularly when he had external as well as internal evidence to go on; since, as he could recall years later, Harte had said to him "with a cynical chuckle that he thought he had mastered the art of pumping up the tear of sensibility." "The idea conveyed," Twain continued, "was that the tear of sensibility was oil, and that by luck [no pun intended] he had struck it" (*MTE* 265).

The problem for Twain was that in 1870 Harte was still a good friend to whom he felt indebted for literary assistance; he was a force in contemporary literature, and a critic to be looked up to by an aspiring realist. It seemed that Harte alone of all their crew could rebuke the entrenched British romanticists with precisely the irritating suavity with which they liked to put Americans in their place. Twain was also drawn to Harte because he represented to him an enviable compromise between literary sophistication and Western earthiness. Having noticed that that was exactly why Boston was so taken with Harte, Twain felt he could pan the same literary gold.

He might even profit from Harte's mistakes, for when he inquired rather closely into his success formula he was appalled to discover that in addition to being no true friend of realism, Harte was an interloper, in truth a sentimental romanticist, the very foe whose blood the realists had been calling for. While their friendship lasted Twain kept quiet. Once it gave way, the dammed-up torrent of abuse that broke over Harte's head was something to behold. The insincerity of Harte's character ran together with the insincerity of his work ("he had nothing to feel with . . . his heart was merely a pump" [*MTE* 265]); and Twain could not have been more intoxicated had he been given the chance to rattle the bones of old Sir Walter himself. Wanting to know from Howells, at the high tide of his hatred (in 1878), what German town Harte would "filthify with his [consular] presence," Twain rhapsodically ticked off his vices:

> Harte is a liar, a thief, a swindler, a snob, a sot, a sponge, a coward, a Jeremy Diddler, he is brim full of treachery, & he conceals his Jewish birth as carefully as if he considered it a disgrace. How do I know? By the best of all evidence, personal observation. . . . If he had only been made a home official, I think I could stand it; but to send this nasty creature to puke upon the American name in a foreign land is too much. (*T-H* I 235.)

Quite as important as his tirade was the question Twain anxiously appended to it: "Have you heard any literary men express an opinion about the appointment? Who were they—& what said they?" (236). Although Harte's literary fortunes had sagged, he was still widely published and well thought of in the late 1870's, so that while Twain felt he knew his man, he had a sneaking suspicion that the people who should did not. Under these circumstances, open criticism might in reality have made Twain look worse than it did Harte, an intolerable risk. Consequently, Twain's having bottled up a much-needed criticism somewhat intensified the heat of his grumbling. A good part of what he said about Harte was rancorous and directed more at the man than his works.[2] Nevertheless, the results were less deplorable than they might have been, for the failings in Harte's fiction (the

---

2. I should hasten to point out that it does not fall within my province in this discussion of Twain's criticism of Harte to suggest how true or false were his charges against Harte's character. That Twain's merciless vilification of Harte is unfair on the face of it, however, anyone can see for himself. For a full investigation of this matter one should consult Margaret Duckett's book, *Mark Twain and Bret Harte* (Norman, Okla., 1964).

Miss Duckett makes the long overdue attempt to right the scales that Twain—and those who took him literally—heedlessly weighted against Bret Harte's reputation as a man. Her chapters on the disastrous *Ah Sin* collaboration and its aftermath (10, 11, and 12) are particularly useful. However, in her zeal to see justice done, Miss Duckett has regrettably—though understandably—made herself so unstinting an apologist for Bret Harte, through right and wrong, and so vehement a

pretentiousness, artificiality, and insincerity) were all of a piece with the failings Twain perceived in his character. They were indeed the effect of that cause. The rancor, on the other hand, worked as hyperbole, supplying both sauce and subtlety to the criticism. What Twain lost in moderation he gained in freedom, and freedom was of the essence; it was the one indispensable quality of his grumbling. With it came probing truths. Probably no other portion of Twain's criticism is so instinct with the substantive virtues of grumbling as is his criticism of Harte, with whom the grumbling was freest because most of it was personally intended and privately uttered.

When all is said and done, one could of course wish that Twain's criticism of Harte had been more consistent, and occasionally more objective too. The state of their personal relations and their positions in the literary world relative to one another were the chief barometers of Twain's regard for Harte's writing. At the beginning of their friendship Twain was too deferential; at the end of it, when he regarded Harte as a mortal foe, he tended to carp at his faults. The course of this criticism is most advantageously viewed in the context of Twain's relationship to Harte over the span of fifteen years from 1864 to 1879. During those years the two men found themselves thrown into rivalry for leadership of the new movement of Western realism, to which

---

prosecutor of Mark Twain, that in writing Harte up and Twain down, as Harte had done in revising *Ah Sin*, she often stretches her evidence rather thin, and summons up all imaginable probabilities and hypotheses, with the result that the scales become as badly weighted against Twain as they had formerly been against Harte. (This she belatedly recognizes, but does nothing to correct, after 278 pages of relentless blackening and whitening, and again after 54 more pages of it.) Her method of attack is repeatedly to turn the tables on Twain: if he accused Harte of being a liar and drunk, she will find a way of showing that Twain was a bigger liar and drank more; if Harte failed to fulfill the terms of his contract with the *Atlantic*, she will insist that Twain did not do much better by the *Galaxy*. As for Twain's literary judgment of Harte (a matter infrequently mentioned) Miss Duckett intimates that Twain had an adverse comment on "Tennessee's Partner" not because it was a poor story, but possibly because it might be construed as reflecting upon his friendship with Harte. How? Twain may have been the model for Harte's conception of Tennessee, to whom, supposedly, Harte would be Tennessee's partner. Do not the Tennessee lands entitle Twain to that name? (p. 50).

Harte had made the first major contribution with his heart-of-gold motif, and to which Twain was ultimately to make the most lasting contribution with his innovations in the use of the vernacular style for an elevated theme. On the long view, the two men were really most apart therefore in the area where they seemed most together. The key to Twain's criticism of Harte was his realization of this fact.

His principal statements on Harte occur in certain letters to Howells, in his autobiographical dictations, and in marginal notations in his personal copies of *The Luck of Roaring Camp and Other Sketches* (1870) and *The Twins of Table Mountain* (1879). These notations comprise the only continuous effort at literary criticism among all the marginalia in Twain's library,[3] and as a body they record Twain's most sustained inquiry into the quality of work done by a ranking contemporary writer.

3. A fair portion of this library is now stored with the Mark Twain Papers, and my judgment here is based on what I have seen there and in the Berg Collection of the New York Public Library. Some of the books Twain marked are of course in private hands, and one always finds a stray volume or two turning up in a dealer's list.

Since I have earlier alluded to a number of these marginal comments, I should, in connection with the importance of the Harte marginalia, make some summary statements about the whole of them. In kind, Twain's margins run the gamut from dedicatory remarks (like the one to his mother, his "most charitable critic," in a first edition of *Innocents*) to a running debate with Henry H. Breen, the writer of a style manual (*Modern English Literature: Its Blemishes and Defects*), on the question of plagiarism. In content, Twain's marginalia include humor, skepticism, views on morals, justice, and civilization, and literary criticism. Quite interesting is the sight of Twain's pencil censoring in books in his private library matters that seem salacious or that refer too plainly in print to man's physical nature. Outside of those notes with an element of literary criticism, which, except for the ones on Harte, are sporadic, Twain made noteworthy statements in three kinds of books: (1) books on astronomy and evolution from which he seemed to have been acquiring background for works like *The Mysterious Stranger* and "Captain Stormfield's Visit to Heaven"; (2) an assortment of memoirs and histories, among the more engrossing of which, for Twain, were *The Memoirs of the Duke of Saint-Simon* and *The Greville Memoirs, A Journal of the Reigns of King George IV and King William IV*; and (3) a group of histories and biographies dealing with Joan of Arc, which he consulted to immerse himself in the facts and atmosphere of her times.

It will be best, I think, to work our way into the criticism from the standpoint of the personal relationship, by which it was mainly conditioned.

II

When they were introduced to one another in May, 1864, by George Barnes, editor of the San Francisco *Call* (the *Call*, for which Twain was working, and the U.S. Mint, for which Harte was working, occupied the same building), Twain was, as he recalled, "a fading and perishing reporter" (*MTE* 265). He had just left a highly compatible job on the *Enterprise*, he was unsettled in life, though almost thirty, and had given no sign that he was anything of a writer. Harte's remembrance of Twain at their introduction was of a listless, curly-headed yokel, who tried to hide his embarrassment behind an air of eccentricity.[4] Twain was nobody, and not only was Harte somebody, he was rapidly establishing himself as the most prominent writer in California, which really meant the most prominent one west of the Mississippi. Harte had been in California for ten years, spending his time not on the frontier, but in the cities, particularly San Francisco, as opposed to Twain's three years amid the alkali dust of Nevada. By the time he met Twain, Harte was said to be ready for a national audience,[5] and having obtained it by publishing "The Legend of Monte Del Diablo" (a polished Irvingesque sketch about Spanish California) in the *Atlantic* (October, 1863), he had already disassociated himself from the *Golden Era*, of which the *Enterprise* had merely been a frontier satellite. Harte was, in short, a lion, entertained by the best families on the Coast (for example, the Frémonts), so that when he was induced to write for the newly founded *Californian*, the editor, Charles H. Webb, could say with pride, in giving Harte one of several stints as guest editor, that his name was a "household word on the Pacific Coast."[6] When, several months after

4. Henry C. Merwin, *The Life of Bret Harte* (Boston, 1911), p. 39f.
5. So said Fitzhugh Ludlow in 1863 (George R. Stewart, *Bret Harte: Argonaut and Exile* [New York, 1931], p. 123).
6. *Ibid.*, p. 126.

their meeting, Harte asked Twain to contribute to the *Californian*, Twain was duly impressed. Writing home in September, 1864, he crowed: "I have engaged to write for the new literary paper— the 'Californian'. . . . I quit the 'Era,' long ago. It wasn't high-toned enough. The 'Californian' circulates among the highest class of the community, and is the best weekly literary paper in the United States—and I suppose I ought to know" (*Letters* I 100).

Twain had become infatuated with the parvenu respectability desired as much by the literary as by the business community of San Francisco; and everything implied by the realization of such a desire seemed to be consummated in the writings of Bret Harte. Harte had broken the ice; he had made the doings of rugged low-life Westerners palatable to respectable readers. As he rode the crest of local fame, he had been in Twain's eyes "a contented Bret Harte, an ambitious Bret Harte, a hopeful Bret Harte, a bright, cheerful, easy-laughing Bret Harte, a Bret Harte to whom it was a bubbling and effervescent joy to be alive" (*MTE* 267). This Twain remembered in 1906, when he could say almost nothing good about the man. He had been even more liberally disposed in January, 1871, recognizing an indebtedness to Harte, despite the fact that, as he said, "Bret broke our long friendship a year ago without any cause or provocation that I am aware of" (*Letters* I 183).[7] It seems that a poem paralleling Harte's much-imitated "Heathen Chinee" had appeared in the Buffalo *Express* under the name Carl Byng, and Twain was thought to have been the author. To Thomas Bailey Aldrich, who chided him for its being such a poor imitation of the "Chinee," Twain wrote: "I did hate to be accused of plagiarizing Bret Harte, who trimmed and trained and schooled me patiently until he changed me from an awkward utterer of coarse grotesquenesses to a writer of paragraphs and chapters that have found a certain favor in the eyes of even some of the very decentest people in the land . . . " (*Letters* I 182f.).

7. That was not the only insult Twain suffered from Harte. At a luncheon that Ralph Keeler, a former Californian, gave for his better-known friends—Aldrich, Fields, Harte, Howells, and Twain—Howells recalled that, amidst the mutual ribbing, what stood out was "Bret Harte's fleering dramatization of Clemens's mental attitude toward a symposium of Boston illuminates. 'Why, fellows,' he spluttered 'this is the

This was the highest tribute Twain paid Harte. In fact, on the matter of help, Twain paid no one as high a tribute, not even Howells, who had done a good deal more for him. What Twain might specifically have had in mind when he alluded to Harte's trimming, training, and schooling it is rather hard to know. He could have been referring to the help Harte gave him with *Innocents*, but the connotations of "schooling" suggest that he was probably thinking of the work he had published in the *Californian*, where Harte was in a position to make regular editorial suggestions. For the two years from October 1, 1864, to September 29, 1866, Twain contributed sixty-two sketches to the *Californian*, a total for one journal that is surpassed only by the number of items he published in the *Enterprise*. When one sifts through a fair selection of these sketches looking for the

---

dream of Mark's life' " (*Literary Friends and Acquaintance* [New York, 1900], p. 310f.). In the same year, 1871, on an early visit to Twain's newly established residence in Hartford, Harte was remembered by Twain to have come for a loan and to have remained to pass insults on the house, furniture, and domestic arrangements (*MTE* 274). For Harte's side of the matter, see Stewart, *Argonaut and Exile*, pp. 233, 237; and, of course, Duckett, *Mark Twain and Bret Harte*, Chapters 6, 11, *et passim*.

Although it may not have been the act that Twain considered a breach of friendship in 1870, the tone of condescension that crept into Harte's review of *Innocents* in that year may well have hurt his pride. Harte had thought the book contained "mannerism that is only slang, some skepticism that lacks the cultivation which only makes skepticism tolerable, and some sentiment that is only rhetoric." He also wrote, "To subject Mr. Clemens to any of those delicate tests by which we are supposed to detect the true humorist, might not be either fair or convincing." He found the humor of "John Phoenix" "more cultivated" than Twain's (*Overland Monthly*, LV, O.S. [January, 1870], 100f.; reprinted in *Mark Twain, Selected Criticism*, ed. Arthur L. Scott [Dallas, Tex., 1955], pp. 13–16).

Finally, in the light of this review, it should be recalled that Harte had read the manuscript of *Innocents* for Twain and had told him what "chapters to leave out" and Twain had "followed orders strictly." Harte had greatly praised the book to Twain, but apparently took umbrage (the cause is not quite clear) at Twain's wanting him to be the first one on the coast to review it—the idea supposedly being that he would do a good turn for a friend. In consequence, it would seem, Harte wrote Twain *"the most daintily contemptuous & insulting letter you ever read . . ."* (letter to Charles H. Webb, November 26, 1870, quoted by Frederick Anderson in his Preface to *"Ah Sin": A Dramatic Work by Mark Twain and Bret Harte* [San Francisco, 1961], p. viif.).

marks of such schooling as would purge Twain's writing of coarseness and make it acceptable to cultivated readers, one does observe some notable departures from his usual style. Indeed, his prose seems, on close inspection, to be remarkably saturated with Harte's mannerisms, including the long and elaborate syntax, the formal diction, and the tone of literary refinement borrowed from the eighteenth-century classical tradition.[8] At first Twain used this style seriously in an attempt to write gracefully, and with an attitude of urbane amusement (as in the first of the passages given below); but then, as often happened with him, he began to caricature his own newly acquired habit when he noticed that the discrepancy between its loftiness and his clownish persona could be turned to humorous account (as in the second passage). Neither passage would normally be identified as Twain's work, and both might well be assigned to Harte if one knew that they were written for the *Californian* in 1864. What seems an effect of judicious elegance in the first passage is rapidly transformed into a parody of pretentious verbosity in the second:[9]

> If the projectors of this noble Fair never receive a dollar or a kindly word of thanks for the labor of their hands, the sweat of their brows and the wear and tear of brain it has cost them to plan their work and perfect it, a consciousness of the incalculable good they have conferred upon the community must still give them a placid satisfaction more precious than money or sounding compliments. (October 1, 1864, *SOS* 121.)
>
> Love's Bakery! I am satisfied I have found the place now that I have been looking for all this time. I cannot describe to you the sensation of mingled astonishment, gladness, hope, doubt,

---

8. With the exception of Miss Duckett (*Mark Twain and Bret Harte*, (Chapter 22), the few critics who have considered Harte's possible influence on Twain have thought it to be negligible, or extremely general. J. DeLancey Ferguson saw no difference between the material Twain had written for the *Enterprise* and what he did for the *Golden Era* and the *Californian* (*Mark Twain: Man and Legend* [New York, 1957], p. 99f.). E. Hudson Long agreed with him (*Mark Twain Handbook* [New York, 1957], p. 331). Neither made a comparative analysis of Twain's style in those journals, nor has anyone else.

9. The objective in each of the essays from which these passages are taken is one of sophisticated comment on local events (Harte's favorite type of journalism), and the formal prose stands out in each by virtue of its occurring in a piece that also contains Twain's more familiar style.

anxiety, and balmy, blissful emotion that suffused my being and quivered in a succession of streaky thrills down my backbone, as I stood on the corner of Third and Minna streets, last Tuesday, and stared, spell-bound, at those extraordinary words, painted in large, plain letters on a neighboring window-curtain —"LOVE'S BAKERY." "God bless my soul!" said I, "will wonders never cease?—are there to be no limits to man's spirit of invention?—is he to invade the very realms of the immortal, and presume to guide and control the great passions, the impalpable essences, that have hitherto dwelt in the secret chambers of the soul, sacred from all save divine intrusion?" (October 22, 1864, *SOS* 136.)

There are numerous other like passages in which Twain seemed to be alternately striving for elegance and parodying it through a mixture of the formal with the informal, so that it is difficult at times to be completely certain of his purpose because he was obviously not certain of it himself. The elegance would appear to be a result of the schooling, and the parodies a tacit rejection of it.

At this point Twain resisted thinking ill of Harte. Had he not felt himself under obligation to him, and had he been more confident of his own values, he might have converted his satire on formality into a commentary on Harte's style. But possibly that would have been too much to hope for at a time when Harte represented so much of what Twain wanted to secure for himself in the way of audience and reputation. Vanity had gotten the better of Twain. His letter home of January 20, 1866—which contains his statement about wanting to be back on the river— tells us a good deal about why he was not quite ready to entertain the idea that, deep down, he and Harte did not really worship the same gods. He bemoaned the fact that the East should have made a great to-do over "a villainous backwoods sketch" like his "Jumping Frog" story, while ignoring the "tolerably good" things he had written—presumably material that smacked of "literature," and not of the frontier. Some of that better writing he was planning to bring out with Harte in a volume of sketches; and it was Harte, he was pleased to report, who had approached him about the matter, promising to "take all the trouble" of seeing the sketches into print. Twain's contributions were to have been culled from *Enterprise* stories, the poorest of which, interestingly, he claimed to have burned. In addition, Harte and Twain were thinking of collaborating on a burlesque of a forthcoming collection of California poetry made up of items rejected from a recent anthology Harte had edited. The juiciest morsel Twain tried to toss off as lightly as he could: "Though I am generally placed at the head of my breed of scribblers in this part of the country," he wrote, "the place properly belongs to Bret Harte, I think, though he denies it, along with the rest." Finally, to show the folks back home how his cup of respectability ran over, he mentioned his regret, in a postscript, at having missed the maiden voyage of the *Ajax* to the Sandwich Islands because "the cream of the town were aboard."[10]

So much for the Western Mark Twain, Bret Harte's friend and compatriot in the dawning campaign of realism—the aspirant toward respectability, who was soft on Harte's non-realistic prose style.

III

In 1871, the year after Fields, Osgood and Company had finally succeeded in landing the Western stories they had been seeking from Harte and were to publish in the famous volume called *The Luck of Roaring Camp and Other Stories*, Harte made his triumphal appearance in Boston as the celebrity to whom the *Atlantic* contracted to pay all of ten thousand dollars for exclusive rights to his literary output for the forthcoming year. In that moment, according to Twain, "one of the pleasantest men" he had ever known turned into "one of the unpleasantest." He became "showy, meretricious, insincere; and he constantly advertised these qualities in his dress" (*MTE* 264). Certain it was that no writer in Twain's day had risen so high and fallen so low within so short a time as Harte had. Although Twain, almost alone, could see early evidence of its coming, the decline

10. Copyright © 1967, Mark Twain Company. Paine only published a portion of this letter, with no indication that he had anywhere abridged it (*Letters* I 101f.). The parts of it referred to here that Paine did not publish are those about the burning of the *Enterprise* stories, the burlesque of California poets, the book he was doing in secret, and the postscript on the *Ajax*. The complete letter is in the Mark Twain Papers.

was forecast in Harte's failure to make good on the spirit of his contract, under which it was expected that he would furnish at least one story or poem for each of the twelve monthly issues of the magazine.

In retrospect, Twain claimed to have been immediately disillusioned with Harte in the East. But as far as the romanticism in his writing was concerned, Twain did not find him out overnight. Lingering envy, a feeling of rivalry and admiration for Harte's place in the world, along with a willingness to give credit for the good things he had done, initially deterred Twain from making an all out condemnation of Harte, even in private.

In the first place, he could not have missed what Howells sensed about the difference in the Eastern reception given himself and Harte, that he, "Mark Twain," "seemed not to hit the favor of our community of scribes and scholars, as Bret Harte had done, when he came on from California. . . ." Harte was looked upon as a literary man worthy of instant recognition, Twain as a humorist, a species of writer who was always in need of earning what little recognition he might deserve. Somewhat miffed, Twain was determined to be regarded as at least as much of a writer as Bret Harte. In 1870, he was eager to free himself from newspaper work in order to do some "higher-class writing" for a "first class New York magazine."[11] Exactly a year later he was quitting that magazine, the *Galaxy*, and pronouncing himself interested in the writing of books only. That the image of Harte was egging him on can be seen from his pointing to Harte, immediately following this pronouncement, as somewhat of a cynosure—"the most celebrated man in America today." Several days later, he was saying he was afraid he might cheapen his work if he appeared too frequently in magazines; and his reason for wanting to absent himself from public view was that he was biding his time until, as he put it, "Bret Harte simmers down a little." Then he intended "to go up ahead again," by which, one assumes, he meant where he had been with *Innocents*. He had to be at his best to overtake Harte, and so he was going "to go slow" he repeated, for he planned to "'top' Bret Harte again

11. *Literary Friends and Acquaintance*, 351. Letter to Elisha Bliss from Buffalo, March 11 [1870], *Berg* (Copyright © 1967, Mark Twain Company).

or bust."[12] These motives must have had a good deal to do with Twain's scrutinizing Harte's finest work, the stories and sketches in *The Luck of Roaring Camp*, and his writing marginal comments on them. The desire for emulation thereby gave way to disillusionment in the crucible of criticism.

As an early estimate of one of the first dedicated realists by a fellow realist, during the seminal years of American realism, Twain's criticism of Harte's stories takes on fundamental importance. Those stories were and are still considered excellent specimens of their kind and of Harte's fiction. Twain thought rather well of the title story, but his waning enthusiasm and increasing criticism of the others resulted from a close application of the criteria of realism. When Bradford Booth examined Twain's marginal notes, he correctly regarded Twain as a reader who was at first more apt to admire than to find fault, but he underplayed the increasing acidity of his remarks, and made nothing of the erosion of Twain's good will.[13]

Twain's marginalia in *The Luck* come to some 435 words. In addition, one finds various passages simply scored. All told, there are forty-one separate comments, of which nineteen are favorable and twenty-two critical or questioning.[14] Fourteen of the nineteen favorable notes are on the title story, none exceeds

12. Letter to J. H. Riley from Buffalo, March 3 [1871], *Berg*; letter to Orion Clemens from Buffalo, March 11 [1871], *MTP*; transcript of original letter made by George Brownell (Copyright © 1967, Mark Twain Company). Twain repeated the sentiments expressed in the letter of March 11 in yet another letter that Paine published from about this time. He said that he was withdrawing from the New York *Galaxy* in hopes that the public's missing him for a while might increase the demand for *Roughing It*, on which he was working (*Letters* I 185).

13. It was not quite true that, as Booth held, Twain merely picked up carelessness here and there in Harte's dialogue but generally maintained "a lively sense of his friend's merits as a writer of vigorous and colorful narrative" ("Mark Twain's Comments on Bret Harte's Stories," *AL*, XXV [January, 1954], 492-95).

14. In his presentation of the marginal notes, Booth did not tabulate or group them according to kind, and he omitted several of the smaller items. My figures include all comments and every instance of scoring. All page references have of necessity to be to the first edition, the one Twain read, published in Boston by Fields, Osgood & Co., in 1870. Its pagination is different from that of subsequent editions, which include the story "Brown of Calaveras" (pp. 89–106 of the later editions).

a brief, assenting "good," "all good," or "good, & characteristic,"
and almost all approve Harte's depiction of the California setting
and character types, which, as Twain would claim many years
later, Harte was able to "put . . . into his tales alive" because he
had gotten his material by "unconscious absorption" (*LE* 146).
In the beginning Twain was, in other words, heartily convinced
of his friend's realism, his imaginatively bringing to life people
and places drawn from their common experience. Twain was
also quite willing to grant something that Harte was rather vain
of—his sensitivity in recording the interplay of human feelings.
His most explicit approval was accordingly reserved for the un-
assuming final sketch in the book, called "Boonder." It was his
last observation, made after 127 note-free pages: "This is in
Bret's *best* vein," he wrote, "—it is his 'strongest suit.'" Presumably, what Twain enjoyed was a minor specimen of Harte's
Dickensian blending of quiet humor with subdued pathos, an
effect that had been rather strained in his more ambitious pieces.
("Boonder" was an ungainly mongrel who attached himself to a
family, which grew fond of the rascally creature and then found
him killed by the first train run by a railroad whose intrusion he
had protested.) However, by what it signified about the other,
more significant items in the volume, Harte could not have been
flattered by the compliment on "Boonder."

The impression of over-all dissatisfaction is augmented by the
fact that four of the notes on "The Luck" (the story, that is) are
critical, while in the remaining stories that are commented upon
the yield is eighteen critical notes against five laudatory ones, a
reversal suggesting that the more Twain read of Harte, the less
he liked him. This surmise is supported by the pattern of his
notes. Almost all of them are confined to the first seventy-two
pages. On page 72 "Tennessee's Partner" ends, and since Twain
gave that story his sternest criticism, disappointment and flagging interest probably impelled him to skip and read more
selectively from there on. In addition to "The Luck" and
"Boonder," the stories commented upon are, in order, "The
Outcasts of Poker Flat" (twice favorably and once unfavorably),
"Miggles" (once favorably and six times unfavorably), "Tennessee's Partner" (once favorably and ten times unfavorably),
and "A Lonely Ride" (once unfavorably).

The qualities Twain found particularly disturbing were not merely elementary lapses in realism (though they were that too); they were the epitome of all that he—and supposedly Harte, as well—had held against the sentimental romanticism of Goldsmith, Cooper, and Scott: faulty observation, non-observation, the subservience of fact to sentiment, and the milking of moral feeling for its own sake. The significant revelation of Twain's notes is that he compares the intent with the actual result of situations in which Harte wanted to give the impression of realism and, by overdoing it, went wrong exactly where he tried to go right. Moreover, Twain was as much as invited to focus on authenticity by Harte's professions of strict realism (his narrators continually insist upon the accuracy of what they report) and his dependence on picturesqueness. It is true that Twain seems at times to ferret out inobtrusive details, but it is in just such details that his delicate ear picks out the all-betraying false notes.

A few key comments will illustrate. It was ridiculous, Twain thought, for one of Harte's stage drivers to address his passenger as "Sir." "One of those brutal California stage-drivers," he pointed out, "could not be polite to a passenger,—& not one of the guild ever 'sir'd' *anybody*" (112). To Harte's placing Piney Woods (the naïve young bride of "The Outcasts of Poker Flat") as a waitress in "Temperance House," Twain objected, "Impossible save in derision" (24). Whereas Harte named the establishment "Temperance House" in order to certify the girl's respectability, every Westerner would know, as Rodman Paul has pointed out, that the most prominent building in the mining camps "was nearly always a drinking and gambling resort that was often a hotel, and sometimes a brothel as well."[15] In "The Luck" and "Tennessee's Partner" Twain was struck by the patent wrongness of "bowers" as a localism for Jacks in poker (2, 71), since the term was customarily associated with euchre. Equally unnatural to Twain was the atmospheric scene in "The Luck" in which Harte had his miners lying under the trees

15. *California Gold* (Cambridge, Mass., 1947), p. 80. Twain, by the way, used the name "Temperance Tavern" facetiously in *Tom Sawyer*. Its haunted room, Tom suggests, on having run upon a drunk Injin Joe asleep there, must be haunted with whiskey (*TS* 257).

"in the soft summer twilight." "This must be a mistake," he wrote, "—I think there is no twilight on 'the coast'" (14). Twilight there may have been, but, as Twain recalled it, it was not the soft, lingering kind. That was a detail Harte had simply created for effect. In *Roughing It*, Twain had indicated that night came "not with a lingering twilight, but with a sudden shutting down like a cellar door, as is its habit in that country" (I 252). Harte had a generally poor sense of physical relationships. It got pretty bad when he had Tennessee's partner nail down the lid of his friend's coffin after the coffin had been deposited in the grave. Come what might, Harte was going to get the partner down into that grave; and so Twain wondered, tongue in cheek, whether Harte was not asking the man to perform a "human impossibility—unless he . . . buried the poor devil perpendicularly" (68f.).

Twain did not wish, he said, "to be hypercritical," nor had he been, for, having applauded examples of workable realism in "The Luck," he judged the other stories by that standard and was disappointed. In "The Luck" he had specifically liked the typicality of the mining camp scene and of the easy mingling of the heterogeneous characters, and also the typical behavior of the usually disorganized miners in suddenly becoming so officious about their responsibilities as foster parents that they would call a meeting and frame a resolution for the adoption of the child (89). Regardless of whether Harte had experienced what he had written about or had indeed gotten his mining camp information from Anton Roman,[16] the literary temptation to manipulate the real for the purpose of suggesting the typical had led him considerably astray. Harte often seemed to have become enamored of the effect he wished to produce. Nowhere was this admiration more precarious than in his attempt to represent typical frontier speech, to which Twain made considerable objection. (He eventually complained more persistently about Harte's dialect writing than about any other flaw.) The speech in "Miggles" did not sound right to Twain's sharp ear mainly because its singularity had the appeal of quaintness rather than of real speech. "The girl's 'dialect' is not good," he noted, "but, it

16. See Anton Roman, "Reminiscences of Bret Harte," *Overland Monthly*, XV, N.S. (September, 1902), 221.

has at least *one* saving feature—it is difficult to explain *why* it isn't good, or point out the precise errors. It has a grand general badness." A brief example may show what Twain had in mind. In one sentence Miggles says, "I'll trouble you for that thar har-pin," and shortly afterwards, "Who'll bear a hand to help me get tea?" In the second sentence the rhythm seems a little clogged by Harte's throwing in the superfluous "bear a hand" solely for the regional nuance. "I'll trouble you" suggests a politer style, and the plain "bear" doesn't sound right after "thar" and "har." Twain picked up a number of such inconsistencies and some related ones, such as those in Harte's version of typical Western idioms, like the contrived metaphor he used in the tense episode of Tennessee's capture: " 'What have you got there?—I call,' said Tennessee quietly. 'Two Bowers and an ace,' said the stranger, as quietly, showing two revolvers and a bowie-knife" (59). In addition to his using the wrong term again, it was poor judgment in Twain's view for Harte to favor a minor similarity at the expense of the over-all exactness of the figure: "to have said 'a *pair* of *Jacks* & an ace' would have been good enough poker talk, but a wonderfully poor poker *hand* to make a bluster about."

The subtlest and most comprehensive instance of Twain's exposing an untypical dialect comes in Tennessee's partner's courtroom defense of his friend. To Twain the speech was "much more suggestive of Dickens & an English atmosphere than 'Pike County.'" And so truly it was, when one analyzed it. With its balanced syntax, smoothly modulated rhythms (obtained even through its halting pauses), and Cockney locutions ("thar ain't any liveliness as he's been up to, as I don't know"), one can easily mistake this kind of talk for that of any of a number of Dickens' characters, from Bill Sikes to Barnaby Rudge:

> "I come yar as Tennessee's pardner,—knowing him nigh on four year, off an on, wet and dry, in luck and out o'luck. His ways ain't allers my ways, but thar ain't any p'ints in that young man, thar ain't any liveliness as he's been up to, as I don't know. And you sez to me sez you—confidential-like, and between man and man,—sez you, 'Do you know anything in his behalf?' and I sez to you, sez I,—confidential-like, as between man and man,—'What should a man know of his pardner?'" (62f.)

How such a speech was to be properly written, incidentally, Twain would soon demonstrate in *Roughing It*, in the impromptu eulogy delivered by Scotty Briggs, a similarly circumstanced character (II 68f.).

Harte's romanticism was most blatant in the areas of motivation and narrative logic. In his criticism of these matters, Twain instanced the embarrassment of Harte's adding touch after touch to the softheartedness of his frontiersmen. As he tried to account, for example, for the contributions on behalf of the child in "The Luck," Twain observed "the gambler unquestionably gave more money than any one else, & it should have been mentioned—the idea conveyed, is that he gave *only* the ['very beautifully embroidered lady's'] handkerchief" (6). After declaring that Roaring Camp "looked suspiciously on strangers" and discouraged immigration, Harte had had the miners wanting to build a hotel there and "to invite one or two decent families" for the boy's sake. Again, Twain felt Harte was going out of his way to exploit sentiment and asked: "Then why the hotel? For the one or two families?" (16). On reading "Tennessee's Partner," Twain was similarly concerned with the internal justification of events—to say nothing of the unconscionable sentimentality of the story. At the hero's decline, he wished there had been greater dispatch in winding things up: "This sentimental old miner should have passed away earlier—many, many years earlier" (71). As one would expect, Twain's longest comment was on the awesome goodness of the partner, for which Harte must take first prize for bathos in local color:

> Does the artist show a clear knowledge of human nature when he makes his hero *welcome back* a man who has committed against him that sin [adultery] which neither the great nor the little ever forgive?—& not only welcome him back but love him with the fondling love of a girl to the last, & *then* pine and die for the loss of him?
>
> It is granted that when old bosom friends get to hating each other, they hate like super-vicious devils—but it is new that the human Unpardonable Sin should turn the victim's *love* to rampant *adoration*. (71f.)

Twain used a pertinent term to describe this "blemish." He said it "makes the main history simply impossible." A realistic story, he implied, should have the possibility of "history." Or, more specifically, it might be said that by sticking to his proposed "history" Harte would have been able to winnow true realism from romantic realism.

The artistic attainment of "history" was a concept that would figure quite prominently in Twain's appreciative criticism, for as his vision of the meaning of realism matured he became less concerned with day to day reality (the correspondence of literature to ordinary life), and more concerned with historical reality as a vital record of recurrent experience (the correspondence of times past to time present). For the time being, in his comment on the stories in *The Luck of Roaring Camp*, Twain's idea of history accorded with the general understanding among writers of local color, including Harte, that historicity was a norm of realism. Just as Harriet Beecher Stowe intended in *Oldtime Folks* (1869) "to interpret to the world the New England life and character in that particular [early] time of its history which may be called the seminal period,"[17] so did Harte offer his stories a year later with the "motive . . . to illustrate an era of which Californian history has preserved the incidents more often than the character of the actors" (Preface to *The Luck*, p. iv). Twain declared Harte unfaithful to his laudable purpose. As he would suggest in his notebook at a later date, the sentimentality of the heart-of-gold motif had utterly confounded Harte's effort to give a literary-historical treatment to the realities of Western life. After poking fun at "non-existent dialects" that undergo constant variation, Twain turned to the unlikely morals of Harte's characters and to his unhistorically representing their exceptional conduct as their typical conduct:

> some of the whores & burglars said, "We owe him [Harte] *one* grace, anyway. We have been the filthiest lot of heartless villains all our lives that ever went unhung—now instead of using the sufferings of the really good & worthy people whom we have robbed & ruined as the basis of his pathos, he hunts out (no, not that,)—he *manufactures* the one good deed possible to each of us, & in this way he has set the whole world to snuffling over us & wanting to hug us. We owe Harte a deep debt of gratitude—

17. *The Writings of Harriet Beecher Stowe* (Boston, 1896), IX, xxiii.

the reverence in which gamblers, burglars & whores are held in upper classes to-day is all due to him & to him only—for the dime novel circulates only among the lower ranks."[18]

IV

While Twain did not have the material to form a general estimate of Harte's work in examining the stories in *The Luck*, he did see some things that would eventually be recognized as basic limitations. It was significant that he saw these problems at all at a time when Howells, Fields, Lowell, and others remained very solidly impressed with Harte. He also located areas of recurrent weakness, for the melodrama of "Tennessee's Partner" was to be repeated in "The Iliad of Sandy Bar" (1872), which treats the love-hatred of former partners and has the same setting and as many pathetic fallacies; and Harte finally did enough stories of that kind to grow weary himself of endings that left his heroes, as he said, "dying in an attitude on my hands."[19]

Lamentably, much as he railed against Harte's inconsistencies, Twain was not consistent himself in his appraisals of Harte subsequent to his criticism of *The Luck*. Or maybe he just forgot how he had felt about that volume. In any case, neither his criticism of the stories nor his memory of personal insults, like the ones he mentioned to Aldrich and Webb, prevented him in 1872 from intimating the highest regard for Harte as a writer. He placed him among the upper tier of authors, along with Holmes and Howells, acknowledged favorites, and continued to think him one of "the big literary fish" (*T-H* I 160) on through 1876. Otherwise, he would not have wanted to write a play with him in 1877, during which collaboration, despite a deterioration in their personal relationship, Twain credited Harte with showing an enviable facility with plot and dialogue (*MTE* 277f.). It is useful to know that, under the circumstances, Twain could be this honest in his estimate of Harte as a writer.

18. Unpublished Notebook No. 14 (February–September, 1879), 18. Twain had several notes on Harte in this notebook. Two of them became the core of stories he told about him in the autobiographical dictations, and the other went: "Bret's saintly wh's & self-sacrificing sons of b's" (Copyright © 1967, Mark Twain Company).

19. Stewart, *Argonaut and Exile*, p. 223f.

The backbiting which broke out during the revision of the play was nothing new. It merely brought to a head resentment that had been building up for a number of years. The two men had been at odds earlier over delays in the writing and publication of Harte's novel *Gabriel Conroy* (1875), which was handled by Elisha Bliss and the American Publishing Company, in which Twain had an interest. In March, 1877, Harte wrote Twain a stinging letter implicating him in Bliss's poor sale of the novel, charging him with having obtained a financial advantage from Bliss for landing the book, and spurning Twain's incredible proposition of twenty-five dollars per week and board while they wrote another play together.[20] Although Harte and Twain jointly attended rehearsals of *Ah Sin* prior to its opening in Washington on May 7, 1877, contact between them had ceased somewhat before the play folded at the end of August. Recounting how their collaboration had proceeded, Twain was still as

20. DeVoto made brief mention of this letter and the break in relations (*MTE* 281, n. 6). Smith and Gibson deal more fully with both and quote Twain's reaction to the letter, written on the back of its last page: "I have read two pages of this ineffable idiocy—it is all I can stand of it" (*T-H* I 186). Miss Duckett produces the full text of this letter (*Mark Twain and Bret Harte*, pp. 134–37). Paine published only one letter from Twain to Harte, and it may well be the only one that survives (May 1, 1867, *Letters* I 124). In the Mark Twain Papers there are ten letters from Harte to Twain, running from April 1, 1872, to April 2, 1877. (All are published by Duckett, pp. 76f., 81, 84, 94f., 97, 98, 99, 124f., 134–37, 141f.) The last of them concerns a proposal for the production of *Ah Sin* with J. T. Ford in Washington, Baltimore, and Philadelphia, financial arrangements for the play, and their supervision of rehearsals. It has none of the testiness of the previous letter. All of the other letters are pleasant and friendly. In August, 1874, Harte told Twain of the fancy prices he was getting for his stories from the newspapers (six hundred dollars for "The Rose of Tuolumne"). He said it was good for the profession that he demanded those prices, and that Twain should do even better with his more popular fare. Having heard about the dramatization of *The Gilded Age*, Harte thought Twain might be getting a play on the boards before he did, and was happy for him. In another letter (December 16, 1876), Harte said that he was revising *Ah Sin*, heightening his own material and subduing Twain's and that they ought to take advice from their wives in the construction of women characters. The letter was written with obvious good feelings toward Twain and his wife. The next letter, the one of March 1, 1877, was the provocation for a flareup that could have come at any time; one is only surprised that they were not at one another's throats a good deal earlier.

generous in praising Harte's work (he had no talent for drama himself) as he was scathing in denouncing his character (*MTE* 277–79).

Up to this time the only piece of direct literary criticism Twain had added to his notes on *The Luck* filled an obvious gap in his examination of Harte's style. He pointed out its stuffiness as evidenced by circumlocution. Momentarily abashed at how, in spite of himself, he might use "three words where one would answer," Twain joked about becoming as "slovenly" as Charles Francis Adams if he didn't watch out, but at least felt assured, as he said, that "I never shall drop so far toward his and Bret Harte's level as to catch myself saying, 'It must have been wiser to have believed that he might have accomplished it if he could have felt that he would have been supported by those who should have &c., &c., &c.'" (*T-H* I 112).

It was in 1879, after the careful reading of a collection of Harte's short stories and a novelette, that Twain again attempted some extended criticisms of his writing. In the case of the stories, reported on in a letter to Howells, there was a recurrence of Twain's earlier vacillation, as he was at one moment lashing out at Harte's affectation, absurd dialect writing, and sentimentality, and at another finding occasional "evidence of genius." The collection of stories, *An Heiress of Red Dog and Other Tales*, contained much the same kind of Western tales that Twain had read in *The Luck*; and since fidelity to realism was what he praised in the earlier group, it would seem from his upbraiding Harte for his pretenses and his "struggle after the pathetic" that Twain was explicitly being turned this way and that by the fact that Harte's romantic defection made him an enemy from within the realist camp. That defection and Twain's criticism of it interestingly parallel the line of development in their typical themes: whereas with Twain thematic progression is from innocent romance to enlightening realism, with Harte it is from clear realism to cloudy romance. "What *mightn't* this ass accomplish," Twain asked, noticing on second reading a "decided brightness on every page" of *An Heiress*, "if he would do his work honestly & with pains?" If his comment on the stories did not amount to a great deal in itself, it did result in his volunteering, "I mean to weed out some of my prejudices & write an article on 'Bret

Harte as an Artist'—& print it if it will not be unfair to print it without signature" (*T-H* I 261f.).

Twain had unlimited opportunities and ideal circumstances under which to do the intended article, for from 1876 to 1881 (when Howells turned the editorship of the *Atlantic* over to Aldrich) he could have had almost carte blanche to write whatever he wanted to in the way of an anonymous critical essay for the Contributors' Club column. While he did, on Howells' request, furnish the first piece to appear in that column (on Anna Dickinson's return to the stage) and subsequently printed other critical notes there, it was not until June, 1880, that Twain alluded to Harte. However, instead of doing the job he had laid out for himself the year before, it seems that upon ridding himself of prejudice all he could muster was one irrelevant paragraph in an eleven-page article devoted to misplaced adverbs, tautology, and priggish heroines; and in that paragraph he cursorily lauded Harte for his true realism in the description of Western scenery and chided him for his false realism in reproducing a dialect that "no human being, living or dead, ever had experience of."[21]

From all that one can tell, an obstacle to Twain's publishing a full-scale criticism of Harte was that there was no way for him gracefully and naturally to bring his grumbling mask into play with a peer who was not publicly understood to be his foe. The humdrum paragraph in the *Atlantic* indicates that when inhibited Twain could write fairly tepid stuff. It simply was not possible for him to give the full treatment to a subject like Harte when he lacked the adrenaline of grumbling. As luck would have it, though, Twain had the chance to grumble at will, in what may have been preparation for the unwritten essay, in the margins of *The Twins of Table Mountain*. Although less subtle, his grumbling functioned there quite as well as it would had it been a public mask. Twain's discontent also made the grumbling more heated. Not only was he disgusted with Harte at about the time that he received a copy of *The Twins*, but he was also unhappy with himself, bogged down as he was by the writing of a travel book that would not move, haunted by self-doubt (he hadn't produced

21. "The Contributors' Club," *Atlantic Monthly*, XLV (June, 1880), 849–60.

a decent book in four years and feared he might be played out as a writer),[22] and hounded, on and off, by illness, money worries, inclement weather, and the detestable French. On Sunday, August 17, 1879, the day that the New York *Sun* published *The Twins* (through the good offices of Harte's friend Charles A. Dana), Twain was in England having another bad day. Bothered by arthritis, he had had to listen, through a cold and rainy morning, to an intolerable sermon: "Topic treated in the unpleasant, old fashion: Man a mighty bad child, God working at him in forty ways and having a world of trouble with him" (*Biog* II 647). It is likely that *The Twins* had been released a day or two earlier (to secure British copyright) by Chatto and Windus, Twain's publisher, who sent him a copy, as they recently had of *An Heiress of Red Dog and Other Tales*.

Harte, who was feeling rather poorly himself,[23] had obligingly written a thoroughly bad story. It must have been catnip to Twain, considering the ferocious mood he was in. Alongside *The Twins of Table Mountain*, even the poorly plotted *Gabriel Conroy* and *Two Men of Sandy Bar* (the play) seem forgivable failures. The story is about orphaned twins, Randolph and Rutherford (Ruth for short) Pinckney, who live in a cabin on the top of Table Mountain, where they have spent some three years prospecting unsuccessfully for gold.[24] As the tale opens, Rand is returning from the valley, which he scorns as the source of immoral influence. His fears that his brother may be in love with Mornie Nixon, daughter of a notorious drunkard, are well founded, for she is already pregnant when she tries to make her way up to the cabin and is rescued by Rand from a trail that is crumbling away. Ruth, meanwhile, thinking Mornie to be in Sacramento, is off looking for her there. Members of a theatrical

---

22. See Blair, *Mark Twain & Huck Finn*, Chapter 11. Twain had in passing voiced the same despair in the letter in which he had complained of Harte's appointment to the consulship in Crefeld, Germany (*T-H* I 236).
23. *The Letters of Bret Harte*, ed. Geoffrey Bret Harte (New York, 1926), p. 154.
24. Table Mountain is in the vicinity of Jamestown in Tuolumne County, just below the Calaveras County border, which is the Stanislaus River, and two and a half miles south of Jackass Hill, where the Gillis boys had their cabin and were at different times hosts to both Harte and Twain.

troupe to which Mornie once belonged arrive to help care for mother and child, and one of the actresses, Euphemia, flirts with Rand and gets him to rescue *her* from the crumbling trail. On Ruth's return he faces a brother who wishes him to renounce Mornie and the child, as well as a group of hostile townspeople headed by the girl's father. After further complications, the doctor attending Mornie pacifies the townspeople and helps to reconcile the various hostile parties. Ruth is united with the mother and child, but Rand loses Euphemia to an actor she had vowed to marry.

In all, Twain made fifty-eight distinct comments on *The Twins*, including a few self-explanatory underscorings. Many of these comments are on realism, dialect, motivation, and related questions, and are in that respect similar to those he had made on *The Luck.* However, this time all of the comments are critical, and there is a needling, satiric innuendo in most of them. Thus, at the innocuous announcement of an evening rehearsal at Table Mountain by the theatrical troupe, Twain gibes, "Imagine it" (47).[25] Of greatest annoyance to Twain were the catchpenny tricks that Harte invented to vary the real with the romantic. The worst of these was his use of alternate blanching and blushing as a means of externalizing emotion. In the course of picking out eight such changes of color,[26] Twain exposed a repetitiveness that destroyed the sincerity of the emotions Harte was trying to portray. And it was not that he had hit upon a mere oddity. Rechecking brings out yet other instances and confirms the suspicion that Harte relied almost exclusively on blanching and blushing to indicate deep or sudden shifts of feeling, while a spot check of other stories turns up enough specimens of the device to

25. All page references are to the first edition of *The Twins of Table Mountain* (London: Chatto and Windus, [1879]), a paperbound issue, which was the one in which Twain made his marginal notes. Each of the unpublished notes cited in this chapter is copyrighted (Copyright © 1967) by the Mark Twain Company.

26. These occur on pp. 38, 39, 70, 86, 91, and 96, with 96 having two separate underscorings and a comment on a third instance of coloring. At least four other such instances of coloring can be located in *The Twins*. A more easily available text than the first edition is that of the second American issue of the story in *Condensed Novels and Stories* (Boston, 1882), and in this text the page numbers are 212, 225, 227, and 230.

suggest the facility with which Harte resorted to it.[27] In *The Twins*, specifically, Twain at first wondered why Rand would inexplicably lose his color on being taken for his brother and then just as inexplicably recover it in the ensuing confusion ("Why did he blanch before & why does he blush, now?" [39]). But when Harte had Rand's cheeks fire up in sympathy with Euphemia's blushing and described it as "so utterly unexpected of him," Twain objected, "Why this person is *always* blushing" (86); and a reasonably observant reader would have seen by then that he *was* a completely indiscriminate blusher. Before Twain is finished with it, coloration becomes the opposite of what it was supposed to be; it becomes farcical. Next to a passage in which Rand sank on a rock, buried his face in his hands, and then "rose, wiped his hot eyelids, and staggered toward the cabin" (because he had been warned not to mistreat Mornie), Twain wrote in the margin, "A very sentimental person & much given to blanching, blushing, & crying. Also 'staggering'" (70). At another point, as the thought that the girl may not recover brings Rand "trembling to his feet," after having twice changed color, Twain acidly inquired, "Did he blush—or turn pale?" and added, "Did he think it was his business to nurse the woman?" (96).

Too much of the story revolves around Rand. His romantic moralism is not just overdrawn, it is maudlin and inconsistent. Yet Harte insisted that his actions were realistic, in fact, "natural." Twain was abashed. After such a shy and puritanical

---

27. I have checked on coloration in the twenty-three stories in *Tales of the Argonauts* (Riverside ed.; Boston, 1907), II, and have found that whether a person was surprised, embarrassed, guilty, injured, angry, in love, perplexed, or delighted, blushing and blanching were about the only methods Harte used to represent their feelings. The only other symptoms were moist or glistening eyes, and those often accompanied crimson faces. The most grotesque instance of pigmentation was the following: "Peg's face on one side turned a deep magenta color, on the other a lighter cherry, while her nose was purple, and her forehead an Indian red" (p. 284). She was embarrassed. To boot, Harte had earlier given this girl freckles, pale blue eyes, a large mouth, and irregular teeth. In total the volume contains thirty-three instances of coloration, found on pp. 10, 20, 91, 122, 132, 145, 155, 172, 173 (2), 175, 176, 181, 182, 183, 188, 218, 221, 232, 233, 235, 256, 275, 285, 291, 293, 310, 331 (2), 346, 400, 416, and 417.

boy had placed "his large hand" on the shoulder of a girl he had just met, Twain read in disbelief that Rand was "a perfectly natural man," and wrote in mock agreement, "Very 'natural' man" (30); and at Harte's calling him "young and inexperienced," he scoffed, "He is young & inexperienced, but puts his paw on a strange girl's shoulder." Harte botched the whole scene. As the girl "instantly stepped back a single pace and drew her left foot slowly and deliberately after her" *before* lifting and dropping "the daring hand" "in mid air," Twain glumly demanded, "What became of his hand while she was stepping back a pace? Did it remain?" (*ibid.*). Once Euphemia had awakened a spark of romance in the boy, formerly an unapproachable prig, he suddenly had his arm "around her waist, and his astonished, alarmed face within a few inches of her own," at which Twain threw up his hands: "One never knows what this nondescript will do next—except that it will be something foreign to human nature" (88).

Throughout, Harte was trying to show the awkwardness and emotional instability of the boy, but, ironically, he made the mistake of trying to render his actions real by overloading them with supposedly "realistic" details. Hence the romanticism of technique Twain complained about. Harte did this again and again. When he brought Ruth back from Sacramento with a "bent figure" and "stooping shoulders and [a] haggard face," Twain simply observed, "This is a boy—Twin to the other boy" (111). To Rand's conjecture that his brother was likely "haggard, weary and footsore, on his hopeless quest, wandering in lonely trails and lonelier settlements," Twain rejoined, "He could walk from Table Mountain to Sacramento in two days & follow a broad & frequented public road" (82).[28] In the ending, Harte worked too hard for the effect of verisimilitude and failed to bring off an old sentimental trick—the fusing of Mornie's dream of her lover's return with his actual appearance. Amidst the unsubtle confusion Twain asked impatiently, "Where does the 'dream' leave off & the reality begin?" (120f.).

28. There was also a main stagecoach route in the vicinity. Flagrant errors of fact and geography were not uncommon with Harte. Stewart points out several obvious examples (*Argonaut and Exile*, pp. 50, 223, 304).

And so it went, with one situation after the other. When Harte tried to write dialect, he was so unsure of himself and so intent on being realistic that he made a character's initial speeches dialectal beyond recognition, and then, unable to sustain the subterfuge, virtually dispensed with dialect altogether in succeeding speeches. After noting repeated difficulties of this kind, Twain scored the worst example of it in the speech of a bartender. At first, Harte had him saying things like, "I'd like to ask ye how ling ye kalkilate to hang around," and "Ole Nixon has been cavoortin' 'round yer. .... Sabe? Now let me ax ye two questions" —at which point Twain declared, "No man ever used a dialect like that—it resembles the speech of no tribe, extant or extinct" (108). Then, at the conclusion of the story, the bartender says, "Gentlemen, call for what you like: the Mansion House treats to-day in honour of its being the first time that Rand Pinckney has been admitted to the Bar," whereupon Twain grumbled, "Even *this* creature has dropped his dialect" (120).

As before, Twain was annoyed by Harte's carelessness in the handling of physical relationships. Some of this criticism was mere nit-picking. But most of it dealt with the focal issue of sensory credibility, and specifically with imaging, which was the most cogently aesthetic standard to be invoked by a realistic criticism. Could one visualize this act, Twain asked, hear this speech, experience this movement, or feel what these characters felt? Such questions emphasized that the shabbiest thing Harte could have done was to romanticize realism, which he did intentionally by his sentimentality and unintentionally by trying to out-realize realism. This troweled-on realism of Harte's had survived criticism because the non-Western reader was a fairly soft touch for it, especially, as will be noted, if he happened to be an Eastern or a British reviewer. The strangest part of it all was that in *The Twins* Harte for once should not have had to worry about authenticity. His setting was the same general area in which, in 1855, he had spent all of his seven months in the diggings. Thus it is a sobering commentary on Harte's well-advertised knack for treating the real that familiarity should have proved to be his undoing. It made him reckless and pretentious. These qualities Twain noticed in three major episodes, and his comments on them were the kind that only a really observant fellow Westerner and former resident of the Table Mountain area could have provided.

Of the three episodes, two—the fantastic rescues along the cliff's edge—are the most exciting in the book, while the other is supposed to contribute to local color. The un-localized local color stems from a whim of sentiment. A desire for moral detachment from the settlement below makes the boys locate themselves on the top of the mountain and do their work there. However, this requires an impossible mining procedure. For one thing, the "cement," which Harte correctly defined in a footnote as "the local name for gold-bearing alluvial drift [in] the bed of a prehistoric river" buried in the mountain, had been fairly well exhausted by 1868, the time of the story. None the less, instead of having his boys try pocket mining or one of the abandoned tunnels in the side of Table Mountain, Harte had them attempt what not even the mining companies, with all of their expensive machinery, would have attempted—that is, to sink a vertical shaft in the top of a mountain that was about 400 feet above the "pay gravel," and that was capped by some 140 feet of solid latite!

Twain was troubled by a certain vagueness in the description of the mining. When he read that Rand "had attacked the walls on either side of the lateral 'drift' skillfully, so as to expose their quality without destroying their cohesive integrity," he underscored "on either side" and noted, "Truly this is a wise miner" (24), his point being that it was only from the straight end, rather than the sides, that Rand could expect to hit anything really new. There was no mention of tools in this digging, and no specific depth was given to the shaft on which the twins had been working for three years, though it had a ladder in it. Hearing voices, Rand came up the ladder a dozen steps and, "seizing the rope that hung idly from the windlass, he half climbed, half swung himself to the surface." Twain was annoyed to find that he would thereafter continue to hang onto the rope—"Why—& how?"—once he was standing and could move about on the surface. (Being captivated by Euphemia, Rand held onto the rope for almost all of their four-page conversation, which also annoyed Twain.) Having had his fill, Twain opened up on the entire situation, and particularly on the mining: "A ladder in a shaft which is so deep as to be dark? . . . —& a windlass, too? What kind of mining *is* this? And do they [naturally] climb the rope of the latter?" (25).[29]

Harte did not know his ropes in the mining district and he did not know rope—which fouled his first rescue episode. Rand, it seems, came down an "almost perpendicular 'slide'" to reach the pregnant girl on the crumbling trail, and, fastening one end of a rope to "a jutting splinter of granite," he began to "'lay out,' and work his way laterally along the face of the mountain." Twain was particularly skeptical of the utility of a rope in that lateral movement: "How in the world could the rope assist him in such a performance?" Harte next had him pass the rope around the girl's waist and half-lift, half-swing her "from her feet," while both of them moved backwards and downwards away from the jutting point to which the rope remained tied and towards the place where she had left the regular trail. Perplexed by the function of the rope, which could only exert an increasingly adverse pendulum effect on their lateral movement, Twain further remarked, "This is a queer way to use a rope. The rope was worse than useless, it was an incumbrance" (52). Also, finding it absurd for Mornie to be made to "lean against" a sheer cliff "for support" during their ascent, Twain ironically noted, "She probably found it efficient" (53). The rescue was concluded on an appropriately sentimental note, and, as Twain pointed out, Harte was not above using a bit of contortion to achieve it: Mornie's hair lies "caressingly" across Rand's "breast and hands," but at least one of his hands is in no position to be touched by the hair of a girl he is half-carrying and half-supporting.

The second rescue was even more phenomenal. Upon hearing Rand's account of the first, Euphemia sets out for the dangerous trail herself, with the protesting Rand following "mechanically":

> Once or twice the trail crumbled beneath her feet, but she clung to a projecting root of *chapparal*, and laughed. She had almost reached her elected goal when, slipping, the treacherous chapparal she clung to yielded in her grasp, and Rand, with a

---

29. There was a line through the word "naturally."

cry, sprung [sic] forward. But the next instant she quickly trans-
ferred her hold to a cleft in the cliff and was safe. Not so her
companion. The soil beneath him, loosened by the impulse of
his spring, slipped away; he was falling with it, when she caught
him sharply with her disengaged hand, and together they
scrambled to a more secure footing.

Underlining the last part of this passage, Twain wrote, "This is
more than marvelous—it is impossible" (93). Euphemia pointed
out "significantly" that they had been saved "*without a rope*"
[Harte's italics], to which Twain added, "Just so!" (*ibid.*).

V

From his distrust of Harte's realism, it may be inferred that
Twain could conversely be as captivated by "the real" as Henry
James was in the late 1870's, when he called it "the most satisfying thing in the world."[30] Whether Harte was a man to share
their satisfaction is another matter. Assuredly, by 1879 he was
no longer the Promethean realist he had seemed to be just nine
years earlier. Yet he was always vain of his realism, and the less
secure he was about it, the more vain he became. His reputation
rested upon it. In 1872, for example, after his disappointing year
with the *Atlantic*, he had lectured Howells about taking editorial
liberties with a poem of his, "Conception de Arguello," saying,
"I want you to accept my facts without fear and without re-
proach. I am careless in *composition* at times, but I am *never*
careless with my facts, general outlines, details or color."[31] In
the main, critics were no help to Harte, for they generally did
accept what he implied he was doing as a realist. It has been
remarked that since there was no one in the East competent to
say whether Harte's stories ran true to life or not, critics were
for the most part simply taking Harte's word for it.[32] Some
Eastern critics actually encouraged the artificial in Harte by
preferring his style of realism because, gentleman that he was,
he could be entrusted not to soil the page with anything that was

30. *French Poets and Novelists* (London, 1884), p. 202.
31. Bradford A. Booth, "Bret Harte Goes East: Some Unpublished Letters,"
    AL, XIX (January, 1948), 329.
32. G. Harrison Orians, *A Short History of American Literature* (New York,
    1940), p. 199f.

really disreputable. He suited Boston to a "T": he did not abuse his license as his imitators did, "with a nauseating realism, unredeemed by the genuine humor and sentiment which had saved it in his case from vulgarity."[33]

Harte pressed the matter of genuineness with sufficient presumption to make it stick. The first purportedly "searching, adverse criticism" of his works,[34] by E. S. Nadal in 1877, contained fulsome praise of just the type of realistic effects Twain had seen him distort. Despite faulty characterization, melodrama, and a journalistic style, Harte remained, in Nadal's view, a "marked genius." It was as if he and Twain had not read the same writer. Nadal said, "the gifts of Bret Harte are vivid imagination, color, dramatic dialogue, power to attract and power to entertain, a good sense of nature, a lively and daring humor, and considerable keenness of perception. His power of dialogue is surpassed by no living writer. The similitude of the talk of his characters to real speech is apparent in all his books."[35] Even in one of the more truly critical evaluations of Harte, made possible by the first collected edition of his works, it was still felt that, whatever the overlay of sentiment and the lapses in realism, Harte "used his material at first hand, and . . . relied confidently upon his own observation and knowledge." This, by the way, was the opinion of the reviewer in the *Atlantic*, who was fully aware of Harte's having romanticized California life and who had perceived that "while separate incidents have often a vivid native realism, the web of the stories is woven upon a loom which is hopelessly foreign from the author's invention."[36] Apparently, the further east one got, the more convinced critics were that Harte's realism was wholly reliable, and the more prone they were to believe that he always based himself on firsthand experience. An English reviewer was positive that "Bret Harte wrote of things he had seen, of men he had known; wrote, as is so rarely done, of what he had felt or experienced. . . . With a keen eye, a searching scrutiny, he seizes and retains every feature, every

33. *Harper's*, XLII (April, 1871), 777.
34. Stewart's phrase (*Argonaut and Exile*, p. 238).
35. *North American Review*, CXXIV (January, 1877), 81, 85.
36. "Harte's Sketches and Stories," *Atlantic Monthly*, L (August, 1882), 264, 266.

salient tone of the story he relates; he paints the *mise en scene* in short but powerful and graphic sketches. . . ." Furthermore, his characters "always remain faithful to their nature and individuality."[37]

There would appear to be some understatement in the contention that "criticism in the seventies, groping for clear principles found itself hesitant, self-conscious, provincial and timid."[38] How great the need was for someone to discuss Bret Harte with a little boldness of spirit could not be better illustrated than by the unbelievable gullibility of the major British and American reviews of *The Twins of Table Mountain*, in the London *Athenaeum* and *Scribner's Monthly Magazine*, respectively. The reviewer for the *Athenaeum* was for the most part content to relate the plot and in his one critical statement to say, "There is some pretty coquetry on the part of a young lady called the 'Marysville Pet' [Euphemia], and the two or three scenes which the story contains are described with Mr. Bret Harte's usual terse vigour."[39] The editors of *Scribner's*, which had serialized *Gabriel Conroy*, retained a generally good opinion of Harte. The magazine had published other items by Harte, among them "The Great Deadwood Mystery," which appeared with *The Twins* and three other stories in the Houghton-Osgood book under review in January, 1880 (possibly by Richard Watson Gilder, chief editorial assistant to Josiah G. Holland). The reviewer cared less for "A Legend of Sammstadt" than for the other stories in the collection, which were set in Harte's "old ground." There, "Mr. Harte is at times quite as strong as ever. Who else can give the startling contrasts of Western life so resolutely, so pitilessly? And who can work so well the pathetic and noble vein, at the same time, in the ignoble block?" "The Great Deadwood Mystery" is not as good as it might have been, the reviewer holds. "But," he goes on,

37. *Potter's American Monthly*, XVII (October, 1881), 306.
38. Robert P. Falk, "The Rise of Realism 1871–1891," in *Transitions in American Literary History*, ed. Harry Hayden Clark (Durham, N.C., 1953), p. 400.
39. "Novels of the Week," *The Athenaeum*, No. 2706 (September 6, 1879), 302.

in "The Twins of Table Mountain," Mr. Harte strikes again the full note of his genius. Whether it be plot, characterization or description of Western landscape, each part is admirable. This story alone would be enough to make a reputation: the author is entirely himself; there is no trace of Dickens, Hawthorne, or any other writer; it is marred by no strained, foreign, or hackneyed words; the scene is novel, the humor fine, the pathos exquisite; short story though it be, it is an honor to American Literature.[40]

No need now to ask where was Twain when American realism had had such need of him, and particularly of his criticism of Harte. He did not read enough criticism to know that; for he considered himself a writer and not a critic. Suffice it to observe that he not only pinpointed the vagaries of Harte's spurious realism and showed where and how it went wrong, but he also explained why it went wrong. In the course of developing a thesis about his own conduct in writing ("I confine myself to life with which I am familiar when pretending to portray life"), Twain reported: "I've been a prospector, and know pay rock from poor when I find it—just with a touch of the tongue. And I've been a *silver* miner and know how to dig and shovel and drill and put in a blast. And so I know the mines and the miners interiorly as well as Bret Harte knows them exteriorly" (*Biog* II 915f.). Harte had never really tasted any pay rock, and had never sweated over a shovel and gotten dirty or become one of the boys, as Twain had. He had never known frontier experience as a participant, and so could not treat it *inside*, as Thoreau would have said. Harte was an imposter, the kind that, as Wallace Stegner has noted, the hobos call a "scenery stiff."[41] The distinction between observation that has been lived and has gone into the writer's blood and observation that has been the result of looking on is one of the major insights Twain was to provide, in speaking of Harte for posterity in his final and inimitably grumbling comments on him:

> It was at Yreka and Jackass Gulch that Harte learned to accurately observe and put with photographic exactness on paper

---

40. *Scribner's Monthly*, XIX (January, 1880), 473f.
41. "Western Record and Romance," in *The Literary History of the United States*, ed. Robert E. Spiller *et al.* (rev. ed.; New York, 1953), p. 867.

the woodland scenery of California and the general country aspects . . . and it was also in these places that he learned, without the trouble of observing, all that he didn't know about mining, and how to make it read as if an expert were behind the pen. It was in those places that he also learned how to fascinate Europe and America with the quaint dialect of the miner—a dialect which no man in heaven or earth had ever used until Harte invented it. With Harte it died, but it was no loss. (*MTE* 262f.)

I have examined in this section the various components of Twain's grumbling; its being, among other things, a dramatic form, an expression of anti-conventionalism, a burst of comic zest, a technique of subtlety and emphasis, a source of insight and enlightening candor, as well as an ax-grinding, realistic criticism. The qualities this criticism markedly lacks and that it should have, in order to be as generally relevant for *criticism* as it is significant in form and meaning, are—to put the matter in its simplest terms—a sense of time, of comparative relationships, and above all a philosophic dimension, if that is not too solemn a phrase for it. Clearly, much of Twain's criticism seems intelligent without having much intellectual heft to it. However, from all that one can gather, Twain avoided the intellectual on principle. That was an attribute of his Americanness, one might say; and what Tocqueville sagely concluded to be the inherent "philosophical method of the [unphilosophical] Americans" was a concerted resolve "to seek the reason of things for oneself, and in oneself alone; to tend to results without being bound to means, and to strike through the form to the substance."[42] A critic with the American mind of Mark Twain can, in this respect, be more basically intellectual than one who has been trained in traditional philosophic method. There is, at any rate, more of the intellectual in Twain's appreciative criticism than in his other criticism. For what he considered one of the highest literary arts was that of vivifying history, of evoking what was essentially and universally Life in the flux of time. Toward that intellectual art, realism of the sort discussed in this chapter was an intelligent stepping stone.

42. Alexis De Tocqueville, *Democracy in America*, ed. Phillips Bradley, trans. Henry Reeve, rev. Francis Bowen (Vintage ed.; New York, 1955), II, 3.

PART III

Twain's Appreciative Criticism: From History into Life

You soon realize that India is not beautiful; still there is an enchantment about it that is beguiling, and which does not pall. You cannot tell just what it is that makes the spell, perhaps, but you feel it and confess it, nevertheless. Of course, at bottom, you know in a vague way that it is history; *it is that that affects you, a haunting sense of the myriads of human lives that have blossomed, and withered, and perished here, repeating and repeating and repeating, century after century, and age after age, the barren and meaningless process; it is this sense that gives to this forlorn, uncomely land power to speak to the spirit and make friends with it; to speak to it with a voice bitter with satire, but eloquent with melancholy. The deserts of Australia and the ice-barrens of Greenland have no speech, for they have no venerable history; with nothing to tell of man and his vanities, his fleeting glories and his miseries, they have nothing wherewith to spiritualize their ugliness and veil it with a charm.*

(FE *II 153*.)

11

Macaulay: Living History by Antitheses

Twain's addiction for strong-arm criticism did not dull the sensitive, appreciative side of his nature. On the contrary, a good case can be made for its having been enlivened by that criticism. It was, after all, *because* he was so negatively exacting that his praise hovered just short of the lyrical when he saw how steadily lucid, precise, and alive with images Howells' descriptive prose could be. Plainly, he was able to admire with the same passion that he hated. This is not to say that appreciation made him less critical—Macaulay, for example, was invoked in contraposition to Goldsmith—but rather that being hard to please increased his readiness to embrace the rare real thing. There was, of course, as I have pointed out earlier, much greatness (such as James's) to which he was crassly immune, and there were some minor lights upon whom his enthusiasm was wasted. However, Twain's admiration can by and large be trusted when it is not wholly detached from the hardheadedness of his grumbling, the habit of which, if anything, made him sharper than he might otherwise have been, more selective, and more prone to judge by lasting standards.

Another contribution of his experience as grumbler was that he did not hesitate to applaud writers who were experimenting with novelty of form and idea, as were, in their several ways, Edgar Watson Howe, Émile Zola, and Adolph Wilbrandt. On reading *The Story of a Country Town*, he was impressed by the attained sense of life, and only wished Howe had more faithfully persevered in his endeavor to portray the unchronicled realities of small-town America. In the case of Zola, whose sordidness had stung the small, dark prude in him—and battened the Franco-phobe—Twain made the new a test of his own prejudices, and confessed that Zola's dim view of human nature illuminated and catalyzed certain of his repressions. With Wilbrandt's play, *Der Meister von Palmyra*, he entered so completely into the telescopic presentation of history that the curiously mystic and pessimistic lesson it adduced became a palpable symbol energized by the novelty of discovered knowledge. An interesting consequence of the revelation of *Meister*, with its deflation of pride and hope of progress, was that in discussing the play Twain's thinking seemed to gyrate from radical rebellion to a traditionalist despair that change could accomplish anything: an evil fate was the one certainty, stoicism the one course of honor.

The racking depression Twain had suffered in the aftermath of going broke and losing his dearest daughter had predisposed him to glorify Wilbrandt's paradigm of history. It was under the spell of the same general depression that in 1896, a few years before he saw the play, he wrote one of his infrequent tributes to a member of the Victorian establishment, Thomas Babington, Lord Macaulay, whom people by the end of the century were beginning to consider parochial, mannered, and old-fashioned. Wilbrandt's was generalized, ideal history. Macaulay's was real. It was drenched with the sights and smells and common sense of diurnal reality. Yet Macaulay, no less than Wilbrandt, gave Twain intimations of timelessness with which to shore up his intellectual defenses against the ravages of time. This meant a great deal to Twain, and, as with Howells, he was induced to eulogize Macaulay because he thought he was insufficiently esteemed.

Among the qualities that pleased Twain most, the realization of history as life stood highest. It is with variations on that achievement, as seen in certain works of Macaulay, Howells, Howe, Zola, and Wilbrandt, that this section of Twain's appreciative criticism will be concerned. Since his evaluations of Macaulay, Howe, and Zola were private, there was no reason for him to work obliquely through a critical persona. Similarly, as appreciation, by its very nature, needs no protective point of view, the persona was also proportionately less perceptible in his public approbation of Howells and Wilbrandt.

II

If there was one writer Twain would rather have been other than himself, I believe it would have been Macaulay. He read and reread him early and late, in season and out, and never tired of what he called the "glittering pageantry" of his prose.[1] "Macaulay is present," Twain observed, "when we follow the march of his stately sentences" (*IA* II 245). When George OttoTrevelyan's *Life and Letters of Lord Macaulay* appeared in 1876, Twain discussed it before his Saturday Morning Club in Hartford. He quoted liberally from Macaulay's essay on Bacon in "Is Shakespeare Dead?" in an attempt to show that Bacon was qualified to have written the plays, and he alluded to "Horatius at the Bridge" in *A Connecticut Yankee* (314). Particular favorites were Macaulay's *History of England* and the essays on Warren Hastings and Robert Clive. He used a passage from the essay on Hastings in *Following the Equator* and commended the *History* in the journal from which he wrote that book. It is quite possible that Twain's tributes to British colonial rule in *FE*, in some ways his most anti-imperialist, anti-occidental, and at times anti-British book, may owe something to his acquaintance with Macaulay's idea that England had brought order, justice, education, and, in short, the true fruits of civilization to a barbarous and chaotic India—a judgment backed by Macaulay's own laudable service there. Perhaps the best demonstration of the kind of appeal Macaulay had for Twain is to be inferred from his having come under Macaulay's influence, both aesthetically and philosophically. A reading of the essays on Hastings and Clive inspired him to write a lyric and symbolic poem (no small feat for Twain). In addition, all three of Twain's historical novels, *The Prince and the Pauper*, *A Connecticut Yankee*, and *Joan of Arc*, were composed on the Macaulayan theory that history should provide an imaginative vivification of the past. With reference to *A Connecticut Yankee*, he said, "I am only after the *life* of that day, that is all: to picture it; to try to get into it; to see how it feels & seems" (*MTMF* 258). Or, as he remarked about *The Prince and the Pauper*, "my idea is to afford a realizing sense

---

1. Dixon Wecter, "The Love Letters of Mark Twain," *Atlantic Monthly*, CLXXX (November, 1947), 38.

of the exceeding severity of the laws of that day by inflicting some of their penalties upon the king himself" (*T-H* I 291). He was trying, as Macaulay had, to offset the idealization and sentimentality of the historical romances, with which nineteenth-century historians felt themselves to be in competition. While working on *Joan*, for example, he at one point "tore up the fragment of history" he had written because it "sounded too much like a romance."[2] In *A Connecticut Yankee*, he specifically relied on the Whiggish concept of progress, which Macaulay had done so much to popularize, and on a moral interpretation of history which William Hartpole Lecky had directly inherited from Macaulay. There was a like equivalence in method, for in noting how he wanted to deal with history in the *Yankee*, Twain asserted that his main object (like Macaulay's) had been to present a "*contrast*"; modern times being a commentary on ancient times, with the "juxtaposition emphasiz[ing] the salients of both" (*MTMF* 257f.).

All told, one would be hard put to find another writer who suited Twain more completely than Macaulay did. Merely to list some of the peculiar virtues and vices generally ascribed to Macaulay is to draw up a profile of Twain's literary alter ego. Macaulay has been called a common-sense moralist and the very personification of Whiggery; a Philistine and hater of art (the prince of Philistines, according to Arnold), a man without sensibility, and, some believed, without spiritual idealism or refined sentiments either (Carlyle, as might be expected, said he lacked "vision"); an opinionated observer, a good hater, a fluent talker, a feared disputant, and expert at vituperation; a lover of details with a gift for graphic description, an excellent raconteur, the master of a lucid style having the flavor and ease of speech; an enemy of romance and theoretical philosophy; a writer who preferred experience to abstraction and scorned the speculative mind; a political liberal, an advocate of the cult of progress, a rationalist, a man of incurable prejudices; a partisan historian, who took no great trouble to conceal his opinions, who wrote history as if it were fiction, and who loved facts and was guilty of much inaccuracy in their use; and an imaginative literary

2. Unpublished Notebook No. 27 (March, 1893–July, 1894), 26 (Copyright © 1967, Mark Twain Company).

critic who gave a lively impression of the writers he described, but did not much like writing criticism.

No doubt Twain was, before the turn of the century, as enchanted as any other "liberal" might have been with the informing thesis of the *History of England*, which, if it did not quite show, as charged, that God was on the side of the Whigs, had at least succeeded in tracing all of the blessings of nineteenth-century life back to the Glorious Revolution and its Lockean innovations. Moreover, in a manuscript in which he tried to work out the "laws" of history, Twain took up a doctrine that had been acted on by Macaulay, as well as Carlyle: the doctrine that, in Twain's words, "to write a minute history of persons of all grades and callings, is the surest way to convey the intelligible history of the time."[3]

But the key *artistic* interest Macaulay had for Twain lay in his genius for transforming history into life, a gift which he thought had also empowered Howells to write an expressive description of Venice. Few of Twain's experiences were so aesthetically satisfying as those in which he felt himself to be pervaded by the restored past, teeming with its former life and color. Realism in this exalted sense (over and above authenticity of details and the faithful representation of experience) had no higher calling for either Twain or Macaulay. Its importance in the total breadth of Twain's concept of realism, which, as we have seen, could otherwise be rather narrow, has never really been appreciated.[4] Something of his feeling for the higher, Macaulayan

3. "Book Two, Eddypus," 10, *MTP* (cited by Roger B. Salomon, *Twain and the Image of History* [New Haven, Conn., 1961], p. 21).

4. It would be well to keep in mind that the broader view of realism that Twain appreciated for itself and in Macaulay's work co-existed with his appreciation for the lesser aspects of realism, and that it was by no means a new-found interest with him. Apparently, it was influential in making his own past available to him for the uses of fiction. Reminiscences stirred by a letter from Will Bowen in 1870 put the Hannibal years before him as the embryonic basis of the world of Huck and Tom. "The fountains" of his "great deep" having been "broken up," he said:

> The old life has swept before me like a panorama; the old days have trooped by in their old glory again; the old faces have looked out of the mists of the past; old footsteps have sounded in my listening ears; old hands have clasped mine; old voices have greeted me, & the songs I loved ages & ages ago have come wailing down the centuries! Heavens what eternities have swung their hoary cycles about us since those days were new! (*Letters to Will Bowen*, p. 17.)

realism of historical realization Twain projected in the meditative passages of *Following the Equator*. As he tried, for example, to account for the inscrutable fascination of India, in a period when he was more often morose than not, Twain alluded to a consciousness that the very pulsations of living history were all around him, that if India could not be called beautiful, it could cast a beguiling spell which one felt to be *"history"*:

> it is that that affects you, a haunting sense of the myriads of human lives that have blossomed, and withered, and perished here, repeating and repeating and repeating, century after century, and age after age, the barren and meaningless process; it is this sense that gives to this forlorn, uncomely land power to speak to the spirit and make friends with it; to speak to it with a voice bitter with satire, but eloquent with melancholy. (II 153.)

Transcending Twain's intuition here is the state of mind which induced it—i.e., his attitude towards history—and its ultimate source. This attitude, whether or not he was fully aware of it at this point, as he was at others, harks back directly to the most significant change in nineteenth-century historiography, which is none other than the change inaugurated by Macaulay. For it was in opposition to the method of classical eighteenth-century historians like Hume and Gibbon, who wanted to define broad historical movements, chart political changes, and characterize the tone and *Weltanschauung* of an age, that Macaulay both advocated and wrote a new imaginative history, where the emphasis fell on social history, the routine of daily life, and the interaction of the personalities of influential men. Above all, the Macaulayan method, as exemplified by Twain, produced a sensory awareness of the passage of man through time and of the particular things he touched and that touched him en route. In this way did the technical realism of details serve the larger realism at work in the recreation of history.

III

Macaulay's concept of history and his reputation should be pursued a little further before we take fuller note of Twain's enthusiasm for him, because Macaulay saw his own historical method as the historians' hope for reclaiming a lost province that

232

had been taken over by such brilliant usurpers as Sir Walter Scott. In this context, what Twain's separate remarks about Macaulay and Scott signify is that the former's history became the reagent of the latter's historical romances.

The Macaulayan concept of history as set forth in his essay on "History" (1828) is that it "begins in novel and ends in essay." Since it comes "under the jurisdiction of two hostile powers"—"the Reason and the Imagination"—instead of being shared between them, it has alternately fallen under "the sole and absolute dominion" of one or the other and consequently has sometimes been "fiction" and sometimes "theory." The fault of "modern" histories, he held, is that they tended to be dryly factual, and too general and theoretical. What ensued in his own times, Macaulay argued, was that the dominantly imaginative and, to his way of thinking, the superior species of history was falling by default into the hands of rank amateurs—the writers of historical romances. The example of Scott had become well-nigh overpowering: "Sir Walter Scott . . . has used those fragments of truth historians have scornfully thrown behind them in a manner which may well excite their envy." It is therefore necessary for "a truly great historian" to "reclaim those materials which the novelist has appropriated." Indeed, just prior to this statement, he had put the case more strongly: the historian should give "to truth those attractions which have been *usurped* by fiction."[5]

When he came to write his *History of England from the Accession of James II* many years later (the first volume appeared in 1848 and the last in 1861), Macaulay avowed that his aim had been "to write a history so popular in its appeal that it would supersede the latest novel on the tables of young ladies. . . ." And so vast was its success that that is just about what his

---

5. My italics. "History," *Critical and Historical Essays* (Boston, 1900), I, 235f., 272–78, 281f. The *Critical and Historical Essays* are in six volumes (X–XVI) of *The Complete Writings of Lord Macaulay*, in the Houghton, Mifflin Standard Library edition (Boston, 1900). In all references to the *Essays*, I use the symbol *CHE* and the subnumeration I to VI. The famous essay "History" was a review of Henry Neele's book, *The Romance of History*. Views similar to those here cited were set forth in Macaulay's review in the same year (1828) of Hallam's *Constitutional History* (*CHE* I 285ff.).

History did.[6] Although Macaulay never completely lost his large popular following, romantic critics with strong theoretical leanings—as, for example, Poe, Carlyle, and Emerson—were generally dismayed by his materialism and superficiality, finding him optimistic for the wrong reasons;[7] whereas after the 1860's there was a gradual waning in his once-dazzling popularity. Meanwhile, his slight favor among literary critics and the advent of a new breed of "scientific" historians led to an increasing scorn of his method, or rather of his seeming lack of a correct one.[8] A definite trend against Macaulay was discernible in the 1880's. Historians saw him as an example of how not to write history, and genteel critics objected that he could not comprehend "piety of mind."[9]

The decline in Macaulay's reputation was one factor behind Twain's defending him in the notebook diary he used for writing *Following the Equator*. Another factor was the specifically pietistic disapproval of Macaulay, an attitude which may have had some bearing on Twain's directly contrasting Macaulay's *History* with Goldsmith's *Vicar* (his praise of the *History* was written on the verso of the diary page that contained his squib on Goldsmith). The library of the ship carrying him from India to Mauretius (where he would be reminded of the cloying *Paul et Virginie*) was to be saluted, he declared, both for its *not* having a copy of the *Vicar* (with its "long waste-pipe discharge of goody-goody

6. Harper's, for example, competing with five other editions, reported, after an initial sale of sixty thousand copies of the first two volumes of its edition: "Probably, within three months of this time, the sale will amount to two hundred thousand copies. No work, of any kind, has ever so completely taken our whole country by storm" (George Otto Trevelyan, *The Life and Letters of Lord Macaulay* [London, 1893], p. 509). Not since *Waverley* had a book had such a sale. In 1861, when the entire five volumes were out, the two-hundred-thousand-copy figure was reached within a few months (Hart, *The Popular Book*, p. 116).

7. Emerson held that Macaulay "explicitly teaches that *good* means good to eat, good to wear, material commodity . . ." (*English Traits* [Boston, 1903], p. 247).

8. See A. V. Dicey, "Macaulay and His Critics," *Nation*, LXXIV (May 15, 1902), 388f.

9. Said James Cotter Morrison in his *Macaulay*: "We never leave him conscious that we have been raised into a higher tone of feeling, chastened and subdued into humility, courage, and sacrifice" (["English Men of Letters"; New York, 1883], p. 55).

puerilities and dreary moralities") and for its *having* a copy of Macaulay's *History*, in reading which one became oblivious to the present ills of the world. A third factor was that historical romances, with which Macaulay had originally vied, were mushrooming anew in the nineties and their extravagance seemed more flagrant than ever. In particular, Twain had made some notes on several of Stanley Weyman's historical romances, which he read on the next leg of his sea voyage, on leaving Mauretius; and though he was entertained by Weyman (the English Dumas), he felt that he was careless with facts and had his Frenchmen pretentiously behaving like Englishmen.[10] Furthermore, according to Twain, those who criticized Macaulay were much like those who praised Goldsmith, in that it would take a person with a fairly dull mind, or someone who had not really *read* them, to do either. This is his statement on the *History*, the ideal of absorption it embodies, and the absorbing reading it affords:

> [one can say a] hearty good word for even this poor smirking, sniveling, hypocritical little library; for it has Macaulay's England; & a library can not justly be called dull which has that in it. In our day people say its style is too studied, too precise, too trim, ornate, dress-paradish; but how do they find that out? For the moment one opens any volume of the five, at any place in the volume, he sinks into a [cosy trance of enjoyment] into profound unconsciousness of everything this worldly—flights of time, [duties, suffering neglect] & waiting duties, the [pangs] [usurption] pains of disease, of hunger [& thirsts], the [griefs] burdens of life, the encroachments, the insults of age,—everything vanishes out of his consciousness except the [happy & satisfied sense of being entertained; entertained pungent & pervasive tingling] sense of being pervasively content, satisfied, happy. I have read that History a [good many] number of times, & I believe [it has no dull places in it].[11]

---

10. Twain alluded to *The Red Cockade* (1896) and *Under the Red Robe* (1894). His criticism was deleted from the *FE* manuscript, 1593f., *Berg*; in the published text the corresponding place from which it was cut was II 331. Other novels he mentioned reading on the trip were Stevenson's *Prince Otto* (1885), Henry Kingsley's *Geoffry Hamlyn* (1859), Israel Zangwill's *Master* (1895), and Marcus Clarke's *For the Term of His Natural Life* (1874). He disliked the first two and liked the last two (Unpublished Notebook No. 29 I [January–April, 1896], 3–5).

11. *FE* MS, 1549, *Berg* (Copyright © 1967, Mark Twain Company). Here as in other manuscript material brackets indicate cancellations. Twain's

IV

In coming under the influence of Macaulay's essays on Clive
and Hastings, Twain merged his own bias with Macaulay's and
built creatively on it, both in subject and in the structuring of
ideas. This occurred in a poem and in the Indian section of
Following the Equator.

It was not just India and Macaulay separately that had been
entrancing to Twain, but also Macaulay on India—that is, on
British rule in India. Whenever Twain wrote about a place he
visited, he usually did his homework and read what the "authorities" had had to say about it, so that he could poke around for
some impertinent details to embarrass them with. Not so with
Macaulay and the heroic portrait he had drawn of Warren
Hastings, a man whose reputation had been gravely impaired by
Burke's harrowing denunciation during the impeachment proceed-
ings mounted by the Tories. Even when, playing devil's advocate, Twain, in 1901, put the worst face on the activities of Hastings and the East India Company, he did so in order to make a
searingly ironic comparison between the charges Burke had
heaped upon Hastings—without regard for extenuating circumstances—and the fact that there was no Burke to press similar,
overdue charges against Richard Croker and Tammany Hall,

---

reason for printing his opinion of *The Vicar* and withholding his opinion
of Macaulay is partly that he wanted to be ironic—he loathed the boat
and its library, and so would rather praise it for what it lacked than
what it had—and partly structural, for the excitement of India, with
which he had associated Macaulay, was now behind him and he was
picking up where he had left off in Australia, with sardonic comments
on "civilization."

Macaulay, interestingly, had about as little use for Goldsmith as
Twain had. In his *Britannica* article on Goldsmith (1856), Macaulay
noted that "he knew nothing accurately"; and he did the same kind of
job on "The Deserted Village" that Twain would do on *The Luck of
Roaring Camp*, criticizing inconsistencies in Goldsmith's description,
where it bore "no resemblance to the originals." Macaulay also disliked
The Vicar as much as Twain did. He thought its "fable" was "one of
the worst that ever was constructed," that it was "wanting in probability and consistency," and that its conclusion was "a tangle of
absurdities" (*Miscellanies* [Standard Library ed.; Boston, 1900], III,
43–46).

whose guilt, unlike Hastings', was a dead certainty.[12] On the whole, Twain rather took to heart Macaulay's brilliant vindication of Clive and Hastings against their stay-at-home maligners.[13] Both men had had to stand up to charges of corruption and venality in their declining years, with Clive broken in health and Hastings bankrupted by the effort to defend himself, when almost singlehandedly, as Macaulay had it, each man had risen from the rank of clerk to subdue the entire subcontinent, institute political and fiscal reforms, and hold India for England while she was losing her American colonies.

When Twain, in 1893, under the shadow of financial failure, read aloud to his wife and daughter from Macaulay's essays on Clive and Hastings, he brooded over "how great they were and how far they fell," and conjured up "an imaginary case . . . of some old demented man mumbling of his former state" (*Biog* III 1499). As Twain described the man and repeated some of his mumblings, Livy and Susy asked that he write the situation up, and he did, producing a poem called "The Derelict."

The importance of the poem (outside of its biographical implications) is that, while scarcely remarkable as poetry, the basic allegory contains a pattern implicit in the essays on Clive and Hastings. Into them Macaulay had injected a familiar dramatic formula in compensation for the insipid biographies he was reviewing: the rise of a seeming nondescript to high position and his fall when, after honorable service, he has to withstand charges

12. In "Edmund Burke on Croker and Tammany." This was first presented as a speech before the Organization Committee of the Acorns (a reform movement in New York municipal politics) at the Waldorf-Astoria Hotel on October 17, 1901, and shortly thereafter it appeared as a fifteen-page pamphlet.

13. The essays on Clive and Hastings were both book reviews in the *Edinburgh Review*, the one of Major General Sir John Malcolm's *The Life of Robert Lord Clive* (London, 1836), and the other of Rev. G R. Gleig's *Memoirs of the Life of Warren Hastings, First Governor-General of Bengal* (London, 1841).

Macaulay was not an uncritical adulator of his subjects. He thought Gleig's book was full of "undiscerning panegyric," and he would not gloss over the fact that Hastings did not have a stainless character, having engaged, as he did, in such devious practices as putting out the British army to the Nabob of Bengal for hire, and conspiring with Chief Justice Impey to remove a political enemy. The essay on Clive appears in *CHE* IV 314–406; the essay on Hastings in *CHE* V 114–242.

of malfeasance. It was typical of Macaulay to make history yield a compelling literary motif, and rather typical of Twain to be sensitively aroused by such a motif. He constructed a metaphor that might express the Macaulayan protagonist's rebuke to his detractors and memorialize a heroic moment in history. On a more specific level, the contrast he developed exactly parallels the content of the passage from the Hastings essay cited in *Following the Equator,* wherein Macaulay had noted how "the natives" had turned on Hastings when he was down. The basic situation is unfolded in Twain's opening stanza:

> You sneer, you ships that pass me by,
>   Your snow-pure canvas towering proud!
> You *traders* base!—why, once such fry
>   Paid reverence, when like a cloud
> Storm-swept I drove along,
>   My Admiral at post, his pennon blue,
> Faint in the wilderness of sky, my long
>   Yards bristling with my gallant crew,
> My ports flung wide, my guns displayed,
>   My tall spars hid in bellying sail!
> —You struck your topsails then, and made
>   Obeisance—*now* your manners fail.[14]

---

14. Paine published the first stanza with a few minor changes (*Biog* III 1499f.). All but the last stanza of the poem was given by Jervis Langdon in his pamphlet, *Samuel Langhorne Clemens: Some Reminiscences and Some Excerpts from Letters and Unpublished Manuscripts.* The last stanza is supplied by Arthur L. Scott. Here, then, is the rest of the poem (Scott's text, *On the Poetry of Mark Twain,* pp. 105–7), in which the theme and metaphor of the first stanza are further developed:

> Well, go your way, and let me dream
>   Of days long past, when I, like you,
> Was strong and young, and life did seem
>   Made all for joy; when I, like you,
> Did skim the sea all bravely clad,
>   And whether skies in splendor shone,
> Or palled the world in gloom, was glad:
>   O golden days, where are ye flown!
>
> For thirty years I served the wars
>   And trod the deep in sinful pride
> Begot of my brave battle-scars
>   And cherished stains where heroes died.
> Remotest oceans knew my fame,
>   Remotest lands paid court to me
> With thundering guns and spouting flame
>   And welcoming hosts on bended knee.

On rereading "The Derelict" some sixteen years after he wrote it, Twain remarked, "it is like reading another man's work." He was quite aware of having extrapolated Macaulay's dramatic method along with his subject: "There is no figure for the storm-beaten human drift as the derelict—such men as Clive and Hastings could only be imagined as derelicts adrift, helpless, tossed by every wind and tide" (*Biog* III 1500).[15]

For thirty years. Then came a day
  When all my pride full low was laid,
And all my honor men did slay
  As 'twere a worthless thing. They said
"This ship is old, and fails apace;
  "Her form is warp'd, her spars astrain,
"Her sails but rags—it were disgrace
  "To let *her* bear the flag again."

The ingrates sold me! and I sank
  From that high service of the State
To sordid commerce; taking rank
  With *your* sort; bearing freight
Of hams and soap and corn and hay,
  And manned by sloven longshore clods
Profaning decks where once held sway
  The Nelson breed of warrior gods.

Some while I wistful watched to see
  If my wide world had me forgot:
If fleets would dip their flags to me,
  And fortresses salute. O lot
Full hard to bear was mine! No soul
  Remembered me! No topsail strikes,
No color dips! My humble rôle
  Now 'twas, to dip to these, and strike *my* kites!

Well, thirty years I wrought in trade,
  And alway shabbier I grew;
And then once more I fell a grade,
  And carried swine—as freight *and* crew.
Full forty years I bore this cross
  And led this life of nameless shame,
Then foundered in a happy gale,
  And derelict became.

The years they come and the years they go,
  As I drift on the lonely sea,
Recking no more than the winds that blow,
  What is in store for me;
For my shames are over, my soul at peace,
  At peace from loathsome strife,
And I wait in patience for my release
  From the insult of this world's life.

15. For the personal reference of his sense of being a "derelict," one should consult his letter to Howells of January 22, 1898. It was because he and

To return now to *Following the Equator*, one finds it a strangely irreverent book for Twain to have been writing so close upon the completion of his most reverent book, *Joan of Arc*. The differing treatments of history in these two works are equally surprising. In the one, he had made a typically Macaulayan heroine of his central figure, a valiant young derelict who, glowing with the finest spirit of her age, was beset by a pettifogging officialdom. In the other, the writing of which was therapy for his sorrow over losing Susy, he dethroned the Whig concept of history as a record of "Bright Improvement" (I 87) and kicked the dust of his disillusionment over it. His attack on "civilization" could not have been more scathing. It began at Hawaii, the first Pacific landfall (where he observed that, thanks to Captain Cook and American missionaries, the island paradise had exchanged its native evils for those of civilization, which had decimated its population); and the attack deepened as it spread through the accounts of sadism in the Australian "convict dumps," the annihilation of the peaceable Tasmanians, the murder lust of Thuggee cultists and other religious horrors in India; until, about two thirds of the way around the world, Twain could hardly stand it any more, and sighed like an aged Huck Finn: "If I had my way I would sail on forever and never go to live on solid ground again" (II 314). In the Indian section, by far the most complex part of the book, sheer unassimilated bewilderment resulted in contradictory reactions and a problem in structure. To resolve it Twain availed himself, interestingly, of the one rhetorical device most commonly used by Macaulay and of the realistic, worldly-wise bias of his essays on Clive and Hastings.

In brief, the problem was that with almost everything he saw Twain could at one and the same moment be both revolted and stirred to the depths of his being. In the earlier Indian chapters, however, he was decidedly more stirred than revolted, at times almost against his will and assuredly against the major emphasis of previous sections of the book, in which he had positively refused to find anything good in any society. As he looked back on Bombay during composition and at some "distance" in time, his

---

Howells had each lost a daughter that Twain said they were "a pair of derelicts" (*T-H* II 670).

mind reeled with visual imagery, in which the past became all too hectically present, so that he was powerless to give it meaning: "I seem to have a kaleidoscope at my eye; and I hear the clash of the glass bits as the splendid figures change, and fall apart, and flash into new forms, figure after figure, and with the birth of each new form I feel my skin crinkle and my nerve-web tingle with a new thrill of wonder and delight" (II 37).

His first attempt to organize his impressions and deal with their incoherence was deceptively simple. The "remembered pictures" floated past him "in a sequence of contrasts," and he merely put down the conjoined marvels and horrors in sets of antitheses:

> This is indeed India; the land of dreams and romance, of fabulous wealth and fabulous poverty, of splendor and rags, of palaces and hovels, of famine and pestilence . . . the country of a hundred nations and a hundred tongues, of a thousand religions and two million gods, cradle of the human race, birthplace of human speech, mother of history, grandmother of legend, great-grandmother of tradition, whose yesterdays bear date with the mouldering antiquities of the rest of the nations. . . . (II 26.)

Twain would come to find, as we have seen earlier, that India was more than the "mother of history." She was, in an appropriately Hindu setting, its perpetual avatar. Throughout the Indian journey that was one of the main things her contradictions seemed to mean to Twain, and, for him, to experience them was to get the feel of living history. Not only was Twain's idea the object of Macaulayan historiography, its very form—the summational juxtaposition of antithetical qualities—was Macaulay's trademark, as may be gathered, for example, from the way he reacted to an alarmingly callous murder. It sounded to him like "a terribly realistic chapter out of the 'Arabian Nights,' a strange mixture of simplicities and pieties and murderous practicalities, which brought back the forgotten days of Thuggee and made them live again; in fact, even made them believable" (II 76).

However quietly Twain may at first seem to have appropriated the famed Macaulayan antithesis, if one looks carefully enough, his borrowing becomes more and more apparent. In no other part

of the book is his style so conspicuously punctuated by antitheses. And, with respect to content, there are a number of
interpretive references in Macaulay's essays on Clive and Hastings that are echoed by Twain with varying degrees of specificity
—such as that Bengal was Eden-like and its people languid and
"thoroughly fitted . . . for a foreign yoke" (*CHE* IV 344f.; *FE* II
217, 243); that the cruelty of the Surjah Dowlah, who was
responsible for the Black Hole, brought on Clive's revenge and ultimately inclined him to use devious strategems to counter Eastern deviousness (*CHE* IV 347–53; *FE* II 218f.); that Britain's
veracity formed the backbone of her oriental empire (*CHE* IV
362; *FE* II 217), while the Indian was born to deceit (*CHE* V
130, 149; *FE* II 80) and the Indian nobility to treachery and
luxury (*CHE* V 188; *FE* II 51f., 66–68); that the sacred Benares
was honeycombed with superstition, hypocrisy, and commercialism (*CHE* V 179; *FE*, chaps. lx, lxi, lxii); and that the
Indians, a child-like race (*CHE* V 201; *FE* II 27f.), benefited
from British rule (*CHE* V 201; *FE* II 202). Twain's criticism of
the educational system in India also resembled Macaulay's
criticism of the legal system (*CHE* V 168f.; *FE* II 298–307).
More than anything else, though, one notices the regularity with
which Twain represented his ambivalence in antitheses, eventually needing only catchwords from them to categorize his
feelings (see *FE* II 243).

Not all of Twain's Macaulayan antitheses were the same,
however. The second such full-scale catalogue of balancing contrasts was expressly different from the awed tone of the first one.
The change was in part due to experience and the return of
Twain's earlier mood; in part it may also have been due to
certain hints derived from Macaulay. The catalogue was followed
by assessments of Hastings and of British rule that were clearly
taken from Macaulay and that repeat his antithetical form; and
its tone harks back to that of a quote from the essay on Hastings
which Twain had used shortly after the first catalogue. To some
extent, therefore, Macaulay would seem to have given Twain a
basis for the more consistently realistic and morally critical tone
of the latter parts of his Indian section, which brought it into
line with other sections of his book.

The second catalogue has the function of moral stock-taking at Allahabad ("Godville") preliminary to the recklessly irreverent chapters on Benares, the site of priapus worship and pestilential holy waters, and also, as Twain sees it, of the ultimate in antitheses: a religiosity whose intensity is matched only by the smell of the noisome sump where its rites are held. In anticipation of this satire, the unfavorable members of Twain's antitheses provide a destructive comment on each of the more favorable members, and vice versa:

> It is the Land of Contradictions, the Land of Subtlety and Superstition, the Land of Wealth and Poverty, the Land of Splendor and Desolation, the Land of Plague and Famine, the Land of the Thug and the Poisoner, and of the Meek and the Patient, the Land of the Suttee, the Land of the Unreinstatable Widow, the Land where All Life is Holy, the Land of Cremation, the Land where the Vulture is a Grave and a Monument, [and] the Land of the Multitudinous Gods. . . . (II 160.)

In the Benares sequence Twain set aside all pretense of wonderment over India, except in the ironic sense. (Adding to the idea of the holiness of life, for example, he said that "all life seems to be sacred except human life" [II 197]). It is at this point that he thinks again of Hastings. In his summary of Hastings' activities at Benares, wonderment over the feats of small bands of courageous Englishmen replaces his wonderment over India. Relating the episode of Hastings' collecting a huge fine from the Rajah of Benares with no more than a few hundred native troops and three young English lieutenants under his command, Twain marvelled at his *sang-froid*:

> The incident lights up the Indian situation electrically, and gives one a vivid sense of the strides which the English had made and the mastership they had acquired in the land since the date of Clive's great victory. In a quarter of a century, from being nobodies, and feared by none, they were become confessed lords and masters, feared by all, sovereigns included, and served by all, sovereigns included. It makes the fairy tales sound true. (II 200f.)

Although Twain went considerably beyond Macaulay in elaborating Hastings' amazing feats in Benares and probably did not use Macaulay as his immediate source for this passage, his conclusions are Macaulay's, gotten either at first or second hand;

and along with them, he also took over Macaulay's formulaic antithesis: a negative idea (A) is followed by a positive one (B), and then another positive one (C) is balanced by a negative one (D) that supports (C): "Some of [Hastings'] acts have left stains upon his name which can never be washed away, but he saved to England the Indian Empire, and that was the best service that was ever done to the Indians themselves, those wretched heirs of a hundred centuries of pitiless oppression and abuse" (II 202).

In terms of narrative method, the Macaulayan antithesis gave Twain a means of imposing the symmetry of historical perspective upon the disorder of recalcitrant, and often contradictory, facts. He got the feeling of having seen the totality of human experience, and of having encompassed the whole moral gamut. It was in this connection that the Macaulayan viewpoint seems to have been one of the first correctional influences, along with personal experience, on Twain's early attitude towards India. He was faced with the complex and structurally disruptive problem that he should elsewhere have found civilization to be only a more complicated and often more dread barbarism than the one it replaced; whereas in India, under an equable British surveillance, he seemed to reverse himself, finding native barbarities to be infinitely worse, but the culture infinitely more attractive, than occidentalism. What Macaulay supplied was a more realistic appraisal of the Indian character, which was more in keeping with Twain's disillusioning principle that human nature was pretty much the same the world over. The immediate provocation for his going to Macaulay was that it seemed utterly incomprehensible to him that mild-natured Indians could ever have been Thugs, and that there should be enough of that murderous spirit left among them "to keep it darkly interesting" (II 80). Finding it difficult even to believe the newspaper accounts of Indian depravity, he remembered that "Macaulay has a light-throwing passage upon this matter in his great historical sketch of Warren Hastings, where he is describing some effects which followed the temporary paralysis of Hastings' powerful government brought about by Sir Philip Francis and his party." The passage Twain then quotes describes a kind of moral baseness that Twain was particularly averse to and which had inspired his poem on the derelict: those who had formerly quailed before a great man fell upon him when he was deprived of some of his power. This is the quoted passage:

> The natives considered Hastings as a fallen man; and they acted after their kind. Some of our readers may have seen, in India, a cloud of crows pecking a sick vulture to death—no bad type of what happens in that country as often as fortune deserts one who has been great and dreaded. In an instant all the sycophants, who had lately been ready to lie for him, to forge for him, to pander for him, to poison for him, hasten to purchase the favor of his victorious enemies by accusing him. An Indian government has only to let it be understood that it wishes a particular man to be ruined, and in twenty-four hours it will be furnished with grave charges, supported by depositions so full and circumstantial that any person unaccustomed to Asiatic mendacity would regard them as decisive. It is well if the signature of the destined victim is not counterfeited at the foot of some illegal compact, and if some treasonable paper is not slipped into a hiding-place in his house (II 80f.; *CHE* V 149.)

It may seem odd that Macaulay should have had to give Twain an *ad hoc* lesson in realism, but that was no small part of his appeal. As Harry Hayden Clark suggested, Macaulay's democratic spirit "combined with his belief in material progress and common-sense intellectualism, all imbibed by a reading public running into millions, must have constituted a considerable force for the rise of realism in America."[16]

16. "The Vogue of Macaulay in America," *Transactions of the Wisconsin Academy of Sciences, Arts and Letters*, XXXIV (1942), 276.

12

Howells and the Poetics
of Appreciation

I

William Dean Howells had read Macaulay, one of the "literary passions" of his youth, with such "personal devotion" that he looked upon the reading as a "long debauch." Having steeped himself in the *History* and essays, and having left almost nothing "unenjoyed," he reformed his prose style—which, significantly, had formerly been "modeled upon that of Goldsmith and Irving" —in order to emulate Macaulay in the writing of "short, quick sentences" cast in a predominantly Anglo-Saxon diction.[1]

This may or may not have had a bearing on Twain's placing Howells, who ranked high among his own literary passions, on as elevated a plane as he had placed Macaulay. But clear it was that he appreciated Howells for having much the same style and ends that had pleased him in Macaulay: effortless precision, vividness, and the art of "concreting abstractions." Twain's point of departure in the *Harper's* essay on Howells (1906), and really the gist of it, was that Howells had for some forty years (or roughly since the death of Macaulay and the appearance of the *History*) provided the reading public with a "sustained exhibition of . . . clearness, compression, verbal exactness, and unforced and seemingly unconscious felicity of phrasing" (*WIM* 228). By its quiet concentration Howells' style transmitted the sense of participation Twain valued most in descriptive and historical writing. Nothing came between the reader and the thing described. Hence, he relived Howells' Venice or Boston with the same fervor with which he relived Macaulay's England. More than that, he relived Howells' appreciative impressionism with an equivalent poetics of critical appreciation. Just as Macaulay

1. *My Literary Passions* (New York, 1895), p. 116f.

had inspired him to write a poem, so did he match the aesthetic impact of Howells' prose—its mode, as he said, of "translating . . . the visions of the eyes of flesh into words that reproduced their forms and colors" (*WIM* 233)—with a translation of analytic insight into the illuminative absolute of poetic metaphor. Just such a translation graced the first representative paragraph Twain cited, one in which Howells wrote more like Macaulay than he did in almost any other place.

In their treatment of the past as present, Macaulay and the Howells of *Venetian Life* (1866) and *Tuscan Cities* (1886) (books Twain was especially fond of) had each perfected a style that at once consumed and was consumed by its subject. Twain's responsive appreciation of Howells was the counterpart for criticism of what their style was for the revitalization of history. Metaphor solidified his meaning by reproducing the definitional precision for which he congratulated Howells, as well as its source, which was crystalline clarity.

His first and simplest metaphor of what it meant for Howells to have set the world a model of *"sustained"* excellence in prose style nicely specifies the nature of that virtue and why it should be underrated—i.e., because Howells' exceptional consistency ironically undercut the uniqueness of his having always written with such constant clarity: "There are others who exhibit those great qualities as greatly as does [Howells], but only by intervaled distributions of rich moonlight, with stretches of veiled and dimmer landscape between; whereas Howells's moon sails cloudless skies all night and all the nights." The second skill Twain mentions, "verbal exactness," draws from him no less than three metaphoric sequences, which allude, in turn, to the cognitive, psychological, and illuminative powers of the right word, "that elusive and shifty grain of gold." The result is compression and fineness of analysis; the analysis is complete and completely exact:

> Others have to put up with approximations, more or less frequently; he has better luck. To me, the others are miners working with the gold-pan—of necessity some of the gold washes over and escapes; whereas, in my fancy, he is quicksilver raiding down a riffle—no grain of the metal stands much chance of eluding him. A powerful agent is the right word: it lights the

reader's way and makes it plain; a close approximation to it will answer, and much traveling is done in a well-enough fashion by its help, but we do not welcome it and applaud it and rejoice in it as we do when *the* right one blazes out on us. Whenever we come upon one of these intensely right words in a book or a newspaper the resulting effect is physical as well as spiritual, and electrically prompt: it tingles exquisitely around through the walls of the mouth and tastes as tart and crisp and good as the autumn-butter that creams the sumac-berry. One has no time to examine the word and vote upon its rank and standing, the automatic recognition of its supremacy is so immediate. There is a plenty of acceptable literature which deals largely in approximations, but it may be likened to a fine landscape seen through the rain; the right word would dismiss the rain, then you would see it better. It doesn't rain when Howells is at work. (229.)

II

It is probably a little rash to speak of Twain's conceits as "metaphysical," for while the underlying pattern of *discordia concors* is there, the brisk wit and conversion of thought into sensory perceptions are really Thoreauvian in nature. But if it means anything to type this kind of critical analysis, and, within reason, I think it does, it must be apparent that in their separate studies of persons and places the techniques of Macaulay, Howells, and Twain ultimately converge on the dynamics of contrast as a way of knowing, and of knowing, more than anything else, how it feels to experience the closeness of some distant reality. Without necessarily seeing anything of himself in Macaulay and Howells, Twain in 1906 could not have helped being drawn to a technique they shared when it so perfectly coincided with the one he planned for the autobiography he was writing in that year. Reason enough for that technique to be the unstated theory around which his most inspired appreciation would rotate.[2]

Macaulay, with his inveterate Manicheism, might, as a matter of course, talk about history as a drawing up of the "antithetical characters of great men, [and a] setting forth how many con-

2. He may also have conceivably recalled, from the passage he quoted from *Venetian Life*, that he and Howells had both worked the technique of contrasts in writing about the same location some forty years earlier.

tradictory virtues and vices they united" (*CHE* I 235). However, the doctrine of contrast as thematic action, as the entelechy that makes history spring to life and the form Twain thought most persuasive in Howells' descriptive writing, is best delineated in the instructive realism—a treating of the past as if it were really present—that Macaulay wanted historians to reclaim from the historical novelists. "To make the past present," Macaulay asserted,

> to bring the distant near, to place us in the society of a great man or on the eminence which overlooks the field of a mighty battle, to invest with the reality of human flesh and blood beings whom we are too much inclined to consider as personified qualities in an allegory, to call up our ancestors before us with all their peculiarities of language, manners, and garb, to show us over their houses, to seat us at their tables, to rummage their old-fashioned wardrobes, to explain the uses of their ponderous furniture, these parts of the duty which properly belongs to the historian have been appropriated by the historical novelist. (285.)

This was written long before the passionate pilgrims of James's generation had begun to pour over Europe in quest of their past, or of aesthetic education. But for those who, like Howells and Twain, could be awakened to the call of arrested history, the simultaneity of past and present resulted in a meaningful psychic engagement, and it gave them a literary theme as well. It was from the time that he heard of the rumored destruction of the Ponte Vecchio, Howells observed in *Tuscan Cities*, that he felt his "accumulating impressions of Florentine history had centered about it as the point where that history really began to be historic," and that he "really began to be serious with [his] material and . . . found it everywhere in the streets." "Even if," he continued, "one has no literary designs upon the facts, that is incomparably the best way of dealing with the past. At home, in the closet, one may read history, but one can realize it, as if it were something personally experienced, only on the spot where it was lived." Howells then recapitulated Macaulay's ideal of the re-experienced past as a theme that could give him something worth writing about, and something that in Europe was infinitely superior, by contrast, to the record of presently experienced common life which he valued at home:

> In this pursuit of the past, the inquirer will often surprise himself in the possession of a genuine emotion; at moments the illustrious or pathetic figures of other days will seem to walk before him unmocked by the grotesque and burlesquing shadows we all cast while in the flesh. I will not swear it, but it would take little to persuade me that I had vanishing glimpses of many of these figures in Florence. One of the advantages of this method is that you have your historical personages in a sort of picturesque contemporaneity with one another and with yourself, and you imbue them all with the sensibilities of our own time.[3]

Twain made similar comments in *Innocents Abroad*, *Following the Equator*, the Hawaiian section of *Roughing It*, and even in parts of *A Tramp Abroad*; but the place where he laid down the notion of interacting contrasts as making ideal provision for unity and revelation was of course in his *Autobiography*. He trusted that his *Autobiography* would be kept eternally fresh and be assured of a long life because with the "form and method" he had chosen for it "the past and present are constantly brought face to face, resulting in contrasts which newly fire up the interest all along like contact of flint and steel" (*Autob* II 245). He wished to "make the narrative a combined Diary *and* Autobiography. In this way you have the vivid thing of the present to make a contrast with memories of like things in the past, and these contrasts have a charm which is all their own" (I 193). As he noted, "news is history in its first and best form, its vivid and fascinating form" (I 326).

III

Although Twain was trying to elucidate the basis of his life-long enthusiasm for Howells' prose style, the passages he cited in the *Harper's* essay were at least as significant as examples of history brought to life through schematic contrasts as they were for their style alone.[4] One might not be far wrong in supposing

3. *Tuscan Cities* (Leipzig, 1900), p. 16f.
4. Twain also treated such other matters as Howells' humor and the rightness and variety of his "stage directions."
   Much as he praised Howells' novels in correspondence ("you are

that Twain picked the passages at random, possibly by simply going through works close at hand until he hit upon pieces of writing that somehow jogged his aesthetic consciousness into an awareness of itself and of the by then obsessive task he had set himself in writing the *Autobiography*. The only premeditation involved in his choices would seem to have come from his need to document Howells' consistency by gathering passages from his late, early, and middle phases. So he took one from an "Easy Chair" review (1905) of Louis Dyer's *Machiavelli and the Modern State*, one from the third chapter of *Venetian Life*, and one from *The Undiscovered Country* (1880). Since Twain could not have gone looking for passages in which Macaulayan techniques informed the art of Howells' prose, his finding two such passages in the three he chose tells us a good deal about the form that stimulated his appreciative imagination.

The presence of Macaulayan qualities in the "Easy Chair" column is fairly obvious. First of all, being wholly unfettered by the demands of run-of-the-mill reviewing, Howells took up Dyer's *Machiavelli* after the time-honored fashion of a Macaulayan review, in which a new book becomes the pretext for some wide-ranging disquisition on history, society, or morals. In this case, Howells dealt with all three matters. Concurring in the estimate Dyer had made in his last chapter of the duality of Machiavelli's morals, Howells observed that Dyer had essentially followed an analysis "first luminously suggested by Macaulay." Then, after compressing that analysis into a Macaulayan antithesis in the paragraph quoted by Twain, Howells himself fell in with some of the more notable aspects of Macaulay's essay

---

really my only author," he remarked, on the rebound from a distressing encounter with *Middlemarch* and *Daniel Deronda* [*T-H* II 533]), Twain gave an indication of how exclusively his appreciative criticism would be centered upon the conversion of facts into life, the reduction of thought to "a concrete condition," by his preferring to dwell upon the graphic quality of Howells' prose rather than upon the structure of his fiction. From the generality of his comments on such novels as *A Foregone Conclusion, The Lady of the Aroostook, The Undiscovered Country, A Modern Instance,* and *The Rise of Silas Lapham,* it would appear that Twain simply enjoyed the fiction for its own sake rather than as a subject for critical analysis (*T-H* I 21, 245, 427, 407f.; II 537).

form, remarking, for example, how Machiavelli's "very limitations" added to his charm ("the malevolent, the monstrous Machiavelli of tradition . . . ends by becoming a loveable personality"), and subsequently considering a moral proposition typical of Macaulay, that rule by "greed and might" in international relations enables individual men to evade the sting of conscience.

For his part, Macaulay, in his essay on Machiavelli (a review of J. V. Périer's translation of *Oeuvres Complètes de Machiavel*, Paris, 1825) had decried the popular view of him as a calculating fiend and had traced the apparent contradictions in Machiavelli's nature to the historical circumstances and moral climate of his times, when the use of mercenaries had rendered craft and guile of greater political importance than martial valor. Insofar as he celebrated the marvelous richness of character displayed by the Renaissance Italians, Macaulay anticipated the fascination of Burckhardt, Browning, Symonds, and others who would participate in the late nineteenth-century vogue of rediscovering the Renaissance. Dyer's book emanated from that vogue. Its aims, and those of Howells in discussing it, are point by point quite close to Macaulay's, in that each of the three writers states and disposes of the popular view of Machiavelli, balances his virtues against his vices, finds that the former have been overlooked though they outweigh the latter, and considers the ramifications of Machiavelli's political morality.

Clearly, the most enchanting aspect of Machiavelli's character and the one that would make him an ideal subject for Macaulay's antitheses was the fact that, as Macaulay put it, "the whole man seems . . . a grotesque assemblage of incongruous qualities, selfishness and generosity, cruelty and benevolence, craft and simplicity, abject villainy and romantic heroism" (*CHE* I 143). Instead of simplifying these inconsistencies and presenting Machiavelli as a sort of split personality (as had been done often enough), Macaulay saw them as "interwoven" and discerned the historical explanation of them in the prevailingly decadent rationale of Italian morality. Macaulay's method of systematic contrasts becomes more than an organizing principle; it becomes a historical concept unto itself, the diastole and systole of life Italian style.

The paragraph taken by Twain from Howells' "Easy Chair" column is more thoroughly Macaulayan than any other quotable passage he might have found there. In it Howells makes abundant use of antitheses, particularly in characterizing Machiavelli; he offers a historical explanation for Machiavelli's morality; and he deplores the low regard in which Machiavelli is commonly held, when there is so much to be admired about the man:

> Mr. Dyer is rather of the opinion, first luminously suggested by Macaulay, that Machiavelli was in earnest, but must not be judged as a political moralist of our time and race would be judged. He thinks that Machiavelli was in earnest, as none but an idealist can be, and he is the first to imagine him an idealist immersed in realities, who involuntarily transmutes the events under his eye into something like the visionary issues of reverie. The Machiavelli whom he depicts does not cease to be politically a republican and socially a just man because he holds up an atrocious despot like Caesar Borgia as a mirror for rulers. What Machiavelli beheld round him in Italy was a civic disorder in which there was oppression without statecraft, and revolt without patriotism. When a miscreant like Borgia appeared upon the scene and reduced both tyrants and rebels to an apparent quiescence, he might very well seem to such a dreamer the savior of society whom a certain sort of dreamers are always looking for. Machiavelli was no less honest when he honored the diabolical force of Caesar Borgia than Carlyle was when at different times he extolled the strong man who destroys liberty in creating order. But Carlyle has only just ceased to be mistaken for a reformer, while it is still Machiavelli's hard fate to be so trammeled in his material that his name stands for whatever is most malevolent and perfidious in human nature. (*WIM* 230f.)

Twain develops the several points he has to make about this paragraph—it has clarity, exactness, and rhythmic ease—and again packs them into nuggets of metaphor: "how seemingly unadorned, yet [it] is all adornment, like the lily-of-the-valley; . . . how compact, without a complacency-signal hung out anywhere to call attention to it." However, the "choice" phrase he returns to as the hallmark of Howells' artistry is a lily-of-the-valley antithesis that patently smacks of Macaulay: "an idealist immersed in realities who involuntarily transmutes the events under his eye into something like the visionary issues of reverie." With brilliant metaphoric definition, Twain uses this phrase to demonstrate the difference between a mechanic, who would make a "cabbage" of the idea, and an artist, by whose touch it would become a "flower." The great Macaulay could not have improved upon Twain's antithesis: "With a hundred words to do it with, the literary artisan could catch that airy thought and tie it down and reduce it to a concrete condition, visible, substantial, understandable and all right, like a cabbage; but the artist does it with twenty, and the result is a flower" (232).

IV

The other two excerpts were word pictures. Twain used them to show that Howells was a master at "concreting abstractions" and producing "photographs" that were "accurate" and had "feeling in them and sentiment," like "photographs taken in a dream." The one from *The Undiscovered Country* was a Dickensian pastiche in which Howells personified the houses of a once-fashionable Boston district that had fallen on bad times: "Every house seems to wince as you go by, and button itself up to the chin for fear you should find out it had no shirt on. . . ." What Twain did so well in this appreciative criticism, and what he did to make the cited passages shine anew for Howells "with a lustre that they never had before" (this Howells remarked on reading Twain's essay [*T-H* II 813]), was to bring out every latent hue and surface of an unobtrusively jeweled prose. One gasps with Howells at how much is revealed by Twain's informed connoisseurship. He had—be it said—played stranger roles in his time, but none of them did he play more sensitively.

The passage to be reckoned with is the one from *Venetian Life*, where, as Twain saw it, Howells had caught "the spirit of Venice" in the overlay of past and present, and in the vista so obtained had sketched the expanse of reality to be imaged in historical contrasts. But this Pateresque contrast is not the only one in *Venetian Life*. To better understand its function, we should know what Howells had been doing in the others. His object in *Venetian Life* had been (in the tradition of Emerson, Hawthorne, Lowell, and James) to present "in fidelity" what he had seen and therefore empirically knew of European life;[5] and, as he intimated by statement and example in the opening chapters (most forcefully in the third, from which Twain quoted the last two paragraphs), he wanted to steer a course between realism and sentiment. The realism included his deflating both the tales of intrigue and torture about Renaissance Venice (with its "reputation for vindictive and gloomy cruelty") and the tourists' responses to the "proper Objects of Interest." It took in such other matters as the Venetians' refusal to acknowledge the discomforts of winter, and even extended to several bits of irreverent humor at the expense of well-known religious paintings, one of them a Titian (44, 42). The sentiment lay in "the charm of the place [that] sweetens your temper, but corrupts you," and rested, as the realism did, upon overt and implicit contrasts, many of them arising from ambivalent states of mind: for example, Howells was at first "unhaunted by any pang for the decay that afterward saddened [him] amid the forlorn beauty of Venice"; he felt "the past and present [were] mixed . . . and the moral and material were blent in the sentiment of utter novelty and surprise" (27). At every turn Howells structured his impressions by the interaction of opposites. In this respect and in his vivid descriptions, which seemed to light up for Twain what Ruskin called the Sixth Lamp of Architecture, the lamp of memory, Howells' techniques broadly resembled Macaulay's;[6] and they were not vastly different from those that Twain himself would use, within a year of the publication of *Venetian Life*, in his letter on Venice for the *Alta California*, which he amplified in his two Venetian chapters of *Innocents Abroad* (xxii and xxiii).[7]

5. "Advertisement to the Second [American] Edition" (Boston, 1867), p. 5. The edition I cite is the Continental, Tauchnitz, "Authorized Edition" (Leipzig, 1883).
6. Howells, in fact, had made an analysis of the Italian national character that was much like the one Macaulay had made in his essay on Machiavelli. Whereas Macaulay contrasted the ideal of valor among northern nations with the Italians' greater respect for "superiority of intelligence"—so that they would be more contemptuous of an Othello than of an Iago—Howells similarly contrasted an Anglo-Saxon tendency toward savagery with the Italians' polished manner, civilization, and easy yielding to temptation (cf. *CHE* I 156; *VL* 342).
7. Letter of July 29, 1867 (*Traveling with the Innocents*, pp. 59–65). One notices a basic resemblance in contrapuntal form, a balancing of

Howells and Twain had thus around the same time independently arrived at a dialectically inclusive poetics of appreciation, as may be seen in their corresponding first reactions to Venice at night. Each had been drawn to the sight of the "marble palaces" rising from the water's edge (*VL* 27; *IA* I 280); each had noted how the drab and dirty city seen under the "glare of day" was transformed "under the charitable moon," when "her stained palaces [became] white again . . . and the old city seem[ed] crowned once more with the grandeur that was here five hundred years ago" (*VL* 30–32; *IA* I 283); and each had felt an ominous "hush, a stealthy sort of stillness" amidst the lively Venetian night, which was "suggestive of secret enterprises of bravoes" (*VL* 27f.; *IA* I 281). Like Twain, Howells had specifically proposed to know the city "differently from those writers who have described it in romances, poems, and hurried books of travel"; though, again, as was the case with Twain, his attitude of realism did not prevent him from being smitten by "its peerless picturesqueness, its sole and wondrous grandeur" (*VL* 10).

In the passage Twain selected for analysis in the Howells essay, the confluence of realism and humor with sentiment and historical projection reaches a climactic intensity. The Venetians are embarrassed by the snow and want to make it disappear as fast as they can, but the beauty which it covers Howells realistically sees as decked out in another beauty. Outwardly, his description seems yet another fanciful vignette like many others of its kind —e.g., Emerson's "The Snow Storm" and parts of Whittier's "Snow Bound." But as one contrast shades into the next, Howells' picture becomes an animated scene mingling past and present. Its stage manager plays off nature against art and balances European graciousness with a cultured, Bostonian version of American humor, which, as Twain later observed, is the sort that "flows softly all around about . . . and makes no

---

enthusiasm with realism, even though Twain chose to believe the lurid stories of the "justice" dispensed by the Venetian oligarchy, the Council of Three, while Howells discounted them. For Twain's theory of interspersing serious and comical matter and of using a serious and comical depiction of the same idea, see *Love Lets* 165f., *MTMF* 227, and *T-H* I 248f.

more show and no more noise than does the circulation of the blood" (235).

In Venetian streets they give the fallen snow no rest. It is at once shoveled into the canals by hundreds of half-naked *facchini*; and now in St. Mark's Place the music of innumerable shovels smote upon my ear; and I saw the shivering legion of poverty as it engaged the elements in a struggle for the possession of the Piazza. But the snow continued to fall, and through the twilight of the descending flakes all this toil and encounter looked like that weary kind of effort in dreams, when the most determined industry seems only to renew the task. The lofty crest of the bell-tower was hidden in the folds of falling snow, and I could no longer see the golden angel upon its summit. But looked at across the Piazza, the beautiful outline of St. Mark's Church was perfectly penciled in the air, and the shifting threads of the snowfall were woven into a spell of novel enchantment around the structure that always seemed to me too exquisite in its fantastic loveliness to be anything but the creation of magic. The tender snow had compassionated the beautiful edifice for all the wrongs of time, and so hid the stains and ugliness of decay that it looked as if just from the hand of the builder—or, better said, just from the brain of the architect. There was marvelous freshness in the colors of the mosaics in the great arches of the facade, and all that gracious harmony into which the temple rises, of marble scrolls and leafy exuberance airily supporting the statues of the saints, was a hundred times etherealized by the purity and whiteness of the drifting flakes. The snow lay lightly on the golden globes that tremble like peacock-crests above the vast domes, and plumed them with softest white; it robed the saints in ermine; and it danced over all its work, as if exulting in its beauty—beauty which filled me with subtle, selfish yearning to keep such evanescent loveliness for the little-while-longer of my whole life, and with despair to think that even the poor lifeless shadow of it could never be fairly reflected in picture or poem.

Through the wavering snowfall, the Saint Theodore upon one of the granite pillars of the Piazzetta did not show so grim as his wont is, and the winged lion on the other might have been a winged lamb, so gentle and mild he looked by the tender light of the storm. The towers of the island churches loomed faint and far away in the dimness; the sailors in the rigging of the ships that lay in the Basin wrought like phantoms among the shrouds; the gondolas stole in and out of the opaque distance more noiselessly and dreamily than ever; and a silence, almost palpable, lay upon the mutest city in the world. (*WIM* 233f.; *VL* 47f.)

That which Howells did for the snow storm in Venice, Twain did for his description of it. His figure of the "visions of the eyes of flesh" is a key to his own method, for so fully does Twain enter into the sense and spirit of Howells' scene that his appreciation makes a tangible analogy of the reality Howells created and moves on the same level with it:

> The spirit of Venice is there: of a city where Age and Decay, fagged with distributing damage and repulsiveness among the other cities of the planet in accordance with the policy and business of their profession, come for rest and play between seasons, and treat themselves to the luxury and relaxation of sinking the shop and inventing and squandering charms all about, instead of abolishing such as they find, as is their habit when not on vacation.

While Howells' prose style has not been neglected, he has never been looked upon as a striking *stylist* in the way that his friends James and Twain have. In addition, therefore, to filling a critical void, Twain's essay on Howells admirably displays the "unforced . . . felicity" which has always been taken for granted in a style where the craftsmanship shows so little because all of it is so completely at work. In terms of its own artistry, Twain's criticism (and there has been nothing quite as good on Howells) was not only a job well worth doing, it was exceedingly well done. The metaphors he used to define the insight and drama produced by Howells' prose had appropriately to do with either the luminous, representing the effect of insight, or with the scenic, representing the effect of drama. Over all, Twain's metaphoric criticism had a natural flow somewhat like that of Howells' humor. Yet its form could only have been attained by something of the inspired discipline that goes into the making of a poem. Poetry and its devices were to Twain the ultimate expression of meaning. Metaphor he considered to be the very condition of enlightenment;[8] and having been keenly moved, for example, by Mildred Howells' poem on determinism, "At the Wind's Will," he wrote Howells five months before publishing his poetic tribute

8. "Metaphor to use a metaphor by way of illustration," Twain wrote, "may be likened to the succession of lightning-glares that accompany a literary thunderstorm; they light up the landscape to the reader . . ." (*More Tramps Abroad* [London, 1897], p. 191).

to him: "What a lumbering poor vehicle prose is for the conveying of a great thought! It cost me several chapters to say in prose what Mildred has said better with a single penfull of ink. Prose wanders around with a lantern & laboriously schedules & verifies the details & particulars of a valley & its frame of crags and peaks, then Poetry comes, & lays bare the whole landscape with a single splendid flash" (*T-H* II 800).

We shall yet observe how profound an aid to the intellect Twain would make of the poetic intuition in praising Wilbrandt for his dramatization of the historical antitheses that roll down the ages towards a determinism that knowledge alone makes bearable. The determinism Twain affirmed on seeing *Der Meister von Palmyra* was the natural sequel to the underground truth he appreciated in reading Howe and Zola.

13

Howe and Zola:
The Opposing Truth

I

No one, least of all Twain, has been cajoled into thinking his oppositionism was not infinitely more than a pose. It was, as I have indicated, a trade, a creed, an epistemology. To see it provocatively worked tickled his innards—a joy forever—for the will to oppose had taken the place of his nostalgia over youth and had assumed its purity. It became the call of outgrown Innocence and unannealed Truth. The call of a schoolboy who notes that "Faith is believing what you know ain't so," of Huck and Jim, even Joan, and of Satan, and his blood brother, the irascible Mark Twain, whose epic feats of denunciation gave those within earshot "the fierce, searching delight of galvanic waves" (*Biog* I 213).

The oppositionism Twain appreciated in other writers was of several kinds. With Macaulay and Howells, it was mainly a matter of artistic technique (seen in the fusion of antithetical qualities and in metaphors) and of purpose (an incarnation of the past, and of unrealized life in general). With Howe, the opposition lay in his subject and in characterization and tone. Twain hailed the inside job Howe had done of exposing the un-recounted history of life in wasteland America. Zola, though similar to Howe in his attack on the village, also remained in a class quite by himself. He was monster oppositionism, in form, thought, word, and image, in every conceivable respect—the works. His novels were allegories of it. On reading *La Terre*, Twain at first stood almost in the same relationship to Zola that disbelieving and outraged country people might have stood in relationship to Howe. But once the stark light of Zola's all-revealing naturalism broke over him, Mark Twain was Young

Goodman Brown taking up company with Old Scratch in the woods.

Different as they were, the reason that Howe and Zola got under Twain's skin was that they dealt in the sordid, underground truth, which, if conceivable and known, still seemed, as Twain put it, "so grotesquely outside of the nineteenth-century possibilities" (*LFE* 219). It wasn't Zola's "scientific" truth, nor, on the other hand, was it Hawthorne's truth of the human heart, Emerson's subjective truth, or Melville's moral truth—though, like theirs, this underground truth had the more than true reality of literature. Positively and simply, Twain seemed to feel that opposition itself was truth. Its prize was a something which the oppositional writer wrung from the blackness of the human soul. As a realized entity, the opposing truth was a condition of its provenance; it was history written as literature. A major critical point Twain made in discussing Howe and Zola was that the history they wrote achieved whatever definable truth it might contain by being impregnated in a *tale*. Just as Wallace Stevens considered poetry the supreme fiction, so did Mark Twain consider fiction the supreme history.

From both the critical and creative standpoints, the chemistry of fiction was, in Twain's reading of Howe and Zola, demonstrably quickened by naturalistic convictions. Like Zola, Twain believed that man was not so much an agent of evil as naturally unamenable to morality. On reading a book about evolution (*The Universal Kinship*, by John Howard Moore, 1908), he remarked, "we have no *real* morals, but only artificial ones—morals created and preserved by the forced suppression of natural & healthy instincts" (*Biog* III 1363). The scapegoat for this brickbat was small-town American Protestantism. Its conception of goodness was lampooned by an incredulous Satan in "Letters from the Earth," and was made alternately pathetic and pathological in many of Twain's villages, from Obedstown, St. Petersburg, and Dawson's Landing to Bricksville and Hadleyburg—a meandering satire which even crept into his Catholic Domremy and Eseldorf. In Howe's *Story of a Country Town* and Zola's *La Terre*, Twain found composite versions of village life that squared with his own. He had found support, and was relieved to see other writers trying to tell the truth too.

II

In September, 1883, Edgar Watson Howe, thirty-year-old editor of the Atchison *Globe*, had fifteen hundred copies of his novel, *The Story of a Country Town*, printed in the newspaper's print shop. He had started his embittered book in the preceding year, writing it at night, after work, in his kitchen. Being eager to know whether the book had in it what he thought it did, he sent it around to newspaper editors and such other persons as he thought might enlighten him.

On February 2, 1884, Twain received a copy. This book, which supposedly started the "revolt from the village," could hardly have reached him at a more opportune time. He was traversing the nation and taking in its small towns on a lecture tour with the local colorist George Washington Cable. His most recent writing had been on the second part of *Life on the Mississippi* and the final section of *Huckleberry Finn*, in both of which books he had spread before the world the unlovely and unloving round of village life in America.

His return to Hannibal, as described in chaps. liii to lvi of *LOM*, was particularly shaded by gloomy and guilt-ridden reminiscences of just the type that (in varying degrees) had evoked the feeling of emptiness and despair in Howe, Kirkland, Frederic, and Garland. Somewhat like Garland, Twain had gone back home with the "feeling of one who returns out of a dead-and-gone generation," fearing that the faces of former friends would be "old, and scarred with the campaigns of life, and marked with their griefs and defeats, and would give [him] no upliftings of spirit" (*LOM* 393, 394). His apprehensions were amply confirmed. Many of his friends, he discovered, had indeed either "gone to the dogs" or had been "whipped" by life "in every battle, straight along." The "best-natured and most cheery and hopeful young fellow" had left his wife and two children and gone off to Mexico, where he died "without a cent to buy a shroud, and without a friend to attend the funeral" (395). Still another childhood friend had died in an insane asylum, where she had lived the last thirty-six years of her life after having been frightened by pranksters, one of whom Twain as a boy had seen come up behind her wearing a shroud and doughface (397). On

262

the other hand, "a perfect chucklehead; perfect dummy . . . [and] stupid ass" had become "the first lawyer in the State of Missouri" (396). Here, needless to say, were the sarcasms on Sunday-school *exempla* come to life, the ironic details struck off with the touch of a Stephen Crane or an Ambrose Bierce. Twain kept at it for an entire chapter, summoning up the vices of the Sunday-school-trained companions of his youth. The two drownings, the one of the sin-laden Lem Hackett, who "went to the bottom like an anvil," and the other of poor little Dutchy, the prize Sunday-school pupil whom the boys had treacherously taunted into staying down too long, had each been followed by a terrorizing thunderstorm which in young Sam's Calvinist ravings foretold the divine wrath awaiting him and the other unregenerate boys of the village. At chapter's end, Twain told of the compulsion he had to appear before the current crop of Sunday-school scholars, and of his doing so, while in memory he dwelt morosely upon the "Model Boy" of his day, whose "exterior godliness," insufferable priggishness, and utter emptyheadedness had ensured him success in life. Before leaving town he noticed how the good women had aged—it had been "very wearing" on them "to be good"—and recalled certain lost, half-cracked types of the sort one might meet in a *Spoon River Anthology*, a Winesburg, or Tilbury Town: Stavely, the saddler, who flew down to greet each steamboat with a "rush of imaginary business," and the lying, "sentimental, melodramatic fraud" of a carpenter, who confided that he had taken the lives of some thirty persons named Lynch.

Whether or not Howe knew *Life on the Mississippi*, as he did *Roughing It* (his favorite) and *The Gilded Age*,[1] he had reason to hope that his own " 'Missouri' story" (set in the prairie land in the northwestern corner of the state) might interest Twain. Less than two weeks after receiving the book, Twain had read it and prepared an approving letter, appending certain "private" suggestions for the correction of obvious faults. The public part of the letter, which Twain said Howe could use as he wished,[2] was

1. Howe mentioned his reading of these works in his autobiography, *Plain People* (New York, 1929), pp. 147, 149f.
2. Howe immediately quoted from both parts of the letter in his newspaper, and he also used it with the 1917 edition of his book, along with

concerned with four matters: the clarity and fluency of Howe's prose; his truthful depiction of the barrenness of small-town life; his masterful, but insufficiently exploited, characterization of Big Adam, a gruff and plain-spoken farm hand; and his too great dependence on "history" alone, instead of on "history" controlled by fiction. In the private section, Twain advised Howe against the repetition of a striking image, called attention to a grammatical lapse, advocated the removal of his apologetic preface, pointed out the potential that Big Adam might have for the stage, and regretted weaknesses of characterization in the handling of Lytle Biggs, a would-be entrepreneur and Big Adam's employer, and of Jo Erring, the narrator's young uncle, around whom the second part of the book revolves.

On examining the associational drift of Twain's analysis, one notices how he isolated its major problem in direct and basic terms. Considerable stress was given to Howe's subverting the pastoral illusion. But the reason Big Adam got so much play (from Twain) was that, because he mocked the pretensions of his betters and notably differed from the other characters by his unconventionality, Twain saw in him an untapped resource for Howe's oppositional motif. Adam was an example of history being resorbed into character. More generally, one can observe the coming together in Twain's mind of ideas about vividness and simplicity, subversion and realism, and fiction and interest.

This is the public part of Twain's letter, in full, followed by those remarks in the private part which deal mainly with characterization:[3]

> I like your book so much that I am glad of the chance to say so. Your style is so simple, sincere, direct, & at the same time so clear & so strong, that I think it must have been born to you, not made. Your pictures of that arid village life, & the insides

---

parts of a letter he had received from Howells. Complete information on this, along with facts of composition, publication, and Howe's personal involvement in the book, may be found in Claude M. Simpson's fine scholarly introduction to the recent Belknap Press edition of *The Story of a Country Town* (Cambridge, Mass., 1961). On Howe's use of the letters of Twain and Howells, see p. xiii, n. 12. All page references are to the 1884 text as reprinted in this edition.

3. The text is that reprinted by C. E. Schorer, "Mark Twain's Criticism of *The Story of a Country Town*," *AL*, XXVII (March, 1955), 109–12.

& outsides of its people, are vivid, & what is more, true; I know, for I have seen it all, lived it all.

Your book is a history; your scissors could have turned it into a tale—& that would have been better, maybe, for many can write a history, whereas few can write a tale. You could have knocked out an obstruction here & there, & then your history would have become a story, flowing with gathering speed & uninterrupted current.

By the small space which you give to Big Adam, I judge you did not perceive that you were contributing a mighty figure to the procession of originals that is marching out of the ark of American literature to possess the land. Your other characters are good, they are well done, & worth the patient art you lavished upon them; but when Big Adam strides by, it is Gulliver in Lilliput. You give the others big space in the book, & Adam little: now then, bring him on the stage again, & reverse these proportions; so shall you deserve well of the nation. You see I can speak calmly; but when I read passages about Big Adam to George W. Cable, he forgot himself & shouted "Superb, superb —he is colossal!"

You write as a man *talks*; & very few can reach that height of excellence. I think a man who possesses that gift is quite sure to write a readable book—& you have done that.

Private

. . . You have allowed the tears to plash on the floor once in the preface & thrice in the book. The figure is very striking— & jokes & striking figures should not be repeated. You might retort that Adam's corks should not be repeated, then; but not so—no time to explain why, but you know why. I'd rather hear Adam draw an imaginary cork than another man a real one— even at my thirstiest. (You ought to write a drama at once & make Adam the central figure—keep him on the stage all through the piece—there's dollars in it if you get the right man. . . .)

Next time, I wish you'd leave out Biggs, or anybody else whose diversions interrupt the story. *Nothing* should ever be allowed to break the speed of a story.

Mateel carried my heart & sympathy right along, & into her grave with her; but from the beginning to the end I was pretty generally down on Joe [sic]; & when Mateel made her appeal to him—oh, but damnation I cut him dead, there & then, & we have never spoken since. Usually I don't care a rap what becomes of the people in a story, [just so I have a reasonable hope that they are all going to h   ] but I was interested in these folks. . . .

I am talking pretty freely, but I mean no harm. You may have caught the only fish there was in your pond—it's a thing that has occurred before—but I am not able to think so. . . .

The centrality of Twain's criticism rests on his citing Howe's failure to achieve a workable synthesis of two forms. Almost every flaw he mentions goes back to that point. Twain diagnoses the exact nature of this disparity, which is that, while the oppositional truth Howe writes about is "historical," fiction has a potentially more effective organization for it than history does, in that it provides the economy of an internal unity and direction. The truth "goes" better as fiction. This matter can best be appreciated by reacquainting ourselves with Howe's two plots.

In the first, Howe tells the story of Ned Westlock and his relations with his father, his mother, Agnes Deming (the schoolteacher he would marry), and the two towns where he grew up, Fairview and Twin Mounds. This plot is chiefly historical, being an account of rural and small-town life, and having much of Howe's own life in it.[4] By general agreement, it contains his most powerful material. What he calls in a chapter heading "the peculiarities of a country town" are first glimpsed in the physical scene of a Fairview to which Ned's parents had migrated in hopes of improving their lot by "growing up with the country," but where the fairest prospect—the site of the Reverend John Westlock's meeting house, with its shrubless graveyard—is "the bleakest point in the county" (8). The chief occupation in Twin

---

4. As will be seen from my summary, there are a good number of situations in *The Story of a Country Town* that hark back to events in Howe's life as given in *Plain People*. The town of his youth in Harrison County, Missouri, had actually been Fairview (*Plain People*, p. 4f.); Howe's father had built and preached ("without charge") in the combined church and school that stood in a corner of their field (5); his father was, much like the Rev. John Westlock, a "cross and dissatisfied man," who was severe with his wife and children (10), who never "exhibited affection" for them (174), and who was turned out of his church because of gossip about him and a widowed sister-in-law (62f.); and Howe's mother resembled Ned's mother—he said, "of the pale, tired, unhappy women I knew in my childhood, none could compare with my own mother" (57). Although Howe had a young maternal uncle named Nate with whom he had played and one named Joe Irwin, on both of whom Jo Erring was superficially modeled (the latter less than the former), the morbid jealousy of Jo Erring was Howe's own psychological quirk.

Mounds is complaint. The people read little except the Bible and that only to find something to bicker about (141). What rejoicing there is depends upon their learning of someone's failure.

Howe's dramatization of the bitterness of life is finally concentrated in the lives of Ned's father and mother. A physically ominous person, John Westlock is rigid, unfeeling, bigoted, self-righteous, and hypocritical. Although he has preached that only sinners are miserable, Westlock is thoroughly miserable himself, and deserts his wife for a woman whose great passion is to reform sinners and drunkards. Ned's most poignant memories, though, are of how the women suffered from overwork and an unrelenting melancholy. No woman bears a heavier cross than his mother. Faithful to a cruel husband who from the first had been indifferent to her, she keeps a nightly vigil in the hope that he may return, only to die two days before he does.

Howe handled his historical matter with forceful simplicity. At its best it was good fiction too. Indicative, for example, of Howe's skill in giving it a *theme* is the reverie wherein Ned relates his sadness and guilt over not being able to empathize with his mother. The reverie is set off by his mother's observation that, after having moved to Twin Mounds, she does not feel they are any happier than they had been before:

> It was the only reference she had ever made to the subject to me, and I did not press it, for I feared she would break down and confess the sorrow which filled her life. A great many times afterwards I could have led her up to talk about it, fully and freely, I think, but I dreaded to hear from her own lips how unhappy she really was. Had I those days to live over . . . I would pursue a different course, but it never occurred to me then that I could be of more use to her than I was, or that I could in any way lessen her sorrow. She never regretted that I no longer slept in the house, nor that I was growing as cold toward her as my father, which must have been the case, so I never knew that she cared much about it. Indeed, I interpreted her unhappiness as indifference toward me, and it had been that way since I could remember. Had she put her arms around me, and asked me to love her because no one else did, I am sure I should have been devoted to her, but her quietness convinced me that she was so troubled in other ways that there was no time to think of me, and while I believe I was always kind and thoughtful of her, I fear I was never affectionate. (150.)

267

The great effectiveness of this scene is that Howe *shows* us what he had elsewhere been *telling* us about, and he shows us by convicting his narrator of the very lack of humanity that the narrator himself had been telling us about.

A good part of the problem that Twain analyzed in distinguishing between Howe's "history" and a "tale" is that what had to be told was not always assimilated into what was shown. This is nowhere more evident than in the second plot, in which Howe seemed to be shifting from history to fiction but in actuality tied himself to semi-autobiographical exposition, inasmuch as he had experienced a personal dissatisfaction very much like Jo Erring's.[5] Howe realized that he needed more story after the Westlock complication had run its course. (Only once in the second part of the book—in Chapter 16—did he return to direct commentary on the country town.) His problem was, however, that Jo's dissatisfaction was not necessarily typical of the country town, so that it did not properly compose a *story* of small-town life in the same way that "the fall of Rev. John Westlock" did. Using the distinction between history and a tale, one feels that whereas the latter should be generally truthful without having to be specifically true, Jo Erring's tale is simply too special and peculiar to be informative as general truth. He is possessed by an ideal of purity in love that drives him to a neurotic form of jealousy; to wit, since to be happily married a couple must have been in love but once, infidelity becomes retroactive, reaching back to a prior engagement when the girl had "permitted the familiarities which are common under such circumstances" (112). Those are Jo's thoughts at the point when he acknowledges his love for Mateel Shepherd, the new minister's daughter.

In the third year of his marriage to Mateel, when her former fiancé, a contemptible idler named Clinton Bragg, sends Jo one of the love letters she had written Bragg at the age of sixteen,

---

5. Howe confessed, "There is more of the author in 'Jo Erring' than in any other portion of 'The Story of a Country Town,' and 'Jo' did much to weaken it" (*Plain People*, p. 216f.). Howe had been quite distressed to learn that he had not really been his wife's first love. She had, like Mateel Shepherd, been loved and kissed by a schoolmate at the age of sixteen. For more on this matter see Simpson's Introduction, p. xvi, n. 19, pp. xix–xxi.

Jo is to all intents and purposes driven mad. After forcing his wife to leave him, he prays for her return and keeps his door locked in the event she does. He divorces her on grounds of desertion, and when Mateel marries Bragg in a desperate moment, Jo apprehends them on the road and strangles him. He is sent to prison, where he takes poison and dies, and Mateel, worn out by nervous exhaustion, soon follows him to the grave.

One senses that Twain's loathing for Jo was accompanied by disappointment, since he was "interested in these folks," in contradistinction to those he didn't "care a rap" for—the latter being the overly squeamish types he complained about in his reading of Oliver Goldsmith, Jane Austen, Margaret Deland, and Henry Kingsley. In addition to possessing most of the sentimental vices, Jo Erring, like Lytle Biggs, slows up the pace of the action and is the subject of a wrongly constructed historical motive. Howe became obsessed with him for his own sake, rather than for the sake of the story. Twain's central point with Howe was much like what it had been with Macaulay and Howells: fiction brings history to life and makes it true and interesting. It was not history alone, or fiction alone, but the two together that led to a meaningful realism (in the most inclusive sense of that term). And it was character, as one could tell from Twain's statements about Adam and Biggs, that held the key to a fusion of history and fiction.

Of special pertinence, then, are the roles Howe assigned these two characters in his exposition of the revolt from village life. Biggs has the kind of ancillary expository value that places him on a level with Howe's delineation of the social scene. Twain properly thought him to be diversionary, a historical excrescence. Biggs was also exceptionable on the more intrinsic grounds that he infringed upon Big Adam's role and confused it. Although he was intended to be shallow and hypocritical, as his name was meant to suggest, Lytle Biggs was stuffed with *bon mots* that gave him the appearance of a cynicism and oppositionism he did not really possess. He prided himself on being a man who told people "unpalatable truths" (74) and came out with expressions that might seem worthy of a place in "Pudd'nhead Wilson's Calendar"—e.g., "I have observed that happiness and brains seldom go together" (294). However, despite Howe's telling us that Biggs was "not the kind of man he claimed to be" (74), the subversiveness of his "philosophy" was utterly incongruous with Howe's making him a despicable rogue, who swindled the farmers he sold supplies to, after promising to rescue them from their former profiteering suppliers.

For all his unrelatedness to plot, Biggs occupies a good deal more space in the novel than Big Adam does. The farm hand does not make more than half a dozen appearances, and he is there mostly for brief interludes, to bring the narrator messages. A solid oppositional character, it is Adam who lets the reader in on Biggs's swindling and tells Ned that he seems to make his money by organizing the farmers "for one thing, and [being] a member of the Legislature for another" (81). Adam is the only person in the book with a genuine sense of humor; he is rough, a frontier type (with a mocking way of pretending to uncork and empty a bottle of whiskey); and since he is generally looked down upon, one can see the possibilities he has as a commentator on the pretenses and peculiarities of Howe's townspeople. In relation to his employer, Adam is really "Big" and admirably suited to the big use that Twain suggested for him.

When he revised his book, in 1927, and adopted the perspective of a "literary critic," Howe came to appraise it in terms that largely coincided with Twain's. He contrasted the "mainly" fictional intent of his "novel" with the historical aim of "accuracy" (*Plain People*, p. 214f.), and he conceded that "such natural ability" as he had in writing was probably "not inclined toward the novel form" (208). He even felt "compelled . . . to desert poor 'Jo Erring'" (217). Erring's mania seemed to him hard to take after he had read the first part (of which he was justifiably proud), and he concluded that "poor 'Jo's' unreasonable jealousy does not belong in a novel from which the author hopes for permanent fame" (216).

Howe had been so completely swayed by what he called Twain's "wholesome advice about writing" (212) that in replying to Twain's letter he acknowledged most of the "defects" he had pointed out and, in revising the book, acted on almost every piece of advice Twain had given him.[6] For the most part, he came down hard on Lytle Biggs, despite the fact that critics like Howells and Horace Scudder had, respectively, found him "delightful" and one of Howe's "genuine creations."[7] In the clearest instance of a structural improvement based on Twain's criticism, he cut an entire chapter given over to Biggs's truisms, which had come between one in which Jo is harassing and justifying himself for having compelled his wife to leave him and the climactic chapter in which he kills Clinton Bragg. Furthermore, in the few additions that Howe made, he principally gave more space to Big Adam, bringing him into the major action by having him get into a fight with Clinton Bragg, which leads to Bragg's arrest. As a final testimony of the trust Howe placed in Twain's criticism, he actually wrote a play with a special part in it for Big Adam (*Plain People*, p. 213).

III

The job that Howe had done on rural America Émile Zola was to do on the French provinces several years later in *La Terre*. He did it as part of a piece-by-piece anatomy of the entire social organism, which, when completed, would include exposés of the family, church, and army, in addition to those of finance and industry. But in *La Terre*, the programmatic debasement of man had reached its nadir. There one found a tale of bottomless greed

6. In his reply to Twain's letter, by the way, Howe said that, had he laid the book "aside for six months, after finishing it, and gone at it again when [he] was not too tired and indifferent to remark its faults, it would have been a much better book; there would have been less of 'Jo' and more of 'Adam' in it" (*Story*, p. xi). As for actual revisions brought about by Twain's criticism, Howe removed the egregious preface, the repeated references to tears "plashing" on the floor, and an anti-temperance discourse (ostensibly aimed at Clinton Bragg, in Chapter 17) which was clearly one of the "diversions" by which the story was interrupted. Howe also corrected an ungrammatical distribution of "wills" and "shalls" that Twain had noticed.

7. "Recent American Fiction," *Atlantic Monthly*, LV (January, 1885), 126; "Two Notable Novels," *Century*, XXVIII (August, 1884), 632. Although Howells thought Jo was "admirably imagined," his estimate of the book was otherwise completely just. He emphasized the brilliant realism of Howe's portrait of the small town and observed that the Reverend Westlock, rather than Jo, was the "great figure" in the book.

and filial perfidy among members of a peasant family, who did not scruple to cheat, oppress, rape, torture, and murder their own kind, and who, in the manner of Howe's villagers, revelled in each other's misfortunes.[8]

Twain was perturbed by Zola's book and more deeply engaged by it than he had been by Howe's. What affected him most was that the story seemed susceptible of the broadest historical interpretation, which was nothing less than total dehumanization, applicable not alone to men of other times and places, but —soberingly—to the sunlit provincial America which, for all its chuckleheadedness, he had once regarded with affection. After the ghastly enchantment of the book had sunk in, he looked about him like a man who had heard the oracle. As he remarked at the end of his comment, "How strange it is to reflect that that book is true. But it is. You have to confess it at last." If it took Zola to expose "your own people to you," that was because "you were asleep, and had forgotten; [and] he has waked you up" (*LFE* 220).

To cope with the larger vista, Twain had to go beyond the kind of intelligence he had applied to *The Story of a Country Town*. While seeming to reverse his analysis of the relationship of history to fiction, he widened it by concentrating on historical, over and above aesthetic, meaning, with history being considered as the end, rather than just the means of fiction. In doing so, he picked up an emphasis that many of the critics seemed also to have caught. One reviewer, for example, using criteria similar to Twain's, observed that "as a story we cannot conceive of any-body's finding [*La Terre*] interesting; it is dull, slow, unpleasant and bestial; but as a study, one reads between the lines and is filled with pity and a wholesome sense of warning."[9] It is hard to believe anyone could have found the book dull or slow (for one thing, it has a good deal of humor, which is so earthy as to be well-nigh gothic)—but no matter. The idea of its being a

8. One particularly spiteful member of the family, an old aunt, Marianne, nicknamed "La Grande," so arranged her will that the division of her property would be guaranteed to result in perpetual bickering, discontent, and no doubt physical violence, perhaps even murder, among her heirs.

9. "Zola's 'La Terre,' " *Critic*, IX (May 26, 1888), 255.

symbolic study is unquestionably apt. That was how Twain regarded *La Terre*. For while its basic situation is founded on a Lear motif, the fact that Zola's Lear is deliberately represented as totally bereft, with neither a Kent nor Cordelia anywhere in sight, is a crucial sign that the story was meant to be read as social anagoge. Since anagoge is inseparable from story, it was necessary for Twain, as for most readers, to concede the point of view that united them and behold poor groveling humanity through the darkening prism of Zola's naturalism, which was reality made fantastic.

Thus, if Twain was to be receptive to Zola's oppositional truth —which was what finally gripped his imagination—he had first to earn it by accepting the naturalness of the unnatural. And he did. Indeed, Twain's enthusiasm for *La Terre* was proportional to his having to overcome his own prior resistance to a plot made up of every conceivable rebuff to ordinary human feelings. One can understand the nature of Twain's reaction by recalling the action of the novel:

Old Fouan, having held on to his nine and a half hectares (950 acres) until he was too weak to tend them, decided to divide the land among his daughter (Fanny Delhomme) and his two sons (Hyacinthe and Buteau), on condition that he receive an annual rent of 950 francs, which the children cut to 600 and, except for Fanny, almost never paid. The last payment Buteau made (a little over half the amount due) was wheedled out of his enfeebled mother by Hyacinthe, which so enraged Buteau that, following his father's precedent, he gave her a blow that packed her off to the grave. Under constant nagging, Fouan left his daughter's home and went to live with Buteau and his wife, Lise. The old man was put up in a cold, damp room used for the storage of vegetables, and Buteau stole his income and systematically cut down on his food. Eventually the two quarreled over Buteau's exploitation of his wife's sister, Françoise. Violence ensued, and the old man ran to Hyacinthe's place. There he grew so fearful of the roughness with which his son and granddaughter searched him for the "hoard" they supposed him to have that he had to return to Buteau. When he asked that Buteau give back the bundle of securities stolen from him during an illness, he was thrown out and wandered alone through a bitter autumn night.

Lashed, like Lear, by rain and icy winds, and unable to stand the punishment for a second night, he crawled back to Buteau's. Meanwhile, Buteau and Lise wanted Françoise's land and feared it would go to the child she was pregnant with. (She had married Jean Macquart.) Lise, having heard that birth could be aborted through the act of conception, helped her husband to rape Françoise, who, after a struggle, enjoyed it. In the subsequent quarrel, Lise threw her sister down on a sickle, which stabbed her in the side and killed her. Fouan, who witnessed the struggle, told Jean. Buteau overheard and directed Lise to smother the old man in his sleep. Thinking his discolored face might give them away, they partly burned the body, in which there was still a flicker of life, an incident which, unbeknownst to the parents, was secretly observed by their children—*voilà*!

When Twain read *La Terre* cannot be exactly determined, but there is good reason to reject Bernard DeVoto's guess that the six manuscript pages he had written on the book belong to the period 1905–9, or are to be put "several years earlier" (*LFE* 292). Since Twain made a note of *La Terre* in his private notebook early in December, 1887, the year of its publication, and beside it wrote the name of a New York book dealer and importer of French books and often made such notations of books he ordered, and since he mentioned that a review "attracted [his] attention to the book" and said he read it in French, one is inclined to think that he probably got the book and read it about that time—either in December, 1887, or January, 1888.[10] He seems to have learned something of its contents in the summer of 1887, when its serial publication caused five of Zola's disciples to denounce him in the famous *Figaro* letter of August 18. Having followed the book with considerable interest, he wrote his critique almost immediately after finishing it, which accounts for the urgency and intimacy of his tone and for his air of treating a topical controversy.

10. The notebook entry read: "La Terre, Zola. N. Y. W. R. Jenkins." It appeared between items dated December 1 and December 9 (Unpublished Notebook No. 22 [November, 1887–June, 1888], 44). William R. Jenkins both published and imported French books. As *La Terre* was first published in book form in late 1887, Twain must have ordered it

It is very likely, therefore, that Twain was reading *La Terre* before the onset of his own misanthropy, such as it was, or, in other words, while he was still more inclined to think better of man than worse. He was a businessman of some opulence and status in the late 80's, who had visions of making millions on the Paige typesetting machine and of being able to retire and forget about having to write books for a living. This admirably fits the picture, since for *La Terre* to have enlightened him in the degree that he claimed it did, the book had, among other things, to shock him out of certain of his Whiggish complacencies.

The late 80's also provide a thematic context for Twain's comments on Zola. In fact, Zola may have helped him to revise his analysis of history at a time when his anti-royalist attitudes —enlivened by his hatred of the French—had reached their peak. Egged on by Matthew Arnold and Sir Lepel Griffin (*T-H* II 600f.), he was preparing to expose the wanton cruelty, grossness and shams of the aristocratic tradition against which American vulgarity, as seen in its press, was being held up to scorn. While working his retort into *A Connecticut Yankee*, in the summer of 1887, he wanted to write an appendix in support of the view that no real ladies and gentlemen existed prior to the nineteenth century, and he made a note that he should "look into . . . Zola's [book] to show that [among the] Modern French" none existed afterwards either.[11] Once he had actually read the

---

rather soon after it appeared. The review is alluded to in the manuscript comment itself, the text of which is, as previously indicated, published in the *LFE* volume, 218–20. Also pointing toward an early acquisition of the book is Twain's reference to a text of some 518 pages, the number of the first and second (1889) French editions. The suppression, after a scandalous court hearing, of the somewhat bowdlerized English edition, translated and published by the Vizetellys in 1888, and the two translated American editions in that year (by T. B. Peterson and Bros. in Philadelphia and Lair and Lee in Chicago) would have increased Twain's desire to read the book in the original French as well as his satisfaction in having done so, had he read it before the trial and before the translations had appeared.

11. The appendix, a one-page typescript, is in the Mark Twain Papers, Paine 92. Howard G. Baetzhold accurately dates it as having been written in the summer of 1887 ("The Course of Composition of *A Connecticut Yankee*: A Reinterpretation," *AL*, XXXIII [May, 1961], 200).

book, though (and he could only have meant *La Terre*[12]), he changed his idea that France alone was an exception to the rule that true ladies and gentlemen sprang from the liberated lower orders. Interestingly enough, by the time he had ended the *Yankee*, his simplistic antithesis between aristocratic villainy and democratic nobility had completely broken down: Arthur had been ennobled and the maniacal Yankee was vanquished by Merlin after he had become a tin-hat dictator bent on ramming republicanism down his subjects' throats. There is at least an outside possibility that his reading of *La Terre* was one of the factors that made Twain turn on his American democrat and brutalize him. By a similar process, the thinking which on re-reading Carlyle's *French Revolution* had in 1887 (with help from Taine and Saint-Simon, he said) made an out-and-out "Sans-culotte" of Twain, and "a Marat" to boot (*T-H* II 595), and which had consolidated his hatred of the French nobility and his concomitant worship of nineteenth-century progress, seems to have been crossed and perhaps checked by Zola's disillusion-ing picture of the French folk, on whose behalf he presumably became sans-culottist. How long Twain entertained the negation of progress or how much of a dent Zola made in his defense of the common man cannot be known for sure, since his views on both subjects continued to oscillate, as they had even in the 1870's. His doubling back on his original intention in *A Connecti-cut Yankee* did forecast a change of mind, however, and his reaction to *La Terre* forecast the form that the change would ultimately take: absolute despair, leading to an acceptance of the ineluctable depravity of the entire race, including the ordinary Frenchmen who had wrought *the* great modern revolution. For the time being, the most natural locus of attack toward which Twain was deflected by *La Terre* was the American village that he and Howe had already desolated, an objective for which Zola would furnish corroboration akin to natural law.

12. *La Curée*, also published in 1887, is the only other possibility, but it cannot be established that he knew it, whereas his attention had been drawn to *La Terre* by the denunciatory letter in *Le Figaro* of August 18, 1887.

IV

On reading *La Terre*, Twain had at first followed with horrified fascination what seemed a study in nightmarish wickedness and boundless obscenity.[13] Then, becoming more contemplative, he eased his way toward a hypothesis that enabled him to transcend his animus against the French and make the supreme oppositional synthesis in deriving positive understanding from his negativism. To observe how this synthesis developed, one must begin with the narrower aspects of Twain's negativism, and of Zola's, which inspired the synthesis and cleansed away the pettiness.

Initially, Twain's curiosity about *La Terre* had been aroused by the more superficial aspects of Zola's oppositionism, mingled with his own Francophobia. He looked upon it mainly *as* a curiosity, having read, he said, "the rather doubtful statement" in a review that its serial reproduction in a French newspaper (*Gil Blas*) had had to be stopped, for the incredible reason "that the tale was so foul that the French people could not stand it." When he read the book itself, he was least astonished by its overt sensationalism. To the naturalism, however, Twain responded with disbelief and defensive alarm: "did it not seem to you impossible, unbelievable that people such as those in that book are to be found in actual existence in any Christian land today? Were you able at any time, from the beginning to the end, to shake off the feeling that the tale was a hideous unreality, a tumultuous and ghastly nightmare, through which you were being whirled and buffeted helpless?" (218). Even the leavening salacity with which Zola had drawn some hilariously Gargantuan scenes appeared more to abash than amuse Twain, despite the fact that he had long since written *1601*, and had more recently been delighted with Saint-Simon's *Memoirs* and Cleland's *Fanny*

13. Critics still contemplate *La Terre* with the same feeling of nightmarish horror. Angus Wilson, in 1952, wrote: "Even now, the greatest of the novels—*L'Assommoir, La Terre, Germinal*—have the quality of nightmares; how much more appalling must they have been for the contemporary reader. And, as from nightmares, there was no means of escape. Each world of horror was airtight, a little cell . . ." (*Émile Zola: An Introductory Study of His Novels* [New York, 1952], p. 53).

Hill.[14] Probably he had written off the comedy because *La Terre* was so depressing, and Zola's humor only deepened the cruelty of it all. In any case, while the cause of his sending for the book was to find out the "real reason" the French were shocked by it, he himself came away with the most shocking and indeed "hair-lifting" revelation imaginable. Speaking confidentially to his fellow reader, he asked with a sensation of helplessness:

> Did the thought at any time come crashing into your dismayed mind, "What if this is no dream, but reality, and a picture of phases of life to be found here and there in *all* Christian lands!" This *is* a startling thought, isn't it? Well, I have just finished that book, and what I have said above indicates what happened to me: that is to say, chapter after chapter seemed to be only frightful inventions, crazy inventions of an obscene mind; then came the conviction that the tale was true, absolutely true, photographically true; and finally came that hair-lifting thought which I have mentioned [i.e., that it was no dream, but "reality . . . found . . . in *all* Christian lands!"]. (218.)

The painfulness of his having to accept Zola's story as true lay in its locked-in nihilism. Zola not only exceeded Howe in insisting on the baseness of human nature, he almost violated probability to get it across. *La Terre* was saved for Twain only by his willingness at length to give in to the mechanism of its oppositional motive. By the questions he used to assert his shock ("did it not seem to you impossible, unbelievable . . . ?"), he confessed his initial proneness to judge Zola by the very conventionalism his book was written to oppose. As Twain began to realize that, his amazement turned to deference for a truly "fearful book."

Furthermore, in *La Terre*, Zola stood forth as a standard-bearer of the oppositional party in literature to which Twain felt that he too belonged. Hacking away at the very roots of Rousseauism, Zola posited that the peasants' contiguity with the earth they coveted accounted for their uniformly pernicious behavior. Their natural endowment was an inbred ferocity of the kind which animals pass on to their offspring, and which parents and children consequently use against one another.

14. He had made a note "St. Simon in French" in his Unpublished Notebook No. 15 (July 1880–March, 1881), 28. In a letter to Osgood of March 30, 1881 (*Berg*), he said he had been "charmed" by *Fanny Hill*.

Instead of breeding Arcadian virtues, the return to nature made men progressively more brutal, until, as Zola disclosed, it became quite impossible to regard atavism with romantic calm.

The next stage in Twain's evaluation of *La Terre* is a prime example of the therapy of oppositionism, illustrating how it clears the mind of misconceptions. We see Twain universalizing his insight and moving toward a conclusion that would previously have been repulsive to him: an equation of French with American villagers, and with the most puritanical of our villagers at that:

> Now what I am coming at, is this: are there any villages in America whose people resemble the community described in Zola's book? If one is asked this question suddenly, he will feel a shock, and will answer, "Impossible!" But let him stop and think. Perhaps he will not answer up so confidently, next time. After reflection, after calling up particulars lying here and there half-buried in his memory, he will probably grant that there are in America villages that "resemble" that one, in some ways, even in many ways. Well, that is a sufficient concession. Will he go further, and name the state? And if he will, will he name Massachusetts? Yes, under certain limitations, he will name Massachusetts. He will proceed in this way. He will say that without doubt Zola has suppressed the bulk of his villagers—the worthy and the good—and has confined himself to the few and awful. If that was his way, then it may be granted that he could have got material for a modified and yet dreadful enough *La Terre* out of the "few and awful" minority findable in a Massachusetts village. When you have granted that, in the case of Massachusetts, do you feel daring enough to deny it in the case of any other state in the Union? Hardly, I suppose. (219.)

Having taken Zola's revelation this far, Twain was prepared to go all the way and expand it into a historical donnée. In his climactic summary, he not only synthesized seeming opposites, but, once the flood gates of understanding opened, he was willing to believe that most people knew of other suppressed evils even worse than those set forth by Zola. The medium of understanding, and that which convinced Twain of the utter magnitude of the French, and human, propensity toward degradation, was an image of living history. It was his awareness of a cycle of infinite repetition, a sensation that had illuminated so large a segment of time for him in his Indian experience. Beginning with a rejection of what seemed so peculiar as to be implausible,

Twain's vision suddenly grew like the spreading dawn, and he marveled at what he discovered:

> It is very, very curious—the results that gradually come out, when Zola's fearful book sets you to thinking. The first chapter amazed you [a young girl brought a cow in heat to be mated with a small bull, and had to physically assist him]; when you read it, it seemed so grotesquely outside of the nineteenth-century possibilities. But reflection changes your mind. You turn over your moss-grown facts, and know that those circumstances have been repeated in America. Once? Oh, no, several hundred thousand times. How far will your thinking carry you? And what will you arrive at? This: that there is hardly an incident or a conversation in the book that has not repeated itself hundreds and hundreds of times in America, and all over America. And then you will go still further and remember some other things that have happened in America—things still more hideously revolting than ever the most atrocious thing in Zola's volume. (219f.)

V

Did Twain know of "more hideously revolting" things that happened in America, one wonders, or did he merely imagine that they could be recalled if one tried hard enough to recall them? It would seem that Twain both knew *and* recalled small-town happenings that were revolting enough, both before and after he read *La Terre*. In 1879, the year that he made a note to get a copy of *L'Assommoir*, "illustrated,"[15] and a few years before he read Saint-Simon, the Congregationalist Church of Hannibal distributed among its members a little pamphlet alleging that a man active in Sunday-school service had had "improper relations" with a married woman of the congregation, whose husband was intimate with still another married woman. The writer of the pamphlet unflinchingly mentioned all of the embarrassing details of the "case" and alluded to the precise gestures and contact purported to have transpired between the guilty couple, who also were accustomed to having prayers when they were together. The matter had been brought to light by a quarrel between the adulteress and the woman her husband was

15. Unpublished Notebook No. 14 (February–September, 1879), 32.

having a liason with, after denials by the Sunday-school teacher had squelched some of the rumors. When the pamphlet came into Twain's hands, he pinned it to the flyleaf of his copy of Casanova's *Memoirs* and noted that he had known both women as children, that they moved in the town's highest social circles, and that they were undeniably guilty (*MTP*).

We have noticed the melancholia that accompanied Twain's return to Hannibal in 1882. Returning in the imagination some fifteen years later, he brooded even more bitterly over village life and wrote the series of reminiscences entitled "Villagers—1840–3." Those had supposedly been the halcyon years and Hannibal the boy's paradise; but all he could recall were lonely, neglected, perverse, and dissipated people, miserable types not unlike Howe's, and others whose personal tragedies often remind one of the fate of Zola's peasants. In some instances, he remembered situations at least as bad as Zola's, such as those of three mad brothers, one of whom lived in a bark hut, while a second hacked off his offending left hand, and the third wound up in an asylum after marrying, becoming a doctor, and seeming to lead a respectable life. There were tales of sad women, like the one who married a swindler and lost her youth and cheerfulness in waiting with her baby for him to be released from prison. In another case a docile, "heart-hurt" beauty was closely groomed by her parents to become the wife of a lawyer, who then shut her up for two more years of education, after which, on being forced out against her will, she broke a leg, became a cripple, bore children, and remained a permanent recluse. The men fared no better. An easy-going fellow married a "loud and vulgar beauty" and refused to see, as everyone else did, that she was committing adultery under his nose with the doctor friend who boarded with them. An unbelieving Kentucky lawyer who went home to marry but failed to appear for the ceremony was found a year later clothed for the wedding in the family's cemetery vault, to which he used to go regularly to visit his mother's tomb. Also included in these vignettes was one of the several versions of the scene at Twain's father's deathbed; in it, John Marshall Clemens supposedly made his first show of overt affection by singling out his one daughter to receive a final embrace and parting kiss, while his wife and sons looked on. Interestingly, Twain adduced precisely the motive that Zola had given to explain the ruination of his villagers: the lust for money, which, during the gold rush, had lured many a resident of Hannibal to dissipation and a pauper's grave in California. Obviously, Twain had little difficulty in "calling up particulars lying here and there half-buried in his memory" to justify his conviction that Zola had exposed his own people to him.

Eventually, Zola became one of Twain's heroes and ranked with Joan of Arc for demanding justice in the Dreyfus affair.[16] Twain might more properly have acknowledged a private service Zola did him. For beyond confirming his disgust with the damned human race, Zola's account of a besmirched peasantry had so completely penetrated a blind spot in Twain's critical sense that he for once sublimated his neurotic hatred of the French. As late as 1900, for example, Twain said he still could not (possibly he would not) speak the language,[17] though of course he read it with ease; and in addition to making various sneers in his notebooks ("one gets his notion of the F[rench] from their books & history"), he claimed that all a person had to do to write a French novel was to concoct thirty-seven cases of adultery and have everyone live happily to the end.[18] Knowing *La Terre* by no means cured Twain of his prejudice.[19] But it did rid him of the provincial pleasure he had taken in declaring that a nation generally revered for its refinement was assumedly proven by history to have outrivalled the Comanches in the arts of "cruelty" and "savagery."[20] Whereas he had formerly patronized the lower-than-Comanche

16. *MFMT* 130; *Noteb* 342; Unpublished Notebook No. 32 I (January, 1897–August, 1898), 7.
17. *Mark Twain's Letters to Mary*, ed. Lewis Leary (New York, 1961), p. 6.
18. Unpublished Notebook No. 14 (February–September, 1879), 27. Unpublished Notebook No. 21 (February, 1886–May, 1887), 32 (Copyright © 1967, Mark Twain Company).
19. He did not readily take criticism of America from the French. Upon reading Paul Bourget's *Outre Mer* in 1894, he pointed out that since only a native novelist could render the national "soul," he had read *La Terre* in preparation for going to Paris (*LE* 164).
20. "The French and the Comanches," an excised chapter from *A Tramp Abroad*, published in *LFE* 183–89.

Frenchman—"Let us take to our hearts this disparaged and depreciated link between man and the simian and raise him up to brotherhood with us" (*LFE* 189)—after reading *La Terre*, Twain was quite willing to lower the American villager to a status of brotherhood with his French counterpart.

Thus, the high point of Twain's experience in reading *La Terre* was that it more genuinely broadened his concept of human history than had his reading of any of the historians he liked, including Macaulay. Significantly, he did not take a stubborn satisfaction in Zola's pessimism as such, as he did later on with his own. He rather chose to use it instructively. He had read *La Terre*, as Howells in his review had urged that it be read, as a "student of civilization," with "scientific curiosity."[21] At the moment when Twain observed that the particular condition of Zola's villagers was pervasive, he made an imaginative projection that satisfied his desire to know the essence of facts—the reward of oppositional truth. By so exercising his historical sensibility he acted on its most vital tendency, which was philosophic. In the next logical turn that Twain's criticism took, beyond his interpretation of *La Terre*, the philosophic tendency was to be given full play. This occurred when he attended a performance of Adolph Wilbrandt's *Der Meister von Palmyra*.

21. "Editor's Study," *Harper's Monthly*, LXXVI (March, 1888), 641f.

14

Wilbrandt: The Tragic Conquest of Evil

I

In *Der Meister von Palmyra* Twain contemplated a potentially more horrifying exposition of evil than he had in *La Terre*. *La Terre* had inclined him to set aside geographic and national differences: Zola's peasant was Everyman remade in the image of evolution's nature. Wilbrandt's play, which Twain had seen in Vienna at least twice in 1898 and about which he had written an article, entitled "About Play Writing,"[1] offered him the tantalizing prospect of obliterating distinctions in time as well. Given the scheme of the play, wherein Twain saw the "wearisome and monotonous . . . repetition of [the] stupid history" of human life "through the ages" (209), the abuses of one age differed only circumstantially from those of another. Far from being depressed by this, Twain found the play "deeply fascinating," and, with the rest of the audience "sat rapt and silent" "under its spell" (202f.). He was in fact jubilant over the remorseless honesty with which Wilbrandt pursued his "tragic" theme that death was a hero's guerdon for those who endured the indignities of history.

Twain's critical appreciation of *Der Meister von Palmyra* was based on the recognition that tragedy (broadly construed) implied an aesthetic resolution of the problem of evil, and that the heroic triumph over time implied a moral resolution to the dilemma of deterministic pessimism. These possibilities became apparent to Twain because the mode of the play contained a definitive and culminant representation of living history. From act to act, there is, with each jump in time, a visible effect of

1. The article first appeared in *Forum*, XXVI (October, 1898), 143–51. It was reprinted in *The Man That Corrupted Hadleyburg and Other Essays and Stories*, ANE, XVIII, 202–15. Page references are to the latter text.

aging and decay upon the characters and scene, resulting, as Twain observed, in such a "profound illusion of [the] long lapse of time" that "you live it yourself! You leave the theatre with the weight of a century upon you" (205). In addition, an iterative pattern is wafted through the separate periods of history that gives it the immediacy of a dream. "The play," Twain said, "gave me the sense of the passage of a dimly connected procession of dream-pictures" (203). As Wilbrandt used metempsychosis to vivify the illusion of historical flux (one character is put through five incarnations), Twain thought that to be "the strength of the piece" (*ibid.*). The over-all strength of its appeal to him lay in a reciprocity of personal and aesthetic interests.[2] As far as Twain's aesthetic interest is concerned, the reincarnated character is, in relation to his other appreciative criticism, a splendid illustration of the projection of living history, and that projection was achieved through a fusion of antithetical qualities. Wilbrandt's character was at first a "religious enthusiast," then "a capricious featherhead, a creature of shower and sunshine," and, in the three subsequent "lives" Twain saw an increasingly complex combination of her several former selves (203f.).

Twain correctly called *Meister* Wilbrandt's "masterpiece," and in acknowledgment of its elevated purpose he also correctly described it as less of a play than a "stately metaphysical poem" (202). Wilbrandt invited the viewer to look at life *sub specie aeternitatis*. On his philosophic warp, he wove several strands of late nineteenth-century pessimism, but unlike those of Spengler,

---

2. The play was associated in his mind with the unappeasable grief he continued to feel over the death of Susy. Toward the end of December, 1898, he wrote in a letter to Howells,

> Susy hovers about us this holiday week, & the shadows fall all about us of
> "The days when we went gipsying
>   A long time ago."
> Death is so kind, so benignant, to whom he loves; but he goes by us others & will not look our way. We saw the "Master of Palmyra" last night. How Death, with his gentleness and majesty, made the human grand-folk around him seem little & trivial & silly! (*T-H* II 685.)

Twain said that after writing his "Bible," *What Is Man?*, in 1898, "Man" was no longer "the respect-worthy person he was before; & so I have lost my pride in him & can't write gaily nor praisefully about him any more" (*T-H* II 689). This was a more general cause for his finding confirmation of his personal views in Wilbrandt's play.

Chekhov, Hardy, Housman, or Adams, Wilbrandt's, like Nietzsche's, was rather closely tied to the ethics of classicism. He set forth the intellectual consolation of stoicism and the spiritual consolation of death as the individual's means of avenging himself upon the cyclical futility of time. In 1898, Twain could scarcely have hoped for a more gratifying subject. He availed himself of God's view of history, and the unending panorama relieved him of having to plead the special character of human turpitude, as he had in the most distinguished of his own pessimistic works, "The Man That Corrupted Hadleyburg," written in Vienna at about the time that he saw Wilbrandt's play. His citing the cogency of the dream-world reality was partly due to his general fascination in the 90's with manifestations of the subconscious and related psychic states and to his specific interest in psychosomatic medicine, memory, telepathy, and the like. He had, of course, been experimenting with the mysteries of the unexpended emotional life in dream stories like "My Platonic Sweetheart" and in the unfinished manuscripts on "The Great Dark," in addition to exploring the phantasmal qualities of normal consciousness in his developing tale of the "mysterious stranger" named Philip Traum, who would pronounce himself and "life itself . . . a dream."

To some extent, therefore, Twain was predisposed to like Wilbrandt's use of the dream spectacle. But apart from a personal susceptibility to the device, he hit upon the key to Wilbrandt's technical success. For without the atmosphere of the dream, the play becomes a thesis drama, and, lacking the subtlety and realism of an Ibsen play, runs almost directly to allegory. The action revolves around an inverted Faust motif. Apelles, the Master of Palmyra, who saves and rebuilds the ancient Syrian town, enters a pact to accept the consequences of deathlessness but eventually has to renege, so that Death, who is at first scorned, gets the satisfaction of being entreated for help and releases the broken hero from his suffering. It all begins when Apelles, on his return from defeating the Persians, lies near the cave of the Spirit that dispenses life and death, and, scoffing at the myth that the Spirit would bestow deathlessness on whomever it wished to favor, Apelles asks for and gets its "gift," ignoring the Spirit's warning that "Life without end can be regret without end." Thereupon, Apelles is visited by a succession of misfortunes that take his friends and family from him and reduce his city to ruins. He steadfastly spurns the escape held out to him by Death, who appears to him at the end of each act, until the loss of his son brings him to his knees, and he implores Zenobia to intercede on his behalf. Being the helper of all who suffer, and having eluded continuous suffering herself only through metempsychosis, Zenobia puts him into a trance that enables him to beckon Death, whom he thanks with his dying breath for coming to him in his great need.

On one level of criticism, the one most conducive to spontaneous appreciation, the play added fuel to Twain's assault on Christian civilization. He would soon, for example, be writing a sardonic "Greeting from the Nineteenth to the Twentieth Century," exhibiting "Christendom, returning, bedraggled, besmirched, and dishonored, from pirate raids in Kiao-Chuo, Manchuria, South Africa, and the Philippines, with her soul full of meanness, her pocket full of boodle, and her mouth full of pious hypocrisies" (*Biog* III 1127; see also the "Pageant of Progress," III 1149f.). While the late 90's were a season of harrowing despair, when the death wish was never very far from Twain's mind, the long overdue destruction of civilization—an implication of Wilbrandt's play—would have been something he would cheerfully have endured the absurdities of Life to see. One is, consequently, not surprised that he should educe the two martyrdoms in *Meister* as typical of the barbarities that have marked religious history, and then, on his own, take advantage of the opportunity to connect them with the modern French, who, ever-prolific in supplying him with reasons to detest them, had just martyred Dreyfus. If one cannot make much of the immediate social criticism, one really is not supposed to, for Twain's flimsy treatment of the French is now subordinated to a representative crossreferencing of classical with modern times. Wilbrandt had opened up the resources of time to Twain as a means both of winnowing his pessimism of ephemera (France is "Civilization" on trial) and of contending with the problems of evil:

> In the first act the pagans persecute *Zöe*, the Christian girl, and a pagan mob slaughters her. [She is the character who goes through

five incarnations, of which Zöe is the first, and Nymphas the
fourth.] In the fourth act those same pagans—now very old and
zealous—are become Christians, and they persecute the pagans:
a mob of them slaughters the pagan youth, *Nymphas*, who is
standing up for the old gods of his fathers. No remark is made
about this picturesque failure of civilization; but there it stands,
as an unworded suggestion that civilization, even when Chris-
tianized, was not able wholly to subdue the natural man in that
old day—just as in our day the spectacle of a shipwrecked
French crew clubbing women and children who tried to climb
into the lifeboats suggests that civilization has not succeeded in
entirely obliterating the natural man even yet. Common sailors!
A year ago, in Paris, at a fire, the aristocracy of the same nation
clubbed girls and women out of the way to save themselves.
Civilization tested at top and bottom both, you see. And in
still another panic of fright we have this same "tough" civilization saving its honor by condemning an innocent man to multi-
form death, and hugging and whitewashing the guilty one.
(209f.)

The simple meaning of Wilbrandt's juxtapositions, as Twain
amplifies it, is *plus ça change, plus c'est la même chose.* What
Twain saw proposed was a clear philosophic advance over his
own latterday nihilism. On the evidence of history, Wilbrandt
would question the reasonableness of an insistent clinging to life,
however debasing, and an abhorrence of death, however honorable.[3] In the production Twain was writing about, a considerable
effort was apparently made to bring out the value of Death as
a chastener of human folly and a medium for reintroducing
personal dignity into life. Death injected moral understanding—
something an intelligent man could live by—into the otherwise
meaningless repetitiveness of history. As Twain suggested,
Wilbrandt's Death made men aware of the standard that
separated living from non-living.

> Wherever there was a turmoil of merry-making or fighting or
> feasting or chaffing or quarreling, or a gilded pageant, or other
> manifestation of our trivial and fleeting life, into it drifted that

---

3. Hence the typically pathetic irony Twain noticed in the action of "a
   pauper couple, stricken with age and infirmities," who pray to the
   "Spirit of Life for a means to prop up their existence and continue it"
   (206).

black figure with the corpse-face, and looked its fateful look and passed on; leaving its victim shuddering and smitten. And always its coming made the fussy human pack seem infinitely pitiful and shabby and hardly worth the attention of either saving or damning. (205f.)

II

The "project" Twain said he had embarked on in describing *Meister* in such detail was to ween the theatergoing public away from its penchant for light entertainment on which the theater page showed that it was glutting itself. He prescribed "a tragedy-tonic once or twice a month," a refreshing "climb among . . . the intellectual snow-summits built by Shakspeare [sic] and those [other tragedians]" (215). America was "neglecting . . . the most effective of all the breeders and nurses and disseminators of high literary taste and lofty emotion—the tragic stage" (214). Nor was this without personal implications.

The dire need of a tragedy-tonic was driven home to Twain in the pathetic fate of the classical satirist in Wilbrandt's play, Timoleus. Noticing the limitations of the satiric dispensation for dealing with the ravages of time, Twain devoted a full paragraph to the irony that "*his* [Timoleus'] life has suffered defeat." It showed that "no one's life escapes the blight." Formerly a scoffer "at the pious hypocrisies and money-grubbing ways of the great Roman lords," Timoleus had, Twain noted, "grown old and fat and blear-eyed and racked with disease . . . [and had] lost his stately purities and watered the acid of his wit" (210). In describing his complete humiliation ("he confesses that principle, when unsupported by an assenting stomach, has to climb down" [211]), Twain comprehended the necessity of a larger, and higher, critical position than the satirist's. The message sank in as he watched the old fellow remove his hacking carcass from the stage.

Twain did not of course confine himself to the strict and technical sense of "tragedy." None the less, he leaned rather heavily upon one generic aspect of tragedy in analyzing the meaning of Wilbrandt's play, and that had to do with the tragic resolution of the problem of evil. In tragedy, as in Twain's view of the tragical matter of Wilbrandt's play, evil is self-evidently dominant in the human psyche. However, made overt and universalized, evil loses its terror for the individual. Indeed, the tragic vision transmits a certain immunity to the poignancy of evil, insofar as it reveals, to use Twain's words, "what a silly, poor thing human life is" (208). The historical persistence of evil, from which tragedy draws its theme, suggests a macrocosmic order, and the individual's experience of the evil that has plagued all men gives him status in that order. In Aristotelian terms, the tragical exposition of evil as much as furnishes a homeopathic cure for it. As for our reconciliation to the fate of the tragic hero, Twain interestingly prepares us for this by citing his preservation of honor in a situation that somewhat parallels the one in Macaulay's portrait of Hastings which had inspired "The Derelict": when Apelles is falsely accused of misappropriating public funds, he "is too proud to endure even the suspicion of irregularity, [and] strips himself to naked poverty to square the unfair account" (210).

Twain made one interesting extrapolation of the tragic resolution of the problem of evil. Taking Wilbrandt's telescopic presentation of history as inclusive of every fundamental view of life, he contemplated the common purpose of tragedy and comedy. The idea "how comic [are life's] tragedies, how tragic its comedies"—perhaps the most trenchant fusion of opposites that he conceived—had occurred to Twain often enough. It hovered around much of his serious writing and was just about the only redeeming feature of some of the bitter satires of his late period. It is quite likely that he never felt the aesthetic impact of the confluence of tragedy and comedy as keenly as he did in the spectacle of *Der Meister von Palmyra*. Nor was he to find a situation that permitted him to regard with greater Adams-like equanimity the notion that "life is a failure."

> This piece is just one long, soulful, sardonic laugh at human life. Its title might properly be "Is Life a Failure?" and leave the five acts to play with the answer. I am not at all sure that the author meant to laugh at life. I only notice that he has done it. Without putting into words any ungracious or discourteous things about life, the episodes in the piece seem to be saying all the time, inarticulately: "Note what a silly, poor thing human life is; how childish its ambitions, how ridiculous its pomps, how trivial its dignities, how cheap its heroisms, how capricious its course, how brief its flight, how stingy in happiness, how opulent

in miseries, how few its prides, how multitudinous its humiliations, how comic its tragedies, how tragic its comedies, how wearisome and monotonous its repetition of its stupid history through the ages, with never the introduction of a new detail, how hard it has tried, from the Creation down, to play itself upon its possessor as a boon, and has never proved its case in a single instance!" (208f.)

Although Twain's pessimism has frequently been misunderstood, this is no place to attempt a clarification of it. However, it should, in all justice, be noted that when he had sufficient distance on the problem, as he had in the aesthetic experience of seeing Wilbrandt's play, he did not turn his back on life any more than he attempted to destroy its moral meaning. He merely observed how ridiculous it was to be personally hurt by life, and thought a person ought to be able to accept it at its worst. To make that acceptance significant the vision of history as a record of the universal tragedy of man was indispensable. His essay on Wilbrandt therefore constitutes the intellectual high point of his appreciative literary criticism. Having viewed the play at the age of sixty-three, on the threshold of old age, Twain was to find no other dramatic performance that more deeply gratified him.

Unfortunately, the resolution to the problems of evil and pessimism that was held out to him by Wilbrandt was but briefly enjoyed. It had no lasting effect on his progressively souring mood and proved of little use to him in his writings. The sad postscript to his seeing *Der Meister von Palmyra* is that several years later, when Twain came to write his own synoptic version of Wilbrandt's theme in a tale called "The Five Boons of Life," bitterness pushed him beyond the tragic conquest of evil through a morally willed death and landed him on the sands of Pyrrhonism. A "good fairy" brought five gifts to a young man—Fame, Love, Riches, Pleasure, and Death—and asked him to choose. After each of the first four choices had brought him nothing but disillusioning grief, he at length asked for Death, and was denied. "Oh miserable me!" he cried. "What is there left for me?" to which the fairy replied: "What not even you have deserved: the wanton insult of Old Age."[4]

4. *$30,000 Bequest*, pp. 160–65. For another positive conception of the role of death ("sole of the gods of all the heavens") see Twain's poem, "Apostrophe to Death" (1905) (*On the Poetry of Mark Twain*, p. 126f.).

Perhaps the idea inspired by Wilbrandt did not stay with Twain very long for the reason that the more one dwells upon it the further it gets from the experience it summarizes and the more it tends to evaporate into theory. Mere duration, however, has to be measured against depth and breadth. If Wilbrandt's death is not an exact equivalent of the existentialist concept of it as a moral protest against non-living, Twain none the less brought out a good deal of what the play might have in the way of a moral-existentialist application. He specifically considered it a remedy for the giddy meaninglessness of popular happiness. Noting that the pleasure-seeking playgoer needed *Meister* as a "tonic," because he seemed to be feasting on "lightsome" drama, Twain urged, "You are trying to make yourself believe that life is a comedy, that its sole business is fun, that there is nothing serious in it. You are ignoring the skeleton in your closet. Send for 'The Master of Palmyra.' You are neglecting a valuable side of your life; presently it will be atrophied. You are eating too much mental sugar; you will bring on Bright's disease of the intellect." Clearly, its method was such that for the populace at large, no less than for the imaginative mind, the moral tonic could not fail to make a vivid artistic impression, "its story [being] as plain as a procession of pictures" (213). So here was America's great comic genius reminding the nation of the true comedian's affinity for tragedy, which, in any case, is the penumbra that inevitably surrounds great comedy.

Finally, his critical appreciation of *Meister* gave Twain an intelligence and perspective which, while they lasted, lifted him above his emotional distress and overshadowed his creative malaise. It will be remembered that Twain's ego suffered greatly—almost irreparably—in the 90's from his financial failure and personal misfortunes; and, as Bernard DeVoto has pointed out, the feeling of disgrace took its toll on his writing. For a number of years after completing *Following the Equator*, he could finish only a handful of the many pieces he had compulsively begun to write. He probably suffered, DeVoto speculated, from "the fear that his talent ha[d] been drained away" (*MTAW* 113). True, his thinking ill of mankind could not have made him think any better of himself. But while his creative efforts foundered on self-pitying, autobiographical dream stories about

292

"The Great Dark"—with great stretches of time being condensed into minutes and the "Superintendent of Dreams" trying to make his psychic captive accept the reality of the dream's terror (*MTAW* 117, 122)—and while he was therefore impotent to deal with the sadness of real life, Twain's critical penetration remained keen and sure and completely the master of its materials. Through his powers of vision and control as critic, Twain made the dark lessons of history analogues of the vanity of all human wishes; and so he could jolly well take the world or leave it. He was, after seeing *Meister*, not a little like Babbalanja in Melville's romance on that theme of human vanity, when the native philosopher noted his voyage in the world was ended "not because what we sought is found; but that I now possess all which may be had of what I sought in Mardi" (*Mardi*, chap. clxxxix). Although he might, like most men, have lost the quest for wisdom and happiness, Twain's critical consciousness could —unaided, and in spite of his despair—bring him considerable wisdom, and obviously some happiness in having it, during periods of appreciative insight of the kind he enjoyed while watching Adolph Wilbrandt's *Der Meister von Palmyra*.

III

As one looks back over the totality of Mark Twain's performance as critic from the "snow-summit" of appreciation he reached on taking Wilbrandt's "tragedy-tonic" (the Wilbrandt essay and the one on Howells were his latest and structurally best developed pieces of formal criticism), the sort of concluding question that I suppose one wants to ask is: what contribution does Twain's criticism make to our estimate of the man, his mind, and his work? Naturally, I would hope that the answer to this question has been progressively unfolded in the chapters of this book. In a more general sense, though, it seems clear enough that Twain was naturally destined to become a critic, in much the same fashion that, as Baudelaire once remarked, "all great poets naturally and fatally become critics." But, to go more directly to the point, if I had to cite just one or two matters that distinguish the contribution that his criticism makes to our knowledge of Mark Twain the man and writer, and were given no more space than a page or so in which to do it, I would offer the following considerations:

First, whether he was using the feckless muggins to expose a laughable conjunction of serious histrionics with sensation in Adah Menken's *Mazeppa*, or was painfully grumbling about Cooper's murdering the rules of romantic fiction, or was illuminating by careful poetic analysis the craftsmanship of Howells' prose style, Mark Twain was apparently determined to make criticism an *art*—in spite of itself. Most of his critical writings were indeed gems. He was therefore a good deal more than a *mere critic*; whereas he has been thought to have had no gift whatsoever for artistic criticism.

Second, for a critic who had certain marked limitations of taste, and who was occasionally unsure of his opinions, Twain not only had much insight and good judgment, but he made surprisingly few errors of professional judgment once he made up his mind to do a job of analytic criticism. Great improviser that he was, Twain displayed a far greater degree of penetration than anyone has heretofore dared to give him credit for—in revealing, for example, the peculiar faults of Western journalism, the false realism of Bret Harte, the woeful influence of Scott on the South, and the fantastic truth in Zola's naturalism. Let him fool and grumble as he might, Twain's mind was primarily that of a man of judgment. He was obviously a true wit, being never so witty as when he seemed not to be.

Furthermore, Twain knew absolutely what he was about. In one of his most conclusive statements on composition, he pointedly urged the superiority of the powers of critical judgment over those of inspiration as the basis for successful writing. "One should never write under an inspiration," he declared in the same notebook in which he had cursed the "devilish" *Vicar of Wakefield*; for, he continued,

> at such a time one is mentally drunk, & his feelings have the upper hand of his judgment. Poets often write under an inspiration, whereas they ought to go to bed & sleep it off. Often the difference between a judgment born of inspiration & one born of sober cerebration consists of a single word—a word put in,

in the one case & left out in the other. A trifling thing, statistically considered, but usually the reverse of trifling when measured by results.[5]

Here then spoke the inner voice of Mark Twain as writer and critic.

5. Unpublished Notebook No. 29 I (January–April, 1896), 22 (Copyright © 1967, Mark Twain Company).

A Bibliography of Mark Twain's Criticism: His "Literary Essays," Miscellaneous Critical Commentaries, and Related Matters

I

"Literary Essays" and Informal Statements
on Language and Literature*

"Report to the Buffalo Female Academy" (1870), in Buffalo *Express*. Reprinted in *Mark Twain on the Art of Writing*, ed. Martin B. Fried (1961), which also contains "A Good Letter: Mark Twain's Idea of It" (1869). Similar analyses of school-girl compositions can be found in: "Miss Clapp's School" (January 14, 1864), in Virginia City *Territorial Enterprise* (reprinted in *MTEnt* 134–38), and in *The Adventures of Tom Sawyer* (1876), pp. 204–10.

"Comments on English Diction" (1870), in *Samuel Langhorne Clemens: Some Reminiscences and Some Excerpts from Letters and Unpublished MSS*, ed. Jervis Langdon (1938), pp. 20–22.

The Whittier Birthday Dinner Speech (1877). Original manuscript text reproduced by Henry Nash Smith in "That Hideous Mistake of Poor Clemens," *Harvard Library Bulletin*, IX (Spring, 1955), 145–80.

"Unlearnable Things," *Atlantic Monthly*, XLV (June, 1880), 849–60 (a discussion of style, with a paragraph on Bret Harte's style). Other comments on Harte in the margins of *The Luck of Roaring Camp and Other Tales* (1870) (cited below in Bradford Booth's *AL* article [January, 1954]), and in a letter to William Dean Howells (June 27, 1878) in *T-H* I 235–36.

"Concerning the American Language" (1882), in *Tom Sawyer Abroad, Tom Sawyer Detective and Other Stories*, ANE XX 396–400.

Criticism of Sir Walter Scott, in *LOM* (1883), chaps. xl, xlv, xlvi.

"Introduction to 'The New Guide of the Conversation in Portuguese and English'" (1883), in *The $30,000 Bequest and Other Stories*, ANE XXIV 239–43.

---

* Obviously excluded from this list are the non-literary items with which Twain had filled out the volume entitled *Literary Essays* (ANE XXII): "Traveling with a Reformer," "Mental Telegraph Again," "The Invalid's Story," "The Captain's Story," "Stirring Times in Austria," "Concerning the Jews," "From the 'London Times,' of 1904," "At the Appetite Cure," and "In Memoriam."

Bibliography

Letter to Edgar Watson Howe containing a critique of *The Story of a Country Town* (1884). See C. E. Schorer, "Mark Twain's Criticism of *The Story of a Country Town*," *AL*, XVII (March, 1955), 109–12.

Letter to Olivia Clemens (January, 1885), in *Love Lets* 227–28 (criticism of a novel sent him in manuscript).

"General Grant's Grammar" (1886), in *Speeches* 135–37, and in *Biog* III 1651–52.

"English as She Is Taught" (1887), in *WIM* 204–55 (for a related discussion of "baboo English" see *FE* II 296–307).

"Zola's *La Terre*" (1888), in *LFE* 218–20.

Note on Uses of Fact in Fiction (1888), in *Noteb* 192–93.

Letter to Walt Whitman (1889), in *Camden's Compliment to Walt Whitman, March 1889*, ed. Horace L. Traubel, pp. 64–65.

Letter to Andrew Lang on writing for "The Belly and Members" (1889), in *Letters* II 525–28.

"In Defense of Harriet Shelley" (1894), in *LE* 16–77.

"Private History of the 'Jumping Frog' Story" (1894), in *LE* 120–30.

"How To Tell a Story" (1895), in *LE* 7–15.

"Fenimore Cooper's Literary Offences" (1895), in *LE* 78–96. See also "The Noble Red Man" (September, 1870), in *CTG* 70–73; *RI* (1872) I chap. xix; and "Fenimore Cooper's Further Literary Offenses" (1895), ed. Bernard DeVoto, *New England Quarterly*, XIX (September, 1946), 291–301 (reprinted in *LFE* 137–45).

"What Paul Bourget Thinks of Us" (1895), in *LE* 141–64.

"A Little Note to M. Paul Bourget" (1895), in *LE* 165–81.

Criticism of Goldsmith's *The Vicar of Wakefield* (accompanied by slur on Jane Austen, 1897), in *FE* I 339f., II 312.

"My Boyhood Dreams" (1900), in *The Man That Corrupted Hadleyburg and Other Essays and Stories*, ANE XXIII 246–54.

Letters to Brander Matthews critical of Sir Walter Scott (May 4, 1903), in *Letters* II 737–39.

"Italian without a Master" (January, 1904), in *The $30,000 Bequest and Other Stories*, ANE XXIV 171–85.

"Italian with Grammar" (August, 1904), in *The $30,000 Bequest and Other Stories*, ANE XXIV 186–96.

"William Dean Howells" (1906), originally in *Harper's*. Reprinted in *WIM* 228–39.

"The Gorki Incident" (1906), ed. Bernard DeVoto, *Slavonic and East European Review*, XXII (August, 1944), 37–38. Reprinted in *LFE* 155–56.

Comments on Bret Harte, Thomas Bailey Aldrich, Bayard Taylor, Rudyard Kipling, and Elinor Glyn (1906, 1908), in *MTE* section entitled "Various Literary People," 254–319.

Mark Twain on Three Weeks (1908), Elinor Glyn's interview with Twain on her novel *Three Weeks*.

The Cathartic Effect of Humor (1922), in *The Mysterious Stranger*, pp. 131–32.

II

Reviews

Book Reviews

Twain published nothing that can qualify as a regular book review. Among his private, incomplete "reviews" are a burlesque review of S. O. Stedman's *Allen Bay, A Story* (1876), and comments on George MacDonald's *Robert Falconer* (1868) and Margaret Deland's *John Ward, Preacher* (1888). The last of these appears in *Noteb* 206.

Twain wrote a notice in the *Alta California* on the collected publication of George Washington Harris' *The Sut Lovingood Yarns* (1867). Reprinted in *MTTMB* 221.

For a mock British review of *Innocents Abroad*, see "An Entertaining Article" (1870), in *Galaxy*. Reprinted in *CTG* 100–2 and in *The $30,000 Bequest and Other Stories*, ANE XXIV 217–28.

For a criticism of a trivial romance, see "A Cure for the Blues" and "The Curious Book" (1892), in *The American Claimant and Other Stories and Sketches*, ANE XXI 388–407, 408–60.

Dramatic and Musical Reviews

Twain seems to have written dramatic reviews of sorts for the San Francisco *Morning Call* and the San Francisco *Dramatic Chronicle* in 1864–65. Though none of these have survived, most of his other reviews of dramatic and musical performances have, and are included in the following list, along with some of his informal comments.

Comments on acting of Edwin Forrest (1853, 1854, 1865) cited by Pat M. Ryan, Jr., "Mark Twain: Frontier Critic," *Arizona Quarterly*, XVI (Autumn, 1960), 197–209.

One-paragraph review of "East Lynne" (July 15, 1863), cited by Austin E. Hutcheson, "Twain Was 'News' to Other Newspapers While a Reporter on the 'Enterprise,'" *Twainian*, VII (November–December, 1948), 3.

"The Menken—Written Especially for Gentlemen" (September 13, 1863), in *Territorial Enterprise*. Reprinted in *MTEnt* 78–80.

"'Ingomar' over the Mountains" (November, 1863), in *Golden Era, Territorial Enterprise*, and *Yankee Notions* (XIII [April, 1864], 125). Reprinted in Ivan Benson's *Mark Twain's Western Years* (1938), pp. 181–83, and in *WG* 58–60.

Report of theatrical activities in Carson City, Nevada (January 13, 1864), in *Territorial Enterprise*. Reprinted in *MTEnt* 131–32.

"In the Metropolis," containing report on theatrical activity in San Francisco (June 24, 1864), in *Golden Era* and *Territorial Enterprise*. Reprinted in *WG* 75–76.

"Still Further Concerning That Conundrum" (October 15, 1864), mock opera review in *Californian*. Reprinted in *SOS* 131–35.

"On California Critics" (February 25, 1866), in *Golden Era*. Reprinted in *WG* 101–2.

"The Model Artists" (February 2, 1867), review of "Black Crook" in *Alta California*. Reprinted in *MTTMB* 84–87.

"At the Shrine of St. Wagner" (1891). Reprinted in *WIM* 209–27.

"On Play Acting" (1898), review of Adolph Wilbrandt's *Der Meister von Palmyra*, in *Forum*. Reprinted in *The Man That Corrupted Hadleyburg and Other Essays and Stories*, ANE XXIII 202–15.

Art Reviews*

"Academy of Design" (May 28, 1867), review of New York Academy of Design's annual show, in *Alta California*. Reprinted in *MTTMB* 238–42.

"Stewart's Palace" (May 28, 1867), on the architecture of the Fifth Avenue marble mansion of Alexander Turney Stewart, "The Merchant Prince." Reprinted in *MTTMB* 246–47.

"The Domes of the Yosemite" (June 2, 1867), review of Albert Bierstadt's painting. Reprinted in *MTTMB* 249–51.

Criticism of Turner (1879), in *TA* I 219.

"Instructions in Art" (1903), in *Metropolitan*. Reprinted in *Europe and Elsewhere*, ed. Albert B. Paine (1923), pp. 315–25.

III

Satiric Criticisms

Sample Criticisms of Journalism and Oratory

On "Mr. Sterns' Speech" (December 5, 1863), in *Territorial Enterprise*. Reprinted in *MTEnt* 93–95.

"The Great Landslide Case" (August 20, 1865), in San Francisco *Call*. Reprinted in *RI*, chap. xxxiv.

"The Facts" (August 26, 1865), burlesque of news reporting in *Californian*. Reprinted in *SOS* 180–87.

"Introduction" (May, 1870), burlesque of feature writing in *Galaxy*. Reprinted in *CTG* 37.

"A Book Review" (February, 1871), burlesque book review in *Galaxy*. Reprinted in *CTG* 122–23.

A group of Twain's early burlesques of various types of journalism were reprinted in *Sketches New and Old* (1873). These are on feuding rural editors, in "Journalism in Tennessee" (45–53); on the

---

* Mostly semi-serious or ironic.

fashion column, in "A Fashion Item" (197–98); on sensation, in "The Petrified Man" (316–20) and "My Bloody Massacre" (321–25); on the interview, in "My First Interview with Artemus Ward" (364–69); on news reporting, in "The Killing of Julius Caesar Localized" (384–88); and on the medical adviser, in "Curing A Cold" (396–402).

Criticisms and Satires on Popular Poetry

"Real Estate versus Imaginary Possessions, Poetically Considered" (October 28, 1865), in *Californian*. Reprinted in *SOS* 188–90.
"Post Mortem Poetry" (1870), in *Galaxy*. Reprinted in *CTG* 53–54, and in *The $30,000 Bequest and Other Stories*, ANE XXIV 246–54.
Parodies on poetry of Julia A. Moore, in *HF* (1885) 143–44, and in *FE* (1897) I 339–41.

IV

Implicit Criticism in Literary Burlesques Incorporated in Books and Sketches

Sample Burlesques of the Romance, Detective Story, and Sunday-School Tale

For illustrative discussion see Franklin R. Rogers, *Mark Twain's Burlesque Patterns as Seen in the Novels and Narratives 1855–1885* (1960); e.g., in *Innocents Abroad* burlesques of the romance appear in the stories of Count Luigi and of Abélard and Héloïse.
"The Story of a Bad Little Boy That Bore a Charmed Life" (December 23, 1865), in *Californian*. Reprinted in *SOS* 202–5.
"A Mediaeval Romance" (1868). Reprinted in *SNO* 221–32.
"The Story of the Good Little Boy Who Did Not Prosper" (May, 1870), in *Galaxy*. Reprinted in *CTG* 44–46.
"Dilworthy at Saint's Rest" (1873), *GA* II 237–40.
The Adventures of Tom Sawyer (1876).
Simon Wheeler Detective (play, 1877; novel, 1878).
"About Magnanimous-Incident Literature" (1878), in *Tom Sawyer Abroad*, pp. 326–33.
"Edward Mills and George Benton: A Tale" (1880), in *The $30,000 Bequest and Other Stories*, ANE XXIV 129–38.
The Stolen White Elephant (1882).
Tom Sawyer Detective (1896).
A Double Barrelled Detective Story (1902).

V

Criticism in Margins of Books in Twain's Personal Library

Coley B. Taylor. *Mark Twain's Margins on Thackeray's "Swift"* [1868 or 1869] (1935).

Bradford A. Booth. "Mark Twain's Comments on Holmes's *Autocrat"* [1869 or 1870], *AL*, XXI (January, 1950), 456–63.

Bradford A. Booth. "Mark Twain's Comments on Bret Harte's Stories" [1870], *AL*, XXV (January, 1954), 492–95.

Chester L. Davis. "Mark Twain's Religious Beliefs as Indicated by Notations in his Books," *Twainian*, XIV (March–June, 1955), 1–4; (July–August,1955), 1–4; (September–October, 1955), 1–4; (November–December, 1955), 3–4. (Marginalia in W. H. Lecky's *History of European Morals*; book obtained by Twain in 1874.)

Julian K. Sprague. "Mark Twain's Personal Marked Copy of John Bunyan's 'Pilgrim's Progress,'" *Twainian* (March–June, 1959), 1–4. (Book obtained by Twain in 1875.)

Assorted marginalia published by Paine in *Biog* III 1536–40.

VI

Some of Twain's Comments on His Own Writing

Letter to Howells (January 30, 1879), on writing *A Tramp Abroad*, in *T-H* I 248–50.

"On Speech Making Reform" (1884?), *Speeches* 1–6.

"My Methods of Writing" (October 15, 1888), in *The Art of Authorship*, ed. George Bainton (1890), pp. 87–88 (also in *Mark Twain Quarterly*, VIII [Winter–Spring, 1949], 1).

"A Wonderful Pair of Slippers" (1890), in *Europe and Elsewhere*, pp. 87–93.

Introduction to *Those Extraordinary Twins* (1894), in *PW* 229–34.

Autobiographic Dictations (1906–7), entitled by Bernard DeVoto "In a Writer's Workshop," in *MTE* 196–253.

Autobiographic Dictations (1906–10), *Autob* I 193, 237–38, 283; II 245–46.

VII

Discussions of Twain's Reading

Minnie M. Brashear. *Mark Twain, Son of Missouri* (1934), pp. 196–224.

Harold Aspiz. "Mark Twain's Reading: A Critical Study." Unpublished Ph.D. dissertation, University of California at Los Angeles, 1950.

E. Hudson Long. *Mark Twain Handbook* (1957), 294–99.

Walter Blair. *Mark Twain & Huck Finn* (1960).

VIII

Articles on Twain's Criticism and His Views on Writing

George Feinstein. "Mark Twain's Idea of Story Structure," *AL*, XVIII (March, 1946), 160–63.

George Feinstein. "Twain as Forerunner of Tooth and Claw Criticism," *Modern Language Notes*, LXIII (January, 1948), 49–50.

Edgar H. Goold. "Mark Twain on the Writing of Fiction," *AL*, XXVI (March, 1954), 141–53.

Sydney J. Krause. "Twain's Method and Theory of Composition," *Modern Philology*, LVI (February, 1959), 167–77.

C. Merton Babcock. "Mark Twain, Mencken and 'The Higher Goofyism,'" *AQ*, XVI (Winter, 1964), 587–94.

Index

Index

Hinckley, Sallie, 42
History of England, 231–35 *passim*, 246
Holland, Josiah G., 1*n*, 92 and *n*, 222
Holmes, Oliver Wendell, 16, 87, 209
Hood, Thomas, 14*n*, 84
Howe, Edgar Watson, 5, 6, 227, 228, 259–72 *passim*, 281
—writings: *Plain People*, 263*n*, 266*n*, 268*n*, 270, 271; *Story of a Country Town, The*, 227, 261, 262, 264*n*, 266*n*, 272
Howells, Mildred, 13*n*, 258–59
Howells, William Dean, 1*n*, 4, 6, 7, 9*n*, 13–17 *passim*, 22, 102, 103, 196*n*, 197, 201, 212, 220, 227, 228, 231, 239*n*, 246–60 *passim*, 269, 271, 285*n*, 293, 294
Hubbell, Jay, 149*n*, 181–82*n*, 185*n*, 209
Huck Finn, 3, 21, 88, 94, 101, 107, 149, 190, 231*n*, 240, 260

India, 226, 232, 234, 236–44 *passim*
Ingomar, The Barbarian, 46–51 *passim*
Irving, Washington, 13, 92*n*

James, Henry, 14, 17, 22, 220, 227, 249, 254, 258
Jefferson, Joe, 31
Joan of Arc, 194*n*, 260, 282
Johnson, Samuel, 13, 92*n*, 122, 185

Kennedy, John Pendleton, 181*n*, 182*n*, 184, 188*n*
Kingsley, Charles, 47
Kingsley, Henry, 235*n*, 269
Kipling, Rudyard, 16

Landrum, Grace Warren, 182*n*, 183*n*
Lang, Andrew, 96
Langdon, Jervis, 113*n*, 238*n*
Lanier, Sidney, 187, 188
"Last Supper, The," 71–72
Lecky, William Hartpole, 16, 101, 163, 189, 230
Lincoln, Abraham, 113, 149*n*, 173*n*
Literary History of the United States, The, 147*n*, 223*n*
Longfellow, Henry Wadsworth, 13, 84, 87, 135
Lounsbury, Thomas R., 90*n*, 134, 141*n*
Lowell, James Russell, 24, 209, 254
Lynn, Kenneth S., 188*n*

Macaulay, Thomas Babington, Lord, 5, 7, 16, 189, 227–56 *passim*, 260, 269, 290
McGuffey, William Holmes, 92 and *n*, 111
Machiavelli, Niccolò, 251–53 *passim*

McKeithan, Daniel M., 72*n*, 73*n*
MacMinn, George R., 30*n*, 31*n*
Maguire, Frank, 30, 31
Maguire's New Opera House, 31, 34*n*, 47
Margaret of Navarre, 164, 165
Marryatt, Frederick, 172
Matthews, Brander, 4, 8, 134, 141, 149–55 *passim*, 158, 159
Mazeppa, 3, 30–37 *passim*, 43, 45, 47, 294
Melville, Herman, 14, 15, 261, 293
Mencken, H. L., 2*n*, 12, 100
Menken, Adah Isaacs, 3, 30–39 *passim*, 42, 46, 294
Michaelangelo, 164, 165
Milner, Henry M., 30
Minor, Benjamin Blake, 171*n*
"Model Artists," 34, 39, 40, 41, 43*n*
Moore, Julia A. ("Sweet Singer of Michigan"), 87, 88. 106, 121
Moore, Thomas, 84
Mott, Frank Luther, 183
Munsey's Magazine, 9*n*

Nadal, E. S., 221
Napoleon, 71, 176, 177, 179
National Academy of Design, 76, 77, 79, 80
Nevada Territory: Constitutional Convention, 56, 59, 60
New Bowery Theatre, 37
Newell, Robert Henry (Orpheus C. Kerr), 33*n*
New York *Sun*, 213
New York Times, The, 37 and *n*, 78, 79
Nook Farm, 11*n*, 90*n*

Orians, G. Harrison, 182*n*
Osgood, James R., 175*n*, 278*n*
Osterweis, Rollin G., 182*n*, 185 and *n*

Page, Thomas Nelson, 188 and *n*
Paige Typesetting Machine, 275
Paine, Albert Bigelow, 16*n*, 153, 200, 202*n*, 238*n*
Parkman, Francis, 163 and *n*
Paul, Rodman, 204
Paul et Virginie, 234
Pepys, Samuel, 16
Peter Parley's Magazine, 91
Phoenix, John [G. H. Derby], 26, 50, 51, 196*n*
Plutarch, 16
Poe, Edgar Allen, 14, 84, 234
Primrose, Rev. Charles (Vicar of Wakefield), 124–27 *passim*, 157

Mark Twain as Critic
by
Sydney J. Krause

Designer: Edward King

Typesetter: Baltimore Type and Composition Corporation

Typefaces: McKeller Caslon and Caslon Bold Italic

Printer: Universal Lithographers, Inc.

Paper: Old Forge F

Binder: The Maple Press Company

DATE DUE